CHAVIN
AND THE ORIGINS OF
ANDEAN CIVILIZATION

CHAVIN
AND THE ORIGINS OF
ANDEAN CIVILIZATION

RICHARD L. BURGER

WITH 263 ILLUSTRATIONS,
18 IN COLOUR

THAMES AND HUDSON

In Memory of Norman Burger (1917–1979)

First President of the Long Island Chapter of the Archaeological Institute of America

Frontispiece The supreme deity of the Chavín cult, from a sculpture decorating the New Temple at Chavín de Huántar.

© 1992 and 1995 Thames and Hudson Ltd, London

First paperback edition, with colour plates 1995

British Library Cataloguing-in-Publication Data

A catalogue record for this book is available from the British Library

ISBN 0-500-27816-4

Printed and bound in Slovenia

Contents

Introduction

When the Spanish reached the shores of northern Peru in 1532, they encountered a vast indigenous empire ruled by the Incas. This state stretched 4,400 km from north to south, roughly the distance between Stockholm (Sweden) and Aswan (Egypt). The Inca realm was bound together by a road system without parallel in 16th-century Europe and the goods traveling along the royal highways were recorded by government clerks using a system of knotted strings called *quipus*. Accurate accounts of regional demography, craft production, public storage, and taxes were also kept. The European invaders marveled at the efficiency of Peruvian statecraft, the quality of Inca weaving, the sophistication of native irrigation and terracing, and the scale and technology of stonework utilized in public constructions.[1] The secretary of the Spanish expedition conceded that the Inca capital of Cuzco "is so large and so beautiful that it would be worthy to appear even in Spain."[2] Poverty, hunger, and crime were, to the shock of the Spaniards, either absent or so rare as to be insignificant.

It was apparent to the Conquistadors, as it is to archaeologists today, that the Incas possessed a truly impressive New World civilization, one rivaled only by the Aztecs of Mexico. However, Inca culture was merely the last pre-Hispanic manifestation of developments stretching thousands of years back into Peruvian prehistory. Barely lasting a century, the Inca empire drew heavily upon the technological and organizational accomplishments of earlier Andean cultures. The Inca rulers never officially recognized these antecedents. On the contrary, they usually insisted that their forerunners in Cuzco and elsewhere had been primitive warlike tribes. The 17th-century colonial scholar, Father Bernabé Cobo, summarized the Inca conception of the earlier inhabitants of Peru as follows:

> . . . formerly, the inhabitants of this kingdom were extremely barbarous and savage . . . They lived with no chief, no order or respect for the law, spread out in small villages and collections of huts, with hardly any more indications of reason and understanding than brutes, to which they were very similar in their savage customs; actually, the majority ate human flesh, and not a few took as wives their own sisters and mothers; they were all very addicted to the devil, whom they venerated and served with diligence.[3]

The Inca nobility used this unflattering characterization to justify to the Spanish their rule and privileges, just as they had once advocated it as part of their rationale for imperial expansion in Peru, Bolivia, Chile, Argentina, and Ecuador.

1 In his 1,000-page letter to King Phillip III of Spain, the indigenous writer and artist, Felipe Guaman Poma de Ayala, illustrated the first generation of ancient Peruvians with this drawing of a human couple dressed only in leaves planting their crops with an Andean footplow or *chaki taklla*.

The distant past was often described as having consisted of a series of ages, in some accounts ending with an episode of cataclysmic destruction. In the second decade of the 17th century, one non-Inca indigenous writer, Felipe Guaman Poma de Ayala, described an evolutionary sequence of four stages leading up to the Incas. It began with an early age in which the people (called Vari Vira Cocha Runa) lived in caves, dressed only in clothing of fiber and leaves, and worked the fields using a *chaki taklla*, the traditional Andean footplow. It was followed by a second age in which the Vari Runa built small stone huts and dressed in skins. Although still primitively dressed, the Vari Runa of this second age were said to already practice farming using terracing and canal irrigation.[4] Accounts like those of Guaman Poma are rich in symbolism and reveal a great deal about Andean ideology and cosmology, but they contain few clues as to the actual development of Peruvian civilization. Ultimately, the responsibility for discovering the origins of Peruvian civilization, and the factors accounting for it, rests with the archaeologist.

But before proceeding further, it may be useful to consider what is meant here by "civilization." This term has a long and complex history in anthropological writings, and played a central role in the early anthropological formulations of E. B. Tylor in his volume *The Origins of Primitive Culture* (1871) and those of Lewis Henry Morgan in his book *Ancient Society* (1877). Both scholars treated civilization as an evolutionary stage. It was "the most complex of human conditions" for Tylor, and the culmination of progressively more complex cultural stages for both men. Civilization was contrasted with barbarism, the preceding stage, which was characterized by simple agricultural societies. In later anthropological writings, such as those of Robert Redfield or Elman Service, the appearance of civilization continued to be equated with the emergence of complex society and, as such, it is seen as *the* critical watershed in human history.[5]

Underlying much of late 19th-century anthropological discourse was the ideologically important proposition that Western society was a linear descendant of Classical civilization, which in turn had its origin in the pristine civilizations of the Near East. Thus the fascination with the origins of civilization lent historical and sociological depth to the construction of the dichotomy between Western and "primitive" non-Western cultures.[6] Yet these scholars recognized that civilization had also developed elsewhere in the world and, once hyper-diffusionary hypotheses fell into disfavour, scholars began to group comparable cultural phenomena together as civilizations, and distinguish between those civilizations that developed *in situ* (primary or pristine civilizations) and those stimulated by contact with other contemporary civilizations.

Earlier this century, V. Gordon Childe attempted to lend rigor to this exercise by specifying the criteria for the grouping, largely on the basis of ten features central to Mesopotamian civilization. But most scholars remained dissatisfied with this formulation, because it did not take into account the profound diversity of the different civilizations. Not only did early Egyptian civilization lack true cities, but the Incas governed their empire without writing, while domestic animals and the wheel were of little importance among the Aztecs.[7] Given this situation, some scholars, such as British prehistorian Colin Renfrew, advocated a modified trait list approach. Renfrew, for example, suggested that civilizations could be defined as those societies with two of the following three features – towns, monumental architecture, and writing. Others asserted that civilizations were synonymous with coercive states or societies with cities.[8]

We eschew these approaches in favor of a definition which intersects with the more common usage of the term "civilization." In this volume, civilization refers to a society with a high level of cultural achievement in the arts and sciences, as made visible in the form of material objects. This definition is broadly qualitative and it is a subjective decision to determine when, in the continuum of cultural development, civilization can be said to have appeared. Civilizations are probably always complex societies since such advanced cultural accomplishments imply the existence of a body of esoteric knowledge and groups of specialized artisans, as well as a surplus of labor and/or food and the social mechanisms to appropriate it for non-domestic purposes. While this view of civilization presupposes a hierarchically stratified society, it does so only in a general sense, leaving the sociopolitical basis of each civilization open for investigation. For example, it is possible to ask whether the city is invariably a precondition of civilization or simply a frequent correlate. Likewise it can be questioned whether the state is necessarily the primary locus of power in all early civilizations or could religious institutions fulfill this same role? Thus, an intentionally loose definition of civilization serves to focus attention on the emergence of complexity and its cultural expression without anticipating (and biasing) the results by incorporating them into the definition of the term. It allows investigators to concentrate on the processes responsible for civilizations and the nature of these civilizations, rather than on the degree of match with a preconceived typological category.

Most scholars agree that the emergence of civilization was one of those great transformations which occurred only rarely in human history, but which shaped the world as we know it. One of the cherished goals of anthropology is the formulation of explanations for the appearance of civilization, but it is unlikely that this will be feasible until the range of variation in the emergence of the world's early civilizations is known. One approach to understanding the causes of civilization is to concentrate on those few instances in which it developed from purely internal or autochthonous factors. These cases, referred to as pristine civilizations, are recognized in Mesopotamia, China, the Indus Valley, perhaps Egypt, Peru, and Mesoamerica. These five or six examples are of special concern to anthropological theory, since all models of general socio-cultural evolution must be evaluated on the basis of our understanding of them.

Peru has probably received the least attention of the areas where pristine civilizations appeared, despite the unusually good state of archaeological preservation there. However, the data available suggest that the developmental trajectory followed in Peru may represent a pathway dissimilar from those documented elsewhere, and that the organization of early Andean civilization may have been fundamentally different from those civilizations in the Old World and Mesoamerica.

If we were to trace Peruvian civilization back to its most distant origins, it would be necessary to begin with the peopling of the New World by the Asiatic hunters and gatherers who unknowingly crossed over the Bering land bridge from

Peruvian chronology

2 Embellished with fine masonry and stone carvings, the archaeological complex of Chavín de Huántar in the northern highlands of Peru was an important center of the earliest Andean civilization. The glaciated Cordillera Blanca and the Huachecsa River can be seen in the background, with the temple constructions and Mosna River in the foreground.

Siberia to North America some 15,000 years ago or more. Between 14,000 and 11,000 years ago, some of their descendants populated the Peruvian Andes. Others reached the southern tip of South America and feasted on the meat of wild horse, sloth, and guanaco. At least 10,000 years of population growth, and social and economic change transpired in Peru before anything resembling civilization began to emerge.[9]

The best known of the early Peruvian civilizations is Chavín. Its name is taken from Chavín de Huántar, an archaeological site in the northern highlands of Peru which is notable for its monumental architecture, finely carved stone sculpture, and elaborate iconography. The distinctive style utilized on the sculptures of Chavín de Huántar appears elsewhere in Peru on clay friezes, hammered gold, woven and painted cloth, and a host of other materials. The quality of these objects and their relatively early date led Peruvian archaeologist Julio C. Tello to propose in the 1930s that Chavín was the oldest of Peru's civilizations. Tello further argued that Chavín provided the cultural foundations out of which all later Peruvian civilizations grew.[10] A modified version of Tello's concept of Chavín was eventually accepted by most archaeologists, and Chavín is frequently presented as the South American counterpart to the Shang civilization in China, the Sumerian civilization in Mesopotamia, and the Olmec civilization in Mesoamerica.[11]

The spread of Chavín art through the Peruvian highlands and coast was presumed to have occurred rapidly because of its stylistic homogeneity over a large area, and it was seized upon as a convenient chronological marker of rough contemporaneity between the distant sites in which it was found. The "horizon" of the Chavín style was viewed as analogous to two later horizons which resulted from the Huari and Inca empires.[12] When John H. Rowe devised a chronological framework for Peru in 1962, he referred to these similar phenomena as the Early Horizon, Middle Horizon, and Late Horizon. In the interest of greater temporal precision, Rowe defined the Early Horizon as the time span beginning with the introduction of Chavín influence into Ica (a small valley on the south coast of Peru) and ending with introduction of the polychrome slip-painted ceramics of the Nazca style into that same valley.[13]

In Rowe's framework, the Initial Period is the block of time before the Early Horizon; it begins with the introduction of pottery into Peru and ends with the appearance of Chavín traits in Ica. The Initial Period and Early Horizon together span roughly 2,000 years of Peruvian prehistory (2000 BC–AD 0). Cotton first appears in the archaeological record of the Peruvian coast at c. 3000 BC, and this provides a convenient marker for the beginning of the Late Preceramic (3000–2000 BC), the period which immediately precedes the Initial Period.

Public architecture and other elements more fully developed in Chavín civilization first appear during the Late Preceramic, and became more numerous during the Initial Period. In fact, many of the traits that Tello believed were diagnostic of Chavín civilization are now know to be much earlier in date. Therefore, in order to trace the genesis of early Peruvian civilization it will be necessary to consider in the chapters that follow the Late Preceramic and the Initial Period, as well as the Early Horizon, before moving on to Chavín itself.

Since Rowe formulated his relative chronology, advances have been made in radiocarbon dating and other chronometric systems for determining the age of artifacts or sites. However, many early Peruvian sites lack dates altogether, and

3 The Peruvian archaeologist, Julio C. Tello, discovered the Chavín civilization and excavated at Chavín de Huántar and many other early Peruvian sites. Tello appears here in front of a pre-Chavín unbaked clay sculpture that he uncovered at Moxeke in the Casma Valley.

at other sites anomalous dates exist which are not consistent with other measurements or the associated artifacts. Rowe's terminology will therefore be employed in this volume, but it will be supplemented by estimated chronometric dates and radiocarbon measurements when they are available.

There is a significant discrepancy between radiocarbon ages and calendar years which is primarily due to past fluctuations in the quantity of unstable C-14 in the atmosphere. It is necessary to correct or calibrate the radiocarbon measurements to obtain calendar dates, and to compare the antiquity of early Peruvian civilization with the Old World, where chronologies are based primarily on calendar dates taken from written records. The radiocarbon measurements and age estimates presented in this volume have been corrected using the widely accepted calibration curve proposed in 1986 by geochemists M. Stuiver and G. W. Pearson, but the original uncorrected results of a selected group of analyses, including all those cited, appear in the Appendix.[14]

The setting

At first glance, Peru may seem an unlikely place for a pristine civilization to have emerged. It is composed of three contrasting landforms – the arid Pacific coast, the Andes mountains, and the Amazonian lowlands. A traveler can move from the shores of the coastal plain through the rugged highlands and down into the tropical forest in 200 km or less, encountering in the transect 20 of the world's 34 life zones. This juxtaposition of dissimilar habitats within such a small area is unique in the biosphere. The sheer height of the mountainous zone (surpassed only by the Himalayas), and the aridity of the coastal plain, which receives less rainfall than the Sahara or Gobi, present an ominous set of obstacles to human occupation. Acre for acre, Peru has one of the lowest carrying capacities found in the Western hemisphere; in fact, only 2 percent of the land is currently considered suitable for agriculture. The biological and cultural adaptation of indigenous Andean peoples to these varied and extreme environments is in itself a remarkable testimony to the flexibility and creativity of humankind. Important early developments occurred in the highlands, coast, and tropical forest, and the peoples of all three areas interacted and were, to some degree, interdependent.

The approach adopted in this volume is that Chavín civilization arose out of the interplay between the societies of the coast, highlands, and eastern lowlands. At its apogee in the last millennium BC, Chavín civilization linked groups from most of the central and northern coast and highlands of Peru. The area involved in Chavín civilization was roughly 200,000 sq. km, approximately twice the size of Portugal. Societies in the adjacent lowlands to the east of the Andes also apparently played a significant, though less direct, role in these events. For those readers unfamiliar with the central Andes, a more detailed consideration of the geography of these three landforms is in order before focusing on the archaeological record.

The coast

The coast of Peru is a narrow strip of warm desert intersected by dozens of small rivers and intermittent streams, whose headwaters lie to the east in the Andes mountains. Its gently sloping coastal plain varies in width from 20 km to 50 km, broadening to 100 km only in the far north and almost disappearing entirely in

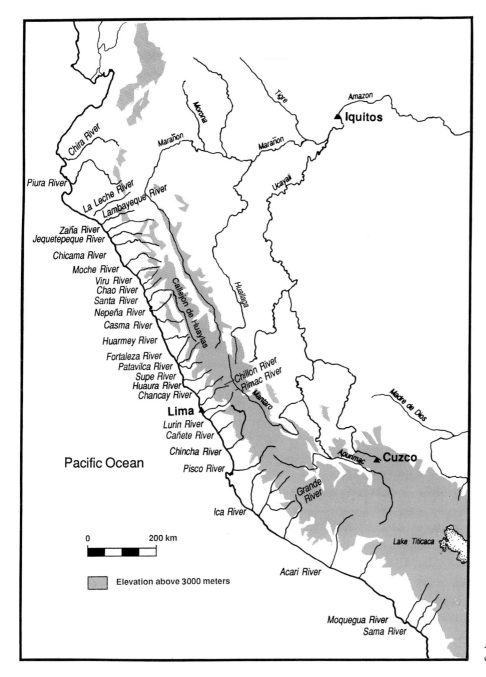

4 Map showing the major rivers in the central Andes and adjacent areas.

the south. The numerous rivers which cross it are short with steep gradients. The upper reaches of the valleys are characterized by narrow canyons or gorges with little, if any, bottomland. Rocky spurs project west from the Andes, creating barren stretches of desert between the rivers. Precipitation on the coast rarely exceeds 25 mm per year and the landscapes of the intervalley zones are almost lunar in appearance. It is possible to walk in these areas for 50 km without seeing a single plant or animal.[15]

The Humboldt Current is responsible for many of the distinctive features of the Peruvian Coast. This ocean current sweeps up to the coast of South America

5 Aerial photograph of the Supe Valley, with the important Late Preceramic site of Aspero visible along the shoreline. The rich maritime resources of Peru's desert coast and irrigated coastal valleys were critical to the development of early Andean civilization.

from Antarctica and its chilly waters support penguins, fur seals, and other decidedly non-tropical fauna. The Humboldt is actually composed of two elements: a wide ocean current with relatively little marine life, and a coastal current only 50 to 100 km wide which hugs the shore. A strong upwelling within the coastal current is responsible for its particularly low temperature. The upwelling brings nutrients near enough to the surface to support trillions of phytoplankton – microscopic plants which are dependent on light and will not flourish at great depths. Thriving in the cool temperatures and low salinity of the Peruvian current, phytoplankton are the bases for a food chain which includes small fish such as anchovies, large fish, like sea bass, ocean birds, like pelicans and cormorants, and marine mammals such as sea lions. The Current also supports large populations of clams on the sandy beaches, and mussels along the rockier shoreline, as well as a host of other shellfish. The maritime resources of Peru are acknowledged to be among the richest in the world. Fishing in the cool coastal current in 1960 yielded 1,680 kg per hectare, almost a thousand times the average of worldwide ocean productivity.[16]

An ocean-atmosphere perturbation, referred to as El Niño, occasionally disrupts this delicately balanced food chain. Each year in January a warm countercurrent from the coast of Ecuador is able to penetrate the far north coast of Peru because of the decreased intensity of the trade winds. The countercurrent brings dolphins, flying fish, and other exotic fauna along with its warmer northern waters, but its impact is generally minor and short-lived. However, once every 16 years or so this countercurrent appears with greater intensity, as far south as the Moche and Virú valleys of Peru's north coast, sometimes having an undesirable impact on both the climate and fishing. At irregular intervals, roughly every 25 to 40 years, major disturbances occur because of the uniting of

6 As this aerial photograph of the lower Ica Valley shows, sand dunes and barren rock slopes frequently border the narrow irrigated river valleys. A small spring supports an island of vegetation amidst the dunes.

the countercurrent with an eastern equatorial current. This rare event warms the sea by as much as 6.6 degrees, killing the phytoplankton and forcing the animals they support to migrate or die. When a major El Niño struck Peru in 1973, the anchovy catch declined by 87 percent. During another El Niño event in 1941, the chief of the United States Fishery Mission to Peru, Reginald Fiedler, observed the waters and shores of Tortugas Bay in Casma choked with millions of dead fish. Though the impact of major El Niños is felt throughout the central and north coast of Peru, they do not necessarily affect the adjacent highland areas.[17]

The Humboldt Current provides Peru with abundant maritime resources, but it also causes the intense aridity of the coast. In the winter of the southern hemisphere (June to November), the moist prevailing winds which blow from the southwest over the Pacific are chilled by the cold upwelling waters of Peru's coastal current. Some moisture precipitates at sea and no new moisture is picked up by the winds before reaching land. As this cool air blows over the coastal plain, it heats up slightly because of the higher temperature of the landmass, expanding its capacity to continue to hold moisture. As a consequence of this, all rainfall is prevented. The warmed air rises along the western face of the Andes and as it cools with increasing temperature, the moisture condenses into thick clouds. Throughout the winter, this stratum of clouds is trapped beneath a layer of warmer air, and they unrelentingly blanket the narrow coast for six months. Precipitation is limited to a fine mist or drizzle which is most intense along the foothills of the Andes, at an elevation between 300 m and 800 m above sea level.

In the summer (December to May) the temperature inversion described above does not occur. The moist maritime air is able to rise unhindered along the flanks of the Andes, cooling gradually until rainfall begins at elevations exceeding 1,600 m above sea level. As in the winter, the coastal plain and lower coastal valleys

7 In the foothills of the Andes, valleys such as the Casma Valley depicted here constrict to form barren canyons or *quebradas*, only occasionally punctuated by small areas of irrigated bottomland.

remain without significant precipitation. Nevertheless, the climate on the Peruvian littoral is humid throughout the year and, as a result of the Humboldt Current, is considerably cooler than tropical areas of similar latitude. The Brazilian coast, for example, is 5.5 degrees warmer than its latitudinal counterpart in Peru.

One of the consequences of a major El Niño is to raise the temperature of the coastal waters enough to provoke torrential rains along the shoreline. On those occasions, more rain can fall in two weeks than in the previous 20 or 30 years combined. Suddenly houses, roads, and irrigation systems are washed away in the wake of the ensuing floods and mudslides.

The natural vegetation of the coastal valleys is arranged in a linear fashion corresponding to increasing elevation, and there is a repetitive patterning of the floral and faunal resources of the different valleys which continues even after agriculture is introduced. Of course, distinctive localized habitats are produced in some valleys by the interplay of local topography and micro-climate, and the resource potential of valleys differs in terms of both the amount and kind of products which can be produced. Some valleys have an especially productive mid-valley zone, referred to as the *yunga* (500–2,500 m), which is warmer, sunnier, and more sheltered than lower elevation lands. This habitat is ideal for growing coca, maize, tropical fruit, and other crops which do not thrive on the cooler coastal plain.[18] Some valleys on the central and south coast have bands of vegetation specially adapted to the fog and drizzle of the winter months. Fog-dependent epiphytes have evolved which ingest the dust-dew solution from the air through their enlarged and specially modified leaf pores. These areas of fog vegetation, called *lomas*, usually occur between 250 and 800 m in elevation.[19]

Coastal ecology is affected by latitude as well as elevation. The impact of the tropical climate of Ecuador is greater on the northern Peruvian coast and is manifest in the warmer annual temperature, the more frequent occurrence of El

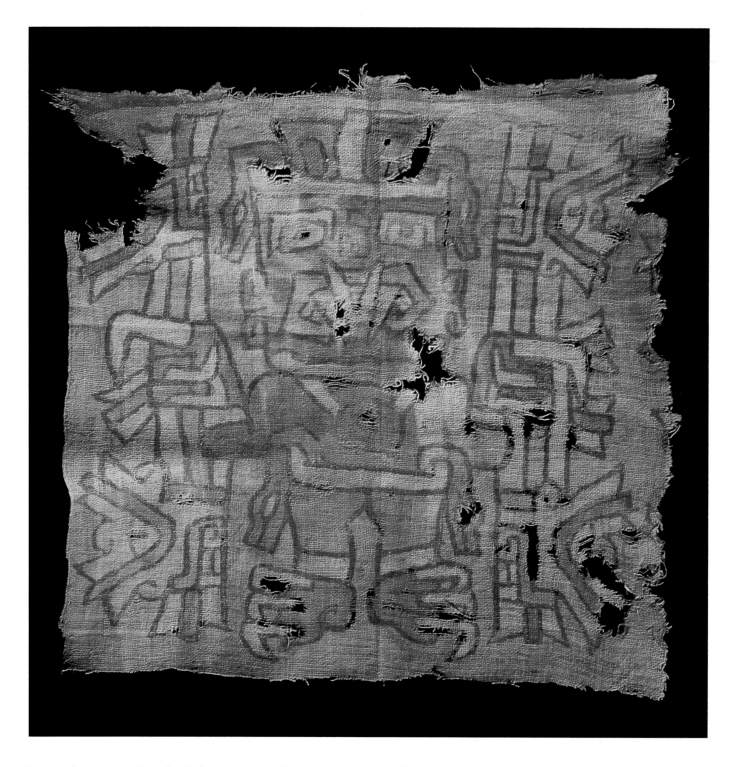

I Painted cotton textile probably from Karwa on the Paracas Peninsula of Peru's south coast. This specimen was one of many representing what appears to be the principal deity of Chavín de Huántar's New Temple. Height 31.75 cm. Photo courtesy of W. Conklin.

II A stone carving from Cerro Sechin in the Casma Valley representing the head of a decapitated victim of a mythical battle. Blood gushes from the victim's eye. Over 3500 years old, the stone frieze decorating the lower terrace at Cerro Sechin constitutes one of the oldest uses of stone sculpture known from the Central Andes. Photo Richard Burger.

III This sculpture from Cerro Sechin represents a severed body stripped of its clothing to symbolize defeat; its closed eye and flexed arms and legs suggest a dead body sprawled on the battlefield. Photo Richard Burger.

IV A stone carving from Cerro Sechin representing a victorious warrior. Photo Richard Burger.

V

VII

V Unbaked clay frieze from the temple of Huaca de los Reyes in the Moche Valley, belonging to the Cupisnique culture of the late Initial Period. Courtesy of Carol Mackey, Proyecto Moche Chan Chan.

VI A multi-colored ocarina modeled in the form of a human with long hair, facial painting or tattooing and an elaborate bead pectoral. This piece exemplifies the poorly understood Tembladera style, best known from looted graves in the Jequetepeque Valley.

VII A classic blackware stirrup-spouted bottle of the Cupisnique culture.

VIII A small pyroengraved bottle gourd (decorated by carving and selective burning) from the Cupisnique cemetery of Puémape. VI–VIII courtesy of the Museo de la Nacion.

VIII

VI

IX

XI

IX The façade of the monumental architecture at Chavín de Huántar was decorated with the sculpted tenon heads that often combine human with jaguar or avian features. This piece is the only tenon head that remains in situ; it is located near the southwest corner of the New Temple (compare ill. 121). Photo Richard Burger.

X View north across the rectangular sunken court at Chavín de Huántar, with the New Temple on the left. Photo Richard Burger.

XI A panoramic view of the ceremonial architecture of Chavín de Huántar with its flat-topped pyramids and sunken plazas. Photo Richard Burger.

XII The eastern face of the New Temple of Chavín de Huántar. Photo Richard Burger.

X

XII

XIII An Early Horizon gold crown, measuring 48 by 13.5 cm, excavated from Tomb 2 at the highland site of Kuntur Wasi, in the headwaters of the Jequetepeque Valley, by the University of Tokyo Archaeological Mission directed by Yoshio Onuki. Courtesy of the University of Tokyo Archaeological Mission.

XIV Hammered gold plaque, 21.5 cm tall, representing the principal deity of Chavín de Huántar's New Temple. Courtesy of Dumbarton Oaks Research Library and Collection.

XV An Early Horizon gold crown found in the tomb of a 50 to 60 year old man (Tomb 1) at Kuntur Wasi. Excavated in 1989, it measures 46.5 by 18 cm. The representation of trophy heads in net bags draws upon a theme popular in the Cupisnique iconography of the north coast (compare ill. 226). Courtesy of the University of Tokyo Archaeological Mission.

XVI Excavations of the earliest period of public constructions at Kuntur Wasi yielded evidence of a late Initial Period building on the summit of the natural hill predating the construction of the large pyramid complex. A large unbaked clay sculpture, 75 cm in height, was recovered inside one of the lateral rooms of the temple. This representation of an anthropomorphic figure with feline attributes was painted in red, green, black, pink and yellow; the intense red color was derived from a cinnabar-based pigment and the unusual green color comes from ground copper ore (malachite). Courtesy of the University of Tokyo Archaeological Mission.

XVII An Early Horizon gold pectoral from Tomb 2 at Kuntur Wasi excavated in 1989 by Yoshio Onuki and his team. This unique piece represents a large feline face and two profile anthropomorphic figures. This image may relate to the mythic tales of twin culture heroes that are known from the Central Andes and beyond. Courtesy of the University of Tokyo Archaeological Mission.

XV

XVI

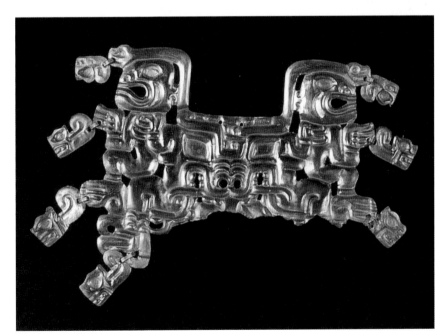

XVII

XVIII A double cloth bag woven with Chavín motifs from white and brown cotton and colored with red pigments; in later times analogous bags were used to hold coca leaves. This piece comes from Peru's south coast. Height 15 cm. Photo courtesy of W. Conklin.

Niño, and in the slightly higher annual precipitation during normal years. In the northern valley of Lambayeque, for example, the average annual precipitation is 100 mm, four times the amount on the central coast. This is not enough to support agriculture, but it does sustain columnar cacti, spiny bushes, and algarroba trees in areas up to 850 m above sea level. At higher elevations in northern valleys like Zaña, there are still vestiges of tropical montane forests, not unlike those on the eastern slopes of the Peruvian Andes or on the shores of Ecuador.[20]

Most coastal soils are relatively fertile and well-drained. They derive from geologically recent Andean sediments deposited as alluvium in the valleys and coastal plain. These soils have remained unleached of their mineral content because of the prevailing aridity. With enough water, the barren desert environments of the coast are transformed into oasis-like gardens which flourish in the unusually mild frost-free climate. Along the edges of the rivers, willows, rushes, and other wild plants are supported by filtrations and seasonal flooding. Cane grows in the brackish lagoons behind the littoral. There are also small areas where vegetation is supported by an unusually high water table or small springs. But for the most part, the coast is dependent on the seasonal rainfall which collects in the upper western slopes and forms small rivers which drain towards the Pacific. Unfortunately, over two-thirds of these watercourses carry no water for at least part of the year, and some are completely dry during most normal years. Almost from its inception, farming on the Peruvian coast has been synonymous with irrigation agriculture.

Throughout the coast, the two factors which determine agricultural productivity are the annual discharge of a river and the configuration of the land surrounding it. The only river in the Pacific drainage whose catchment is not on the western slopes of the Andes is the Santa River, which is fed by the glacial lakes and the highland rains of the Callejón de Huaylas. Instead of draining to the east, like all other highland rivers, the Santa breaks through the western Andes forming a deeply cut valley without a significant coastal plain. Even though the Santa discharges an annual average of $4,594 \times 10^6$ cubic m, more than double the flow of the next largest coastal river, most of its water cannot be used for irrigation farming because of the topography.

The small valleys of the coast presently contain 28 percent of Peru's cultivable land, compared with 55 percent in the highlands. This asymmetry was mirrored, until recently, in the demography of Peru: in 1940, 62 percent of the population resided in the highlands, and the heaviest settlement was between 3,000 m and 4,000 m above sea level. Only 25 percent of the population lived on the coast.[21]

The highlands

The Andes are the backbone of the area discussed in this volume. The Peruvian Andes are high, steep, and rugged. They are made up of many discontinuous ranges with differing orientations. From a geological perspective, the chain is recent, composed of folded and faulted sediments dating to the Miocene and later formations of metamorphic and volcanic origin. Peru's highest mountain, Huascarán, reaches an elevation of 6,768 m. Today, only peaks surpassing 4,800 m elevation are permanently covered with snow and ice, but 12,000 years ago, glaciers covered lands in northern Peru as low as 3,600 m above sea level. The U-

8 Some of the most productive highland lands are located in the *suni* zone above 3,200 m, where rainfall supports high-altitude farming. These steeply sloped fields from the Chavín de Huántar area are used for growing potatoes, oca, and other crops on lands above the entrenched Mosna River.

shaped canyons, rocky moraines, and beautiful glacial lakes of the highlands show the imprint of these earlier times.[22]

In the highlands there is relatively little change in the average daily or monthly temperature during the year. The coldest month (July) has a mean of only 2.8 degrees below that of the warmest month (February). In contrast, there are fluctuations in temperature on most days of 11 to 17 degrees. In the winter, freezing nights are sometimes followed by sweltering afternoons. Sharp diurnal changes are, of course, characteristic of the tropics, and smaller, daily temperature changes also occur on the coast and eastern lowlands.

The highland precipitation pattern (except on the western slopes of the Andes) is unrelated to that of the coast. Moist air is blown over the eastern lowlands from the Atlantic. When the air masses collide with the eastern face of the Andes, heavy rains occur, no matter what the season. During the summer, easterly winds are strong enough to drive the moisture past the eastern slopes and into the intermontane valleys of the Peruvian Andes. As a result, considerable rain falls in these valleys between September and April, with almost no precipitation during the rest of the year. It is axiomatic in Peruvian geography that total rainfall usually decreases from the north to the south and from the east to the west. (Naturally, local topography and wind patterns are also responsible for the diverse highland micro-climates. For example, portions of valleys may receive little precipitation because mountains deflect the incoming air, creating what geographers call rain shadows.) Statistics from a few major weather stations in Peru illustrate this pattern of precipitation. Cajamarca and Chavín de Huántar in the northern highlands have an average annual precipitation of 804 mm and 856 mm respectively, while Huanacayo, in the central highlands, has an average yearly rainfall of 582 mm. Since it takes at least 200 mm of annual rainfall to grow potatoes or maize, normal rainfall in most valleys is more than sufficient to support traditional single-crop highland agriculture without irrigation.[23]

9 In the open grasslands of the *puna*, wild and domesticated camelids graze with deer and other game. In this photograph taken near Ondores in the Junin *puna*, a pile of animal excrement is dried to offset the lack of local vegetation suitable for fuel.

The Andean terrain is bisected by rivers that have formed the highland valleys and basins where most human population is concentrated. The narrow valley floors and steep slopes of these intermontane valleys are well suited to high-altitude agriculture. However, late rains and early frosts can present a serious threat to highland harvests, and irrigation is used in some areas to minimize risks. Nightly frosts occur up to 25 days per month in the winter at elevations above 4,000 m. On the other hand, temperatures rarely, if ever, drop to freezing in areas below 3,000 m. The seasonal frosts and the long tropical growing season preclude the planting of more than one crop per year in most highland valleys. Frosts set the upper limit of highland agriculture, despite the pre-Hispanic development in Peru of frost-resistant varieties of potatoes and other tubers. It is simply not practical to farm most lands above 4,000 m, although special kinds of potatoes are sometimes planted in small sheltered areas as high as 4,300 m.

There are enormous tracts of land above 4,000 m which today are primarily used as pastureland. The year-round grasslands, between 4,000 m and 4,800 m are called *puna*, and these high plains and rolling hills are the natural environment of wild camelids (the vicuña and the guanaco), deer, and an abundance of waterfowl and fish. Prehistoric pastoralists raised domesticated camelids – especially the llama – in this zone as early as 3500 BC. Frosts generally occur in these areas when the skies are clear and solar radiation is quickly lost after nightfall. Snow is unusual because temperatures rarely reach freezing during the rainy season. Even if snow does fall at elevations below 4,800 m, it is invariably melted by the warm temperatures after the early morning.

Further north, the land is generally lower and more heavily bisected by rivers, and the grasslands are consequently scarcer, and different in their composition. This northern high moist grassland environment is often referred to as *páramo* rather than *puna*. In the southern highlands, the dry season is longer and more severe, and the land is somewhat higher in elevation. Though the southern

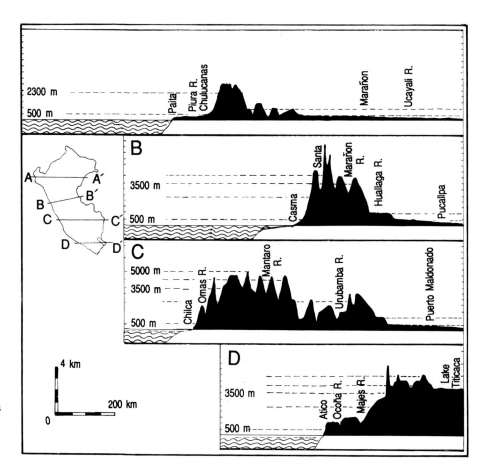

10 The topography of the central Andes varies from north to south as these four transects show, but it is always characterized by massive mountain ranges dropping off precipitously to the narrow coastal plain on the west, and the vast tropical forest on the east.

grasslands are often unable to sustain large herds during the dry season, they are currently the heartland of llamas and alpacas.[24]

The highland region is traversed by a multitude of rivers fed throughout the year by precipitation and glacial runoff. None of these rivers are navigable and fishing is poor. In fact, lacustrine resources always appear to have been of minor importance in highland diet, except near the glacially fed lakes of the *puna*. Rivers, however, are invaluable as a source of water for drinking, cooking, personal hygiene, garbage disposal, and irrigation.

Highland soils are generally inferior to those of the coast. On the *puna*, the soils are usually thin and immature because the original topsoil was scraped off by glaciers and cold weather impeded subsequent soil formation. The soils of intermontane valleys are variable in quality, though usually better than those of the *puna*. The agricultural potential on the valley floors is frequently hampered by high clay content and poor drainage. Erosion is ubiquitous on the valley slopes, and much of the best highland topsoil continues to be washed away and deposited on the floodplains of the Amazon basin and Pacific coastal plain.

The complex highland setting is economically described in the indigenous Quechua language of Peru by a series of terms which correspond to distinct zones of agricultural production. This native nomenclature has been adopted by Peruvian geographer Javier Pulgar Vidal and will be employed here. The *puna* zone (4,000–4,800 m) has already been mentioned. Below it is the *suni* (3,200–

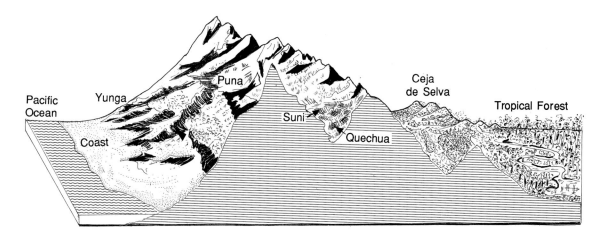

11 Schematic diagram illustrating the position of the major life zones in the central Andes.

4,000 m), in which steep slopes and hollows are devoted to the production of tubers (potatoes, oca, ullucu, mashua, etc.), chenopodium (quinoa, achis, caniwa), lupines (tarwi, broad beans), and grains which were introduced by the Spanish (barley, wheat). The lower slopes and valley floor fall within the *quechua* zone (2,300–3,200 m) in most valleys. In this frost-free environment, maize, squash, and a variety of vegetables can be cultivated, often with the help of supplementary irrigation. The *yunga* is found beneath the quechua in many intermontane valleys (1,000–2,300 m) and on the western slopes of the Andes (500–2,300 m). Highly valued crops like chili pepper (ají), coca, avocado, and fruit are cultivated within this warmer, more protected zone. The elevations cited above are only approximations, and actual elevations vary by as much as several hundred meters, depending on latitude and topography.[25]

The location of these zones relative to each other has always been a critical factor in structuring the production system and the placement of human settlements. In some areas, all four zones are within a day's journey. This arrangement has been described as compressed zonation. Andean farmers in areas of compressed zonation will frequently work small plots of land in each zone in order to achieve something approaching self-sufficiency. In other areas, however, one or more production zones are beyond immediate access and other arrangements must be made to acquire products produced there, either through seasonal migrations, trading alliances, regional markets, or some other mechanism.[26]

The tropical forest and the ceja de selva

The vast Amazonian drainage is by far the largest river system in the world. It covers an area equivalent to the continental United States, and its annual discharge is 15 times that of the Mississippi. Until recently, a dense forest canopy covered much of this region. This lush and seemingly limitless expanse contrasts with the narrow valleys of the arid Peruvian coast and highlands so sharply circumscribed by deserts, rocky ridges, and high-altitude grasslands. Yet within the eastern lowlands there is a critical division between the active floodplains and the slightly higher uplands located between them. Before the 20th century, most of the indigenous tropical forest populations had a riverine orientation focused on the rich floodplains formed by alluvial deposits washed down from the nutrient-rich Andes. These watercourses sustain abundant riverine fauna and the adjacent soils are well suited for intensive agriculture, even for relatively demanding crops such as maize. The rivers provided a critical source of protein in the form of abundant fish, river turtles, caymans, manatees, and capybara (a giant rodent); even terrestrial game tended to concentrate along the shores of the floodplains.[27] Furthermore, the Amazon and its larger tributaries are massive (15 km wide near Manaus) and well suited for navigation. Not surprisingly, native populations used these waterways as their principal avenues of transportation, and vast networks of trade and communication united distant groups.

Unfortunately, the fertile floodplains (often referred to as *varzea*) constitute only about 10 percent of the vast drainage, and a portion of them are ox-bow lakes and swamps unavailable for agriculture. Most of the Amazonian drainage (*c.* 90 percent) consists of forested uplands whose soils are far inferior to those of the *varzea*, highlands, or coast. The upland soils are derived from geologically ancient deposits that have been leached by heavy rains. The consistently high temperatures of the eastern lowlands have hampered the development of humus, and the topsoil tends to be thin, acidic, and nutrient-poor. In many cases, the upland soils become rapidly depleted when cultivated continuously. There is, of course, variability within these uplands and some zones are more fertile than others. Nevertheless, as a whole they appear to have been much more lightly occupied in pre-Hispanic times than the adjacent floodplains.

Although the tropical forest floodplains constitute only a fraction of the entire Amazon drainage, they are still much larger than any of Peru's coastal or highland river systems. Like the Nile or the Tigris-Euphrates, the Amazon and its major tributaries offered annually renewed agricultural resources capable of supporting dense populations. But unlike those Old World water courses, the Amazonian floodplains remain poorly documented from an archaeological perspective. Preservation of most architecture and artifacts in the Amazon is problematic because the continual meanderings of the rivers leads to extensive site destruction. Those sites that escape the ravages of the river usually end up covered by meters of alluvium; if not, they are often obscured on the ground by vegetation and from the air by the dense forest canopy that rises 70–90 m above the ground. The lack of a modern infrastructure in most of the Amazon region has also discouraged the initiation of archaeological research.

Yet, even with the limited evidence available, it appears that tropical forest groups played an important role in the development of Peruvian civilization. As will be seen, many of the cultigens central to early agricultural regimes of the coast and highlands appear to have been domesticated in the Amazonian drainage, and trade goods from the eastern lowlands appear on distant sites with sufficient frequency to demand consideration of this vast but poorly known zone.

The headwaters of several major tributaries of the Amazon, such as the Marañon and the Huallaga, are found along the eastern slopes of the Andes and these river valleys provide a natural link between groups living on the steep Andean slopes and the broad eastern lowlands below. The moisture-laden winds that deposit abundant rainfall over most of the Amazon also produce heavy rains when they collide with the eastern face of the Andes. Thus the tropical forest extends up the eastern face of the Andes. Moreover, river travel by canoe is still

12 The important Early Horizon site of Huayurco in the Marañon Valley, visible in the center of the photograph, was found to have had links with groups in the adjacent highlands and coast.

feasible up to 700 m. Above this elevation there are a series of rapids (called *pongos*) that impede navigation, and the vegetation is denser and more tangled. This zone, extending unevenly up to 2,000–3,000 m elevation, is referred to variously as the montane forest, *ceja*, *ceja de montaña* or *ceja de selva* (eyebrow of the jungle). It is characterized by very steep slopes covered by low trees, mosses and ferns, as well as wild orchids and fuschia. While the soils of the *ceja* are generally good, they can be rapidly destroyed by erosion once the vegetation that covers them is removed. The dense *ceja* vegetation is interspersed with arid canyons which, because of their location or orientation, receive little rainfall. For example, in the Huallaga Valley, the city of Huánuco (2,000 m) receives only 310 mm of precipitation annually, while nearby Tingo Maria is drenched by 3,963 mm per year.[28]

Tributaries of the Amazon like the Marañon and the Huallaga penetrate deep into the Andes, and create situations in which highland, *ceja*, and lowland environments are in close proximity. Similarly, in what now is northernmost Peru, there is a dip in the elevation of the Andes and the *ceja* vegetation of the eastern slopes almost connects with the *yunga* environment on the other side of the continental divide. Islands of tropical forest vegetation appear to have survived in some locations along the western Andes and coast of Ecuador. Thus, coastal and highland groups in northern Peru may have had access to tropical forest resources without lengthy trips into the eastern lowlands.

Archaeologists assume that contemporary observations of the landscape and climate like those just presented illuminate the conditions in which early Peruvian civilization developed. While this may be true, it is unwarranted to

The changing environment

presume complete environmental stability. During the Pleistocene the climate in Peru was considerably colder than in modern times. By 3000 BC the temperatures were roughly the same as those of today. The melting of the glaciers in response to global warming opened up vast expanses of potential agricultural and pastureland in the Peruvian highlands. The snowline retreated 600–700 m in central Peru and 1,000 m in northern Peru. The runoff from the melting glaciers helped produce a sharp rise in the level of the Pacific relative to the land surface, gradually inundating up to three-quarters of Peru's coastal plain. The sea level finally stabilized at the beginning of the third millennium BC.[29]

There have also been more recent world-wide fluctuations in the climate, related according to some scientists to cycles of solar activity. In Peru, even small changes in mean annual temperature would have had a significant impact on human settlement, particularly in highland environments, since the upper limits of agriculture are determined mainly by the frequency and duration of frosts, and the optimal range of elevations in which a crop can be grown is primarily a function of its thermal and water requirements. A drop of 2 degrees in the annual mean temperature depresses the vegetational zonation by 300 m in respect to sea level. Consequently, a cooling trend of modest proportions would turn substantial areas of agricultural land into environments fit only for pastureland. A warming trend, conversely, would open up vast areas of newly productive farmland in the highlands. Augusto Cardich has conducted one of the few detailed studies of post-Pleistocene climatic change in Peru and concluded that, since 3000 BC, the limits of agriculture have fluctuated by 400–700 m.[30]

After studying pollen recovered from late prehistoric sites in central Peru, James Schoenwetter concluded that 300 years ago the lands between 3,700 and 4,200 m would have had an agricultural potential equivalent to lands located today at elevations between 3,400 and 3,700 m.[31] Historical documents likewise attest to climatically-related changes in highland productive activities since the Spanish Conquest. Thus, while the general patterns of climate observed today have existed for at least 5,000 years, it is likely that climatic fluctuations did affect the availability and zonation of crop land. Unfortunately, research on this theme is not well developed and the chronological parameters of prehistoric oscillations have yet to be well defined.

John Eddy has tentatively identified 12 long-term global climatic variations, 5 of which are directly relevant to this volume. Variation 11 (2350–2000 BC) and Variation 10 (1876–1700 BC) are cycles of moderate climate, slightly warmer than current conditions. Variation 9 (1400–1200 BC), Variation 8 (800–580 BC), and Variation 7 (420–300 BC) correspond to periods considerably colder than at present.[32] If Eddy is correct, temperatures during much of the late Initial Period and Early Horizon may have been quite cool, in which case the size of the *suni* and *quechua* zones would have been reduced and their upper limits would have been shifted downwards. But during certain intervals of the early Initial Period and Late Preceramic, conditions may have been even more benign than in recent times.

The impact of temperature fluctuations would have been less notable in the coastal environment, where it would have been mitigated by the influence of the Humboldt Current, and where water availability rather than temperature is the primary determinant of natural vegetation and agriculture. However, Edward Lanning has suggested that besides the world-wide fluctuations in temperature there were periods of desiccation responsible for the prehistoric contraction in the areas of lomas vegetation. Evidence of vegetational change in the coast after 3000 BC is compelling, but many investigators maintain that these are the result of the degradation of the fragile lomas environment and modification of natural drainage patterns by human populations.[33]

It would be a mistake to think of the physical environment as a passive, unchanging backdrop to the prehistoric socio-cultural developments. Peru was, and still is, characterized by considerable tectonic activity caused by the subduction of the eastward-moving Nazca Oceanic Plate beneath the westward-moving South American Continental Plate. The collision of the two is responsible for both the continuing growth of the Andes, and for the subsurface stress which triggers the earthquakes that periodically wreak havoc in Peru. A 1970 earthquake, measuring 7.7 on the Richter scale, resulted in the death of an estimated 75,000 Peruvians. Back in 1746, an 18 m tidal wave totally destroyed Callao, the main port of Peru. These two events are only recent instances of the crises that have characterized the Andean landscape as long as humans have occupied it.[34]

As the Nazca Oceanic Plate forces itself beneath the western edge of the South American continent, it produces a gradual uplift of the coast and, more rarely, sudden uplifts of small portions of the coast. The disequilibrium between the old drainage pattern and the new slope of the uplifted terrain remains unnoticed until the rare heavy rains unleashed by El Niño suddenly precipitate a major transformation in the landscape. Michael Moseley calls this unusual interplay of tectonic activity and climatic perturbations "radical environmental alteration cycles." These episodes have profoundly modified coastal topography and, in the process, destroyed or buried an unknown number of archaeological sites. For example, in the 5th century AD, the living surface of a center of the Moche culture was stripped off and lowered by 4 m, while rich lands near by were buried beneath newly formed sand dunes. Drastic changes in the highland landscape have been produced by land- and mudslides triggered by earthquakes or the breaking of the moraines which dam the glacial lakes. With all of these factors, it is naïve to assume that in Peru the patterning of sites found by even the most dedicated archaeologist provides an accurate picture of the prehistoric settlement system.[35]

Human impact on the Peruvian environment has likewise been significant. People have destroyed much of the native fauna and flora, introduced a wide range of plants and animals from the Old World, reshaped the local topography with terraces, and changed the water table and drainage through pumping and canals. For better or worse, the people of the Andes have manipulated their environment for over 6,000 years, and the landscape is partially a product of their intervention. The origins and development of ancient Peruvian civilization must be viewed within this dynamic context.

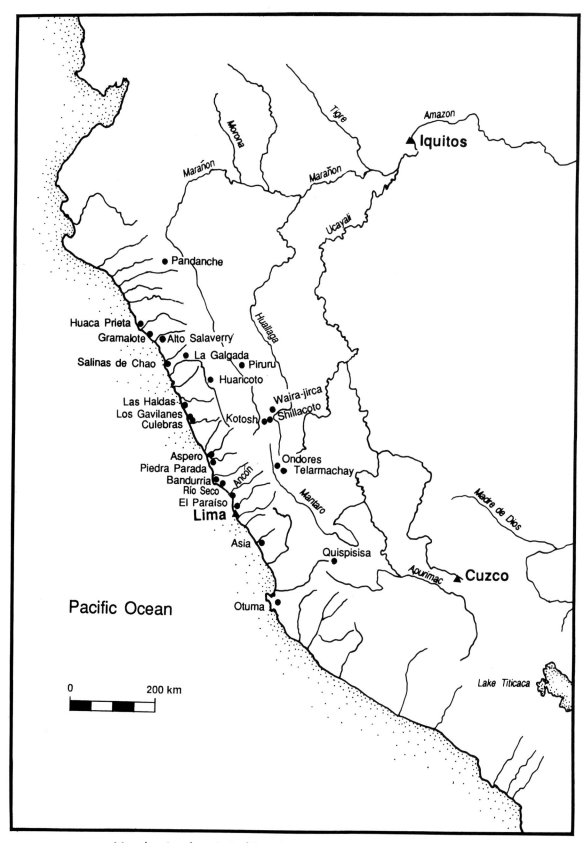

Pandanche

Huaca Prieta
Gramalote ● Alto Salaverry
● La Galgada
Salinas de Chao ● Piruru
● Huaricoto
Las Haldas
Los Gavilanes ● Waira-jirca
Culebras ● Shillacoto
Kotosh
Aspero
Piedra Parada ● Ondores
Bandurria ● Telarmachay
Río Seco
El Paraíso
Lima
Asia
Quispisisa
Otuma

Iquitos

Cuzco

Pacific Ocean

Lake Titicaca

0   200 km

13 Map showing the principal Late Preceramic sites mentioned in Chapter 2.

The Late Preceramic and the Beginnings of Peruvian Civilization

In 1941 archaeologists Gordon Willey and John Corbett were puzzled when a month of excavations failed to yield any pottery either in the large platform mound or in the adjacent midden at the Aspero site in the Supe Valley. The two scholars saw ceramics as the hallmark of a sedentary agricultural society, and conversely assumed that the absence of pottery signaled an economy not based on farming. They further believed that public architecture, such as the Aspero platform, was undertaken only in complex societies practicing intensive agriculture. Conditioned by this rigid conceptual framework and confronted by an apparent contradiction to it, Willey and Corbett dated the Aspero mound on the basis of pottery found in a cemetery near by and presumed a functional explanation for the absence of ceramics at the site. The samples of domesticated cotton, gourds, and maize found in the Aspero refuse seemed to support the view that the mound was coeval with the cemetery. The possibility that monumental architecture had been built prior to the introduction of ceramics and, by extension, before a primary dependency on agriculture, was not even considered.[1]

Nevertheless, the latter possibility became increasingly plausible in the following decades as additional coastal sites which lacked pottery but featured major mound constructions were discovered. Gradually it became apparent that Aspero was not an inexplicable anomaly but rather part of a much larger pattern, which also included the sites of El Paraíso in the Chillón Valley, Río Seco in the Chancay Valley, Bandurria in the Huaura Valley, Piedra Parada in the Supe Valley, and Salinas de Chao in the Chao Valley. Two decades later, investigations by the University of Tokyo at the highland site of Kotosh unearthed large public buildings in stratigraphic layers lacking pottery. Here, the architecture was found beneath the remains of the earliest ceramic cultures in the region.

The introduction of radiocarbon dating made it possible to date these coastal and highland sites without pottery, and the results of such dating confirmed what was already obvious: preceramic cultures in both areas were responsible for the numerous examples of monumental architecture. The oldest radiocarbon measurements from the Huaca de los Sacrificios at Aspero are 2772 BC and 2903 BC, and since the samples were not taken from the oldest construction levels, it is likely that the building began at least 200 years earlier. A sample from the nearby platform mound of the Huaca de los Idolos yielded dates of 3001 BC and 2483 BC.[2] This would make the earliest stone platforms at Aspero contemporary with

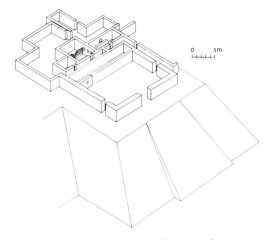

14 Isometric reconstruction drawing of the Huaca de los Idolos at Aspero in the Supe Valley (c. 2750 BC), one of the earliest examples of monumental architecture in the New World. On the platform summit, interior rooms with niches, an altar-like bench, and clay wall decoration could be reached only by way of a walled entry court. The platform walls were probably terraced rather than sloped, and access may have been provided by a central staircase instead of a ramp.

the royal pyramids of the Old Kingdom in Egypt and with the ziggurats of the Sumerians in Mesopotamia. Without any doubt, the Preceramic constructions in Peru are the oldest known examples of monumental architecture in the New World. The pyramids of the Olmec and other Preclassic cultures of Mesoamerica do not appear until over 1,000 years later.

Monumental architecture, one of the criteria of civilization as defined by British prehistorian Gordon Childe (Chapter 1), has been widely used by others as an unambiguous indicator of complex society. As the product of a massive investment of human labor, these constructions imply a substantial population from which labor could be drawn, and an economy sufficiently productive and well organized to be able to support the people engaged in building. A social mechanism capable of mobilizing large numbers of individuals was also needed, since the organization of such projects is inconceivable without the existence of authorities whose right to plan and direct these activities is recognized. Buildings on a monumental scale require that labor be drawn from many separate households within a single community or from several communities or social groups. Collective efforts of this kind are sometimes referred to as corporate labor projects.[3] Many archaeologists assume that only state organizations are capable of erecting truly monumental constructions, and that the use or threat of physical coercion must be one of the mechanisms employed in motivating the workers. A cross-cultural review of ethnographically and historically known peoples does not reveal any instances of truly monumental architecture built in non-state societies. For example, the largest and most imposing prehistoric monuments built on the complex chiefdoms of Moloka'i Island in Hawaii were war temples, but only two of these had platforms with volumes in excess of 5,000 cubic m, and the largest utilized only approximately 15,750 cubic m of stone fill. Such constructions are not comparable to the labor investment represented by El Paraíso, the largest of the coastal Preceramic centers in Peru, which has an estimated volume of over 340,000 cubic m.[4]

Yet before assessing the nature of the societies responsible for the earliest monumental constructions in Peru, we must remember that societies considered in such cross-cultural reviews represent only a tiny fraction of those which have existed in human history. There is no reason to assume that they represent the full range of organizational possibilities or developmental pathways. Various forms of society may have once existed which find no equivalent in the ethnographic or historic record, and some of these may have built monumental architecture in social contexts very different from those with which we are now familiar. As will be seen in this chapter, Preceramic Peru may present one instance in which societies created truly monumental constructions without a coercive state apparatus.

The Late Preceramic period on the coast

Fishing, farming, and trade

The economic foundations of the Late Preceramic cultures of the coast have been well documented over the last decade. The primary elements of this economy were the intensive utilization of maritime resources, floodplain agriculture, and long-distance trade. The importance of fishing and shellfish collection in this economic configuration is unparalleled in other pristine civilizations, but this is not surprising considering the particularly rich maritime resources of the Peruvian coast and the limitations for farming in the arid coastal valleys.

A wide range of maritime resources were exploited along the littoral during the third millennium BC. Principal among these were the schools of anchovies and sardines, the bones of which are abundant in Late Preceramic middens and human coprolites (dried feces). To capture anchovies and other small and medium-sized fish in shallow waters, coastal inhabitants employed small-mesh (seine) nets with apertures of 2–3 cm, and positioned the nets by attaching stone weights and gourd floats. One seine net recovered at Huaca Prieta was calculated to have been 30.5 m long. Simple curved shellfish hooks attached to cotton lines and large-mesh nets were used to capture bigger fish, but there is no evidence that watercraft were used for deep-sea fishing.[5]

In sheer volume, the bulk of Late Preceramic middens is made up of shells from a wide variety of mussels, clams, sea snails, crabs, and other shellfish collected from sandy beaches, rocky headlands, and other littoral habitats. The coastal dwellers also hunted marine mammals, especially sea lions, and ocean birds, including Humboldt penguins, boobies, pelicans, and cormorants. Deer and other land mammals were rarely eaten and must have constituted something of a delicacy. The dart-thrower (atlatl), known from Aspero and Asia (a village site at the mouth of the Omas River), was probably the main hunting device; stone-tipped and fire-hardened wooden spears were also used.[6]

The pervasiveness of marine foods in Preceramic refuse has led many scholars to conclude that maritime subsistence strategies were the mainstay of the economy.[7] Aspero, Salinas de Chao, Bandurria, Río Seco, and other Late Preceramic centers flourished along the shoreline far from the nearest area suitable for agriculture. This contrasts sharply with later pre-Hispanic times, when only specialized fishing villages were established in such spots. The construction of monumental architecture and adjacent habitations along the beach seems to reflect the distinctive subsistence priorities of these Late Preceramic cultures.

The rich resources of the Humboldt Current made it possible to support a large, dense permanent population throughout the year, even with a relatively simple maritime technology. Archaeologist Michael Moseley estimated that the anchovy schools alone could have supported more than 6,500,000 people at only 60 percent of the carrying capacity of the littoral. Of course, such a situation would not have arisen, probably because a diet based purely on anchovies leaves much to be desired in terms of taste and nutrition. Nevertheless, Preceramic coastal dwellers did eat considerable quantities of anchovies, the surplus being ground into fishmeal and stored for later use or emergencies.[8] It also appears that larger fish, and perhaps shellfish, were dried and salted for long-term preservation. The intensive exploitation of these marine resources would have been difficult, even impossible, without cotton for nets and fishing line, and bottle gourds for floats. Cotton and gourds are not native to the arid Peruvian coast, but were introduced from the moister tropical environments to the east and north. Cotton is so common in Late Preceramic coastal sites that some archaeologists refer to this period as the Cotton Preceramic.[9]

Archaeologists have found residues of agricultural foods in the middens of major Late Preceramic centers and smaller shoreline villages. Squash, beans, and chili peppers appear to have been standard fare, but not dietary staples. Fruits

Documented occurrence of food crops and other plants of economic importance at Late Preceramic sites

	Huaca Prieta	Alto Salaverry	La Galgada	Huay-nuná	Los Gavilanes	El Paraíso	Ancón
Potato (*Solanum tuberosum*)				+	*	*	+
Oca (*Oxalis tuberosa*)							+
Ullucu (*Ullucus tuberosus*)							+
Achira (*Canna edulis*)	+		+	+	+	+	+
Sweet Potato (*Ipomoea batatas*)				+	*		+
Manioc (*Manihot esculenta*)					+		
Jícama (*Pachyrrhizus tuberosus*)		+			+	+	+
Peanut (*Arachis hypogaea*)					+		+
Lima Bean (*Phaseolus lunatus*)	+	+	+		+	+	+
Squash¹ (*Cucurbita* spp.)	+	+	+	+	+	+	+
Chili Pepper (*Capsicum* spp.)	+	+	+	+	+	+	+
Jack Bean (*Canavalia* sp.)	+	+	+				+
Common Bean (*Phaseolus vulgaris*)		+ (?)	+			+	
Maize (*Zea mays*)					+		
Lucuma² (*Lucuma bifera*)	+	+	+	+	+	+	+
Guava (*Psidium guajava*)	+	+	+		+	+	+
Avocado (*Persea americana*)		+	+		+	+	
Chirimoya (*Annona Cherimolia*)					+	+	
Pacae (*Inga Feuillei*)		+			+	+	+
Cattail (*Typha angustifolia*)	+		+		+	+	
Bottle Gourd (*Lagenaria siceraria*)	+	+	+	+	+	+	+
Cotton (*Gossypium barbadense*)	+	+	+	+	+	+	+

* Family level identification

¹ Three species of squash, *C. ficifolia*, *C. maxima*, and *C. moschata*, were found at most Late Preceramic sites of the coast.

² Classificatory terms applied to lucuma include *Lucuma bifera*, *Pouteria lucuma*, and *Lucuma obovata*.

like guava, lucuma, and pacae were also common, as were wild foods such as cattail rhizomes.[10] Several domesticated plant varieties (high in yield and carbohydrate content) had been introduced to the coast by this time (2000 BC). Recent microscopic studies of starch grains indicate the cultivation of sweet potatoes and manioc, and earlier research on macroscopic remains documented achira and maize.[11] Notwithstanding the availability of these cultigens, most scholars believe that the agricultural input in the Late Preceramic diet was significantly less and the marine component much greater than in later times.

Research at the shoreline village of Huaca Prieta in the Chicama Valley provides us with an unusually detailed view of early diets. Analysis of partly undigested material still in the intestinal tract of a female corpse found at the site enabled scientists to reconstruct what she had eaten during the final 48 hours of her life. In one of her last meals she had consumed mussels, crabs, sea snails, and sea urchins along with plenty of hot pepper and three types of fruit abundant in her environment.[12]

The considerable time spent net-fishing and diving for deep-water mussels took its toll on the health of the Huaca Prieta residents. The repeated and prolonged exposure to cold water produced audio exoteses in 86 percent of males over 30 years old. This bony growth in the external auditory canal impairs hearing and sometimes causes deafness.[13]

The complementary, rather than primary, role of food crops (which require cooking) in the diet helps to explain why pottery-making was not immediately adopted, despite contact with Ecuadorian groups who had been producing ceramics since 3000 BC. In the absence of cooking vessels, plant and marine foods were roasted over open fires or cooked with heated stones in earthen ovens or gourds. In many cases, cooked foods were only superficially charred and many items were eaten raw.[14]

Cultivation appears to have occured along the banks of the rivers, thereby taking advantage of seasonal inundation following the highland rains. El Paraíso and Piedra Parada were established adjacent to lands suitable for this type of floodplain cultivation, but were still within easy walking distance of the shore. However, most agriculture was probably carried out by people living further inland in dispersed hamlets. A close relationship must have existed between valley farmers and the population living along the littoral since marine produce was as common in the inland valley sites as agricultural goods were in the shoreline communities.[15]

In most valleys, land suitable for floodplain cultivation is very limited, usually less than 5 percent of the land later cultivated using irrigation. It is unlikely, therefore, that the large sedentary populations on the coast could have survived practicing floodwater farming without the unique maritime resource of the Humboldt Current. Conversely, this maritime economy could not have flourished were it not for the acquisition (through exchange for sea resources) of the agricultural products vital to a healthy diet.

In some coastal valleys, Late Preceramic inland populations may have augmented floodplain farming with irrigation agriculture in order to support larger, agriculturally oriented groups. The research emphasis of the 1970s and 1980s on Late Preceramic centers located on or near the shoreline may have led archaeologists to underestimate the importance of coeval inland communities. For example, a host of poorly known early settlements with public architecture have been documented in the Supe Valley, but none has been investigated in depth. A recent pilot study has tentatively concluded that several of these centers, including Chupacigarro Chico, Chupacigarro Centro, and Alpacoto date to the Late Preceramic. These settlements are situated 15–20 km from the coast and are comparable in scale to the large shoreline communities discussed earlier in this chapter. If the Preceramic date of these centers is confirmed by further study, the role of subsistence agriculture in the early coastal developments will have to be reassessed.[16]

The third major component of the coastal economy was long-distance trade, particularly with the adjacent highlands. While the full inventory of highland products acquired through exchange is unknown, it certainly included raw

15 Double-headed birds were popular themes on the textiles of both Huaca Prieta (on the shores of Chicama) and La Galgada (in the upper section of the Santa drainage). Motifs from two looped bags found at La Galgada (a and b) and a twined fabric from Huaca Prieta (c). Note the resemblance in style to the double-headed fish motif on a textile from the site of Asia (d).

materials, food, and craft items. Obsidian, a glassy volcanic rock used for stone tools, occurs naturally only in mountains of over 4,000 m, but small quantities have been found on the coast at most Late Preceramic sites, including Asia, Aspero, Ancón, and Otuma. While probably not essential to the subsistence economy, obsidian is a useful index of the degree of interaction between these societies. The northernmost source of obsidian in Peru was Quispisisa, a deposit located 385 km southeast of Aspero near Castrovirreyna (in Huancavelica) in the south-central highlands. Another example of the import of non-critical raw materials is the wood used in the thresholds of the doorways at Río Seco. They were made from a tree that grows only between 1,450 m and 3,000 m above sea level.[17]

The discovery of potatoes, oca, and ullucu at the Preceramic fishing villages of Ancón and Alto Salaverry suggests the occasional exchange of plant domesticates as well, since these cultigens are characteristic of highland agricultural systems. Finally, a very distinctive type of bi-convex stone bead with two parallel laterally drilled holes appears both at coastal sites (e.g. Aspero and Bandurria) and highland centers (such as Huaricoto and La Galgada), suggesting that trade in manufactured goods existed as well.[18]

The coastal–highland links were probably much more important than this smattering of items would suggest. Pacific shells and fish bones have been found at all of the Preceramic highland sites with public architecture, and the links between the two regions appear to have been extensive. In the recent excavations at La Galgada in the upper Santa Valley drainage, numerous textiles were found which bore similar designs to cloth from Huaca Prieta and Asia.

What factors could have stimulated this interchange between coastal and highland societies? The demand for nutritional ocean products in the highlands may have been one such factor. Endemic goiter and cretinism due to iodine deficiency have traditionally been serious health problems in the intermontane valleys of Peru and Ecuador, and the consumption of relatively small quantities of Pacific mollusks and fish, high in iodine, would have alleviated this problem. In later times, there was an active coast–highland trade in these items, and also in ocean salt. Salt was much in demand by highland agriculturalists living on a bland high carbohydrate diet; moreover, ocean salt, like seafood was also a good source of iodine.[19] The degree to which the pre-Hispanic salt trade was stimulated by nutritional need or culinary taste is difficult to establish, but its importance in later times is undeniable.

It is probably no coincidence that one of the largest coastal Preceramic sites, Salinas de Chao, is located at the edge of an uplifted bay in a spot ideal for salt production; in fact, salt was mined there until recently. Stone mortars would have been an essential tool for processing the sun-dried salt, and the unusually large numbers of spent mortars there suggest that the mining of salt for exchange was underway during the Late Preceramic.[20] At the highland site of La Galgada, a salt crystal was left beneath the head of a woman in one of the earliest burials, and a bed of large salt crystals covered by a layer of charcoal served as the base for two later Preceramic burials.[21] These discoveries not only confirm the existence of long-distance trade in salt during the Preceramic, but also point to the special esteem in which salt was held by highland peoples during this time.

From the perspective of coastal peoples, long-term contacts and reciprocal obligations with highland groups would have helped to buffer them against the unpredictable disruptions of their economy by El Niños. As we saw in Chapter 1, El Niño events can occur four to five times per century on the central coast, and more frequently further north. A sudden decline in ocean productivity triggered by an El Niño would have presented a particularly serious threat to large sedentary populations dependent on maritime resources. The establishment and maintenance of social and economic ties would have facilitated the acquisition of staple food crops (such as potatoes, oca, and ullucu) until the ocean's fertility was restored. Under normal circumstances, bulky highland crops would have been impractical to import in quantity.

The success of the coastal economy and its ability to withstand sporadic environmental crises can be gauged by the large populations it was able to maintain over many centuries. There are extensive midden areas at all of the centers with public architecture. At the Preceramic center of Río Seco, German archaeologist W. E. Wendt concluded that between 2,500 and 3,000 people had been buried in the refuse surrounding the platform constructions; additional burials may exist outside this zone. Tentative estimates for residential populations at each of the major Preceramic sites have ranged from 1,000 to 3,000 individuals. The size of these late Preceramic coastal centers is enormous in comparison with all earlier settlements, and it has been estimated that there were 30 fisherfolk in the Late Preceramic for every hunter-gatherer of the preceding cultural phase.[22]

The mixed maritime-agricultural economy of the Peruvian coast was able to sustain patterns of population growth and density normally associated with more developed agricultural economies. The marked increase in coastal population was accompanied by settlement nucleation. Clearly, the demographic levels and economic prosperity necessary to support large-scale undertakings had been achieved without an exclusively agricultural base. However, these societies lacked the complex division of labor usually associated with great public works elsewhere in the world, for besides possible differences in activities on the basis of age and sex, only the broad division between farmers and fisherfolk seems to have been of significance.

Artifacts and art

In the foregoing discussion, no reference was made to the role of specialized craft production in the economy because it seems to have been of relatively little importance. Although a wide range of Preceramic sites have been excavated, few distinctive objects have been recovered which could not be produced by individual households. The tool inventory was quite simple: besides the fishing paraphernalia already described, the most common artifacts are net bags, unmodified stone flakes, and crudely made unifaces and bifaces which superficially resemble products of the European Lower Paleolithic. Stone mortars and pestles are also found, as are bone needles and bodkins used in textile manufacture. A simple branchless stick pointed on one end, known as a digging stick, was the principal tool of farmers and it remained a standard farming implement on the coast until the arrival of the Spaniards.[23]

Items of personal adornment are rare and generally limited to bone pins and polished bone or stone beads. In Inca times, large earplugs were indicative of male adult status and were presented to young men at the time of their initiation to manhood. Late Preceramic earplugs made of wood have been found at the sites of Asia and La Galgada and, at the latter, white shell had been glued with resin to the surface of the earplug. Shaped or sewn clothing was apparently unknown, but large cotton cloths were wrapped around the body as mantles and skirts. Archaeologists have also recovered other elements of dress, including belts, caps, and sandals. Mirrors were fashioned by grinding and polishing high-grade coal (i.e. anthracite) to a high luster.[24] One of the few elaborate examples of Preceramic handicraft is a small plaque, found at the site of Asia, which has inlaid shell beads and a pyrite(?) mirror on one side and a two-headed bird motif incised on the other.[25]

Cut gourds were used as bottles, bowls, and ladles. Some of these were decorated by scraping off sections of the gourd's epidermis while it was still soft or incising its hardened surface with fine lines. Occasionally, surface decoration was created by a burning incising technique called pyroengraving. The most famous examples of Preceramic pyroengraved gourds come from Huaca Prieta, but even there only 13 out of 10,770 gourd fragments show evidence of decoration.[26]

By far the most developed visual art in these early coastal cultures was that of cotton textiles. These were made entirely manually because the heddle-loom, which incorporates a device to mechanically raise and lower warps so that the wefts can be easily inserted, was apparently unknown on the coast. Consequently, the most popular technique for producing fabric was twining, in which weft yarns turn about the warps instead of interweaving between them. This was an easier and faster way of making fabric without the heddle than weaving, since pre-heddle woven fabric required many more weft insertions than a twined fabric of the same size. At Huaca Prieta, 71 percent of the textiles were twined, while only 5 percent were woven; the remainder were made by looping or netting. Most of the decorated Preceramic textiles from this site were made by twining, probably using a stationary frame or loom. Designs were highlighted by manipulating the variations of color in natural cotton and, more dramatically, by the use of colored pigments, including red, blue, yellow, and green.[27]

The most elaborate examples of twined cloth provide a rare glimpse of Preceramic artistic imagination. Surprisingly, many of these motifs offer antecedents for the art styles of later Peruvian cultures, and several reoccured in Chavín art, such as the frontal anthropomorphic figure with flowing hair or snakes dangling from the waist, profile felines, or the raptor with wings and talons fully extended and head shown in profile. The popularity of two-headed snakes and interlocking stylized birds continued for millennia, and the creation of monstrous images by combining traits of two or more creatures – such as the crab-snake composite from Huaca Prieta – also became a long-standing practice.

The angularity and symmetry of these motifs reflects the limitations inherent in the twining and early weaving techniques, but the resulting effect was seen as aesthetically desirable. In later times, similar motifs inspired by textile designs were applied to metals, stone, and other media lacking these technical constraints.

Unfortunately, most designs are difficult to identify because the dye has faded from the cloth. To reconstruct these images, the positional changes of all of the wefts must be traced and plotted. Archaeologist Junius Bird pioneered this procedure in his analysis of Preceramic textiles from Huaca Prieta. Textile

16 In Chavín art, the supreme deity was shown in a frontal position with long hair and snakes dangling from the waist (see ill. 175). Antecedents for these representations may be present in some Late Preceramic textile motifs from Huaca Prieta (above) and La Galgada (below).

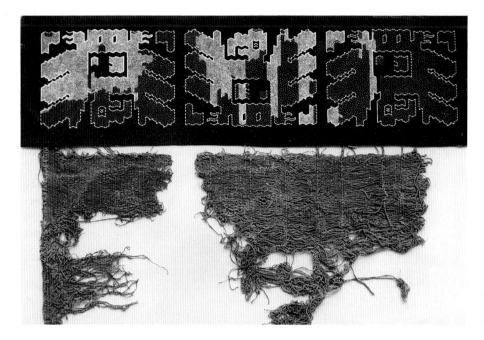

17 Aided by a microscope, Junius Bird plotted the transposed warps of this twined cotton textile from Huaca Prieta to reveal the repeating design of a condor with outstretched wings.

motifs similar to those from this site have been found at Asia, 600 km to the south, and at La Galgada, 140 km southeast.

Are these images merely decorative? Considering the historical relationship of these motifs to later religious art, it seems more likely that the imagery expresses elements of Late Preceramic cosmology and its accompanying myths. Furthermore, the contexts in which the textiles have been found reinforce the view that these were not emblems of elite prestige, but instead were symbols of popular belief.

From this brief review, it is evident that there are very few material indicators which could have served as markers of hierarchical social status. In most societies, the greater the social and economic differentiation, the greater the number of material objects which represent these differences in status. The absence of such markers in the Late Preceramic conversely suggests that the degree of differentiation may have been small.

More abundant expressions of Preceramic creativity may eventually be encountered in large-scale excavations of public architecture. Evidence exists of modeled and painted clay friezes on the raised platforms at Salinas de Chao and Aspero. The discovery of a finely modeled wooden bowl on the summit of Huaca de los Sacrificios and a large cache of modeled unbaked clay figurines on Huaca de los Idolos – both at Aspero – reinforces the impression that rare artistic efforts were destined for the public domain rather than for individual use.[28]

18 A cache of at least 13 small figurines of unbaked whiteish-gray clay was buried between two floors of a small room in Huaca de los Idolos, prior to 2500 BC. It included this small female figure wearing a flat-topped hat.

Mortuary remains

Burial patterns directly reflect cultural conceptions of death and afterlife and the ritual expression of these ideas in this final rite of passage. Interments can further provide a glimpse of the living community since the surviving members perpetuate their own cultural values by organizing these ceremonies. For example, the contrast between the recently discovered tombs of Moche royalty

(AD 200–500) at Sipán, which included offerings of abundant gold jewelry and over 1,000 whole ceramic vessels, and the impoverished pit graves of the peasants of the same society is clear indication of the social differentiation existent in later Andean societies. Similarly, if Late Preceramic societies were stratified along economic and social lines we would expect some sign of it in the way they buried their dead.

Several hundred burials have been excavated from Preceramic sites along the coast of Peru and considerable variation is apparent from site to site, and within sites. It is possible to generalize, nevertheless, that burials are commonly made in shallow ovoid pits in refuse or abandoned houses. Throughout the area, the dead are most frequently placed in a flexed or semi-flexed position reminiscent of a fetus. At Asia, Río Seco, Los Gavilanes, and other sites stones were placed on top of the deceased. This may have been to prevent the return of the deceased's spirit; similar measures are known from cultures around the world. In some sites burials display a favored orientation for the bodies (e.g. east–west at Asia) which probably had ritual significance, but little regularity exists at most sites.[29]

There is a notable absence of lavish burial offerings at any of the Late Preceramic sites. Most individuals were accompanied by little more than a reed mat and some cotton cloth. The worn condition of many items suggests that they had been the possessions of the deceased. A few individuals were buried with special objects, such as an aged woman at Huaca Prieta who was buried in a typical woven mat on top of a small cotton pouch containing two small pyroengraved gourds. The designs on these two objects strongly resemble the motifs on Valdivia pottery from the coast of southern Ecuador, and it is possible that the gourds themselves were imported.[30] Besides rare items like these, however, most possessions could have been produced on a household level without recourse to specialists. Cotton seeds, spindle whorls, and bodkins are found even in the refuse of littoral villages, indicating that these fisherfolk processed cotton grown elsewhere and converted it into cloth and fishing gear. While differences clearly exist between burials, most can be explained in terms of differences in sex, age, or personal achievement. Thus, mortuary patterns, like domestic refuse, do not reveal evidence of social or economic stratification within Late Preceramic society.

The most elaborate burial known from this period was discovered by archaeologist Robert Feldman on the summit of Huaca de los Sacrificios at Aspero. Whereas all the other Preceramic burials found at the site were placed in refuse with few – if any – objects, in this instance an infant less than two months old was buried wearing a shell bead cap, and wrapped in a cotton cloth which was placed inside a basket.[31] This, in turn, was covered with another cotton textile and finally a cane mat tied by cotton strips. The resulting bundle was capped by a four-legged grinding stone, itself the product of several hundred hours of pecking and grinding. The context and special character of this interment have led Feldman to interpret it as a dedicatory offering for the public architecture. This view gains credibility in the light of other unusual objects also buried on the summit of this and other public buildings. It does not necessarily indicate that the dead child was born of high status.

The tombs at Asia are unique among Preceramic burials in providing possible evidence of conflict. Several headless skeletons were unearthed with even fewer grave goods than other burials. Interments of isolated heads were also

19,20 (*Above*) One of the two complete pyroengraved gourds (6.3 cm in diameter) found in a cotton pouch in the grave of an elderly woman at Huaca Prieta; a cotton handle was originally attached to the lid. (*Below*) The decoration on the gourd bears a strong resemblance to that of the Valdivia pottery found along what is now the southern Ecuadorian coast; some archaeologists believe the gourds may have been imported.

encountered. In one of the latter, the facial skin had been torn off; another skull had a hole punched in the forehead so that it could be hung from a cord as a trophy, as was done in later pre-Hispanic times. Weapons were also encountered at the site, most notably a wooden club embedded with sharks' teeth, plus pointed spears and woven slings.[32] These finds do not imply that warfare was an important force at the time, only that it exists. Most major sites flourished for centuries in locations that would have made them vulnerable to attack, and fortifications were completely unknown during the Late Preceramic.

The general absence of sumptuary goods in the burials suggests that there were ideological strictures against the accumulation of wealth by individuals. Social conventions of this sort are common in many relatively unstratified societies, where the channeling of surplus into personal possessions is viewed as antisocial. In such societies, individual or family prestige may derive from generosity, sacred knowledge, and the ability to mobilize labor rather than accumulated wealth. The capacity of the Preceramic economy to generate a surplus is evident, but it was directed almost exclusively towards public, rather than individual, objectives. Foremost among them was the creation of monumental architecture which lay at the core of all major Late Preceramic settlements.

Monumental architecture

Unlike Egypt, organizational innovations in the central Andes permitted the large-scale mobilization of labor before the appearance of marked socioeconomic stratification and the coercive state apparatus that often accompanies it. At the heart of this Late Preceramic innovation was the role of religious ideology in motivating collective efforts, maintaining order, and perpetuating the system. Large corporate labor projects are characteristic not only of the Late Preceramic, but also of much of Peruvian prehistory. The basis of the later projects, and perhaps of the Preceramic ones as well, was an ideology which held that the community, not the individual, owned and controlled the critical resources. Membership of the community was validated through participation in communal activities, and failure to collaborate resulted in social sanctions and eventually in limited access to land and water. The community's right to land was ultimately based on its relationship to a founding ancestor or supernatural. Religious worship was especially important for defining group membership, and this mythical personage figured prominently in local myth and community ritual.

The majority of corporate labor constructions of the Late Preceramic were created to provide a focus for community rituals. One of the principal features of the Late Preceramic complexes was large open areas which, at the better understood sites like Salinas de Chao and Piedra Parada, feature formally defined open-air enclosures or plazas. These areas, whether circular or rectangular, provided settings most appropriate for group gatherings where people drawn from distinct households and communities established and expressed their goals through activities such as feasting, dancing, and ritual performances. In the pre-Hispanic world there was no disjunction between rituals, with their religious connotations, and the day-to-day world of secular affairs. In most pre-industrial societies, and particularly in pre-Hispanic Peru, questions of health, agricultural production, the settlement of conflicts, and other apparently secular concerns were understood as falling within the religious domain. The activities at ceremonial centers were not merely concerned with the relations between the human community and the supernatural. Nor was the social function of religion limited to giving meaning to daily life and strengthening the fabric of society through shared activities and beliefs: it also actively structured many of the productive activities and shaped social and economic decisions. Consequently, it would be misleading to think of religion – particularly in these early "ceremonial centers" – as somehow separate from the economic or political spheres.

From a different perspective, monumental architecture can be seen as the physical and metaphorical embodiment and expression of a community's unity and identity. Like the space programs of modern industrial nations, the size and quality of Preceramic constructions were public displays of the productive capacity and prestige of each society, particularly in relation to that of their neighbors. If prestige during the Preceramic was measured by the amount of labor that could be mobilized, there were few claims as eloquent as the monumental architecture, which was little more than the reification of human labor. As the pyramids grew through cyclical renovations, they would have come to provide an almost supernatural validation of the society's legitimacy. Moreover, the same social mechanisms that were used to tap public labor for corporate building could be utilized when necessary for other public ends.[33]

With this general background, it is worth considering briefly several of the better-known examples of Late Preceramic public architecture on the coast.

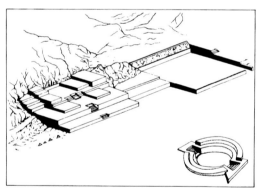

21 Isometric reconstruction of the terraced platforms and sunken circular court of Unit A at the shoreline center of Salinas de Chao.

Salinas de Chao. The public architecture at this 8-hectare site on the shoreline of the Chao Valley consists of a series of rectangular platforms, terraces, and semi-subterranean plazas.[34] The platforms were built on a natural rocky spur which further adds to their imposing appearance, and were constructed of quarried stone bound together by clay mortar and small chinking stones. The relatively coarse masonry walls were, at least in some instances, covered with a light clay plaster. A remarkably wide range of architectural designs were combined in a systematic but non-repetitive manner to form the complex. Some idea of the variety of elements used can be gained by considering the arrangements for access between different levels of the site. This problem was resolved using ramps, inset stairways, and projecting staircases. The use of these alternatives does not seem to follow any particular chronological pattern.

There are two principal public complexes at Salinas de Chao: Units A and B. Unit A consists of a terraced platform 40 m wide, with three flights of staircases leading down the center. Directly in front of the platform is a sunken circular plaza, 10 m in diameter and 2 m deep, reached by two wedge-shaped inset stairways. Unit B, located to the west of Unit A, consists of a terraced platform facing a large rectangular plaza. The frontice of the upper level of the platform was decorated with a clay frieze, 120 cm on a side, incised and painted with a red square with a black center. In a later renovation, the middle terrace of this same platform was adorned with a facing of polished stone slabs. Two flights of stairs lead down the center of this complex into the semi-subterranean plaza which covers 1,080 sq. m. These buildings are surrounded by middens and smaller-scale constructions, thought to be houses. To the east of Unit A is a massive, partially destroyed wall, 2.5 m thick and 1.6 m high which runs 800 m between two mountain ridges, and limits access to the uplifted bay and shoreline.

Aspero. This 12-hectare site features 7 definite platform mounds and 6 other mound-like structures.[35] The largest of these, Huaca de los Idolos, is an entirely artificial construction of stone and clay (10 m high, and 30 by 40 m at its base) with an outer face of angular basaltic blocks set in mud mortar. Excavations revealed that Huaca de los Idolos, like the other mounds at the site, is composed of a series of superimposed room complexes, each filled with quarried rock. Loose mesh bags of crushed sedge or cattail stems were used to carry the stone fill, and were deposited along with the rock. Made using a simple looping technique, these pre-Hispanic disposable containers, known as *shicra*, are characteristic of early monumental architecture on the Peruvian coast. They were never used in domestic architecture.

The flat-topped summit of Huaca de los Idolos is covered by rooms of varying sizes, whose walls have been plastered and, in some instances, painted yellow and red. A stairway leads to the top of the platform where a 2-m wide doorway provides access into a large court. Passageways lead back from this large room into smaller, more restricted chambers, one of which is decorated with a white clay frieze of five horizontal parallel clapboard-like bands. Other features of the summit buildings are walls with cubical niches and low plastered benches. The buried rooms were found in excellent condition and an effort appears to have been made to avoid damaging them at the time of their burial. Domestic refuse does not appear on the floors of these rooms or in the fill.

The special function of these constructions is suggested by the offerings recovered from their summits. Robert Feldman discovered a large cache of 13 unbaked clay figurines between two floors at Huaca de los Sacrificios. Most of these clearly represent females, and four appear to be pregnant. Twined baskets, mats, and fur were found with them and another unbaked clay figurine, probably male, was discovered near by.

A second cache was unearthed on the summit of this mound. It consisted of 135 short carved sticks ranging in length from 1.5 to 8.5 cm, many carved with chevrons and other geometric designs. Their function is unknown, but one possibility is that they served for divining. A fragment of a beautiful wooden bowl decorated with modeled frogs was recovered with the sticks. Caches containing a pecten shell, cotton cloth, and bundles of burnt and unburnt cloth were the most common offerings at Aspero. In later pre-Hispanic times, cloth was favored in ritual offerings, and it would appear that this special practice had already been established by the Late Preceramic. Arrangements of red and yellow featherwork and two string crosses ("ojos de dios") made of cotton thread were also buried in the summits of the platform mounds.

Piedra Parada. Situated only 2.5 km inland from Aspero, this site covers about 15 hectares, and includes four corporate labor constructions, domestic occupation, and middens.[36] Like Unit A at Salinas de Chao, one of the large terraced platforms faces a circular, semi-subterranean plaza measuring 20 m in diameter. At both Aspero and Piedra Parada, there are considerable differences between the orientation of the different mounds.

22 This two-storey building (Unit 1) was one of the nine masonry complexes constructed at El Paraíso in the Chillon Valley. It was reconstructed following its excavation in 1965.

23 Unit 1 at El Paraíso seen (unreconstructed) from the west; the land in the upper portion of the photograph may have been a large open plaza.

El Paraíso. Located on the central coast of Peru, this is the largest known Preceramic period site.[37] Radiocarbon dates indicate that it was built during the final centuries of the Preceramic (*c.* 2000 BC). El Paraíso covers approximately 58 hectares, and 100,000 tons of stones were utilized in building its complexes. Archaeologist Thomas Patterson estimates that it would have taken a minimum of almost 2,000,000 person-days to construct these platforms. Two of the largest buildings, each over 400 m in length, are located parallel to each other on opposite ends of a 7-hectare plaza. At the southern edge of this open area is a relatively small four-tiered rectangular platform complex called Unit I, which has been extensively excavated and restored.

Access from the plaza area to the 16-room complex on the summit of Unit I was provided by two stairways, the larger of which leads into a red-painted chamber. In the center of this room is a sunken rectangular pit with additional circular pits in each of its corners. The cylindrical pits were found filled with carbon to a depth of 80 cm and the entire floor of the sunken rectangular pit had been burnt. Although all of the rooms of Unit I were cleared, its precise function remains unknown. The most common artifacts recovered were grinding stones covered with red pigment. A dedicatory offering sealed in the northwest corner of Unit I consisted of a large stone sprinkled with red pigment and covered with cotton cloth. Alongside it was a gourd filled with food and a miniature version of a *shicra* bag which held small white cakes wrapped in leaves instead of stone rubble.

Despite its immense size, El Paraíso shows a high degree of planning. For example, the walls in Units I, III, and IV are all oriented 24–25° northeast. Similar construction techniques are used in the different parts of the site. Thick roughly trimmed stones of varying sizes were set in clay mortar to form walls up to 1 m thick. The faces of the walls were plastered with gray or pink clay. Rooms were periodically filled in with bagged-fill and ovoid adobes to raise the level of the structure and create a surface for new buildings. The excellent preservation of the *shicra* bags made it possible to calculate that the average load of fill carried from the quarrying area near by weighed about 26 kilos.

Few sections of the lateral mounds have been studied, but archaeologist Jeffrey Quilter encountered engaged columns (partially built into walls) as architectural ornaments in one of the empty rooms he excavated. As in Unit I, there was little evidence of the function of these structures. The chance discovery of loose green, pink, blue, and yellow feathers and down in one floor is difficult to interpret, though it brings to mind an equally enigmatic stick found covered with white feathers at Río Seco, and the colorful featherwork arrangement found at the summit of one of the Aspero mounds. Unbaked clay figurine fragments were recovered at El Paraíso which resembled the female figurines from Río Seco and, to a lesser degree, Aspero.

This overview provides a sense of the monumental scale of Late Preceramic constructions. The building technology utilized is not in itself particularly elaborate, nor do the artifacts associated with these constructions point to greater specialization than would have been thought from the refuse or burials. On the other hand, an enormous amount of collective labor was mobilized to create these monuments for use by the community. It is this communal focus of Andean society and its capacity to mobilize labor towards public ends which distinguishes the beginnings of Andean civilization from most others, and was critical to shaping its development.

The domestic realm

The location of large numbers of middens at sites has led most scholars to conclude that the people responsible for building the monuments must have actually lived around the constructions. Unfortunately, few of these presumed living quarters have been studied. More work *has* been done on the living areas of some of the smaller shoreline villages, however, and – as in the case of monumental architecture – considerable regional diversity exists in the form and construction techniques of the houses that have been documented.

The houses at Huaca Prieta were roughly square subterranean structures of

24 Fiber bags (*shicras*) such as these were used to hold stone fill in the public constructions at El Paraíso. The weights of fill removed from the *shicras* ranged from 17.6 to 36.0 kg.

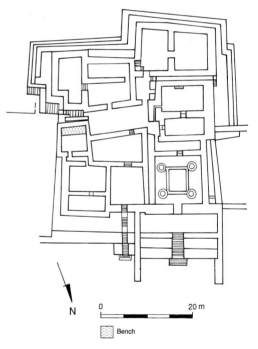

25 Unit 1 at El Paraíso featured two staircases, one of which led to a red-painted room with a burnt sunken rectangular court and four cylindrical fire pits. Its large size and complex layout were the product of 4 to 6 construction phases during the final centuries of the Late Preceramic period.

river cobbles and roofed with wooden beams and whale bone, while the dwellings at Asia are above ground and made of fieldstone, adobe, and clay mortar. At Alto Salaverry, ocean cobbles and boulders of basalt and granite were combined with rectangular adobes and coral blocks to form small semisubterranean rectangular rooms (averaging 1.5 by 2 m), often with a small hearth near their centers.[38]

Frequently, storage pits and hearths are associated with the Late Preceramic residences, indicating that the dwelling units were also the basic units of storage and consumption. In contrast, no large storage facilities have been found in the public constructions. A sunken circular plaza exists on the outskirts of Alto Salaverry, presumably for community gatherings.[39] Its design and construction closely resemble the plazas found at the much larger sites of Salinas de Chao and Piedra Parada.

The Late Preceramic in the highlands

The precocious developments on the coast cannot be understood without reference to contemporary societies in the adjacent highlands. The acquisition and distribution by coastal leaders of highland goods, particularly in times of difficulty must have enhanced the prestige of these leaders. Moreover, the highland demand for maritime products would have opened the realm of production, as well as long-distance exchange, to management by these authorities. It may be significant, for example, that the unprecedented 800 m walls at Salinas de Chao could have served to limit access to the area of the shore suitable for salt production, thereby making it feasible to control salt production and distribution, while at the same time physically marking this ability.

Though the highlands and coast were linked directly by exchange and social interaction, the subsistence basis of the two areas was fundamentally different. Despite these differences, public architecture appeared in intermontane valleys prior to 2500 BC and probably many centuries earlier. The earliest dates associated with temple constructions are 2796 BC from Huaricoto and 2821 BC from La Galgada (both in the highlands), but carbon samples have never been tested from the lowest construction levels at most highland sites.[40] It would appear, therefore, that small, mostly unstratified theocratic polities appeared in the highlands at almost the same time as on the coast. The two developments must be considered as two interrelated elements within a single developmental process.

Subsistence

Rainfall agriculture lay at the core of the highland economy. Five to six months of natural precipitation could support a rich natural flora in the intermontane valleys of northern and central Peruvian highlands, and many of the wild plants native to these high elevations attracted the interest of early hunter-gatherers. The domestication of plants was well underway by 5000 BC, and by 3000 BC it is likely that almost the full range of food plants adapted to highland environments was already available. Examples of numerous early cultigens have been recovered from dry caves in Ayacucho and the Callejón de Huaylas, although the specific composition of the Late Preceramic highland diet remains undetermined due to the poor preservation of remains at most highland sites.[41]

A recent carbon isotope study suggests that maize, a crop which grows well mainly on the valley floors, constituted about 20 percent of the diet in the central Callejón de Huaylas during Late Preceramic times.[42] The majority of crops were probably cultigens better adapted than maize to the more abundant valley slopes e.g. potatoes, oca, and ullucu. A balanced diet was achieved from highland tubers, maize, Andean grains e.g. quinoa, native legumes, and lupines such as tarwi, but hunting was nonetheless widely practiced, and wild game was an important source of meat protein.

The hunting pattern at the site of Kotosh, located at 2,000 m above sea level, is particularly well documented.[43] Approximately 70 percent of the usable meat derived from three types of deer: the white-tailed deer, the brocket, and the huemul. Most of the remainder came from the two wild camelids, the guanaco and the vicuña, though smaller game such as the viscacha and skunk were also caught. The white-tailed deer and the guanaco were available locally, but Kotosh hunters also frequented much higher elevations in search of the vicuña and the huemul, which dwelt above 3,900 m. The riverine fauna in the Peruvian highlands is scarce and fishing was not a major source of food at Kotosh or other coeval centers.

In contrast, guinea pig bones are extremely common in Late Preceramic highland middens. In fact, at some sites their remains are second in number only to deer bones. Though the guinea pig never gained world-wide popularity as a source of food, it was probably the only animal in ancient Peru domesticated specifically for consumption. The wild ancestors of the domesticated guinea pig can still be found in the meadows and marshes of the *puna* grasslands. There is insufficient evidence, however, to determine whether the guinea pigs consumed in the Late Preceramic were sufficiently different from these wild relatives to consider them truly domesticated.

Particularly favored for its delicate flavor and succulent meat, its fatty constitution would have also provided relief from the low-fat carbohydrate diet typical of the highlands. In later pre-Hispanic times, the guinea pig was also widely used in religious ceremonies, divination and curing rituals. Though it has been estimated that guinea pigs constituted 25 percent of the animals consumed at Kotosh during the Late Preceramic, each guinea pig provides only 700 g of usable meat compared to 57.5 kilos from a guanaco and 36.5 kilos from an average deer. Thus, the guinea pig probably provided less than 1 percent of the meat protein at Kotosh, and even less at other sites. (Though native to the Peruvian highlands, guinea pig remains also appear, albeit less frequently, at Late Preceramic sites on the coast. Archaeologist Edward Lanning discovered guinea pig hutches at the shoreline village of Culebras, and based on the associated remains, concluded that the animals were fed on anchovies.[44])

The other two domesticated mammals, the llama and the alpaca, were probably bred for their cargo-carrying capacity and wool respectively. These two animals appear to have been fully domesticated by 2500 BC and were being herded at this time on the high grasslands of Junin in central Peru. In the *puna*, the gradual process of *in situ* domestication lasted for over 2,000 years – evident from the steady decline in the frequency of deer remains and the corresponding increase in camelid remains – until, by the Late Preceramic, deer and other wild game were no longer a major source of meat, despite their presumed abundance in the *puna* habitat.[45]

With the advent of camelid herding, small permanent villages like Ondores on the shores of Lake Junin were established in the *puna* itself, while caves and rockshelters began to be used only seasonally for short periods of time rather than as base camps. There is no evidence that these herders had adopted farming to a significant degree. The analysis of plant remains from one cave shows the continued utilization of wild plants and the conspicuous absence of any cultigens. It would seem, therefore, that on the *puna* there was considerable continuity with the hunter-gatherer lifeways present before fully-fledged camelid domestication. Populations remained small and, not surprisingly, monumental architecture was not a feature of this area during the Late Preceramic.[46]

Though a milestone in Peruvian prehistory, the early domestication of the llama on the *puna* may have had little immediate impact on nearby agriculturalists. As we have seen, the agricultural settlements in the intermontane valleys continued to depend on wild deer as their major source of animal protein long after the *puna* dwellers had shifted to domesticated animals. In fact, deer were still the preeminent meat source at Kotosh and Huaricoto 1,000 years after the end of the Preceramic. Moreover, camelid remains recovered along with cervid remains at these centers appear to be from guanaco and occasionally vicuña, rather than the llama.[47]

The delayed impact of domestication on the valley settlements had serious implications above and beyond dietary considerations. It would be wrong to assume that, once llama were domesticated on the *puna*, there was an immediate proliferation in long-distance llama caravans and woolen clothing. For example, it is significant that no evidence of textiles made from alpaca or llama wool has been found at La Galgada. This site, located on the floor of the Tablachaca Valley, is only 20 km from the grasslands above Corongo, and some woolen

26 Evidence of the *in situ* domestication of the llama has been recovered from caves in the high grasslands of the Junin Valley. These caves were occupied throughout Preceramic times and continued to be used by llama herders during the Initial Period and Early Horizon.

27 Until recently, the domesticated llama was an important source of meat for highland populations, and llama caravans were an essential means of transporting bulky commodities long distance. During a visit to the *puna* mining town of Cerro de Pasco in the late 19th century, the French traveler Charles Wiener drew this picture of a llama caravan at rest.

goods would have been expected among the numerous fibre and cotton textiles discovered. Similarly, llama remains and wool do not begin to appear systematically at coastal sites with any great frequency until about 500 BC.[48]

Judging from the above, it would appear that two very different human societies in the highlands lived adjacent to each other during the Late Preceramic, one in the *quechua* and *suni*, the other in the *puna*. This is not to say, however, that the *puna* dwellers were totally isolated, as the discovery of exotic obsidian and worked Ecuadorian shell at the Telarmachay Cave on the Junin *puna* clearly proves.[49]

Public constructions of the Kotosh Religious Tradition

Highland farmers built substantial public complexes in a wide range of locations. As we have seen, the first example of a highland center with public buildings was discovered at Kotosh (2,000 m), but others have now been uncovered at Shillacoto (1,920 m) and Waira-jirca (c. 1,700 m) in the Huallaga drainage, Huaricoto (2,750 m) in the Callejón de Huaylas, La Galgada (1,100 m) in the Tablachaca Valley, and Piruru (3,800 m) in the Tantamayo drainage. These centers span the gamut of highland zones lower than the *puna*.

All these cases of highland Preceramic public architecture are remarkably similar, despite the distances separating them. They typically consist of small free-standing buildings with central stone-lined firepits. The edifices are either square with rounded corners or round, and their interior chambers are plastered with light-colored clay. Those walls still standing feature symmetrically arranged niches. The floors are made of carefully selected light-colored clay and are often split-level, with the upper level possibly functioning as a bench. At several of the sites, identical structures of this type share a common wall and constitute dual or twin chambers.

These distinctive constructions were created to provide an environment for religious ceremonies, in which the burning of offerings was a critical element. At intervals the chambers were intentionally filled and covered by their builders to permit the construction of a new series of similar buildings at a higher level. The excellent condition of most buried structures, and the care with which they had been covered, led investigators to refer to this practice as "temple entombment." The repeated burial of these chambers gradually produced mounds of considerable size which, when stabilized by outer stone terraces or revetment walls, assumed the appearance of stepped, multi-tiered truncated platforms, topped by small masonry superstructures. At any given time, several similar temple chambers were visible on the summit and terraces of these Late Preceramic platform mounds.

How can we explain the similarities between such widely dispersed public complexes given that the environment, economy, and many aspects of their culture so clearly differed between these sites? Perhaps the most plausible suggestion is that these centers shared a set of religious beliefs which entailed similar kinds of ritual activities and, consequently, required a similar type of ceremonial building. The underlying religious ideology and its material expression in sacred architecture has been called the Kotosh Religious Tradition after the site where it was first recognized. Although there are differences in the ritual chambers, the core architectural element of these buildings that allowed the rites to be performed was always maintained.[50] Like the kivas of the American Southwest, the chamber sizes, construction, and ornamental details vary according to local materials, building traditions, and organizational capacity. A brief review of some of the better-known examples of this architecture and its associations at several sites may give a clearer picture of this pattern and its relation to the monumental coastal architecture discussed earlier.

Kotosh. Located in an arid area whose precipitation is restricted by the local topography and wind patterns (known as a cloud shadow) on the eastern slopes of the Andes, the site of Kotosh was dominated by two artificial mounds.[51] The smaller mound, called KM, yielded evidence of superimposed Preceramic

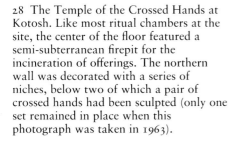

28 The Temple of the Crossed Hands at Kotosh. Like most ritual chambers at the site, the center of the floor featured a semi-subterranean firepit for the incineration of offerings. The northern wall was decorated with a series of niches, below two of which a pair of crossed hands had been sculpted (only one set remained in place when this photograph was taken in 1963).

29 A panoramic view of mound KT at Kotosh after excavation. The arid environment surrounding the site can be seen in the background, and the Temple of the Crossed Hands appears in the center of the photograph. In the lower section of the photograph is the two-room Templo Blanco, the oldest set of ritual chambers excavated at Kotosh. The remnants of two later chambers superimposed above it are also visible.

temples with relatively little later occupation. The distinctive architecture of the temple chambers and the associated artifacts were used to define the Mito culture – the Late Preceramic culture in the Huanuco area. The larger mound, called KT, reached a visible height of 13.7 m and most of its remains belong to the Mito culture. Towards the end of the Mito occupation, this mound had the appearance of a three-level platform supporting numerous small chambers of the Kotosh Religious Tradition. The chambers were made of fieldstone set in clay mortar and plastered with light yellow-brown clay. The buildings were roughly square and oriented to the north or south. Excavations of the lowest platform have disclosed no less than seven superimposed temples, and 5–7 m of cultural stratigraphy under the oldest temple, the Templo Blanco, still remain unexcavated.

The best known of the Mito Phase constructions at Kotosh, the Temple of the Crossed Hands (Templo de los Manos Cruzadas), was discovered on the middle platform directly beneath the Temple of the Niches (Templo de los Nichitos). On the stairway leading to the Temple of the Crossed Hands was a stylized white painting of a serpent. The building itself is roughly square, measuring 9.5 m by 9.3 m on a side, and 2 m high. The upper interiors of the walls were recessed to

30 The Temple of the Crossed Hands, Kotosh. The sculpture of the crossed hands to the right of the central niche was the larger of the two, and shows the right arm crossing the left. The small niche above it was filled with camelid or deer bones.

31 The smaller sculpture to the left of the central niche was carved with its left arm on top of the right, intentionally reversing the position of the other. The contrast in their size and position, as well as their location on the wall, suggests that they may express the principle of dualism or complementary opposition so important in traditional Andean thought.

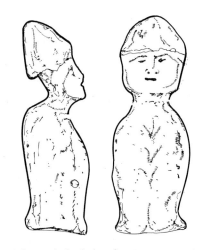

32 This unbaked clay figurine (7.2 cm in height) was found in a niche of the Templo Blanco at Kotosh, and was associated with three other unbaked clay objects.

support a flat roof of small log beams plastered with clay. The red-painted entrance contrasted with the yellow-brown plaster covering the rest of the building and, on entering the chamber, it was necessary to step down to the lower surface of the split-level floor. In the middle of the room was a stone-lined circular firepit set into the floor. Two stone subfloor flues ensured the complete incineration of the offerings, and the firepit was found filled with fine ash.

Facing the entrance, along the northern wall, are five niches. The two niches either side of the large central niche each have a low-relief clay frieze of crossed hands below them. The design and symmetrical arrangement of the two friezes implies that they were consciously created as a pair or dyad, and archaeologist Seiichi Izumi interpreted them as the hands of a woman and a man (one pair of hands was smaller than the other).[52] Perhaps the broader principle being expressed in these unique friezes is one of duality, in which the unity of fundamentally opposing forces is symbolized. The twin temple chambers mentioned earlier may have been an architectural expression of this same concept. Offerings of camelids or deer and guinea pigs were found in the small niches, and two crude anthropomorphic figurines of baked clay were also associated with the construction. Before the Temple of the Crossed Hands was filled with river cobbles, these friezes were carefully protected with a layer of sand.[53]

At Kotosh, 11 Mito chambers have been discovered. Considering the large portions of both mounds still uninvestigated it is probable that over 100 were built at the site. All known chambers have similar ground plans and orientations, but they differ in secondary architectural elements, and seem to have been successively larger. Since the buildings were in excellent condition when they were covered, a non-utilitarian motive for their entombment must be sought.

Religious activity among most agriculturalists tended to be calendrical, and the repetitious pattern of building and reburial at Kotosh suggests a cyclical pattern of ritual renovation and renewal. The burning of offerings in the Andes was a means of transforming material goods into a form which could be consumed by supernatural forces. Fire was simply a ritual agent and probably not, as some have suggested, the object of worship.[54]

33 The exterior revetment walls and terraces of the North Mound at La Galgada after partial clearing. The arid slopes of the Tablachaca Valley can be seen in the background.

Though Kotosh is in many respects an impressive site, it may not have been a Preceramic highland center of exceptional importance. An even larger site, Shillacoto, is located only 5 km away on the opposite bank. Unfortunately, the visitor to Shillacoto today will find it covered by houses and modern garbage from the modern city of Huánuco. Small-scale excavations there revealed two Late Preceramic ritual chambers, similar to the ones at Kotosh, buried beneath Initial Period constructions. Another 20 km downstream, even closer to the montane cloud forest, is the smaller site of Waira-jirca, where exploratory soundings revealed at least two superimposed Mito chambers.[55] It is likely that additional testing would reveal still other centers with Late Preceramic public constructions in the Huallaga drainage.

Huaricoto and Piruru. The site of Huaricoto provides an interesting contrast to Kotosh. Situated on a terrace overlooking the rich valley floor of the Callejón de Huaylas, the ritual chambers here lacked stone superstructures or even stone footings. Instead, the buildings appear to have been made in some perishable material, such as adobe or wattle and daub. Finely made floors of light clay, some split-level, have been found but the stone-lined central firepits lacked subfloor flues. This difference may simply be due to the greater ease of incinerating offerings within the perishable superstructures. Shell, meat, and clear quartz crystal were among the burnt offerings made in ceremonies here. Considerable variation occurs in the orientation of the chambers at Huaricoto and the firepit of one chamber is semi-circular. It would seem that there was little standardization in ceremonial chambers at this site, and only a modest amount of labor was invested in public constructions. Huaricoto, it appears, was a much less organized society than Kotosh and may even have lacked permanent authorities to supervise community rituals.[56]

The most recently discovered example of the Kotosh Religious Tradition is at the site of Piruru, located at 3,800 m in the uppermost agricultural zone (the *suni*), above the banks of the Río Tantamayo. Three Preceramic temple structures were revealed below 4–5 m of later occupation. All the Preceramic chambers have a central hearth with flues, but only one has a split-level floor. The superstructure of this building consists of a low stone wall which supported an upper wall of poles daubed with mud. The size and shape of these three buildings resemble those at Kotosh.[57]

La Galgada. The lowest of the centers of the Kotosh Religious Tradition is La Galgada, located at 1,100 m near the floor of the canyon-like mid-Tablachaca Valley.[58] The arid *yunga* environment of this site could not have supported rainfall agriculture, and there is direct and indirect evidence that small-scale irrigation was being practiced around this site during the Late Preceramic. Because of the steep gradient, it would have been easier to initiate irrigation here than in the lower coastal valleys. Though the climate is reminiscent of the coast, the architecture encountered is very similar to that of highland centers. This is not entirely surprising since the littoral is some 80 km and a lengthy journey away, while rich highland environments are easily accessible on foot within an hour and a half. Another eight major examples of Late Preceramic architecture have been located along the Tablachaca within 10 km of the site.[59]

Like Kotosh, La Galgada had two major mounds, the larger of which was over 15 m in height. This mound was terraced by three successive circular revetment walls and must have been an impressive sight. A succession of chambers with central firepits were built on the summit. At one point five or more chambers were arranged asymmetrically on this upper platform. The earliest of these were made of river cobbles set in clay, while the later ones were constructed from trimmed fieldstone. Most of the buildings were plastered with clay and painted white, but one exception had black painted walls. Like Kotosh, the chambers at La Galgada had high stone superstructures with niches decorating the interior and split-level floors. The chambers likewise had flat log roofs, and even show the same detail of stepping down into the lower floor level when entering the chamber. Most of the Late Preceramic chambers were roughly circular, though for a short interval the sub-rectangular form popular at Kotosh, Shillacoto, and Piruru was adopted and then abruptly dropped. As at Kotosh, buildings were oriented to the cardinal directions, but west and north, rather than south and north. In most of the buildings, the lower portion of the interior wall projected forward slightly to form a dado, while the niches were arranged symmetrically above it. An analogous division of the interior walls was achieved at Kotosh by using a band of projecting stones known as a stringcourse. None of the

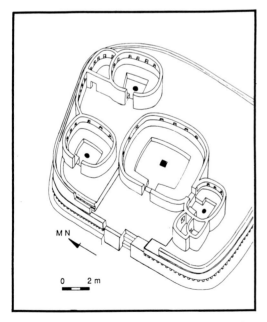

34 Drawing of the ritual chambers on the summit of the North Mound at La Galgada *c.* 2300–2200 BC.

35 This unusual square ritual chamber at La Galgada, constructed before 2300 BC, was plastered with a finishing coat of yellow clay. The building measures only 2.6 × 2.3 m.

numerous chambers at La Galgada show evidence of painted motifs or low-relief friezes.[60]

Valuable clues about the activities which had taken place within these chambers have been found at La Galgada as a result of the dry conditions favorable to preservation. In several cases, the seeds of burnt chili peppers were recovered from the firepit. As cooks of Sechuan food well know, hot peppers release noxious smoke when burnt and we can only imagine the environment in one of the enclosed windowless chambers during ceremonies when these items were dropped into the firepits. Vestiges of the ceremonies including white, orange, and green feather down were found on chamber floors and, in one case, the lower portion of a set of deer antlers was recovered.[61]

An enclosure wall of river cobbles defined a circular court 17 m in diameter. It faced the principal mound and the materials used suggest that it dates from the earlier part of the building sequence. This court has no known equivalent at other Late Preceramic centers of the Kotosh Religious Tradition, but this could be due to sampling problems. Of all the centers, La Galgada had the least amount of later occupation and, consequently, relatively subtle features such as this court can be detected without excavation.[62]

Comparisons with the coast. The contrast between the complexes of the Kotosh Religious Tradition and those of the coastal centers should be apparent. Besides the individual architectural features unique to it (e.g. split-level floors with central hearths and flues), there was a fundamental difference in the overall layout. The highland centers feature single, free-standing buildings usually of a single room; when two rooms are joined in a twin structure, a separate entrance is provided for each, with no internal connection between the two. The coastal centers, in contrast, were comprised of large complexes of interconnecting rooms. While access to the ritual chambers was maximized in the highland sites, it was often restricted in the coastal complexes and became increasingly difficult as one approached the interior rooms. Feldman has referred to this pattern as "graded access." When compared to coastal centers, the Kotosh Religious Tradition's overall lack of formal planning in the arrangement of the ritual architecture and the ease of access to ceremonial chambers suggest that they were built by a very different type of society.[63]

Residences

La Galgada is the only highland site where archaeologists have documented the presence of a habitation surrounding the ceremonial architecture. Fifty rustic buildings were identified as houses, and others were destroyed when a road was built through the site in 1975. The houses at La Galgada were round and covered a surface area of 14 sq. m. The unpainted walls were made of rough fieldstone set in clay mortar. Floors were of natural earth, and formal firepits were not incorporated in the construction, though ash was found both inside and outside the buildings.[64]

In most cases, we have only a fragmentary picture of where the population lived in the highland valleys. It is conceivable that the populace lived in the area surrounding the public architecture as at La Galgada, and that later occupations have shielded these deposits from investigators. Alternatively, in those highland centers not practicing irrigation, the people could have been dispersed across the landscape in small farmsteads and hamlets. Because of the diversity of the highland landscape and the need of communities to exploit non-contiguous resource zones, it was (and still is) common for social groups bound by kin ties to be widely distributed spatially, congregating for special occasions. If this was the case, the ceremonies at the centers of the Kotosh Religious Tradition would have brought together different segments of the normally fragmented society.

Burials

The only site of the Kotosh Religious Tradition where Preceramic burials have been found is La Galgada. The interments include men, women, and children of all ages.[65] Most of the individuals, however, were either under 4 or over 40; it has been estimated that 24 percent of them were at least 50 years old. The dead were buried in temple chambers which had been modified to form tombs before being covered by later ceremonial constructions. Others were placed in gallery tombs between the chambers and the revetment walls. The tombs were apparently entered repeatedly from above. One tomb, for example, had flexed burial bundles on top of slightly earlier extended burials; all four of these interments date to the Late Preceramic.

The earliest burials are reminiscent of the coastal burials in the simplicity of the burial goods. The oldest of the Late Preceramic chamber tombs contained a man and two women, all over 50, buried in tightly flexed positions maintained by wrapping yellow or brown cotton thread around the bodies. The male and one of the females wore cotton caps and were covered with strips of bark cloth. Sprinkled with tufts of human hair, the male was wrapped in a yellow and brown twined cotton blanket and placed within a net of vegetable fiber. Near by, the two females were placed together on a twined junco fiber mat and covered with a basket-weave textile. One woman lacked a cotton mantle, but wore four bone hairpins and was accompanied by pieces of anthracite and rock crystal. The other woman had a basket, rather than a cap, on her head and wore a yellow cotton mantle. She had a single greenstone bead and a curl of salt crystals, but no hairpins. A line of grave goods was placed near the heads of the dead, which included numerous baskets and cotton bags. There was also a gourd bowl, a gourd dipper, and a stone mortar and pestle.

Grave goods at La Galgada became increasingly common later in the Preceramic. The standard set of jewelry buried in the later tombs consisted of bone pins to arrange the hair and fasten cotton mantles, and beaded necklaces of stone and Pacific shell. Turquoise-like stone was imported in the form of finished beads and these were glued with resin to the bone pins.

. Most individuals were also buried with textiles and cotton bags, some of which had unique and complex designs. Red, yellow, blue, and black dyed yarn supplemented the natural brown and white colors of the cotton. As we mentioned, many of the motifs from these textiles are similar to those from Huaca Prieta, although it is presumed that they were locally produced. Beads of Pacific shell and even Ecuadorian *Spondylus* occur frequently, sometimes with special pendants of carved stone or *Spondylus*. One woman, for example, had a white bead necklace with a shell pendant resembling a viscacha; it had an inlaid pink nose, blue turquoise eyes, and a mottled-looking coat of shell and stone inlays.

Although there was an increase in the number of goods buried with the dead in the later Preceramic, this seems to have been applied universally: a comparable set of goods was possessed by people of the same age and sex in the available sample. So, as on the coast, the burials do not suggest that strong hierarchical divisions existed within the society. The very fact that it was considered appropriate to bury a cross-section of men, women, and children inside the sacred architecture bespeaks a strong identification between the populace as a whole and the public architecture it constructed. The abundance of important materials used in jewelry provides convincing evidence for the participation of La Galgada in the long-distance exchange network which operated during the Late Preceramic. The Tablachaca River falls within a natural trade route between the coast, highlands, and tropical lowlands and apparently all the inhabitants of La Galgada enjoyed the benefits of being situated along it.

36 A group burial at La Galgada of a man and two women was made inside a disused ritual chamber. Thanks to the excellent preservation conditions, textiles, baskets, gourds, bark cloth, and other perishable grave goods were recovered.

Ecuador and the tropical forest

The field of interaction during the Late Preceramic period went beyond the Peruvian coast and highlands. Cultures to the east in the Amazonian lowlands and to the north in what now is modern Ecuador also participated in the networks of long-distance exchange and presumably had some impact on the direction and nature of the coastal and highland developments. Most goods produced in the tropical forest were perishable organic materials and we must therefore assume that they will be severely underrepresented in the archaeological record.

The discovery of tropical forest products, such as a necklace of *espingo* seeds found at Bandurria and a fragment of palm fruit of La Galgada, have called attention to these links. The mandible of a piranha (*Sarrasalmus* sp.), discovered in a Late Preceramic context at Kotosh, was another such find. Judging from the

37 The *Spondylus princeps*, sometimes called the "thorny oyster," is a bivalve native to the warm Pacific waters of Ecuador and further north. Its distinctive coral-like pink color is found on the shell's exterior and along a circumferential band on its interior. This exotic mollusk played an important role in prehistoric Andean ritual, and was said to have been one of the favorite foods of the gods.

wear on its normally razor-sharp teeth, it probably served as a burin for working wood or bone. The piranha is not native to the rivers of the eastern slopes and consequently it must have been imported from the floodplains of the tropical forest. Some of the multi-colored feathers found at Aspero, El Paraíso, and La Galgada may also have come from the eastern lowlands. Terence Grieder, for example, believes that the orange and red-orange feathers at La Galgada probably belonged to a macaw or a cock-of-the-rock, both of which are Amazonian species.[66]

The strongest evidence for contact with Ecuador is the discovery of *Spondylus* shell at coastal sites such as Aspero and El Paraíso, and highland sites like La Galgada. An example of a *Strombus* shell, another Ecuadorian mollusk, has likewise been recovered at Telarmachay, a cave in the Peruvian highlands. The final and best-known pieces of evidence are the pyroengraved gourds from Huaca Prieta which were undeniably influenced by the art-style of the Ecuadorian site of Valdivia.[67]

A word of caution is warranted, however, because our rather piecemeal knowledge of these ties with tropical forest cultures to the north and east is unlikely to reflect the breadth of these interconnections. We should remember that most of the cultigens adopted on the coast, and many of those accepted in the highlands, were introduced in domesticated form from the tropical lowlands. Thus, the links suggested by these items merely confirm the continuation of a long-standing relationship critical to the establishment of the Late Preceramic coastal and highland economies.

There was not, apparently, a long transition between the initiation of settled village farming and the creation of large public works in ancient Peru. On the contrary, agriculture – whether in combination with fishing or hunting – seems to have developed hand in hand with collective labor. Life revolved around cooperative efforts, both subsistence and otherwise, and public works were the conspicuous expression of this basic organizing principle.

The large-scale mobilization of labor was made possible by a shared community ideology and its religious and social sanctions, rather than by coercive authorities. As a consequence, the public monuments were designed to meet the spiritual and social needs of the community as a whole rather than to immortalize a particular individual or family. To those who have always cited the case of cultural evolution on the arid Peruvian coast as a product of the exploitation of populations (dependent on central authorities for access to irrigation works) for the benefit of the elite, this Late Preceramic pattern may come as some surprise.[68] Irrigation was absent or insignificant when large-scale public labor began, and thus cannot be considered a critical factor in the emergence of central authority and corporate labor either on the coast or in the highlands. La Galgada appears to be an ideal control on theories which posit irrigation as a critical factor. For in spite of its dependence on irrigation systems, it seems no more stratified than societies dependent on floodwater or rainfall farming, nor do its public authorities appear any more centralized or powerful.

At La Galgada, as at virtually all the other Late Preceramic centers, there seems to have been some sort of weak theocratic authority, which was neither unified nor powerful. On the coast one encounters multiple coeval mounds, and multiple axes of public activities at virtually all sites. This led archaeologist Michael Moseley to speculate that there may have been a pluralistic form of authority. Likewise, the asymmetric distribution of analogous small temple buildings at sites of the Kotosh Religious Tradition suggests that authority derived from, and continued to serve, many social groups.[69]

Yet to build on a monumental scale there probably had to be some kind of corporate authority with recognized power to plan and direct, and agricultural surplus and exotic goods must have passed through the hands of these people.[70] Nonetheless, these authorities did not convert their power and prestige into personal wealth or real political power, despite the increasing success of the institutions over which these leaders governed, and an overall increase in the size and prosperity of the communities which supported them.

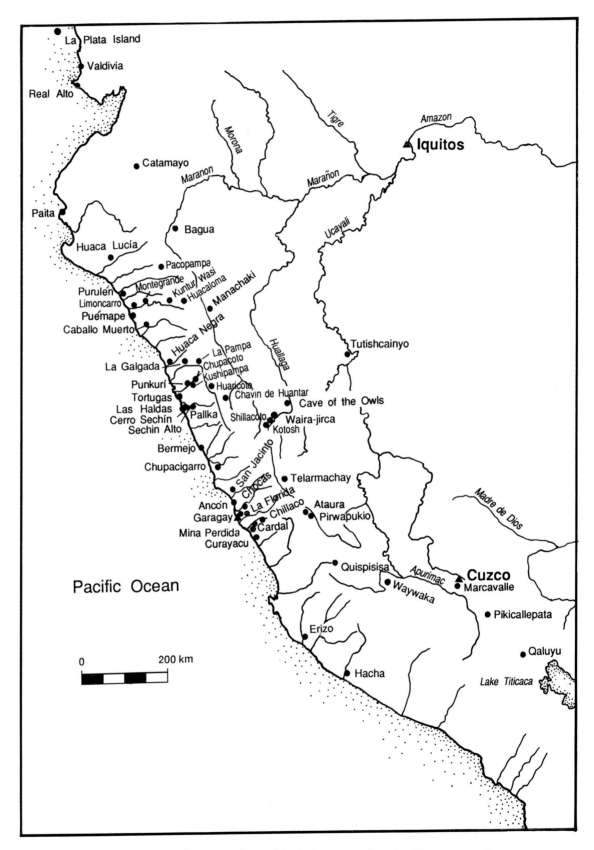

38 Map showing the principal Initial Period sites mentioned in Chapters 3 and 4.

The Initial Period Societies on the Coast

In approximately 2000 BC, the peoples of the Peruvian coast and highlands began to produce pottery for cooking and storage. For archaeologists, the initiation of ceramic production is a watershed because pottery is ubiquitous at sites and resistant to the elements and hence provides a sensitive measure of time and cultural interaction. It is therefore understandable, though not altogether desirable, that ceramic studies have occupied much of the time of scholars studying the Initial Period.

Yet it is becoming increasingly apparent that the introduction of pottery on the coast was simply one part of a much larger socioeconomic transformation which was prefigured at El Paraíso. Along the central, north-central, and north coast, there was a systematic shift of the major centers of activity to inland locations adjacent to the rich lower valley lands, and away from the ocean front. These new locations mirrored the changing economic strategies of coastal societies. While marine resources continued to be important, plant foods came to dominate the diet. The dependence on agricultural crops by large coastal populations implies the existence of canal irrigation, and must have had a profound effect on the organization and scheduling of daily life for most people. With this change came the construction of some of the most impressive public monuments in Andean prehistory.

All the basic elements making this transformation possible already existed in the Late Preceramic. As we have seen, the important cultigens had been introduced and the coastal peoples had benefited from centuries of experience learning how to make these alien crops flourish along the river's edge. Irrigation was already being practiced on a small scale in the La Galgada area, and it is probable that people were also experimenting with it on the coast around such sites as Piedra Parada and El Paraíso. No less important, organizational principles and institutions had been developed in the Late Preceramic to coordinate large-scale public labor and these provided the foundation for the Initial Period corporate activities, like the building of canals and massive pyramid constructions. Lastly, as we have seen, the shoreline economy of the Late Preceramic sustained the growth of large and dense populations, and these demographic levels provided the final critical Andean resource: abundant human labor.

There is no consensus on why the maritime-based economy was reoriented in favor of irrigation farming. At one time it was argued that steady population growth had begun to exceed the productive limits of the Preceramic subsistence system and that people were gradually forced to rely on agriculture in order to maintain their standard of living. This hypothesis, a product of the Malthusian fears of the 1960s, lost popularity as it became evident that the maritime economy could probably have supported a much larger population than existed in the Late Preceramic.[1] Moreover, there is as yet no convincing evidence of overutilization or degradation of the marine resources, or severe nutritional stress on the human population. Another hypothesis invokes environmental change as the cause of the shift. As noted in Chapter 1, there has been a gradual uplifting of the coastline in relation to the ocean due to the subduction of the Nazca Plate below the Peruvian Plate. It has been argued that at Aspero, and perhaps elsewhere, this irreversible trend could have stranded Late Preceramic coastal centers, forcing schools of small fish into deeper waters beyond the reach of the fisherfolk while, at the same time, lowering the watertable relative to the land surface and thereby depleting drinking water and diminishing the productivity of floodplain farming.[2] The fossil bays surrounding several Late Preceramic sites lend some credence to this idea. Nevertheless, one wonders whether relatively minor changes in settlement location and fishing techniques plus some small-scale irrigation might not have been sufficient to compensate for these hypothetical changes. It seems likely that a combination of other non-environmental factors, such as sociopolitical competition, dietary preferences, and the work regime, were more important in the decision to settle inland.

The first ceramics

Pottery-making was adopted in Peru over 1,000 years later than in Ecuador, Colombia, and probably the Amazonian lowlands. Despite their contact with some of these pottery-using peoples, it was not until approximately 2000 BC that ancient Peruvians began to utilize this technology. The perennial shortage of fuel both in coastal and highland environments may have been partly responsible for their reluctance to begin firing ceramics, but with the greater dependence on agricultural staples, the advantages of boiling less digestible cultigens such as beans and starchy tubers seem to have outweighed the investment of time and resources. It will be recalled that some Late Preceramic clay figurines were baked, so the notion of hardening clay by fire had existed in Peru long before the actual production of ceramic vessels.

The earliest pottery in most of coastal and highland Peru bears little resemblance to coeval Valdivia ceramics, so it would be incorrect to assume that pottery-making simply diffused south from Ecuador.[3] Instead, we find a complex pattern of independent experimentation in some areas of the central Andes, and influences from the tropical lowlands to the east and north in others. The earliest assemblages known from the Peruvian coast are technologically primitive. Their rims and body walls are almost egg-shell thin, only 2–3 mm, and their forms imitate the restricted vessels and open bowls made from gourds. The best-known examples are from Erizo in Ica, Ancón and La Florida in Rimac, and Huaca Negra in the Virú Valley. These assemblages show a striking similarity in their forms and production technology. Yet there are differences between them, particularly in decoration. Ceramics from La Florida, for example, sometimes display decoration with broad shallow incisions, while the early Ancón pottery features black painting.[4] The earliest known pottery in the highland section of the Santa drainage (the Toril style from Huaricoto) was similar to the oldest pottery from the *yunga* (e.g. the ceramics from La Galgada) and portions of the nearby coast (e.g. The Early Guañape style from the Virú Valley).[5]

Toril pottery illustrates the rather rudimentary nature of the early ceramic assemblages. There are only two basic forms – shallow bowls and neckless cooking pots (known as neckless *ollas*). The exteriors are mottled in color due to the incomplete control of the oxygen supply during the firing. The surfaces, though burnished, are uneven and remnants of the polishing marks remain. Large lumps of quartz were embedded in the body of the vessels, which expanded during the firing process causing star-shaped cracks and weakening the thin brittle walls of the vessels. The Toril assemblage at Huaricoto was sandwiched between Late Preceramic layers, and strata containing the more sophisticated late Initial Period style. The much greater variety of form and decoration and the absence of technological difficulties in the late Initial Period assemblage reinforces the impression that considerable *in situ* experimentation was involved in pottery-making in the Huaricoto area, and probably elsewhere.[6]

This pattern is very different from the one documented for Huánuco, at the sites of Kotosh and Shillacoto. The earliest pottery there, known as the Waira-jirca style, is very elaborate. The artistic and technical quality of this assemblage suggests that it drew upon an already evolved pottery tradition, and the style of the vessels suggests that this influence came from the tropical forest to the east. It will be recalled that Kotosh is located at the edge of the *ceja de selva* (the cloud forest which shrouds the lower eastern slopes) and would itself be overgrown with dense jungle if it were not for the cloud shadow in which it is located. At present, the *ceja* vegetation begins a few kilometers to the east.[7] Trade sherds from the tropical forest have been recovered at Shillacoto and Kotosh. In the Cave of the Owls, located at only 500 m above sea level in the midst of the jungle, a small number of Waira-jirca-style sherds were recovered along with the local tropical forest ceramic style.[8]

Unlike the coastal and highland assemblages described thus far which are rarely decorated, surface adornment is common in the Waira-jirca style, particularly bands of parallel lines (known as hatching) filled with red, white, and yellow mineral pigments after firing. To the west, early ceramic styles feature vessels with simple profiles, but in Huánuco there are many forms with composite silhouettes created by carination between the side and bottom of the vessel or by basal or labial flanges. While these features are alien to the coast and highlands, most have antecedents or parallels in the tropical forest, particularly among Early and Late Tutishcanyo styles of the Central Ucayali and the local materials from the Cave of the Owls.[9] The Waira-jirca assemblage also incorporates globular or egg-shaped cooking pots characteristic of the coastal and intermontane valley styles, further evidence for its multiple sources of inspiration. Nevertheless, the elements described above, and additional features such as the ovoid or triangular forms of the vessels in horizontal cross-section, testify to the profound influence of the jungle pottery tradition on the development of some early highland ceramic styles. Thus, it is not surprising that the figurative representations on Waira-jirca pottery feature tropical lowland animals such as the jaguar, spider monkey, capuchin monkey, spectacled owl, and snake.[10]

The earliest known ceramic style in the northern highlands of Peru was found by German archaeologist Peter Kaulicke at the site of Pandanche, near

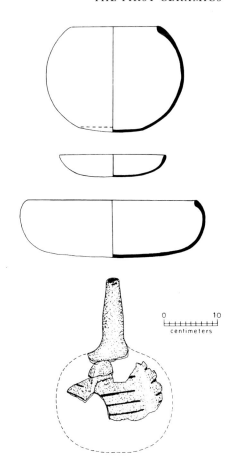

39 Ceramics from La Florida. The earliest pottery from the central coast featured technologically simple pottery, with shapes that imitated the natural forms of bottle gourd vessels.

Pacopampa. As at Kotosh, Shillacoto, and Huaricoto, Pandanche-style ceramics were found between Late Preceramic and later Initial Period layers. The Pandanche ceramics have relatively simple forms similar to those of the coast, but also have carinated globular cooking pots and jars with convex curved necks. These oxidized vessels are most commonly decorated by fine brushing to form designs and textures, often in combination with incised or finger-impressed appliqué strips.[11] Stylistically, Pandanche pottery most closely resembles that from coastal Ecuador, especially late Valdivia (Valdivia 8) and early Machalilla ceramics, although it is possible that future research in the southern Ecuadorian highlands and eastern lowlands will produce even clearer antecedents.

Thus, the complex quilt of local ceramic styles which appears at the outset of the Initial Period bears witness to contacts with the north and east, as well as to the creativity of the local communities. At the outset, pottery remained scarce in many areas and early Initial Period coastal sites still have quantities of fire-cracked rock, suggesting that some Preceramic cooking techniques were retained even after pottery was introduced.

The diversity of Initial Period ceramic styles gives a sense of the cultural heterogeneity which characterized this period. Generated by a high degree of community self-sufficiency, and reinforced by competition with neighboring groups, there developed a strong sense of local identity which was expressed through these myriad pottery assemblages. Indeed it was not unusual for a single valley or portion of a valley to have its own distinctive pottery style. However, many local communities were also part of larger systems, and this accounts for the development of the wider pattern of regional identities and styles. This regional differentiation was already evident by the Late Preceramic and it persisted until the arrival of the Spaniards.

In all societies, several levels of socio-cultural integration exist which culminate in an all-inclusive social system. During the Initial Period, the highest level appears to be that of regional social systems comprising a multitude of culturally related but politically autonomous centers, each with their own hinterland. Most day-to-day interaction was probably limited to members of a single center; this constituted the local system. Economic interdependency between nearby communities in different habitats linked them at an intermediate level. Face-to-face contact with people of different centers within the same regional system was more restricted, but may have included occasional exchange of handicrafts, marriage ties, and attendance at large public events. Though these broader ties did not obliterate local identities, they did generate regional cultural patterns, particularly in public architecture, which have been identified by archaeologists. Naturally, these amorphous social systems were not closed, and some overlapping and contact existed with adjacent regions. This chapter will focus on the distinctive cultural patterning of the three regional systems that developed along the central, north-central, and northern Peruvian coast.

The central coast and the tradition of U-shaped public architecture

The best-known of these early regional architectural traditions is the U-shaped pyramid complex first recognized by Peruvian architect Carlos Williams in 1971. These monumental constructions constitute the core of all major Initial Period sites in the lower, and in some cases, mid-valleys of the Lurín, Rimac, Chillón, Chancay, and Huaura Valleys; a few related constructions have also been reported further north in Supe and Pativilca. Thus far, approximately 20 U-shaped pyramid complexes have been identified, though only a small number have been studied in detail.[12]

The scale of this public architecture is substantially greater than that of the Late Preceramic. The Huaca La Florida in Rimac, for example, represents an investment of at least 6.7 million person-days, and this excludes the labor needed to level the area and to plaster and/or decorate the outer surfaces of the buildings.[13] La Florida is by no means the largest of the U-shaped pyramidal mounds. San Jacinto, in the Chancay Valley, is four times larger, and it would have required almost 2 million cubic meters of material just to level its 30-hectare plaza.[14] Prior to their identification, many of these mounds were presumed to be natural hills because of their enormity. The U-shaped monuments have a number of formal features in common. They comprise massive terraced platform mounds flanking three sides of a large rectangular plaza. The central mound is frequently the largest, but the layout does not display exact axial symmetry since the two lateral arms are always different in size, and a single opening invariably exists between the central pyramid and one of the lateral arms. The summit of the pyramidal mounds is reached by steep stairways from the central plaza. On the top are decorated chambers in which religious rituals were carried out. Between Lurín and Chancay, all the U-shaped complexes are oriented northeast, varying between 13 and 64 degrees east of north.[15]

The layout of these monumental constructions probably developed from that of El Paraíso, with its long low parallel wings, enormous central plaza area and northeastern orientation. However, Initial Period constructions differ from this local antecedent in having a much larger central building at the apex of the "U" (compared with El Paraíso's relatively small Unit 1) and by connecting the central structure with one of the lateral arms.[16]

The construction technique of the U-shaped complexes was likewise derived from earlier local building practices. At centers such as La Florida, sloping or battered walls of uncut fieldstone set in clay mortar were still used to define platforms with buildings on their summit. The core of these structures often

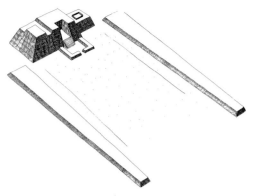

40 At the beginning of the Initial Period (*c.* 2000 BC), the U-shaped Huaca la Florida in the Rimac Valley, depicted in this isometric reconstruction, was one of the largest complexes in the Andes.

41 The clearing of a looter's trench at the U-shaped center of Mina Perdida in the Lurín Valley revealed over 30 construction phases spanning the entire second millenium BC. This photograph shows the remains of four superimposed central staircases, the oldest made of cubical adobes, the penultimate of cubical adobes with stone surfaces, and the final one of stone blocks (the man holding a rod stands on a step of the final staircase).

consisted of stone blocks, small hemispherical adobes, and river cobbles, sometimes enclosed in fiber bags like those used at El Paraíso. Significant variability did exist in the construction technology employed between coeval centers. For example, the early Initial Period platforms of Mina Perdida in the Lurín Valley were built with small cubical adobes rather than fieldstone.[17] As in the Late Preceramic constructions, the public buildings show an emphasis on the careful finishing of walls with layers of clay plaster. Platforms were expanded horizontally by building new retaining walls parallel to those of the prior building phase, and by filling the space between them with rubble. Concurrently, the mounds were raised by filling old summit buildings and capping them with a new clay surface, thereby converting them into a platform base for a new set of similar structures. As at Kotosh and La Galgada, a cross-section of these U-shaped mounds invariably reveals a sequence of superimposed clay floors and revetment walls separated by rubble.

There is rarely evidence of damage to the structures at the time of their burial, and the newer constructions generally replicate the design of the older buildings. This pattern of ritual entombment has already been touched upon in the discussion of Preceramic monumental architecture (Chapter 2). The resulting cyclical growth of pyramids through accretion is characteristic of early Peruvian public building, and contrasts with pyramids elsewhere – like that of the Great Pyramid at Giza – that were the product of a single episode of intense activity over several decades.

Huaca La Florida is the oldest of the classic U-shaped centers dated thus far. It is associated with some of the earliest pottery known from the central coast. Pockets of habitation refuse have been isolated at the base of the central mound and material has also been recovered from the platform constructions. Analysis of these collections indicates that construction of the monument was under way early in the Initial Period, and though the mounds show evidence of several construction stages, the structure appears to have been built, utilized, and then abandoned within a relatively short time, perhaps no more than a few centuries. Radiocarbon dates from the site suggest that there was no significant break between the building of terminal Preceramic centers such as El Paraíso and the initiation of U-shaped pyramid construction.[18] Structures similar to La Florida continued to be erected on the central coast for at least 1,000 years. For instance, one of the final building stages at Cardal in the Lurín Valley has been dated to c. 940 BC.[19] Clearly, the tradition of U-shaped public architecture on the central coast is one of considerable antiquity and longevity, as well as areal distribution.

But what was responsible for the popularity of the U-shaped layout? It is widely believed that this design reflects and expresses basic cosmological principles underlying the religious worship at these centers, like the cruciform design of a medieval cathedral. In the pre-Columbian world, however, the purpose of such cosmological models is not solely descriptive or symbolic; it was also designed to focus and influence supernatural power for the benefit of the community. Archaeologist William Isbell has argued that the meaning communicated by the U-shaped design is basically the same as that found in the later buildings of Inca Cuzco, and is found today among certain tropical forest groups. He believes that the parallel arms of the U express the opposing and yet complementary forces within society and the cosmos, and that the central building at the apex of the U represents the synthesis of these opposing forces. In this view, the plaza becomes a neutral field mediating between opposing cosmic domains while the center of the central mound is the critical point of synthesis and resolution.[20] While such interpretations correlate with what we know of indigenous Andean thought, they are difficult to evaluate empirically without extensive excavation. Nevertheless, the attribution of powerful religious significance to the U-shaped monumental constructions has been amply confirmed by the large-scale excavations at Garagay and Cardal, as we shall see.

Garagay. Located 8 km inland in the lower part of the Rimac Valley, Garagay has recently been engulfed within the modern city of Lima. The surviving portion of the site covers 16 hectares, 9 of which comprise its central plaza area. Beginning in 1974, the central mound (Pyramid B), the right arm (Pyramid A), and the small circular court in front of Pyramid A were investigated by William Isbell and Peruvian archaeologist Rogger Ravines.[21] The ceramics and four radiocarbon measurements ranging from 1643 BC to 897 BC suggest that Garagay was established in the middle part of the Initial Period, after nearby Huaca La Florida was abandoned.

Excavations revealed that the central earthen mound at the apex of the U (Pyramid B) was actually a stepped flat-topped pyramid with steep plastered stone walls defining its outer face. Construction eventually reached a height of 23 m and covered a surface area of 385 × 155 m. The central mound overshadowed the right and left lateral arms, which only reached heights of 6 m and 9 m respectively. Walls projecting from the middle of the central mound define a vestibule between the vast open plaza and the steep central stairway providing access to the pyramid. The main stairway was plastered in white clay and was found in undamaged condition. The steep incline and delicate surface of the stairs suggests that they were used only by a small number of individuals on rare occasions. The central stairs lead to an open landing overlooking the plaza.

A doorway leads back from this space into an atrium set into the center of the pyramid's summit. Unfortunately, the final atrium of Pyramid B has been badly damaged by erosion and the construction of a television antenna, but it is known to have been decorated with polychrome friezes. Votive offerings left in the floor of that building have been recovered. Perhaps the most fascinating of these was a small piece of granodiorite wrapped in cotton thread, plastered with gray clay, slipped with shimmering specular hematite, and then painted with the image of a supernatural being with huge upper canines, and eyes with eccentric pupils. Cactus spines were tied to its sides, as if representing staffs. Embedded in it was a small *Spondylus* shell bead brought from Ecuador. The investigators have linked this piece to the main supernatural image of the Old Temple at Chavín de Huántar and go on to suggest that the earlier construction phases at Garagay should therefore predate the Chavín de Huántar temple.

The now demolished atrium had been built directly above an older atrium of similar design (referred to as the Middle Temple). The atrium is roughly square, 24 m on a side, with lateral inset stairways flanked by pilasters and probably a central stairway in the rear. The walls of the room were originally about 1.6 m high and sloped outwards by 12 degrees. Wooden posts set into lined circular pits helped to sustain some sort of roofing, although it may not have covered the lowered center of the room. Colored friezes sculpted in low-relief decorate the walls and pilasters. Along the excavated north and east walls, archaeologists

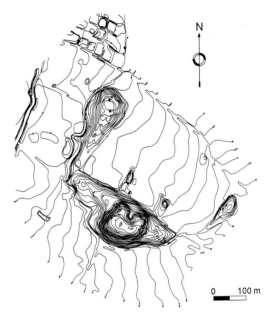

42 Following the abandonment of Huaca La Florida, the center at Garagay (seen in this topographic map) emerged as the largest U-shaped construction in the Rimac Valley.

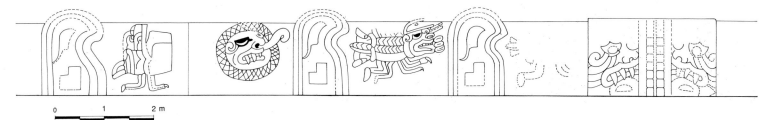

0   1   2 m

43 The polychrome friezes decorating the atrium of Garagay's Middle Temple feature a fanged supernatural with spider attributes, possibly linked to divination and water for irrigation.

44 Detail from the clay frieze that decorated the walls of the Middle Temple central atrium at Garagay. This head of a supernatural with spider attributes was painted yellow, blue, red, and white. The cross-hatched band surrounding the head represents a spider web and the nasal extrusion corresponds to the pedipalp of the arachnid (it may also represent the nasal discharge associated with the inhalation of hallucinogenic snuff).

discovered a series of profile figures separated by geometric motifs. The figures are monstrous supernaturals, combining elements of spiders with anthropomorphic faces; some also have large fangs, often interpreted as feline. The frieze is modeled in fine clay and painted with vivid yellow, white, red, pink, and grayish blue mineral-based pigments. Unbaked clay sculptures of this kind are delicate, and repairs and renovations were common at Garagay. In some spots there are ten layers of painted clay, the original color combinations carefully maintained.

The staircase, the votive offerings, and the images on the walls of this summit chamber leave little doubt that the monumental architecture at Garagay was designed to provide an environment for religious ceremonies, some of which could have been attended and seen by only a small number of individuals. But what cosmology underlay these rituals and what were the goals of the ceremonies? The large canines of Garagay's friezes suggest the ferocity and power of the supernaturals being worshiped and, along with the eccentric irises, served as markers of the supernatural beings during much of Peruvian prehistory. The prominence of arachnid elements is particularly notable. Spiders were used in late pre-Hispanic times (and still are in parts of modern highland Peru) to predict the onset of rainfall and other agricultural matters. In fact, in Inca times there was a special class of diviners, called *pacchaŕicuc*, who used spiders to foretell the future.[22]

The idea that the U-shaped pyramid constructions housed rituals to preserve agricultural fertility had been suggested even before the discovery of the spider imagery. There was speculation that the orientation of the temples was towards the mountains and, more specifically, towards the source of water used in irrigation.[23] Completely dependent on unpredictable highland rain for survival, coastal societies probably attempted to control these natural forces by making offerings or, in Andean terms, "feeding" the deities responsible for them, thereby creating a sense of reciprocal obligation. It is likely that these temples also served as points of divination and perhaps astronomical observation to help coordinate planting, irrigation, and harvesting.

In two of the small circular pits in front of Garagay's arachnid images, small doll-like figurines were left as offerings. Their fanged faces are made of clay and painted, and they are dressed in textiles. One of the figurines, referred to earlier, has two large fangs and carries two large cactus spines on its back, suggesting the staffs of the principal deity. Significantly, the spines come from the San Pedro cactus, a source of the vision-producing mescaline still used by shamanic curers in Peru. These spines were also found encrusted in adobes left in the fill of the Middle Temple of Garagay's Pyramid B. It seems plausible that a drink containing mescaline may have been ingested during rituals to facilitate direct communication with the supernatural realm. Ravines tentatively dates these figurines to the Middle Temple of Pyramid B or an even earlier construction phase, which indicates the considerable antiquity of the anthropomorphic deity.

The summit of Garagay's Pyramid A yielded additional evidence of ritual activity.[24] The complex architectural history of this mound has yet to be published in detail but it consists of at least four construction phases. Early in its history, walls were decorated with naturalistic friezes in low relief. One atrium wall has a remarkably realistic representation of a cotton net, with the looped nodes carefully depicted. This motif has been interpreted as a fishing net, but another possibility is suggested by the Initial Period art of the north coast, where net bags are shown filled with human trophy heads rather than fish. Significantly the entrance to this early atrium was decorated with a pair of anthropomorphic warriors grasping circular shields.

This construction level was covered by another, in which the exterior face of the central atrium consisted of a series of large niches, which may have once held three-dimensional cult objects or sculptures. The pilasters which flank these niches were decorated with monochrome clay friezes. Symmetric sets of three profile faces were created facing towards the entrance into the atrium, made with broad incisions on a flat plastered surface. These friezes differed from those of Pyramid B in style as well as technique, for they are highly conventionalised and sometimes difficult to decipher. The motifs combine anthropomorphic faces with avian, feline, and more abstract attributes. Rather than appending these attributes to the faces in mask-like fashion, as was the case in the Middle Temple of Pyramid B, the elements were integrated into the visage, sometimes replacing the nose. These images, charged with religious import, were eventually enveloped by at least two later summit constructions. A small painted clay mask of an anthropomorphic face with large upper canines was recovered from the rubble fill of one of these later constructions.

The motifs known from the public iconography on Garagay's summit also appear on the domestic pottery utilized at fishing villages such as Ancón and Curayacu. This suggests that a wide community shared these symbols and

45 On the summit of Mound A at Garagay were found two unbaked clay sculptures of anthropomorphic figures grasping circular shields. Note the naturalistic modeling of the hands and feet.

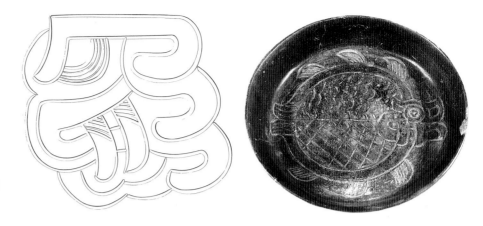

46 Religious motifs from the public architecture of the U-shaped complexes were also represented on the household pottery of fishing villages. The design shown here decorated a large jar from Ancón.

47 The interior of this blackware bowl from Ancón is decorated with the incised image of a supernatural with sea turtle attributes, a motif as yet unknown in the public art of the Initial Period ceremonial architecture on the central coast. Diameter 23.4 cm.

48 Hollow and solid female figurines with elaborate hair styles were used in household contexts, perhaps for curing ceremonies. This large hollow figurine (47 cm high) from the fishing village of Curayacu is an unusually fine example.

underlying beliefs. But public iconography offers only a partial picture of religious ideology, for some themes, like that of a supernatural with sea turtle attributes, appear on pottery but have yet to be documented in public contexts. More striking still are the numerous hollow and solid pottery figurines depicting nude women found at Initial Period sites throughout the central coast. Particular attention was given to the coiffure, breasts, and navel. Most are small, but there are some large carefully modeled examples, such as one discovered at Curayacu. Fragments of these figurines are usually found in domestic refuse and, judging from this context, they may have played a role in household rituals, rather than community worship.[25]

Cardal. The Lurín Valley is the southernmost valley in which multiple U-shaped centers have been found. One of these centers, Cardal, has been investigated recently by the author.[26] It is situated in the lower valley, 15 km from the Pacific and 37 km southeast of Garagay, at an elevation of 150 m above sea level. Judging from the 26 radiocarbon measurements available, Cardal was occupied between *c.* 1300 BC and 900 BC; it is therefore roughly contemporary with Garagay.

A fairly clear picture of Cardal's architectural layout has emerged from the investigation. A ceremonial road following the site's central axis approaches the pyramid complex from the northeast. The road passes between two massive rectangular enclosures and two sunken circular courts before reaching the raised central plaza. Across the 3-hectare open plaza is a massive set of 34 stairs which ascend directly to the summit of the central pyramid. The stairs are capped in white clay and two black painted lines on the middle stairs reiterate the site centerline. The steps of this 6-m wide staircase are so narrow and steep that it is almost impossible to climb them and, as at Garagay, their near perfect state suggests that they were seldom used. Four superimposed central staircases were unearthed, and a fifth one can be inferred from the stratigraphy; each set corresponds to a different construction period.

The final staircase led to an open antechamber and a central atrium with the same basic design as the Garagay atrium, but lacking the pilasters and wall decoration. Nevertheless, a frieze fragment of a frontal anthropomorphic face with upper fangs was found on the atrium floor. Below this badly damaged final atrium was a well-preserved earlier complex with the same layout, but superior

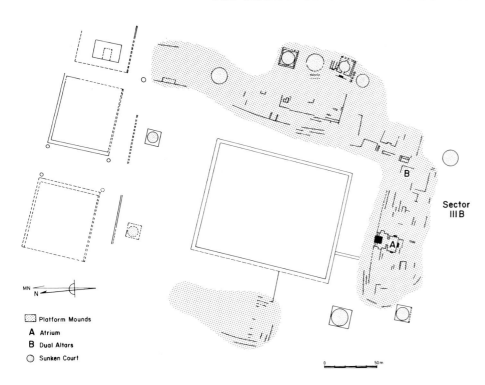

49 Ground plan of the U-shaped complex of Cardal during its final period of use (*c.* 1000–900 BC), after the addition of dual rectangular plazas and ten sunken circular courts.

50 Aerial photograph of the central mound at Cardal during the excavation of the central staircase and atrium.

51 The central staircase at Cardal, leading to the principal atrium area. Three superimposed staircases are visible in the photograph, the last of which has been badly damaged.

52 Isometric reconstruction of the central stairway and decorated open antechamber of Cardal's penultimate atrium (*c.* 1100 BC).

Platform Mounds
A Atrium
B Dual Altars
◯ Sunken Court

Sector IIIB

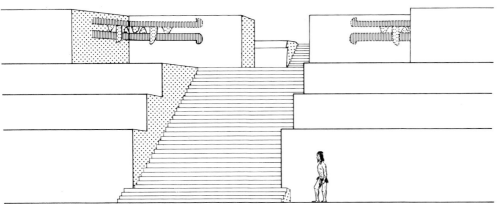

construction. A clay frieze modeled in low relief and painted with red and yellow pigment decorates the open landing at the top of the stairs. Artists sculpted a massive mouth band with interlocking teeth and large upper fangs on either side of the entryway into the central atrium. This awesome motif is clearly visible from the central plaza an is actually best observed from below. The frieze was renovated up to six times, sometimes involving changes in the color pattern. The entire frieze was coated with a thin layer of white clay before it was buried.

Passing in between these enormous gnashing teeth, the viewer enters a roughly square atrium with a rear staircase and two symmetrically arranged lateral staircases. The walls of the room are slipped with a light brown clay, and the only ornamentation is a ledge-like bulge covering the upper walls of the room. Absent is the elaborate terracing of the floor, the pilasters, the small circular pits, and the interior friezes known from nearby Garagay. Yet the overall similarity in the summit architecture between the two U-shaped centers is still striking. Moreover, a clay frieze uncovered on the right arm of Cardal shows a variant of the repeating geometric motif found at the Middle Temple at Garagay.

Excavations at Cardal near the juncture of the central pyramid and the right arm revealed additional religious architecture with no known parallel. A medium-sized rectangular summit building had been constructed on a low platform. The focal point was a pair of identical stepped altars placed back to back in separate rooms in the center of the building. Burnt offerings were found on and around the altars and on the restricted staircase leading into the building. When seen from the side, the form of the altars is identical to the step-fret or step-block motif that was widely used as a decoration on Initial Period ceramics. While it could be argued that these pottery designs represent altars, it seems more likely that both the pottery motifs and the form of the altars symbolize a higher level religious concept; for example, they could represent a sacred mountain.

Participation in ceremonies on the pyramid summit at Cardal was restricted, so the focus of most public activities must have been in the open areas below, particularly in the central plaza. Surfaced with hard white clay, the plaza was probably the scene of banquets, dances, and ritual battles, as well as religious ceremonies; through these activities, social norms were reaffirmed, links between distinct groups were forged, and disruptive tensions within the society were dissipated.

The layout of Cardal also furnished smaller more intimate environments in which individual segments of the larger society could join together. Eight semi-subterranean circular courts, each no more than 13 m in diameter, ring the outer edge of the complex. At least superficially, they are reminiscent of the multiple kivas in a Hopi pueblo, each used by a specific clan or secret society. Investigations at Cardal reveal that these structures were plastered and painted and, like the central plaza, kept clean. In two of the four excavated courts, a votive offering was left in the center; in one case, a human skull, and in the other a ceramic bottle decorated with interlocking snakes. In a third circular court, a T-shaped hearth was found in the center. Along with the huge central plaza and outlying rectangular enclosures, these courts attest to the high priority given to the construction of well-defined public spaces. Although it is difficult to determine empirically the nature of the public activities carried out in these public spaces or the composition of the social groups using them, the importance

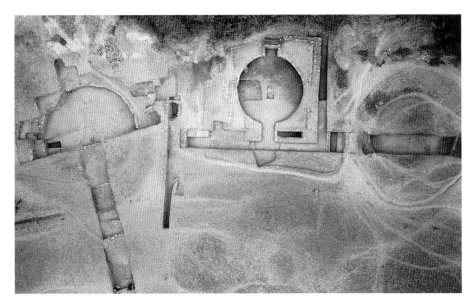

53 Like the *kivas* of the American Southwest, the sunken circular courts at Cardal seen in this balloon photograph offered intimate environments in which small segments of society could gather. These three courts are located on the outer terrace of the site's eastern lateral pyramid platform; the fully excavated middle court featured a T-shaped firepit in the center of its floor.

of these areas to daily life, and the ritual overtones pervading this public sphere, is incontestable.

Settlement and subsistence

The U-shaped centers of the central coast represent an enormous investment of human labor expended above and beyond that dedicated to providing basic human needs. It has been estimated, for example, that the Initial Period pyramid complexes in Lurín, Rimac, and Chillón represent over 12 million person-days of work.[27] Obviously, these societies had a stable economy and a large population, otherwise it would not have been feasible to channel this quantity of labor into the public realm without jeopardizing the survival of the community. On the other hand, it is erroneous to view public works projects of this scale as the *inevitable* outcome of particularly productive subsistence economies, since large, dense populations of farmers exist in parts of Africa and elsewhere which have never engaged in comparable undertakings. Social mechanisms must therefore have been developed to mobilize "surplus" labor during the dead season in the agricultural cycle, and to extract surplus food production for the communal banquets associated with the building activities. Before considering these elusive organizational factors, it is necessary to consider more closely the economic base of these Initial Period societies.

Three types of Initial Period settlements have been encountered: large centers with public architecture such as Garagay and Cardal; small shoreline villages like Ancón and Curayacu; and small inland hamlets such as Chillaco and Palma (in the mid-section of the Lurín Valley). These three kinds of settlements were linked together by exchange networks to form small-scale internally self-sufficient subsistence systems. The Initial Period refuse from Ancón, for example, is dominated by the remains of domesticated food plants, yet there is no arable land in the immediate vicinity, nor is there artifactual evidence suggesting that these people ever engaged in agriculture. The excavations at inland sites such as Cardal and Garagay have yielded enormous quantities of marine shells and fish bones, as well as the remains of sea lions, pelicans, and cormorants. In fact, shoreline resources provide almost all the animal protein consumed at Cardal and other large centers, yet most are too far from the ocean to regularly exploit the littoral habitats, and no fishing paraphernalia has been recovered from them. Locally available game such as deer, and land snails from the nearby area of fog vegetation, were eaten on occasion to create a somewhat more varied diet.[28]

Two examples of the third type of settlement, the inland hamlet, were found in the *yunga* environment of the entrenched middle section of the Lurín Valley. Both sites cover less than 1.5 hectares and it is unlikely that the population at either one exceeded 150 people. Chillaco at 1,100 m and Palma at 1,350 m were ideally located for the cultivation of coca and chili pepper. These crops do not grow well in the lower valley because of the heavy cloud cover and relatively cool temperatures, but they flourish in the sunny and well-protected mid-valley.[29]

It is possible that some of the mid-valley sites may have been agricultural communities specializing in the production of items for exchange purposes, such as coca. The presence of abundant ocean products over 50 km inland at Palma and Chillaco demonstrates that these small settlements were integrated into the valley food-exchange system.

At least two varieties of coca were grown in pre-Hispanic Peru: one (*Erythroxylon novogranatense* var. *truxillense*) was cultivated between about 200 m and 1,800 m elevation in the coastal valleys and the other (*Erythroxylon coca* var. *coca*) mainly between 500 and 1,500 m elevation on the eastern slopes of the Andes. The coca leaf appears for the first time on the central coast late in the Initial Period. The oldest known specimen of this addictive cultigen is a chewed quid which still displays tooth marks.[30] Traditionally, the coca leaf was masticated with powdered lime or ashes as a mild stimulant, to suppress fatigue and give a sense of increased energy and contentment. (The conversion of the coca leaf into concentrated cocaine by chemical means is a relatively modern development and the strong psychological and physical effects of this drug are not comparable to that of the unrefined coca leaf, which is still chewed by millions of farmers in the Peruvian and Bolivian highlands.)

There are also small-scale civic-ceremonial centers in mid-valley locations: Malpaso (or Piedra Liza) in Lurín, Yanacoto and Santa Rosa de Quives in Rimac, and Chocas in Chillón. Chocas resembles the U-shaped complexes in the lower valley, but it differs in orientation. Malpaso lacks both the distinctive U-shaped layout and northeast orientation. These differences may be due to chronological factors, but they could also express cultural differences between the mid- and lower-valley populations.[31]

The substantial populations responsible for constructing the 20 or so pyramid complexes of the central coast have been difficult to find archaeologically. Some may have lived in yet unlocated hamlets on the valley floor which were later destroyed by intensive agriculture or hidden by alluvium. Others appear to have resided in nucleated settlements behind the public architecture, e.g. at Cardal and Mina Perdida in Lurín. It is important to realize that the U-shaped complexes were not empty ceremonial centers drawing labor from vast hinterlands. There are major constructions in virtually all the central coast valleys and many of them appear to be contemporary. In the relatively small valley of Lurín for example, Mina Perdida, Cardal, Manchay Bajo, and perhaps

Parka were utilized at roughly the same time, although they are all within an hour's walk of each other. Since still other pyramid complexes were being built and used in neighboring valleys at the same time, these other drainages cannot be posited as sources of labor. It would appear, therefore, that each of these civic-ceremonial complexes was constructed and utilized by a local social group.

Each of these groups must have numbered over 1,000 to create monuments of the proportions described, and consequently they could not have been supported solely by floodplain agriculture. There would have been little arable land near most of the U-shaped centers without some kind of water management. The scale of irrigation works, however, may have been small, perhaps no more than short, gravity-flow canals siphoning water off from a spring or the nearby river. At La Florida, for example, a single 4-km canal would have quadrupled the amount of agricultural land. Most of the settlements with U-shaped architecture were probably on the outer margins of the cultivated land, but with the later expansion of irrigation systems, the ruins of these centers have been converted into agricultural fields.

Not surprisingly, there appears to be a direct relationship between the amount of irrigable land and the scale of Initial Period monumental construction.[32] The valleys of Chancay and Rimac which have the largest annual river discharge and the most cultivated land also have the largest pyramid complexes. The medium-sized Chillón Valley and small Lurín Valley have complexes of correspondingly less size. It is reasonable to assume that the larger valleys supported greater populations and could consequently appropriate more labor.

As mentioned previously, historian Karl Wittfogel and others have attempted to explain the origins of civilization in Peru and elsewhere as the outcome of the administrative demands of irrigation. Yet in the case of coastal Peru, the small-scale hydraulic systems of the type believed to have existed in the Initial Period would not have required a large bureaucracy to construct or maintain them. There are numerous ethnographic examples from Peru and elsewhere in which the responsibility for building and regulating such systems belongs solely to the local community.[33] On the other hand, the inherent qualities of water management probably did influence the nature of these early coastal societies. Building even relatively small hydraulic works requires more labor than a single household can muster. Moreover, all canals require annual repairs and the removal of silt that invariably accumulates in them. Unless maintenance is carried out each year along the entire canal, the availability of water is jeopardized. Therefore, there is an inherent need for supra-household cooperation in the initial construction and later maintenance of this agricultural infrastructure, a need which does not necessarily exist in areas dependent on rainfall agriculture. Finally, unequal distribution may leave those plots down-valley without sufficient water for their crops, hence the additional need for mechanisms of social control. As seen in the previous chapter, social systems emphasizing cooperative labor developed on the coast prior to the dependence on irrigation agriculture, but when the latter did occur, it must have reinforced social coherence and cooperative labor, and led to their further development.

The crops grown by coastal farmers were basically the same as those cultivated during Late Preceramic times. The quantity of plant foods consumed, however, appears to have increased dramatically. One new introduction on the central coast, at least judging from the macrobotanical evidence, was maize. At

54 Balloon photograph of a household area uncovered behind the main pyramid at Cardal. The stone footings of a small storehouse and a partially destroyed rectangular domestic structure are visible. The open patio area where most activities were probably carried out had numerous unlined pits, some of which were used for burials.

Ancón, where there is a large sample of well-preserved plant remains available for the entire early sequence, maize first appears in the late Initial Period levels. It occurs already fully developed; incomplete cob fragments range from 50–60 mm in length and up to 16 mm in diameter. This is as large as many strains of maize used subsequently on the central coast. In spite of this, maize is not common in the late Initial Period refuse. But whatever the specific makeup of the Initial Period diet, the development of irrigation agriculture (combined with fishing and shellfish collection) supported a major increase in population: the number of people living on the central coast by the end of the Initial Period must have been many times that of the Late Preceramic, judging from the number and size of the archaeological sites.[34]

At both Ancón and Cardal, houses were simple quadrangular structures, only 2.5 m on a side, with low stone footings supporting upper walls of perishable materials. Cooking was carried out in adjacent buildings or areas, and subterranean storage pits were common around the buildings. At Cardal small free-standing bin-like constructions were constructed several meters behind the houses. At Ancón the walls were made of small stones set in seaweed and marsh grass, while inland at Cardal they were constructed of fieldstones and occasional small hemispherical adobes set in clay mortar. Food was stored, cooked, and eaten at these household units, and the refuse from these activities was thrown out in front of the buildings. The residential areas also appear to have been the focus of productive activities, including the occasional fabrication of bone and stone items for household use. At Cardal, spindle whorls and charred cotton seeds were recovered from the refuse, as were stone clod-breakers or digging stick weights. These materials suggest that people were not only engaged in cotton cultivation, but were processing the raw fiber around their homes, and transforming it into thread and cotton textiles.[35]

A recent study of Initial Period domestic pottery from Ancón has found that although the size of serving dishes remained the same, the size of cooking vessels steadily increased until, by the late Initial Period, the pots were triple their original size. This pattern suggests a steady growth in the size of individual households. It would be interesting to have complementary information on the changes in the size and structure of household architecture to independently evaluate this inference.[36]

The economic foundation of Initial Period society on the central coast and elsewhere was fundamentally agrarian. The manufacture of products for exchange apparently had a negligible role, and though a considerable agricultural surplus must have been produced, it was not used to support craft specialists. Instead, it was funneled into the agricultural infrastructure and the public monuments expressing the power and prestige of the community. Since almost all the critical foodstuffs and raw materials were locally available, production for long-distance exchange was not a vital subsistence activity.

Obsidian from the south-central highlands was used for cutting tools, but it was scarce and consequently highly valued. Obsidian artifacts and used flakes were rarely discarded, and the clearest evidence of the material's utilization comes from the minute chips produced when resharpening these instruments. Exotic items acquired through long-distance trade do occasionally appear, particularly imported pottery and jet mirrors made from anthracite coal. Less frequent are valuables used as personal ornaments, such as colored feathers and *Spondylus* beads. There are also unique exotic items, like the figurine with articulated arms and inlaid shell eyes found in a woman's grave at Ancón. Its body was carved from chonta wood, a material found only in the tropical forest east of the Andes.[37] These items underline the fact that the societies of the central coast were not isolated from other spheres of interaction. Yet long-distance trade does not appear to have been an important element in the local economies, and other kinds of intersocietal interactions – some of which may have been accompanied by gift exchange – were probably far more significant.

Burials and social organization

In some respects, Initial Period culture on the central coast was remarkably conservative. The sharp increase in public labor and the change in agricultural technology that permitted a rise in production and population did not lead to the development of occupational specialization and increased division of labor, nor did social hierarchies emerge to manage the increased population density. On the contrary, the organization of Initial Period coastal society represents a gradual transformation of that of the Late Preceramic.

Some sense of the character of this society may be gleaned from the mortuary remains. At the fishing village of Ancón, three classes of burials were encountered.[38] For most people, death was a community affair and its members were buried together in a spatially separated area which comprised the burial ground. There was little distinction between graves. Most individuals were buried in shallow pits on their side in a flexed position. Wrapped in cotton cloth and placed on a reed mat, the deceased was usually accompanied only by a used cooking vessel containing food for the afterlife. Red ocher was daubed around the head and, as in the Preceramic, the body was covered with stones.

One adult male, about 30 years old at the time of death, was set apart from the rest by his dress and offerings. A cebus monkey covered with mica flakes had been placed on his knees. In later times these tropical forest animals were cherished by coastal peoples as pets, and were an item of exchange. The monkey's owner was buried in standard fashion, but a string of stone beads with a carved stone pendant, and another of colored feathers and iron pyrites, were placed on his forehead. He also wore necklaces and armlets, and had a fan of red, yellow, and green feathers. Beneath his head was a wooden bowl filled with more feathers, and near by was a single-spout bottle and a decorated bowl. A mortar and pestle with traces of red pigment wrapped in cotton cloth was also found.

A second type of interment was found several hundred meters from the cemetery area. Five 6-month fetuses, probably still-born, had been buried along with a 20–30 year old woman. One fetus was underneath her right hand. An undecorated bowl, a few baskets, and some simple cotton cloth accompanied these individuals. One wonders whether the separation of these bodies from the main cemetery area did not symbolically express the threat to the larger community of unborn children and death in childbirth. Interestingly, segregation along these same lines has been documented by Jeffrey Quilter at the site of Paloma, over 2,000 years before.

The third type of burial appears to be a dedicatory offering, immediately preceding the construction of a semi-subterranean stone residence. The body of a small child, 3–5 years old at the time of death, was interred beneath the corner of this structure in line with one of the walls. The child's eyes had been removed and replaced with mica sheets, its stomach replaced with a gourd, and its heart with a clear rock quartz crystal. If, like the burial atop the Aspero pyramid in Late Preceramic times, this interment was a dedicatory offering, then the child and the associated finery would have been buried to ensure the success of activities in the building above and the social group or groups utilizing it. The practice of leaving dedicatory offerings of animals, and more rarely unflawed young children, in the corner of important constructions survived into the 20th century, despite the efforts of the Christian colonizers.

Recent discoveries at Cardal seem to indicate that an analogous burial pattern existed in the major civic-ceremonial centers. Excavation of the penultimate atrium area of the central mound at this site revealed that it had been converted into a community cemetery following its use, prior to the construction above it of the final atrium complex.[39] Sixteen individuals had been buried in a tightly flexed position face down in shallow pits dug into the atrium floor. As at Ancón, red ocher was frequently sprinkled around the heads and the bodies were apparently wrapped in cloth, placed on fiber mats and then covered with stones. When items accompanied the dead, they were usually a charred cooking pot or a few spindle whorls. One adult male, however, was distinguished from the others by his jewelry. He wore a necklace of sea lion incisors and red-painted bone earspools. A bone tool was left clutched in his hand, but no pottery or other offerings had been included in the grave.

Other isolated burials were found in the residential area behind the central mound, inside pits that had been dug below floor level. Like the burials on the pyramid summit, offerings rarely included more than an occasional cooking vessel or spindle whorl. In one case, a pecked-stone clod-breaker was included with the deceased. It should be emphasized that the burials in the atrium – like those below – were of men, women, and children. Considering this fact, and the paucity of gravegoods or traces of elaborate ritual, these interments are thought to be those of community members rather than of sacrificial victims. If this conclusion is correct, it would seem to confirm the close symbolic relationship between community members and the most visible product of their collective labor: the U-shaped pyramid.

Centers the size of Cardal clearly needed leaders to direct construction, to organize large-scale ceremonies, and to bear the responsibility for a host of administrative and ritual activities critical to the community's survival. The differential burial treatment of a few select individuals at Ancón and Cardal suggests that individuals with special status did exist in the community. On the summit of the main mound at Cardal there are free-standing constructions which appear to be unusually well-built residences, and could have served as permanent or temporary homes for these community authorities. Yet differences in individual prestige and power do not necessarily imply a highly stratified society. It remains unknown how access to these positions was determined, whether it was by kinship, personal achievement, or sacred knowledge. The frequent assumption by some scholars of the existence of elite lineages may be completely unjustified. For instance, the Kogi priests in Colombia, like Tibetan monks, drew their members from the youth of numerous kin groups.[40]

Another important question, more easily resolved archaeologically, is the degree to which the people in prestigious positions were able to translate their authority into personal gain. Judging from the remains at Cardal and Ancón, the leaders were only able to capitalize on their status to a very limited degree. The refuse surrounding the houses on the summit is very similar to that found below, and suggests that consumption patterns were fundamentally similar to the rest of society. Similarly, burial goods effectively distinguish "high status" individuals from the others, but do not represent personal wealth acquired by appropriating the labor of others.[41]

In summary, the evidence available on the Initial Period societies of the central coast suggests a multitude of weakly stratified small-scale societies with highly developed religious institutions and corporate labor practices. The 20 or so civic-ceremonial centers appear to have been occupied by independent and equivalent small-scale societies tied through economic interdependence to shoreline villages and specialized inland farming hamlets, and linked to other large centers by shared beliefs and perhaps also by marriage alliances and occasional cooperation in raiding or defense. These major centers do not seem ever to have been integrated into some sort of overarching hierarchical political structure.

The balkanized nature of central coast society can be illustrated by comparisons of the pottery assemblages. At roughly the same time, the characteristic pottery at Curayacu is decorated with bichrome painting zoned by incisions, while at nearby Cardal it is adorned with unzoned cane-stamped circles. Meanwhile, at Ancón, decoration primarily consists of curvilinear incisions – particularly on bowl interiors. The substantial variation in the layout and orientation of the ceremonial complexes reinforces this impression of local independence and diversity.

Only about 50 km of desert separates the Chancay drainage from the Huaura Valley, but during the Initial Period this insignificant barrier corresponded to a weak frontier between two fields of interaction. Monuments with classic U-shaped configurations occur only rarely north of Chancay. Most public

The north-central coast and the tradition of pyramids with circular courts

55 Located on the sandy slopes above the irrigated valley floor, Chupacigarro was one of the most important public centers in the Supe Valley during the Late Preceramic and Initial Period. The rectangular platforms and sunken circular courts visible in this aerial photograph constitute only a portion of the monumental architecture at this poorly known site.

architecture in the valleys of Pativilca, Huarmey, Supe, and Casma has roots in the local Late Preceramic building tradition known from such sites as Piedra Parada and Salinas de Chao. Public constructions most frequently feature sunken circular courts either in isolation or in conjunction with large rectangular platforms with quadrangular sunken plazas. There are well over 50 monumental sites of this tradition; 36 sites with sunken courts have been found in the Supe Valley alone. Among the best-known are Chupacigarro, Cerro Colorado, El-15, Alpacoto, Era de Pando and Los Taros in Supe; San Jose in Pativilca; and Bermejo in Fortaleza.[42] Unfortunately, none of these large sites have been studied intensively and even their age is uncertain. However, isolated C14 measurements suggest an Initial Period date for Cerro Colorado, El-15, and Bermejo.[43]

While the construction of sunken circular courts was autochthonous to the north-central coast, it spread outside this core area into the highlands and along the coast as far as Moche to the north and Mala to the south. When adopted by alien building traditions, the circular court was usually utilized in new contexts. At Cardal, for example, circular courts were placed on the outer periphery of the mounds rather than on the centerline of the site. They were not added until around 1100 BC, roughly two centuries after the beginning of Cardal's public constructions. The diffusion of architectural elements between the central coast and the north-central coast occurred in both directions. Consequently, the U-shaped design characteristic of the central coast appears in modified form in several classic north-central coast monuments, like La Empedrada in Supe, and Las Haldas and Casma in Sechín Alto. However, the scale of the lateral mounds at these sites was sharply reduced relative to the central pyramid and plaza, thereby deemphasizing the U-shaped ground plan.

The distribution of such complexes suggests that the north-central coast was an independent field of social and religious interaction, but it does little to clarify the function of these centers or the nature of the societies responsible for their construction. The absence of intensive investigation in most of the valleys on the north-central coast presents an almost insuperable obstacle to more meaningful analysis, but fortunately, a series of early sites in this tradition have been excavated in the Casma Valley. Along with surface reconnaissance of other sites, these studies provide a window on the development and organization of at least one valley on the north-central coast during the Initial Period.

The Initial Period occupation of the Casma Valley

The number and size of the Initial Period centers in Casma are impressive. During the early Initial Period, there were at least five centers with public architecture, and during the late Initial Period there were six. The two sites of Sechín Alto and Moxeke each cover approximately 200 hectares, and the main pyramid at Sechín Alto is one of the largest constructions ever built in pre-Hispanic Peru. The Casma drainage includes two rivers, the Sechín and the Moxeke, which join together to form the Casma River only 10 km from the Ocean. Hence Casma is more comparable in some respects to two valleys sharing a single floodplain than to a single river valley. If Casma is compared to two such valleys, Rimac and Chillón for example, or even to a major valley like Chancay, it does not have substantially more early public construction. Thus, while the quantity of public construction in Casma is indeed remarkable, it is not anomalous. Few people realize that San Jacinto and Miraflores in Chancay may represent a labor investment equal to that of Moxeke and Sechín Alto.

The Casma sites are well-known because of the history of research in Peru. Julio C. Tello was the first archaeologist to appreciate the importance of the early centers in Casma, and his 1937 discoveries at Cerro Sechín, Moxeke, and Sechín Alto had an enormous influence on all subsequent research (although his conviction that these were coastal irradiations of Chavín civilization has been disproved by recent research).[44] These three famous sites will be described in some detail before considering the Initial Period of the Casma as a whole.

Cerro Sechín. Located near the juncture of the Sechín and Moxeke Rivers at an elevation of only 100 m above sea level, Cerro Sechín is probably the best-known of the early Casma sites.[45] During the late Initial Period, this monument covered 5 hectares and consisted of a three-tiered stepped platform flanked on each side by two smaller buildings. Tello observed a circular depression in front of this complex which may have corresponded to a semi-subterranean court. The pyramidal construction was quadrangular with rounded corners and measured 53 m on a side. Its outer wall was adorned with approximately 400 stone sculptures; 302 sculptures were recovered prior to the excavation of the southern wall. No other Initial Period or Early Horizon site in Peru has yielded as many stone carvings. The site was oriented to the cardinal directions and the principal access was a northern staircase divided in two by a deep cleft. Several superimposed versions of this central bipartite stairway were encountered by Tello and subsequent investigators. It led to the upper platforms and summit buildings, which have been badly damaged by later occupations.

56 The terraced platform at Cerro Sechín was decorated with hundreds of stone sculptures depicting a procession of victorious warriors and their mutilated victims. Wearing spotted pillbox hats and holding staffs of authority, two guards flank the rear stairway of the site.

57 Cerro Sechín sculpture of a victim writhing in agony while his intestines spill from his body. Height c. 1.7 m.

The stone sculptures were made from granite blocks quarried from a hill immediately behind the site. Each stone was worked by percussion flaking and/or pecking and then abrading, probably with sand and water, until two relatively flat smooth surfaces were obtained. Judging from an incomplete sculpture, the desired motif was then sketched in charcoal before it was indelibly engraved by cutting grooves about 11 mm wide and 7 mm deep. All of this was done in one of the world's hardest known stones without the benefit of metal tools. Most carving was done on irregular rectangular blocks of two sizes: small slabs, roughly 85 × 70 cm, and large slabs, approximately 3 × 1 m. The large sculptures were set upright in the parament (the principal retaining, outer wall of a pyramid or platform) and alternated with vertical rows of the smaller carvings.

The hundreds of individual sculptures were arranged in the platform wall to portray a single mythological or historical scene in which two columns of warriors approach each other from opposing sides amidst the carnage of their adversaries.[46] The military procession is depicted as though it were advancing towards the central staircase from the rear of the building. At the head of each column is a banner, probably emblematic of the victorious group. The two sculptures of banners flank the main staircase, and their original height has been estimated at 4 m. They are substantially larger than the other carvings, and they may have helped to support a carved lintel spanning the entryway.

The representations on the sculptures are of humans, and there is a conspicuous lack of animal attributes or other features that might suggest that supernaturals were being represented. The victorious warriors, which constitute about 7 percent of the carvings, appear exclusively on the large slabs and are easily identifiable from their pillbox headdresses, flowing loincloths, and the staffs and darts they hold. One is shown with decapitated heads hanging as trophies from his waist. The defeated are portrayed as naked, in positions that graphically express their agony. Nude bodies are shown with eyes bulging and hands flailing, their torsos sliced in two by transverse cuts. Sometimes the body lacks its head or, in other cases, blood or entrails gush from the victim. Other sculptures depict severed body parts, such as arms, legs, rows of eyes, and stacks of vertebrae. Decapitated heads are particularly common, comprising about 70 percent of the stone carvings. Usually the head is shown lifeless with its eyes closed, ready to be used by the victors as a trophy, but on some pieces blood still flows from the eyes, mouth, scalp, or neck. These gruesome images were often intentionally oriented upside down or sideways, as if representing human remains scattered on the ground.

This stone frieze is vivid evidence that small-scale raiding existed in the Initial Period, and suggests the degree to which violence played an integral role in the religious and political ideology of these early societies, if not their daily lives. Nevertheless, this does not mean that large-scale organized warfare had yet developed. Most major Initial Period centers are situated in militarily vulnerable locations. No protective walls or moats have ever been documented at these sites, and the building of redoubts for temporary refuge does not appear for another thousand years.

For many decades, the dating of the Cerro Sechín sculptures was a matter of heated debate. Fortunately, joint Peruvian–German investigations under the direction of archaeologists Lorenzo Samaniego and Henning Bischof have now been able to resolve this problem. Excavations in the passageway running along the western wall of the platform uncovered the base of a post still encrusted in the floor. The stratigraphy indicated that the post had been erected shortly after the sculptured revetment wall was built. It had been burnt while the building and its sculptures were still in use. Nearby carvings were discolored by the fire and the charred remnants of the post were sealed by a new floor. Charcoal from the posthole produced a radiocarbon measurement of 1519 BC, which is consistent with a series of radiocarbon and thermoluminescent results from other strata.[47]

Research has shown that the stone-faced platform was part of a late renovation of the Cerro Sechín pyramid. Three prior construction phases have been documented, the oldest of which probably dates to the early Initial Period. The original construction consisted of a terraced platform, 34 m on a side, topped by a summit complex. Conical adobes were the main building material. These large sun-dried clay bricks had broad circular bases and tapered to a narrow point. They were laid in clay mortar, interlocking with each other, with their flat bases plastered to form the wall surfaces. Finger marks left by the brickmakers are still visible on the adobes. Conical adobes were once thought to be typical of Chavín civilization, but contemporary research has shown them to be characteristic of Initial Period public architecture along the north-central and north coast and not of later sites linked to the Chavín horizon.

The summit complex of the first construction phase consisted of a central subrectangular room opening on to an open patio and flanked by smaller rooms. Most of the complex was painted pink outside and blue within. A painted mural of large black felines with red-orange paws and white claws on a yellow background decorated the entryway into this chamber. The facade of the second set of summit buildings was ornamented with a series of pilasters. The clay friezes adorning these combine polychrome painting with curvilinear incisions in the clay. The best preserved depicts a human figure turned upside down, with its eyes closed and a stream of what appears to be blood flowing from the skull. This image is not identical to the later stone sculptures, but it presents a clear antecedent for them in both style and theme.[48]

The stone carvings of Cerro Sechín have sometimes been interpreted as a war memorial, like Hadrian's Arch, but this view seems inconsistent with the recent discoveries. The pilaster was decorated centuries before the stone frieze, yet it appears to depict the same scene. Perhaps the sculptures commemorate some mythical or semi-mythical battle won by ancestral heroes. Often, such real or fictive triumphs remain critical to a group's territorial claims, like the Inca legend of Mama Huaco's victory over the Hualla or, for that matter, Joshua's conquest of Jericho. If this interpretation is correct, the Cerro Sechín monument is not an anomalous historical monument, but simply another example of civic-ceremonial architecture decorated with religious and mythical themes. It is noteworthy that the pillar image is only a secondary detail in the summit complex which otherwise features unambiguously religious images –the painted felines. Likewise, when the basal platform of the third construction phase was cleared, it revealed a painted and incised frieze showing a pair of enormous fish.

The architectural chronology summarized above indicates that, at least at Cerro Sechín, dressed stone architecture was a relatively late innovation replacing construction in adobe, just as stone sculpture was introduced as a substitute for painted and modeled clay friezes. These technological changes appear within an unbroken local cultural tradition expressed by continuity in

58 These gruesome Cerro Sechín sculptures depict: (above) a successful warrior adorned with severed heads (2.8 m high); (below) a large pile of decapitated heads (2.74 m high), and the bleeding head of a defeated soldier (41 cm high).

59 This stone sculpture (45 cm high) of a severed head found at Sechín Alto strongly resembles the carvings from Cerro Sechín.

60 Stone carving (105 cm high) from Chupacoto, Huaylas.

site location, architectural form, building orientation, artistic style, and other features. The stone frieze at Cerro Sechín is one of the oldest dated Andean stone sculptures known at the present time. Similar sculptures have been found near by at Sechín Alto, as well as in the mid-valley section of Nepeña at the site of Kushipampa (Siete Huacas) and above the valley headwaters at Chupacoto, a major center in the highland Callejón de Huaylas.[49]

Sechín Alto. The largest of the early Casma sites is Sechín Alto, located only 2 km from Cerro Sechín. The main mound measures 250 × 300 m at its base and has a maximum height of 44 m; its volume is more than twice that of La Florida in Rimac. It was probably the largest single construction in the New World during the second millennium BC. The core of the mound consists of conical adobes, and looting revealed that, in at least one spot, the early adobe pyramid was decorated by a clay frieze. Most of the mound visible today is faced with large granite blocks set in clay mortar. Some of these blocks are huge, measuring over 1.5 m on a side and weighing over 2 tons. The stone facing of Sechín Alto, like Cerro Sechín, represents a later renovation of the complex. Four enormous rectangular plazas extend 1.4 km out from the central mound, of which three have sunken circular courts in their center. The largest of these has a diameter of about 80 m, judging from aerial photographs.[50]

The dating of Sechín Alto remains problematic, particularly since investigations there have been limited to selective test-pitting and surface surveys. Nevertheless, the style of the ceramics recovered from a 5-m deep pit in front of the mound suggests that the site was occupied during the early or mid Initial Period, a conclusion consistent with a radiocarbon date of 1721 BC associated with these sherds. Judging from the stone-facing and the presence in the first

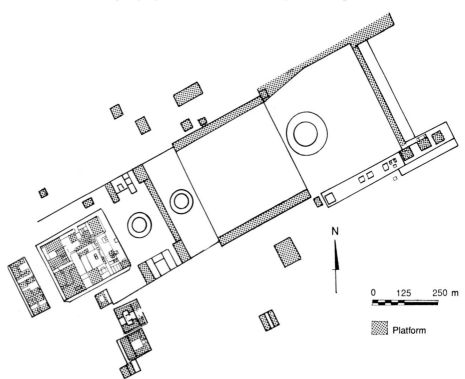

N

0   125   250 m

░ Platform

61 Map of the monumental architecture of Sechín Alto in the Casma Valley. The 35-m high central pyramid towers above the site's sunken courts, rectangular plazas, and lateral pyramids.

62 By the late Initial Period (*c.* 1200 BC), Sechín Alto was one of the largest architectural complexes in the world. Its main pyramid rose to the height of a nine-storey building, and the line of plazas and platforms at its base stretched for over 1.5 km. This aerial photograph of the site can be interpreted in conjunction with the simplified groundplan (ill. 61).

63 The early construction phases of Sechín Alto's main pyramid used conical adobes, but the final episode used large blocks of stone to face the structure's terraced walls.

64 The inland site of Moxeke in the Casma drainage sprawls over 220 hectares and includes two large pyramid platforms as well as substantial zones of domestic occupation.

circular court of a stone sculpture similar to that of Cerro Sechín, the public architecture continued to be refurbished during the following centuries.[51] If this tentative dating of Sechín Alto is correct, the great size of the public architecture could be the product of over a millennium of building.

Moxeke. The largest early center in the southern tributary of the Casma is Moxeke. At the southwest and northeast extremes of the site, separated from each other by 1.1 km, are two major platform-pyramid constructions. These mounds face each other across an immense rectangular terraced plaza. They have the same orientation (N 41° E) and both are bisected by the centerline of the site. Smaller platform mounds and more modest buildings interpreted as residences are visible to the west and east of the plaza area; these too are oriented in the same or similar direction. During the early Initial Period, this entire complex constituted a single center, although its bipolar layout and great size have sometimes resulted in it being mistakenly treated as two separate entities.

Moxeke first gained notoriety following Tello's discovery of painted clay sculptures on the principal mound.[52] The latter measures 160 × 170 m at the base and has a total height of 30 m. Like Cerro Sechín, it is basically a tiered rectangular pyramid with rounded corners. The core of the monument is composed of a mass of conical adobes, but the final rebuilding features massive stone revetment walls. Some walls incorporate carefully shaped and polished square stone blocks known as ashlars.

The clay sculptures were found decorating the outer face of the third platform terrace, some 10 m above ground level. The front wall is punctuated by large niches 3.9 m wide and 1.7 m deep, with the enormous high-relief sculptures filling these niches. The flat wall face between them was adorned with a repeating, conventionalized design made by incision. Black paint in the grooves was used to highlight this motif, which was colored blue, pink, and white. The sculptures had an original height of about 3 m, of which no more than 2 m

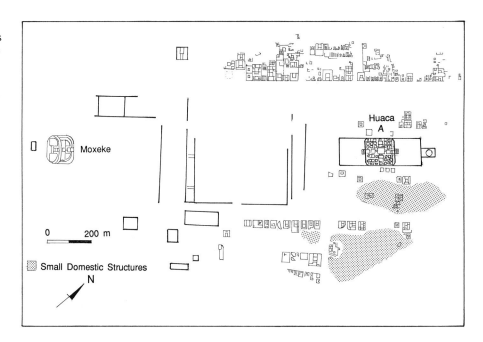

remained when Tello unearthed them. The sculptures flanked the central stairway overlooking the plaza, and show the upper portion of anthropomorphic figures elaborately dressed in tunic, short skirt, and loose mantle. One well-preserved example was painted entirely black and must have presented a vivid contrast to the white back and pink sides of its niche. The adjacent sculpture is similarly dressed, with the addition of a twisted cord sash. In his upraised hands the figure holds bicephallic snakes with forked tongues. Unfortunately, the heads of these figures have been destroyed.

The niches along the northwest side of the building were smaller, and the wall face separating them was left undecorated. The sculptures in these niches represent massive heads. One face with bared teeth is emerald green and has pink vertical lines descending from its black hemispherical eyes. The head in the adjacent niche is expressionless and has its eyes and mouth closed in a manner reminiscent of the Cerro Sechín carvings of trophy heads.

The scale of these imposing clay sculptures was designed to make them visible from below, where most of the public ceremonies must have been held. The central atrium was built on the decorated third terrace, but behind it were additional terrace levels. These created a summit surface suitable for serving as a ritual stage which would have dominated the site. The construction history of the main mound at Moxeke was a long and complex one. Studies like those carried out at Cerro Sechín will be needed to clarify it and to date the famous clay friezes. Fortunately, recent excavations by Shelia and Thomas Pozorski in the northern half of Moxeke, known as the Pampa de las Llamas, have begun to clarify the dating of this sector of the site. The recovery of both twined and woven cloth mixed together in the refuse pointed to an early Initial Period date, and the similarity of the ceramics to those from the shoreline site of Tortugas supports this conclusion.[53] The 23 carbon samples analyzed from the Pozorskis' excavations suggest that the site was occupied between 1800 and 1400 BC, and while these dates confirm the occupation of Moxeke during the early Initial Period, they also indicate that this occupation continued through the middle Initial Period. The cut stone-facing and the presence of corn stalks in the fill covering the clay sculptures of the Moxeke mound indicate continued construction during the middle portion of the Initial Period.[54]

The terraced platform at the northeast end of Moxeke, Huaca A, is quite different from the main mound. The building measures 140 m on a side and 9 m in height. Besides its main staircase, which overlooks the central plaza area, there is a back staircase which leads into a sunken rectangular plaza, and a stone platform in which there is a circular stone court. Huaca A is primarily constructed of rough unworked stones set in clay mortar, hidden by a thick coat of white plaster. Its tiered platforms are covered with a maze of bilaterally symmetric sub-rectangular chambers. The original height of the thick double-faced walls forming these rooms was between 4 m and 7 m, and rows of large niches were characteristic features of the upper walls. All the rooms studied have high thresholds, and the doorways were built to hold wooden bars to block entry. Julio C. Tello and the Pozorskis concluded that Huaca A was primarily designed as a public storehouse, which seems plausible considering its unusual features, but the hypothesis is difficult to substantiate. Upon excavation, most of the chambers proved to be empty, lacking evidence of either stored goods or storage vessels. Thus far, a few turquoise beads, a single anthracite mirror, some

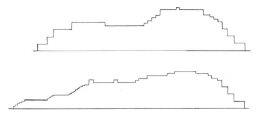

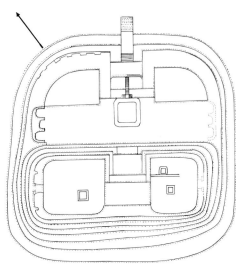

65 The main public structure at Moxeke was a 30-m high tiered pyramid decorated with polychrome clay sculptures.

66 Julio C. Tello unearthed colored sculptures of anthropomorphic figures on the third platform of Moxeke, including this incomplete figure elaborately dressed in a tunic, short skirt, and loose mantle. Width 3.2 m.

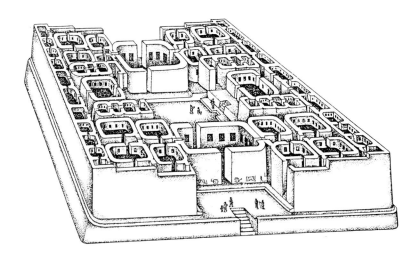

67 Hypothetical reconstruction of Huaca A at Moxeke, a multi-roomed structure that may have been used to store ritual paraphernalia, foodstuffs, and other materials used in public activities at the site.

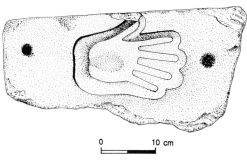

0   10 cm

68 A rectangular stone block carved on two sides with a naturalistic human hand and a double-bodied snake was discovered in Huaca A. Along with the Cerro Sechín carvings, it is among the oldest stone sculptures known from the New World.

textiles, and a wooden figurine have been recovered from platform rooms. Only the presence of unusually large numbers of small rodent bones in some rooms hint at the possible storage of foodstuffs.[55]

Small-scale probes beneath the floors of Huaca A have revealed an earlier set of constructions similar in form and orientation to the rooms above them. If storage was the principal function of Huaca A, it was probably an integral part of corporate activity from Moxeke's inception. But does this structure imply the elite control of critical resources or the existence of a ruling class? Not necessarily. Huaca A could have merely stored sacred paraphernalia and food for outdoor ceremonies and public banquets; ceremonial huts with similar functions are still maintained in tropical South America by the Warao and other tribal groups. Whatever activities were carried out at Huaca A, they were inseparably intertwined with religious authority and ceremony. This fundamental relationship is tangibly expressed at Huaca A by the huge low-relief clay frieze of felines decorating the main entrance of the building. Among the unusual items found associated with the final use of Huaca A was a cut and polished prismatic stone carved on two sides – one with a naturalistic right human hand, the other with a double-bodied snake. The Pozorskis interpret this carved block as an altar. The building level in which the sculpture was found appears to date from between 1500 and 1400 BC, roughly the same age as the Cerro Sechín stone frieze.[56]

Over 70 aligned rectangular platforms ranging from 2–5 m in height and 10–50 m on a side were built in rows along the eastern and western sides of the central plaza. Many of these constructions were never finished, but the more complete buildings feature an atrium and a central room on their summit. Earlier domestic structures were leveled to provide space for these stone platforms. Although clearly public in character, their function remains unknown, and artifacts are rarely found in them when they are excavated.

A chronology for the Casma Valley

The most recent research in Casma distinguishes only between the early Initial Period and the late Initial Period. Early Initial Period sites produced a mixture of twined and woven cloth, while late Initial Period sites yielded only woven textiles. The ceramic chronology for the valley is still poorly understood. The earliest pottery style is characterized by neckless jars with rows of deep punctations circling the shoulder of the vessel. This style is best known from the fishing village of Tortugas, but variants of it are also known from the northern part of Moxeke and the earliest ceramic-yielding layers at Las Haldas. Smaller punctations in area and more curvilinear incised designs, like those published by archaeologist Rosa Fung from Las Haldas (phases 2–3), are typical of late Initial Period pottery from Casma. Unfortunately, more refined ceramic sequences such as the four-phase sequence proposed by Fung and the three-phase sequence of Collier and Thompson, have been undermined by recent stratigraphic investigations, and a detailed alternative has yet to be developed.[57] Therefore, the following discussion is based on gross chronological assessments and will require modification when a better relative sequence is developed.

Settlement and subsistence systems

Cerro Sechín, Sechín Alto, and Moxeke fit into a coherent valley system inextricably linked to the patterns of small-scale irrigation agriculture. Not surprisingly, the settlement pattern bears a strong resemblance to that already described for the valleys of the central coast. Gravity canals are by their very nature limited to a single bank, and even today each of the narrow and irregularly sloped coastal valleys in Peru is irrigated by several small floodwater irrigation systems using intakes at different elevations along the river. In Casma, the location of major centers suggests the existence of analogous waterworks. Most of the good irrigable land is in the lower valley where the alluvial plain widens, and this is where Initial Period settlement was concentrated.

During the early Initial Period, Huerequeque and Sechín Alto were built on the north and south banks of the lower Sechín River respectively, while Moxeke dominated the north bank of the Moxeke River and Cerro Sechín was established where these two rivers merge to form the Casma River. All are located on or adjacent to excellent irrigable farmland. Only Cerro Sechín, which is best situated in relation to the naturally watered floodplain, appears to have been occupied before the Initial Period. Coeval shoreline villages were located in small well-sheltered bays to the north of the Casma River at Tortugas and Huaynuná, and to the south at Las Haldas. There is no evidence of public architecture at any of them for the early Initial Period, and judging from the material culture, these settlements were closely tied to the inland centers.[58]

This same settlement pattern continued into the late Initial Period. Cerro Sechín flourished above the river delta, and Sechín Alto continued to expand along the Sechín's south bank. Huerequeque was abandoned during this period, but two new centers – Sechín Bajo and Taukachi-Konkan – took its place.[59] Along the Moxeke River, the major change appears to be the establishment of Pallka, a mid-valley center 35 km inland at an elevation of 900 m. Although the public constructions there incorporate the sunken circular court, this is located alongside the main mound. The overall layout lacks the strong central axis characteristic of the lower valley sites. Moreover, Pallka's due east orientation is unique, as is its placement on the crest of a ridge. These distinctive features and the pottery recovered there suggest strong links with the neighboring highland region, as well as to the lower valley.[60]

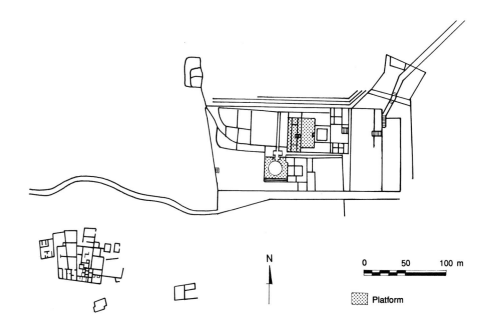

69 The site of Pallka flourished during the late Initial Period and Early Horizon in the mid-valley *yunga* zone of the Casma drainage.

N

0   50   100 m

::::: Platform

Along the shoreline at Las Haldas, a large central pyramid and a series of rectangular plazas and circular courts were constructed, covering older residential areas and extending over some 8 hectares. The late Initial Period ceremonial architecture at Las Haldas is very similar to that at Sechín Alto, but smaller in scale.[61] The expansion of Las Haldas may have been spurred by the abandonment of Tortugas.

The economic links between coastal and inland centers is unambiguous. At Moxeke, located 18 km from the Pacific, excavations revealed that almost all animal protein was obtained from marine resources, principally small fish, mussels, chitons, limpets, and clams; in fact, the arid conditions there preserved fish heads and strips of dried fish. Besides some land snails from the lomas and an occasional deer, there is little evidence that terrestrial fauna were consumed. The daily diet at Las Haldas and Tortugas appears to have been similar to that of Moxeke, relying on a number of good sources of carbohydrates including sweet potato, manioc, achira, and potatoes, supplemented by peanuts, squash, common beans, lima beans, avocados, and hot pepper.

Some minor differences in diet did exist, however, between shoreline and inland communities. For instance, seaweed was common in the refuse at Tortugas and at Las Haldas, and the bones of sea lion and ocean birds were also occasionally recovered, remains which were entirely absent in the lower- and mid-valley sites. At both types of site, cotton fiber and seeds are common in the refuse, but cotton bolls and other unusable plant parts were only recovered inland, presumably closer to where cotton was actually cultivated. Similarly, investigations at Las Haldas yielded a variety of fishing gear, including several grades of looped cotton netting, fishing weights and floats, and shell and cactus spine fishhooks. Neither these items, nor the fish being caught, suggest that Initial Period marine technology had changed significantly from that of the Late Preceramic.[62]

Economic links were not limited to foodstuffs and cotton fiber, but included locally manufactured products and exotic materials. The discovery of similar carved stone bowls at Moxeke, Las Haldas, and the other early Casma sites reflects the circulation of goods between the valley and shoreline communities. The ties linking the various Casma communities were far more complex than mere economic interdependency, and the shared material culture of these sites, expressed in a common ceramic style and similar architecture, underlines the strength of these ties.

Socio-political organization

While there is considerable reason to believe that the groups of Casma were drawn together by a web of ideological, economic, and socio-cultural links, there is little evidence of a larger political unit encompassing these culturally related, but ostensibly autonomous centers. Some scholars, such as Jonathan Haas, however, have assumed that only true states could have constructed sites like Sechín Alto. The emergence of a state apparatus is notoriously difficult to establish conclusively on the basis of archaeological evidence, but the existence of standardized government architecture and artifacts emblematic of bureaucratic status are perhaps the most conspicuous indicators of the later pre-Hispanic state in Peru. The general absence of such emblems in early Casma, and the considerable variation between the various centers, would seem to bear testimony to a very different kind of society. While there are significant differences in scale between the sites in Casma, these can be better explained as a product of ecological and historical factors, particularly the length of time over which a site has been occupied. Rather than assuming that these sundry sites were organized into a political hierarchy dominated by a single center, such as Sechín Alto, I favor a view in which these centers are seen as a patchwork of tiny independent pre-state polities, each primarily exploiting the land watered by its own small hydraulic system. These polities were probably linked by marriage ties, shared religious beliefs and ceremonies, and exchange of goods, and may have occasionally cooperated for defensive purposes or in raiding parties.

The maintenance of a discrete state apparatus is inherently costly and wasteful, and most anthropologists and political scientists believe that for this reason a state only appeared after social classes had developed, and the conflicting interests of a complex society could no longer be handled primarily through ideological and social mechanisms. Significantly, Casma has produced little concrete evidence of economic or social stratification during the Initial Period. The archaeological patterning is in most respects quite similar to the situation already described for the central coast. Besides the division of labor between fisherfolk and farmers, there is little indication of occupational differentiation. The absence of workshop debris at sites such as Las Haldas and Moxeke, and the poverty of the artifact assemblages recovered at these and the other Casma sites, seem to rule out full-time craft specialization.

At Moxeke, there appear to be two separate groups of domestic architecture. Both groups consist of small clustered sub-rectangular rooms with central subterranean hearths in their center. One group was situated behind the aligned platforms flanking the central plaza. They are connected with these constructions and share their orientation. Their walls are of quarried stone, plastered, and sometimes painted inside with red pigment. Small storerooms were built behind these buildings, and internal storage was provided by sub-floor depositories and wall niches. In contrast, the other class of domestic architecture is much more irregular and does not align with the rest of the site. The walls of these structures were made of perishable materials, using a low stone cobble footing as their foundation.

The Pozorskis assume that these two types of domestic architecture are contemporary, and have interpreted the differences between them as indicative of the existence of "elite" and "low-status" social segments. It is noteworthy, however, that the refuse of both sectors consists of similar lithic debris, pottery, spindle whorls, and food remains. Solid ceramic figurines were the only class of artifact found exclusively in the "elite" area. Most of the stamp and cylinder seals were found in the "elite" houses, although one was found in the adjacent public architecture. (These seals were probably used for body painting.) Stone bowls and associated pestles were also found in or near the "elite" residences and adjacent aligned buildings, but this distribution may simply reflect the need for ground red pigment for these constructions. Judging from the artifacts alone, therefore, there is little basis for positing the existence of an elite class with greater access to sumptuary goods or critical resources.

On the other hand, the existence of divisions in the society despite similar patterns of consumption remains a possibility. The close links between the occupants of the better-quality residences and the public activities going on in the adjacent platforms and plaza is reminiscent of the situation at Cardal, where distinctive residences may have been built on the pyramids themselves. The direction of construction projects on such a scale and duration as Moxeke certainly would have been difficult without recognized leadership, and it is plausible that these leaders may have occupied the "elite" residences. The presence of such a group, however, does not imply the existence of a true class society or, for that matter, a state.

Nor do the burials thus far recovered in Casma provide evidence of social stratification. Two burials were excavated at Moxeke: one in the so-called elite architecture and the other in the so-called low-status architecture. Both individuals were interred in a flexed position within unlined sub-floor pits. Fragments of pottery were the only grave goods. A burial beneath one of the circular forecourts at Las Haldas differed little from the Moxeke interments.[63]

Casma's neighbors: Nepeña and Santa

The situation in Casma during the Initial Period presents an intriguing contrast with its two neighboring valleys to the north, Nepeña and Santa. Unlike Casma and most of the coastal valleys discussed thus far, neither Nepeña nor Santa appear to have supported multiple monumental centers. This pattern is only partially explicable in terms of local ecology or lack of investigation in these valleys. Nepeña is considerably smaller than Casma, with only about half the irrigable bottomland and less than half of the average annual discharge. The Santa River carries more water than any other coastal valley but, unfortunately for farmers, its riverbed is deeply entrenched and it is only possible to irrigate about the same amount of land as in Nepeña. Both valleys have been the subject of systematic surface survey, as well as selective excavation.

In Santa, archaeologists from Catholic University in Lima located two small centers with sunken circular courts: Condorcerro and Cerro Obrero (Tanguche). Both yielded radiocarbon measurements in the second millennium BC (see Appendix A) and may ultimately prove to date from the Initial Period. A more recent comprehensive archaeological survey recorded 1,246 sites, primarily in the lower valley, but none of them were ascribed to the Initial Period. It is only further upstream in the highland section of the Santa, referred to as the Callejón de Huaylas, and in the tributaries of the river, like the Chuquicara, that Initial Period centers are numerous.

Repeated survey in the lower and middle Nepeña by investigators from the University of Massachusetts failed to identify a single Initial Period site of any size.[64] However, much earlier research by Julio C. Tello in the lower valley discovered the mound of Punkurí, which appears to be the major Initial Period center in Nepeña, and its importance justifies a closer look at the site.

Punkurí. Located 27 km inland on the valley floor, Punkurí has been estimated as covering only 2 hectares. Its most imposing feature is a mound measuring 45 m on a side and 10 m in height. Tello's 1933 excavations revealed a series of superimposed platforms, several of which were decorated with painted clay low-relief friezes or high-relief sculptures.[65] The oldest construction was built of coarse fieldstone set in mud mortar and was oriented 20 degrees west of north, an orientation unlike that of any of the Casma sites.

Punkurí is best known for a larger-than-life sculpted clay feline placed in the middle of the staircase leading up to the second platform level. The snarling head of the feline was painted green but its pupils were shown in blue, the gums in red, and the crossed fangs in white. Its two clawed paws were shown in low relief and were separated from each other by a deep vertical cleft reminiscent of the division in Cerro Sechín's bipartite stairway. Moreover, the style of the Punkurí feline broadly resembles the wall painting on Cerro Sechín's oldest temple.

An elaborate offering had been placed in a sub-floor chamber at the foot of Punkurí's feline sculpture. It consisted of a decapitated woman with a kilogram of turquoise beads covering her pelvis in a manner suggesting the remains of a disintegrated sequined garment. At her side was a decorated stone bowl and pestle, like those found at Moxeke. There was also an engraved *Strombus* shell trumpet, a pair of *Spondylus* shells, and some food remains, including guinea pigs and land snails. The richness of this human votive offering follows the tradition established at Aspero, and contrasts with the majority of burials.

Painted low-relief friezes were encountered by Tello on still earlier constructions at Punkurí. One represents a highly stylized motif similar to those incised on stone bowls. Again, a deep vertical groove was carved in the center of the low-relief frieze. Probably the oldest frieze uncovered at Punkurí shows an avian supernatural with monkeys and fish decorating its body.

70 Taken in 1933, this photograph shows the clay sculpture of a feline unearthed at Punkurí in the Nepeña Valley. It was originally painted in white, black, red, and ocher-yellow.

71 During the Initial Period on the north coast of Peru, deep mortars were carved from basalt and other hard volcanic stone which were – in some cases – decorated with elaborate, highly stylized motifs. While the best-known excavated examples come from the Casma and Nepeña valleys, such mortars have been recovered as far north as the Lambayeque drainage. Mortar (below) and rollout of its design (below left). Height 25.6 cm.

The excavation of Punkurí occurred long before the advent of radiocarbon dating, and details of the pottery recovered there have never been published. The similarities with the Cerro Sechín and Moxeke clay friezes, as well as with the Moxeke stone bowls, point to an early Initial Period date for the early buildings at the site, and the presence of conical adobes in some of the Punkurí platforms is consistent with this interpretation. Obviously, conclusive dating will only be possible after additional research. Yet even if Punkurí is tentatively accepted as an Initial Period center, its modest size and solitary presence suggest that public undertakings, and perhaps population levels in Nepeña, were significantly less than in valleys further south.

The Cupisnique culture of the north coast

72 Stirrup-spouted bottles were the most beautiful pottery vessels produced by the Cupisnique culture, perhaps because they were used in ceremonial drinking and hospitality. This modeled and incised bottle (26.7 cm high) depicts an elderly male, perhaps a mythical leader or shaman.

During his 1929 exploration of the dry Cupisnique ravine between Jequetepeque and Chicama, Rafael Larco discovered a distinctive early pottery style previously unknown. When he subsequently encountered cemeteries at Barbacoa and Palenque in the Chicama Valley with essentially the same kind of pottery grave goods, he proposed that the term "Cupisnique" could be applied to the early culture of Chicama and the immediately surrounding area. Cupisnique pottery is typically a dark monochrome color, usually gray or black, sometimes decorated with naturalistic modeling and/or incised with narrow irregular incisions made while the clay was nearly dry. The most elaborate of these vessels have globular or composite-shaped chambers and stirrup spouts with a trapezoidal form. According to Larco, some were made with a two-piece mold. Occasionally, red post-fire pigment was rubbed into the incised motifs or, in other cases, a post-fire graphite slip was applied to produce an unusual reflective surface.

Since pottery was Larco's primary criterion for cultural definition, he classed the contemporary cultures in other north coast valleys – such as Nepeña, Santa, Virú, and Lambayeque – as non-Cupisnique cultures but which, judging from occasional finds of classic Cupisnique pottery, maintained economic and social links with the Chicama area. Larco observed that the Cupisnique culture shared a similar set of religious beliefs with these other related north coast cultures. He referred to this belief system as the feline cult, and argued that its center was in the Nepeña Valley. Larco's main point, however, was that Cupisnique should be considered as a culture in its own right, rather than just a coastal variant of the highland Chavín culture.[66]

Research carried out since Larco's time has confirmed that Cupisnique-style pottery was restricted to the Chicama area. Meanwhile, the substantial intervalley variability in north-coast pottery styles has become increasingly apparent. In such valleys as Jequetepeque and Lambayeque-Leche, for example, post-fire painting in zones is the preferred decorative mode of the late Initial Period.[67] Moreover, pottery in these multiple coeval north-coastal styles was widely exchanged so that in a Cupisnique cemetery such as the one recently excavated at Puémape it is not unusual to find several different types of ceramics represented in a single burial. Thus one grave included a "Santa Ana" style bottle with a hemispherical stirrup and a conical spout as well as a classic Cupisnique bottle with a trapezoidal stirrup and a concave-curved spout. Some scholars, including Larco, had once incorrectly presumed that these regional micro-styles represented temporal differences.

Contemporary scholars hold a broader, less ceramically-centred view of archaeological culture and consequently it is now common to refer to almost all of the late Initial Period and Early Horizon cultural materials from the Virú Valley to the Lambayeque drainage as Cupisnique, regardless of differences in the local ceramic assemblages. There is some justification for this, since the peoples of these valleys appear to have shared a host of cultural elements whose distribution is largely limited to the north coast. Several of these distinctive types of "Cupisnique" artifacts attest to a special interest in personal adornment. For example, rings of carved bone were sometimes found on two, three, or even five fingers of buried individuals. Similarly, shell ornaments sewn on clothing, ear pendants of carved bone with shell and turquoise inlay, and skirts made of thousands of shell beads, are characteristic of Cupisnique material culture. There are also roller and stamp seals similar to those found at Moxeke, sometimes covered with red pigment, which were probably used for skin painting. Not surprisingly, one of the most common non-ceramic artifacts at Cupisnique sites are anthracite mirrors highly polished to reflect an image.

Items of personal adornment are frequently found with individuals buried in Cupisnique tombs. The dead sometimes have necklaces of exotic stone and shell, including beads of lapis lazuli, clear quartz crystal turquoise, and *Spondylus*. Occasionally carved bone spatulas and small cups of semi-precious stone were also left with the dead.[68] People were buried individually in irregular oval pits dug into subsoil. Their bodies were flexed, either on their side or back, and adults were often sprinkled with red hematite powder. Usually grave goods were limited to one or two vessels, left near the head, but a few individuals were buried with three pots. It should be noted that although the inventory of burial goods is somewhat broader on the north coast than for those valleys further south, their distribution is widespread among the graves, and, as on the central and north-central coast, the pattern of interment does not suggest a highly stratified society.

Stone mace heads, usually with vertical ribs and conical flanges, are another distinctive artifact of the north coast. Mounted on staffs, these would seem

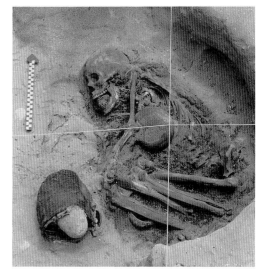

73 Excavations were carried out in 1990 at a classic Cupisnique burial ground at Puémape, located at the mouth of the Cupisnique drainage. This picture illustrates the burial of a female in an unlined pit grave containing a cut gourd vessel, a basket, and a pottery bowl; a ball of cotton thread was placed in her mouth.

74 Among the grave goods at Puémape was this miniature ocarina, modeled in the form of a spotted snake; red and white post-fire paint was used to fill the incisions in the dark-gray clay.

75 A soft-stone roller stamp (4.7 cm high), a ceramic figurine (height 7 cm), a pottery bird-shaped stamp (3.2 cm high), and a polished jet mirror (height 7.3 cm) were some of the Cupisnique artifacts found by Junius Bird in the houses and burials at Huaca Prieta in the Chicama Valley.

better suited as emblems of authority than as practical weapons, though they may well have been used for both.[69] The sensitive low-relief carving of small stone ritual objects is unique to the north coast during this time, and some of the finest Initial Period art objects are the steatite bowls and cups embellished by artisans with complex mythical scenes.

Cupisnique architecture

We can only speak tentatively of a distinctive Cupisnique tradition of public architecture. Generally speaking, the public buildings consist of relatively low tiered platforms, massive central inset stairways, and rectangular forecourts. The creation of elaborate colonnades is perhaps the most distinctive element of early north coast public architecture. As in other parts of the coast, painted adobe sculptures adorned building exteriors, and low lateral mounds often produced a U-shaped layout. The largest of the Cupisnique civic-ceremonial centers display a multitude of independent, unaligned mound complexes, all of which appear to be Initial Period or Early Horizon in date. Caballo Muerto in Moche has 8 mound complexes and Purulén in Zaña has 15. It would appear that although ritual entombment and rebuilding was practiced on the north coast, as will be discussed shortly, it was also common periodically to shift the location of ceremonial building. This produced sites with many relatively small mounds, rather than fewer awe-inspiring constructions.

Some idea of the substantial variation in "Cupisnique" architecture can be gathered by a brief review of the few complexes investigated thus far.

Huaca de los Reyes. The largest of the mound complexes at the 200-hectare Caballo Muerto site, Huaca de los Reyes was oriented 5 degrees north of east towards a mountain peak. Its final form was the product of several phases of building activity.[70] Four radiocarbon measurements made on posts from the highest platform of the site ranged widely from 2042 BC to 965 BC, and averaged 1511 BC. However, the ceramic associations confirm that the complex was built at some time in the late Initial Period. The building material used was irregular stone with clay mortar, and the rough stone masonry was enveloped in light clay stucco. In its final form, the complex includes a 6-m high central platform, three aligned rectangular plazas, several pairs of high flanking towers possibly 10 m high, and three sets of triple colonnades. The columns in the colonnades were nearly square and range from 1.5 to nearly 2 m on a side, and they could have easily stood 3 m high. It was necessary to pass through one of these triple-colonnaded halls in order to move from the middle to the upper plaza at the foot of the central mound. On the basis of experiments in moving clay, water, and stone, the minimum amount of labor necessary to build Huaca de los Reyes can be estimated at 349,924 person-days.[71]

Parts of this elaborate building complex were cleared by Thomas Pozorski in 1973–74, and beautiful adobe sculptures and low-relief friezes came to light on the walls and columns of the central and lateral buildings. The most memorable of these are the gigantic three-dimensional feline heads, each measuring over 2 m in height and 1.8 m in width. Larger than a human being, these white snarling faces with clenched teeth, interlocking fangs, flared broad noses, and gaping eyes still have a powerful and intimidating presence. Altogether, 4 were uncovered,

76 Enormous feline heads and other unbaked clay sculptures adorned the platforms at Huaca de los Reyes.

77 The most intensively studied example of Cupisnique architecture is Huaca de los Reyes, one of the eight mounds at Caballo Muerto. Located at the neck of the lower Moche Valley, this site controlled a critical point of the irrigation and transportation networks.

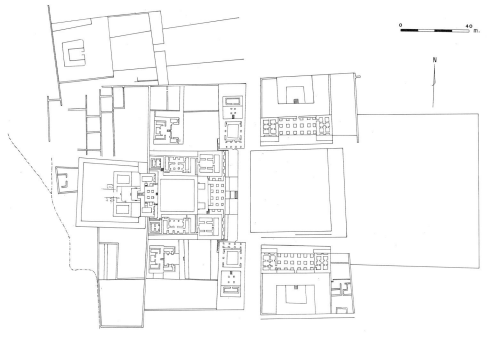

78 With its elaborate combinations of sunken plazas, courts, platforms, colonnades and towers, Huaca de los Reyes (illustrated in this map and isometric reconstruction) demonstrates the complexity and sophistication of the Cupisnique architectural style.

each unique in details. There are also smaller adobe sculptures representing a frontal anthropomorphic figure with snakes hanging from the waist, standing on or flanked by fanged heads. Unfortunately, only the lower portions of the friezes remain. These adobe sculptures provide material expression of the religious milieu in which north coast communal rituals were celebrated, and new evidence for the central role of the feline in north coast cosmology.

Purulén. In the valley of Zaña, the mounds of Purulén sprawl over 3 sq. km, making it the largest known site on the north coast. Most of the building complexes there consist of two or three superimposed stone platforms with a sunken atrium at the summit, and a large inset central staircase leading down to a rectangular forecourt. One of the 15 mounds excavated recently by Peruvian archaeologist Walter Alva featured a 10-m high rectangular platform, measuring 50 × 80 m, and a central staircase 15 m wide. Thick cylindrical columns of

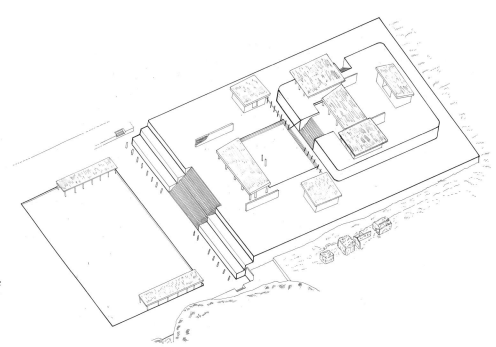

79 A hypothetical reconstruction of the architecture of one of the 15 mounds at Purulén in the lower Zaña Valley.

80 Aerial view of a geoglyph (65 × 35 m) made from thousands of rock fragments, found at Pampa de Caña Cruz in the Zaña Valley.

plastered cane supported a roofed area, and small lateral buildings of cane and clay were erected on the platform summit. Nucleated dwellings surrounded the mounds, and Alva believed the population to have numbered in the thousands. The site of Purulén has been dated to the late Initial Period on the basis of ceramics and a radiocarbon date of 1415 BC.[72]

A remarkable geoglyph was discovered upvalley from Purulén, at Pampa de Caña Cruz. It measures 65 × 23 m, and depicts a monstrous figure with circular eyes, a fanged mouth, and a simplified body. Built on a steep slope, it was designed to be seen from the trail leading up the valley. Its visibility was further enhanced by outlining the figure in dark stones, and using white stone for the face and rose-colored stone for the hair or headdress. The white stone is not local and appears to have been brought from some distance, perhaps from the upper valley. The colored mosaic, made of thousands of small rock fragments no more than 10 cm in diameter, contrasted with the natural soil surrounding it. It would be difficult, perhaps impossible, to date this unusual archaeological feature were it not for the fact that the figure resembles the iconography on pottery looted from cemeteries in the Zaña and Jequetepeque valleys, and a provisional late Initial Period date can be ascribed to it on this basis.[73] The creation of huge mosaic pavements has no known parallel in Peru, but the practice of depicting religious imagery on a giant scale did become widespread later in Peruvian prehistory, the best known example being the ground-drawings of Nazca.

Other Cupisnique settlements

No centers comparable to Caballo Muerto or Purulén are known from the Virú, Chicama, or Jequetepeque valleys. In Virú, the construction of several large rectangular stone buildings (larger than normal residences) probably required group cooperation and coordinated effort, but the buildings do not compare in size or complexity with the mounds at Caballo Muerto. The best known of these Virú corporate constructions, the Temple of the Llamas at Huaca Negra, covers about 300 sq. m.[74] Other sites such as Queneto, Huaca El Gallo, and Huaca La Gallina in Virú, and Jaguay in Chicama may ultimately prove to have major Initial Period monumental architecture, but at present their dating is ambiguous.[75]

The situation in Jequetepeque Valley is much better known. Limoncarro is the only civic-ceremonial center known from the lower valley. Located 20 km inland (150 m above sea level) and pressed against the valley slopes, this U-shaped temple consists of a three-tiered central platform about 5 m high, and two lateral mounds only 1.6 m high, surrounding a 500-sq. m rectangular plaza. Adobe sculptures decorated portions of the architecture, including columns on the southern lateral mound. Nearby, a smaller mound yielded carved steatite bowls and cups when it was destroyed for road construction. The iconography of these vessels will be discussed below.[76]

Huaca Lucía. The northernmost of the coastal centers with monumental architecture is Huaca Lucía in the La Leche drainage. One of the smaller mounds of the massive Batan Grande complex, Huaca Lucía attracted little attention until it was partially cleared in 1979 and 1980. This two-tiered platform originally stood at least 8 m in height and, although the mound itself was modest in proportions, its staircase and colonnade were much larger than normal. The inset central stairway measured 16 m in width, and the 24 cylindrical columns on its summit rose to a height of 3.5–4 m. Built using a core of conical adobes, these massive columns had bracket-shaped tops apparently designed to support roof beams. The architectural elements were highlighted by painting the massive summit colonnade red, plastering the staircase with light clay and decorating the outer wall with a black, red, and dark blue-gray mural.[77]

81 A roofed colonnade of massive red columns topped the summit of Huaca Lucía in the Lambayeque-La Leche drainage. The columns were made of conical adobes set in clay mortar.

Cupisnique art and ideology

Cupisnique beliefs were very much a part of the shamanistic ideology of the Initial Period. Fragmentary glimpses of this can be gleaned from the pottery and public art, but its most complex expression is seen on steatite vessels, such as those from Limoncarro in Jequetepeque; unfortunately it is uncertain whether all of these date to the late Initial Period. The central themes on the stone vessels are two carnivores, the feline and the spider, both of which present a real threat to humans, as well as providing natural symbols for human behavior and values.

A solitary and all-powerful hunter, the feline remains a pervasive symbol in most of tropical South America, and is a common alter ego for shamans and priests. The gigantic head of a feline dominates public architecture at Huaca de los Reyes, and similar representations sometimes decorate the chambers of stirrup-spouted bottles. Feline faces are pervasive as secondary elements in elaborate examples of Cupisnique iconography.

The spider is depicted on Cupisnique stone vessels with exaggerated pincerlike jaws, pedipalps (the reproductive organ of male arachnids), and spinnerets (the organ for spinning silk). The anthropomorphized arachnid supernatural frequently holds a decapitated head or a net bag filled with human trophy heads, and is also often associated with lush plant growth, from which

82 A carved steatite bowl, probably from Limoncarro in the Jequetepeque Valley. It depicts a supernatural figure with spider attributes, holding a severed head in his hand; a net bag of decapitated heads hangs from his head. Diameter 14.6 cm.

83,84 Two Cupisnique stirrup-spouted bottles: (*above*) perhaps illustrating the transformation of a shaman or priest into a feline, 14.5 cm high; (*below*) said to have been looted from a tomb at Talambo in the Jequetepeque Valley, showing a jaguar amidst stalks of the mescaline-bearing San Pedro cactus, 26.7 cm high.

trophy heads, severed hands, and other body parts sometimes grow. These complex images suggest a link between the fertility of the natural world and the ferocity of the trophy-taking supernatural. Images of the feline display a very similar set of associations; the animal appears in some places as the source of plant growth and elsewhere as an emblem on an anthropomorphic figure holding trophy heads.[78] The snake and the raptorial bird are also depicted on the Cupisnique vessels, but usually in a secondary capacity.

One of the most distinctive stylistic features of Cupisnique stone vessels is the division of figures into two non-symmetrical parts. For example, figures will frequently have an anthropomorphic left side and a mainly arachnid or feline right side. Such representations convey the sense of balance of opposites (natural:supernatural, human:animal) and the mystical potential of transformation. Underlying these representations may be the concept of the powers of priests or shamans (or their mythical or divine forebears), who were believed to change forms to facilitate communication between this world and the supernatural realm. One of the most famous pieces of Cupisnique pottery shows a vertically divided visage in which one half appears almost human, while the other shows a dominantly feline aspect.[79]

In many parts of native America, rituals frequently involve the use of psychotropic drugs of some sort to facilitate shamanistic transformation. Significantly, some Cupisnique bottles depict a feline alongside stalks of the mescaline-bearing San Pedro cactus. At Huaca Prieta, Junius Bird discovered a complete set of snuffing paraphernalia (a snuff tray and tube) in a Cupisnique burial, and fragmentary examples of similar artifacts are known from both the north and central coast. Ethnographic analogies lead scholars to believe that these items were used to inhale hallucinogenic snuff, although this has yet to be proven by chemical analysis.[80]

Presumably, many of the images to be found on Cupisnique pottery are taken from the rich mythology of the Cupisnique culture. Perhaps the most common motif incised on bottles is that of trophy heads, linked by a cord or held in a net bag. Modeled vessels often show captives with hands bound behind their backs. These depictions can plausibly be linked to the more complex mythical scenes of supernatural sacrifice shown on the stone vessels. Less intelligible to the archaeologist is the selective depiction of certain foods, like the fruit of the pepino tree, or the realistic portraits of deeply wrinkled human faces.

As Larco recognized, the Cupisnique culture shared many of its beliefs with other contemporary cultures. The centrality of the feline in their pantheon is only the most obvious example of this. Even the Cupisnique spider supernatural can be related to images in the Middle Temple at Garagay. The critical role of trophy-heads and dismembered limbs in the myths, and their intimate connection with vegetation and fertility, similarly have parallels elsewhere, most notably at Cerro Sechín. The existence of certain shared beliefs is also implied by parallels in ceremonial architecture; the U-shaped layout of buildings such as Huaca de los Reyes probably reflects the organizational principles of other coastal groups to the south. Furthermore the practice of "ritual entombment," originally identified with the highland Kotosh Religious Tradition, is likewise found at Cupisnique centers. At Huaca Lucía, for example, a tremendous amount of labor went into carefully burying the main platform in a thick layer of clean sand brought from dune formations several kilometers away.[81]

Montegrande and the mid-valley settlement of Jequetepeque

On the north coast, as on the central coast, most investigations have focused on the easily accessible coastal plain and lower valley areas. Sites in the *yunga* environments of the mid-valley portions of these coastal valleys have received little attention, except as a result of the looting of cemeteries in the Jequetepeque and Zaña valleys since 1963, with particularly intense activity during the 1967–68 drought. From 1978 to 1981, long after the nearly total destruction of these burial grounds, the middle portion of the Jequetepeque between 370 m and 450 m was systematically surveyed because of its impending inundation by the Gallito Ciego dam. Remarkably, 52 Initial Period and Early Horizon sites were located in this small section of the valley, of which 30 have public architecture, while the remainder are cemeteries. The layout of these complexes are usually combinations of low terraced stone platforms 1–4 m in height, and rectangular plazas. Approximately 90 percent of the pottery from these sites is apparently indistinguishable from assemblages in highland Cajamarca, and consequently this dense mid-valley settlement may be a highland intrusion; Jequetepeque is a natural corridor into the highlands, and the coca-producing regions of the mid-valley would have been of special interest to highland groups. It is significant that, in contrast to the lower valley center, colonnades were not a characteristic feature at any of the mid-valley sites. Cylindrical masonry burial towers were used for collective burial at several of the sites, and complex petroglyphs, believed to date to the Initial Period, were pecked into boulders and cliffs near the public centers. These mid-valley traits do not resemble the classic "Cupisnique" cultural pattern, but they do have parallels in the adjacent highland region.[82]

One of the mid-valley Jequetepeque sites, Montegrande, was extensively excavated in 1981–83 by a German team led by Michael Tellenbach. Located 430 m above sea level and about 5 km from the modern town of Tembladera, Montegrande sits on a low mesa overlooking the narrow valley bottomlands. In the center of the 13-hectare site are two low public constructions, Huaca Grande and Huaca Antigua; these buildings strongly resemble the public architecture at the highland sites of Layzón and Kuntur Wasi, both near the headwaters of the Jequetepeque. Surrounding the core of public architecture were 164 dwellings grouped into household clusters around small open patios; less than half of these were occupied at any one time. Montegrande's public buildings were built of rough stone masonry covered with clay plaster and sculpted adobe decoration; while the houses were of cane and mud. Significantly, the houses and platform mounds shared a common orientation, and there is a surprising degree of overall planning in the settlement.[83]

Subsistence and economy

The subsistence pattern on the north coast corresponds closely to that already described for the central and north-central coast. In the Moche and La Leche Valleys, archaeologists have documented the interdependency between relatively large, agriculturally based centers in the lower valley and small fishing villages on the littoral. Highland subsistence items are rare, and the groups achieved economic self-sufficiency at the local level by combining the resources of the shoreline and irrigated valley floor. Maize does not commonly appear in refuse until the late Initial Period and even then it appears to have been of only

85 A whalebone snuff tray and bone snuff tube (16.7 cm long) recovered from an Initial Period house at Huaca Prieta in the Chicama Valley.

86 An incised whalebone snuff tray representing a supernatural figure with crab attributes recovered by Max Uhle in *c.* 1905 near Supe.

minor importance.[84] Surveys in Zaña and Jequetepeque have also revealed dense occupations in the middle sections of the valley, which suggests that this area may have also been an important component in the economy, particularly as a source of chili peppers and, perhaps, coca. The materials recovered from the Jequetepeque sites show strong cultural affiliations with sites in Cajamarca, and it may be that at least in some valleys, the *chaupi yunga* was under the control of highland rather than coastal groups.

The primary source of protein was small fish and shellfish, even at sites such as Caballo Muerto and Huaca Lucía located some 50 km inland. Camelids also appear in the archaeological record, and were apparently hunted in the early Initial Period and domesticated in the late Initial Period. At Huaca Negra in Virú, along the exterior of the Temple of the Llamas, archaeologists William Strong and Clifford Evans discovered a llama buried in a shallow pit with its front legs bound together from the hoof up to the forelimb with a coiled rope, and its hind legs lashed together above the hoofs. Three other llamas were found inside the building, all of which were tied and two of which still wore harnesses. Together with the scarcity of llama bones in the refuse at this and other sites, these fittings suggest that camelids were known principally as pack animals and only secondarily as a source of meat.[85] It is significant that the wool textiles are rare or absent from the coast during this time.

Apparently the organization of different north coast valleys varied, as did the conditions for development. Some of the largest Cupisnique centers, such as Caballo Muerto, are located far from the shore at points where the lower valley begins; these locations are particularly advantageous for controlling the intakes to irrigate the surrounding bottomlands. Other valleys, such as Virú, lack centers of this sort, and the location of Initial Period sites near naturally flooded bottomland led investigators to conclude that irrigation may not have become widespread in Virú until the Early Horizon. In Zaña, relict vegetation similar to tropical forest vegetation on the eastern slopes continued to survive on the western slopes, and this unusual habitat was a special focus of human utilization and settlement.

The economic ties between the north coast and the adjacent highlands were particularly strong, judging from the quantities of exotic pottery and other non-subsistence items exchanged between the zones. The looting of cemeteries in the middle Jequetepeque Valley mentioned earlier yielded a panoply of coastal and highland ceramic styles, including a poorly understood style – featuring polychrome post-fire painting and complex iconography – widely referred to as Tembladera.[86] Cupisnique pottery has been found at central coast sites such as Ancón and at centers in the northern highlands like Pandanche near Pacopampa, Cerro Blanco near Kuntur Wasi, and Chavín de Huántar. A fragment from a finely modeled Cupisnique stone bowl with arachnid iconography was even encountered at Pacopampa, far from its presumed source in the lower Jequetepeque Valley.[87]

87 A multi-colored Tembladera-style bottle said to have been looted from a tomb in the middle Jequetepeque Valley. This resin-painted vessel shows an elegantly attired man playing an ocarina; the feline and avian motifs on the man's tunic closely resemble designs on the Late Huacaloma-style pottery of the highland Cajamarca basin. Height 26.8 cm.

Technological developments

The small-scale societies of the Initial Period offered stable conditions in which technological experimentation was possible, and recent excavations at Mina Perdida suggest that the initial stage of copper metallurgy may have been initiated before 1000 BC. Small pieces of hammered copper sheet were discovered at Mina Perdida in 1991 in the western platform of the late Initial Period public complex. The foil never exceeded a few centimeters on a side and none had been shaped into finished artifacts. Nevertheless, the creation of the thin sheets of copper implies basic metallurgical knowledge as well as an interest in the development of this technology. At Mina Perdida, archaeological investigations recovered pieces of clay and stone that had been modified by high temperatures, as well as isolated chunks of copper ore. These finds suggest that copper may have been smelted rather than obtained as native copper.[88]

As seen earlier in this chapter, another pyrotechnology – the firing of ceramics – had been developed many centuries earlier, and additional breakthroughs continued to be made. The fine late Initial Period ceramics recovered at the cemeteries of the north coast are as beautiful and technologically sophisticated as many later ceramics produced in the central Andes. Good control of clay selection, firing atmosphere, and temperatures are just a few of the many factors that had to be mastered to create ceramics of this quality. Until recently, the production processes were almost completely unknown, since no pottery-producing areas had been identified or excavated.

Many scholars assumed that, like most 20th-century pottery made in traditional Andean communities, the Initial Period ceramics had been fired in the open air without the use of kilns or other specialized structures. But excavations at a 9th-century BC production center in the Batan Grande area of the Lambayeque-La Leche drainage revealed small hour-glass shaped pits lined with refractory clay that had apparently served as updraft kilns. Dozens of these furnaces occur over a 0.25-km area, and this suggests production on a scale much larger than would be necessary for the consumption needs of a single community.[89]

The northern frontier and beyond

On the periphery of the central and northern Peruvian coast was a frontier zone which lacked major population centers and in which regional integration was very weak. Beyond it was the area of the Valdivia and Machalilla cultures where the cultural patterns were fundamentally dissimilar from those of coastal Peru during the Initial Period, despite the presence of relatively dense populations. In 1948, Yale University scholar Wendell Bennett suggested that before the arrival of the Spaniards, much of the territory currently in modern Peru was part of an area co-tradition that he referred to as the Peruvian Co-Tradition. By this he meant that there was a cultural continuum in which the multiple component cultures had been interrelated over a lengthy period of time. In Bennett's view, the cultures of coastal Ecuador were probably part of a different area co-tradition, as yet poorly understood.[90] While Bennett's terminology has declined in popularity, his observations about the long-standing and profound differences between the pre-Hispanic cultural traditions of what are now Peru and Ecuador have considerable merit. The roots of these differences were apparently even more ancient than Bennett had anticipated, extending well into the second millennium BC.

The frontier zone during the Initial Period began at the Sechura desert, a 225-km stretch of arid coastal plain incapable of sustaining traditional agriculture. It lies to the north of the Lambayeque-La Leche drainage and to the south of the Piura drainage. This inhospitable expanse constituted the northern limit of the

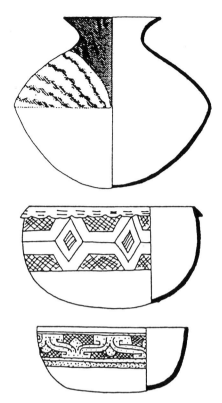

88 Three pottery vessels found at Cerro Ñañañique in the Piura drainage. The red-painted Paita-style jar (top) was apparently imported from the lower valley, where groups produced painted pottery, whereas the two bowls (center and below) are typical examples of the incised vessels favored by mid-valley residents.

Cupisnique culture and, apparently, of Initial Period coastal societies engaging in large-scale public construction. A few fishing communities, dating to the Initial Period, have been located along the shores of the Sechura Peninsula, and small maritime and agricultural villages existed in the Chira and Piura valleys. Unlike many of the coastal rivers to the south, both the Chira and the Piura were blessed with water throughout the year. The ancient frontier area corresponds roughly to a natural zone of climatic convergence. Since at least 3000 BC, the Piura, Chira, and Tumbes drainages had climates intermediate between that of the moist forested slopes of coastal Ecuador and the arid littoral of the northern Peruvian desert. Few valleys would have been better suited for floodplain agriculture than these, but despite this promising situation – or perhaps because of it – none of the Initial Period sites in Chira or Piura appear to have exceeded 2 hectares. A University of Tokyo expedition documented a similar Initial Period settlement pattern for the Tumbes drainage near the modern border between Peru and Ecuador.[91]

Paita is the oldest-known ceramic style from the Chira and Piura drainages. This coastal style had its strongest links with the pottery from the adjacent highlands, rather than with the Cupisnique style of the northern Peruvian coast or the Valdivia pottery of the southern Ecuadorian littoral. While the early phases of the sequence were decorated with incised cross-hatching and other surface texturing, the late Initial Period Paita-style ceramics featured red and black slip painting and post-fire painting, usually on short-necked jars. The communities of the frontier zone had contacts to the north and south, and Paita-style trade pieces occasionally reached the Chicama and Jequetepeque valleys.

While the Piura and Chira valleys supported sedentary agriculture during the Initial Period, El Niños from the north would have brought frequent torrential rains and floods, and dense algarroba forests would have covered much of the coastal plain. The middle and upper valleys of Piura and Chira and the adjacent highlands are torrid and, at least in post-Conquest times, they were also disease-ridden. Even now, the population densities in the highland zones of the valleys are less than half that of the intermontane valleys to the north and south. These river valleys do, however, offer easy access to the Amazonian lowlands from the coast. In this section of the Andes, the highlands narrow to a mere 120 km from east to west and the passes across the continental divide occur at only 2,000 m (less than half the elevation at passes in the Chavín de Huántar region). Lacking the usual high-altitude zones, the savannah-like *yunga* environment of the entrenched coastal valleys actually meets the heavily forested *ceja de selva* vegetation of the eastern Andean slopes. In the upper Chira Valley (known as the Catamayo in Ecuador) remains of small Initial Period villages have been found, and the Catamayo B/C style ceramics point to close ties with the coast and with the Cuenca basin of Ecuador.

A surprisingly large center was established on Cerro Ñañañique (260 m), a hill overlooking the modern town of Chulcanas in Piura's middle valley. During the late Initial Period the inhabitants reworked the slopes of the hill into a series of ascending stone-faced platforms connected by inset staircases, and by the Early Horizon the public architecture began to conform to a U-shaped layout. While this complex was small compared to those further south, it was larger than coeval sites in the Ecuadorian region. In some respects, its groundplan is reminiscent of centers in the upper reaches of Zaña and Jequetepeque.

The factors leading up to Ñañañique's establishment are unknown, but it may have been founded as a gateway community for the goods moving through the Piura Valley across the Andes. The Chira Valley would have also been an attractive route to the coast for goods from the highland valleys of southern Ecuador (i.e. Loja, Cuenca). As we have seen, the late Initial Period was a time of intensified interaction between the north coast, northern highlands, and tropical forest, and Ñañañique may have been founded in response to the increase in long-distance exchange. Significantly, *Spondylus* working debris has been found at the site, and ceramics in the local Ñañañique and Panecillo-phase styles have been recovered from cemeteries in the Jequetepeque and Zaña valleys, as well as at centers such as Pacopampa and Poro-Poro. Judging from the ceramics, the occupants of Cerro Ñañañique also maintained close ties with groups of the neighboring Chira Valley, and with lowland Bagua as well.[92]

A much higher density of population existed on the southern Ecuadorian coast to the north of the frontier zone. Like their counterparts immediately to the south, these were sedentary agrarian cultures with a strong riverine orientation and a significant consumption of marine resources. The abundant rains swelled the coastal river systems of this region making water transportation and year-round floodplain farming feasible. The relevant cultures identified along the southern Ecuadorian coast correspond to the late Valdivia culture (2000–1500 BC) and the Machalilla culture (c. 1500–800 BC).

One of the most intensively studied of these valleys has been that of Chanduy, the focus of a University of Illinois project in the 1970s. Altogether, 12 Valdivia sites and 36 Machalilla sites were registered. With two exceptions, these sites appear to correspond to hamlets distributed throughout the best riverine agricultural land. During Machalilla times, the largest site covered little more than a hectare and the average settlement was less than half a hectare in area. No public architecture has been documented between 1500 and 800 BC, when construction of monumental pyramid complexes along the Peruvian coast was at its height.[93] However, there were at least two earlier centers with a strong ceremonial character in this area during late Valdivia times. Real Alto and Centinela were agglutinated villages situated on ridges overlooking the floodplain. Both were established early in the Valdivia culture and continued to be occupied for nearly a millennium.

Donald Lathrap and his colleagues carried out large-scale excavations at Real Alto and consequently an unusual amount is known about it. Sprawling over some 2 hectares, this center comprises rows of oval houses bordering a large rectangular open plaza. On opposite sides of this public space are two low mounds, no more than 1.4 m high, which supported free-standing buildings of special ritual importance. One mound, called the Fiesta Mound, measured 50 by 37 m at its base. It was resurfaced with yellow clay at least four times, and the building on its summit was refurbished at least eight times. The floor of the summit structure had been cut by pits which held drinking bowls and such distinctive foods as sea turtle and lobster tail. Facing this mound, on the opposite side of the plaza, was the so-called Charnel Mound. On its summit, Ecuadorian archaeologist Jorge Marcos discovered an elaborate stone lined tomb of an adult woman, and an adjacent dismembered male sacrificial victim encircled by seven chert knives. Secondary interments of another seven adult males were found near by in a common grave on the summit.[94]

It is intriguing that Real Alto differs in so many fundamental respects from the Late Preceramic and early Initial Period centers of the Peruvian coast. While both areas share the concept of a central public space maintained for the performance of community ritual, and of the successive rebuilding of community structures at regular intervals, the contrasts are more striking than the similarities. Judging from its location, the charnel house was of critical importance to the community of Real Alto, but it was alien to the Peruvian area, as was the ritual dismemberment of humans as a basic component of community ritual. The central role of authority apparently ascribed to some adult females buried on the Charnel Mound likewise has no known parallel to the south. Perhaps the most suggestive difference between the two areas is that the ceremonial life of the Valdivia and Machalilla cultures did not entail the systematic pooling of group labor for the construction of public monuments, or for any other known purpose. With an estimated population at Real Alto's zenith of 1,500 inhabitants, such endeavors would not have been beyond the physical capabilities of the largest Valdivia community. But the volume of the two mounds at Real Alto is less than 1 percent of the pyramid complexes at the coeval La Florida in the Rimac Valley, 500 km to the south. Thus there were almost certainly basic differences in the mechanisms by which labor could be appropriated and channeled.

Even the units of household production and consumption in the two areas appear to be different. The Valdivia houses excavated are large elliptical buildings made of vertical logs coated with layers of mud. Steep gabled roofs were supported by two interior posts. With dimensions of 12 × 8 m, these dwellings seem too large for single domestic units, and probably housed large extended families like those still found among some tropical forest groups. These houses contrast with the small multi-room dwellings at sites such as Cardal or Montegrande. Thus, the dispersed settlement pattern typical of the Ecuadorian coast in the second millennium BC, likewise bears little resemblance to the pattern of multiple large centers characteristic of valleys on the central and northern Peruvian coast.

Other aspects of the early coastal Ecuadorian cultures were remarkably precocious. For example, excavations on the island of La Plata yielded evidence of Valdivia and Machalilla occupations associated with ceremonial activities and with the maritime exchange of the *Spondylus princeps* shell. La Plata lies 23 km off the Manabi coast, and its exploitation in the second millennium BC is testimony to the maritime skills of the Valdivia and Machalilla cultures.[95] The availability of large *balsa* wood trees suitable for sea-going vessels and the presence of a network of navigable coastal rivers were critical to these developments in the Ecuadorian area.

While the second millennium BC cultures of Peru and Ecuador were quite different in many basic respects, there appears to have been considerable contact between them across the highly permeable frontier zone. The acquisition of the warm water *Spondylus princeps* and *Strombus* shell by Peruvian groups is perhaps the most conspicuous evidence of this link, but evidence of the influence of the Ecuadorian cultures on their southern neighbors is perhaps even more striking. For example, the stirrup-spouted bottle – the quintessentially Peruvian ceramic form that remained popular until the Spanish Conquest – appears to have been developed originally by late Valdivia or early Machalilla groups, and

89 Hypothetical reconstruction of a Valdivia house at Real Alto.

only introduced to the Peruvian coast several centuries later (*c.* 1000 BC). Other cultural features characteristic of late Initial Period north coast peoples may have been inspired by Ecuadorian cultures, including cylinder and stamp seals, napkin ring earspools, and ceramic bottles modeled with images of animals and people. Some of the pottery effigies are quite distinctive, such as the depiction of acrobatic contortionists, and many of these cultural traits were also shared by the peoples of western Mesoamerica. Some scholars propose that the sea trade originating along the Pacific shores of South America was responsible for the spread of these features, and that the Formative Ecuadorian cultures acted as cultural innovators and donors.[96]

The southern frontier

Investigations on the south coast of Peru have also produced evidence of cultural and social patterns fundamentally different from those found on the central and north coast, and this area can be interpreted as the southern frontier of the more densely populated and more tightly integrated regional systems discussed in this chapter. There are no definite cases of monumental architecture south of the Lurín Valley during the Initial Period. In fact, despite site surveys in the Topará, Chincha, Ica, Nazca and Moquegua valleys, very few examples of Initial Period sites of any kind are known to the south of the Lurín Valley. It is unlikely that large settlements with public architecture could have remained undetected until now had they existed along the south coast.

Erizo, in the Ica Valley, is the oldest site with pottery documented from this region. Surface collections recovered thin monochrome neckless ollas with slightly everted rims, not unlike those of Early Guañape. Two radiocarbon measurements on a single piece of carbon averaged 2352 BC. This sample was found with cotton textile fragments and the remains of squash, beans, peanuts, chili pepper, guava, and gourds; no maize was present.[97]

Similar ceramics have been recovered from a small later site in the Acarí Valley, referred to as the Hacha site because of the abundant basalt hoes found on the surface. The late Initial Period occupation at Hacha consists of small rectangular buildings of wattle-and-daub and small hand-made adobes. Several of these constructions were dwellings, but one modest multi-room building has been interpreted as a shrine dedicated to ensuring the success of hunting. Its layout and architectural features are local in character. One room, dominated by a large unvented hearth, was decorated with a painted mural of camelids.[98]

Although Hacha resembled Initial Period sites further north in terms of the crops cultivated, the large numbers of stone hoes and small projectile points recovered there have no parallel at Initial Period sites on the central and north coast. It is likely that the agricultural economy at Hacha was significantly different from these areas. Cultivation was apparently concentrated along the self-watering floodplain using the stone-bladed hoes, and although mollusks and fish were consumed, hunting remained a principal source of animal protein in this lightly occupied coastal region.

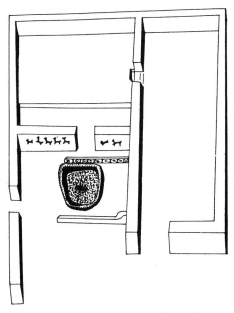

90 Isometric reconstruction of a small building at the site of Hacha in the Acarí Valley, that may have been used for public rituals.

4

The Initial Period Societies in the Highlands and Montane Forest

The developments on the coast during the Initial Period occurred within a much larger social and economic framework, whose demographic core lay in the rich valleys of the northern and central highlands. Large public centers existed in many of the intermontane valleys which were linked together by a loose web of ideological, social, and exchange relations, but apparently lacked an overarching political armature. Designed as the focus of religious and civic life, these highland centers were non-urban, and the massive constructions which characterize them should not obscure the small residential populations or agrarian character of their societies.

In sharp contrast to the coast, the productive base in the highlands was rainfall farming, supplemented by hunting. In fact, the most impressive highland developments were in those regions where irrigation was least critical and where camelid herding was marginal. This economic orientation had been established in much of the highlands during the Late Preceramic and consequently there was considerable continuity in the patterns of settlement, with many Initial Period centers evolving out of smaller Late Preceramic settlements.

The traditional emphasis placed by archaeologists on the most impressive of the highland developments should not obscure the profound unevenness of development during the Initial Period. Between the well-documented highland areas in which precocious developments took place, there were lightly occupied areas with less integration. However, the gaps between the developmental foci did not prevent ties from being forged between the multitude of highland and coastal centers; selected cultural features were held in common by distant groups, and rare natural resources and emblematic craft items were exchanged between them.

On the eastern periphery of this amorphous Initial Period sphere of interaction were small-scale groups living along the fringes of the tropical forest who maintained ties with these highland societies, and presumably provided them with resources from the eastern lowland environments. To the north were the precocious cultures of what is now the southern Ecuadorian coast and highlands. These groups were likewise important to the developments under consideration, both as cultural innovators and the source of specially valued exotic materials. To discuss the Initial Period developments in Peru without including these tropical forest and Ecuadorian groups, as is sometimes done, would be to unjustifiably project modern political and cultural divisions back to a time when, judging from the archaeological record, impermeable political frontiers did not exist. Within this vast socioeconomic field, it is possible to identify clusters of centers with particularly strong cultural similarities, and regional spheres in which interaction was especially intense.

Probably the most studied of these regional interaction spheres is the one centered in the highland valleys of the Department of Cajamarca. It had strong ties with the centers of the Cupisnique culture (discussed in the preceding chapter), and with little-known groups in areas such as Bagua and Huayurco on the forested eastern slopes. The most famous of these northern highland centers, Pacopampa and Kuntur Wasi, have been known in the archaeological literature for over half a century, but they were usually considered to be Chavín centers or even "colonies," mainly on the basis of a few isolated stone sculptures. The magnitude of the pre-Chavín developments in the northern highlands was first revealed by Peruvian scholars Hermilio Rosas and Ruth Shady in 1967 during fieldwork at Pacopampa. Their excavations demonstrated that Pacopampa had been established during the Initial Period, long before the appearance of the hypothetical Chavín influence, and that the integration of Pacopampa into what can be called the Chavín sphere of interaction did not occur until much later. These findings have been supported by the results of more recent projects at Pacopampa, as well as by the investigations initiated by the University of Tokyo at Kuntur Wasi, Huacaloma, and Layzón.

Pacopampa. The site of Pacopampa is located in what today is one of the least developed parts of the Peruvian highlands, and to reach it usually entails journeys on horse or foot along dirt trails. Located some 150 km south of the disputed modern border with Ecuador, Pacopampa is the northernmost Initial Period center with public architecture known in the Peruvian highlands. It is situated roughly 70 km from both the coast and tropical banks of the Marañon River. The Andean mountain chain here is low and narrow, and few spots offer easier access between the Pacific plain and the forests of eastern lowlands.

Pacopampa covers the crest of a hill at an elevation of 2,140 m. Over 1,000 m below is the Chotano River, which eventually joins the Chambaya to form the Huancabamba, a tributary of the Marañon. Archaeological surveys along the steep valley slopes of the Chotano have identified 13 Initial Period sites.[1] All of them are located either in the *quechua* production zone, which in this northern

The northern highlands

91 The builders of Pacopampa (one of the most important Initial Period centers in the northern highlands) terraced and leveled a natural hill to provide a setting for its public architecture.

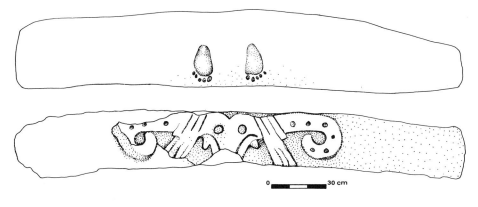

92,93 (*Below*) This large, carved stone sculpture from Pacopampa depicts human footprints on one side and a composite image with feline, avian, and serpent elements on the other. (*Right*) It was only through careful pecking and polishing that the sculptors were able to create the illusion of these footprints in hard stone. According to the 17th-century traveler, Antonio Vazquez de Espinoza, this sculpture was held in great veneration by the Indians of the province.

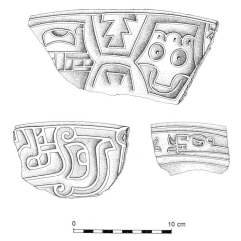

94 Three fragments of bowls of the Pacopampa Pacopampa style were recovered in the El Mirador section of Pacopampa and were decorated with images of felines and serpents.

region occurs at 2,000–2,400 m, or in the adjacent *yunga*-like *temple* zone, found between 1,200–2,000 m. The sheltered valley slopes of the *temple* are favorably suited for tropical crops such as manioc, chirimoya, and even cotton. In fact, during the 18th and 19th centuries, indigenous settlers from the tropical forest repopulated this area using a subsistence system of swidden agriculture.[2] The *quechua* zone is now utilized for growing maize and beans, as well as arracacha (*Arracacia xanthorrhiza*), a root crop rarely grown further south. There is no evidence of Initial Period occupation either in the fertile but torrid *playa* zone adjacent to the Chotano River (1,000–1,200 m) or in the *jalca* zone (2,400–2,800 m) above Pacopampa. At still higher elevations there are cloud forests and wet *páramo* tundra, rather than *puna* grasslands. Wild camelids were not apparently native to the *páramo* environment and deer were the only large game available. The relatively humid northern highland areas like Pacopampa are similarly less favorable for cultivating such high Andean crops as the potato.

The first evidence of occupation in this region comes from Pandanche, a small mound in the *temple* zone.[3] A deep test pit at this 2-hectare site penetrated 4 m of cultural materials to reveal a previously unknown type of ceramic dating to the beginning of the Initial Period, which lay above still earlier layers pertaining to the Late Preceramic. The pottery style, known as Pandanche A, featured thin-walled bowls decorated externally by brushing, impressed appliqué bands, punctated appliqué protuberances (called nubbins), and short incised lines. These decorative modes have parallels in the late Valdivia and Machalilla pottery of southern Ecuador. The sharply carinated bowl forms of Pandanche A ceramics are reminiscent of early ceramics from the tropical forest. Early Initial Period settlements coeval with Pandanche appear to have existed elsewhere in the *temple* zone at sites such as Machaipungo.[4]

The public center at Pacopampa was apparently established during the middle of the Initial Period. From the outset, it was much larger than any of the other sites in the northern highlands, and it drew labor and provisions from the smaller settlements like Pandanche and Machaipungo, which continued to be occupied. By the end of the Initial Period, the public architecture at Pacopampa extended over 9 hectares, and the natural conical-shaped hill on which it was founded was totally transformed by the construction of artificially filled terraces to create a rectangular three-level stepped platform. On the summit were sunken courts and free-standing buildings, all drained by an elaborate stone-lined subterranean canal system.[5] The clearing of one 5-m high terrace wall revealed that all but the upper 60 cm had been built during the Initial Period.[6] Unfortunately, the configuration of the Initial Period layout remains unknown because the overlying later occupations obscure it.

The surface of Pacopampa is littered with fragments of stone sculptures and cylindrical stone columns, some of which probably date to the Initial Period. Among them is a prismatic lintel-like block of volcanic stone decorated on two faces. One side depicts a fanged feline face flanked by avian elements and profile views of a spotted snake body, while the other side shows a pair of naturalistic feet pecked into the surface and polished to create the illusion of human footprints in stone.[7] This unusual sculpture bears only faint similarities to the stone carvings at Chavín de Huántar, its strongest resemblance being to the pre-Chavín carving found at Huaca A at Moxeke in Casma (Chapter 3). Other Pacopampa sculptures, like one showing curvilinear snakes, are equally distinctive and may also have been carved during the Initial Period.

Stylized felines, birds, and snakes were also prominently featured on the late Initial Period Pacopampa-style pottery, awkwardly dubbed the Pacopampa Pacopampa style.[8] The feline: bird: serpent triad was also central to Cupisnique iconography and the earliest sculpture from Chavín de Huántar. Tello saw the three animals as metaphors for the forces of the earth, sky, and water, and their ubiquity in the art of the Initial Period implies a degree of shared beliefs.[9] The source of these beliefs cannot be traced to any single site or region, but rather appears to be a development of ideas already present in many disparate areas during the Late Preceramic. Their prominence on the domestic pottery and public architecture of the Initial Period is testimony to the intimate ties between religious ideology and social life that characterized the cultures of this period.

The style of these images and the ceramic vessels on which they appear at Pacopampa was distinctive, which makes it easy to differentiate from the pottery of other areas. Pacopampa ceramics were decorated with post-fire painting in zones and pre-fire polychrome painting in red, tan, white, and gray, while the rims of bowls were frequently shaped to form waves, steps, and other unusual patterns. The repertoire of surface decoration included pattern burnishing and patches of incised parallel lines, sometimes called combing. The narrow incisions used to create the figurative rectilinear geometric motifs on bowls and other vessels were engraved before firing but often when the clay was almost dry. The resulting thin irregular incisions were often different in color from the polished surface.[10]

Many of the finer portable artifacts recovered at Pacopampa and neighboring sites appear to be items of ritual paraphernalia used in ceremonial activities. For

95 A small pottery cup in the Pacopampa Pacopampa style, adorned with bands of interlocking bird heads and felines.

96 A small stone snuff spoon from the Pacopampa area, perhaps used in the ingestion of hallucinogens; its decoration is typical of the local Initial Period style. Length 5 cm.

97 This small stone tumbler was found at Yarac Sara near Pacopampa, and was incised with a complicated mythical theme (see rollout, left) distinct from those commonly represented on ceramics. Height 6.4 cm.

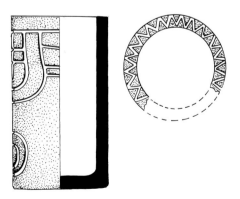

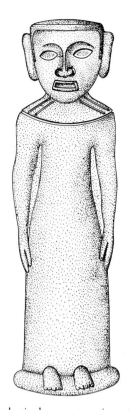

98 Hypothetical reconstruction of a large hollow pottery figurine (c. 45 cm high) unearthed in the El Mirador section of Pacopampa. It represents a male with a distinctive hair style and an unusual full-length tunic.

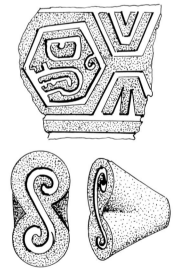

99 Ceramic cylindrical and stamp seals found in a house in the El Mirador section of Pacopampa.

example, Rosas and Shady recovered a small stone spoon, probably used for inhaling snuff, which was decorated with the same frontal "feline" face sometimes represented on the Pacopampa Pacopampa-style bowls. An even more complex example of Initial Period iconography appears on a small stone cup from one of the small village sites near Pacopampa; about the size of a "shot glass," it may have been used for the consumption of ritual beverages, perhaps *chicha* beer.[11]

Worked and unworked marine shell has been surprisingly common in all the excavations at Pacopampa. Considering the time required to travel from the Pacific shore to Pacopampa on foot, shellfish are very unlikely to have been eaten. A more plausible interpretation is that the shells were used in ceremonies related to water and agricultural production. The elaborate subterranean canal systems likewise seem to exceed the exigencies of drainage, and they too may have played a part in rituals of fertility.

The extent of the resident population at Pacopampa during the Initial Period is unknown, but investigators believe that most people continued to live in small villages and hamlets adjacent to the agricultural lands of the *quechua* and *temple* zones. Some habitation areas did exist, however, at Pacopampa. Thus far, only one such area has been studied.[12] On a hill called El Mirador to the west of the monumental architecture, excavations by Peruvian archaeologist Daniel Morales revealed the presence of an ovoid building cut into the bedrock, with stones arranged around its edges to support what may have been a conical thatched roof. Morales interprets this building as an Initial Period residence, possibly occupied by the religious specialists responsible for temple activities.

Among the artifacts associated with this dwelling are large, hollow ceramic anthropomorphic figurines dressed in long sleeveless tunics, which would have originally stood about 48 cm high. The realistically modeled heads of these figurines show long shoulder-length hair, sideburns, abnormally large ears, and straight noses with holes for nostrils. But these were not the only unusual items recovered. There were also crude figurines of dogs, bears, felines, and viscachas, as well as Cupisnique-style seals of both the roller and stamp variety. Also present was an unparalleled number of fine pottery vessels, many of which were not in the local style. The exotic pottery included styles from the coast, eastern slopes and elsewhere in the highlands. An impressive variety of foreign ceramics have been recovered in smaller quantities from other sectors of Pacopampa, and the distinctive styles of these pieces have allowed scholars to trace the wide-ranging ties maintained by the center.

While these patterns of exchange may have been important in terms of maintaining the prestige of Pacopampa and its leaders, a stable and productive subsistence base was vital for sustaining a population large enough to undertake such major public works as the construction of the Pacopampa pyramid. The establishment of the primary center in the *quechua* zone has suggested to some scholars that maize had become the staple by the late Initial Period, although root crops may have been preeminent prior to this time.[13] There is, however, no direct evidence of this, and future studies may prove that other crops such as arracacha were no less important than maize. Judging from the animal bones recovered from the El Mirador excavations, the meat consumed came primarily from deer, with only occasional preparation of birds, dogs, guinea pigs, and chinchilla. An unexpected discovery in the El Mirador refuse was that human remains were second in frequency only to deer. These bones are frequently cut, calcined, and gnawed, and the existence at Pacopampa of some sort of ritual cannibalism must be considered a serious possibility.[14]

The Cajamarca basin. Cajamarca is the largest intermontane valley south of the Pacopampa area. Although the Cajamarca River drains east towards the Marañon, the core of the Cajamarca Valley is located less than 10 km from the headwaters of the Jequetepeque River in the Pacific watershed. The valley floor of the Cajamarca River is broad, fertile, and frost-free. Its high agricultural potential and pleasant climate made it a prized possession of the Incas and it was here that Pizarro captured the Inca emperor Atahualpa. In 1979, the University of Tokyo initiated a decade of systematic investigations in Cajamarca, and present knowledge of the Initial Period occupation in this area derives largely from this research.[15] The early and/or mid-Initial Period in this area is referred to as the Early Huacaloma Phase and the late Initial Period is dubbed the Late Huacaloma Phase, both so named after the site of Huacaloma. No evidence of Late Preceramic antecedents for the Initial Period occupation has yet been discovered in this area, and the materials of the Early Huacaloma Phase are invariably buried beneath larger constructions of Late Huacaloma times.

The ceramics of the Early Huacaloma Phase are similar in many respects to those of Pandanche A, and the Japanese scholar Kazuo Terada has argued that the two styles were contemporary. Early Huacaloma, like Pandanche, is characterized by exterior surfaces decorated with nicked and incised appliqué bands, but there are also differences in forms and decorative modes (e.g. absence of combing, presence of incision) between the two styles.

In the Cajamarca area, there is abundant evidence for early occupation in the *quechua* zone. An Early Huacaloma Phase site was found at 2,400 m and two others were located along the fringes of the valley floor around 2,700 m. However, there are also coeval sites on the high plateau between 3,000 m and 3,200 m and it is likely that a broad range of environments was exploited for farming. Analysis of faunal remains from both the early and late Initial Period refuse from Huacaloma confirms that, as at Pacopampa, wild game was the principal source of meat and deer was the principal game. Cervids systematically constitute over 70 percent of the identified animal bones and would have yielded over 85 percent of the meat consumed, since most other animals were small by comparison. The overwhelming majority of deer remains come from the white-tailed deer (*Odocoileus virginianus*) which are browsers inhabiting wooded zones, rather than the taruca deer (*Hippocamelus antisensis*) found in the high *páramo* grasslands. Thus it appears that most of the hunting was done in forested areas near the agricultural lands within the Cajamarca basin itself. The abundant deer remains also suggest a more heavily forested habitat than exists in Cajamarca today.[16]

The earliest evidence of public architecture known from the heartland of the northern highlands comes from the Huacaloma site (2,700 m). Found in the deepest stratum immediately above sterile soil, the Early Huacaloma phase building is rectangular and measured 5.5 × 3.9 m. It was made of volcanic tuff blocks plastered with cream-colored clay. This clay was applied in thin layers to the exterior and interior of the walls, and was also utilized for the carefully prepared floor. In the center of the room was a round, semi-subterranean hearth where fires had been repeatedly lit, and the surrounding 1.5 m of floor had been scorched red from the heat. No food remains or artifacts were found inside the room, and it is likely that it had been meticulously cleaned. The elaborateness of the construction and its conspicuous lack of refuse led the University of Tokyo excavators to conclude that this building was probably used for religious practices, and that it was related in concept to the ceremonial architecture of the Kotosh Religious Tradition (Chapter 2).[17]

This small building was buried with 2 m of a hard thick layer of clay fill as part of the remodeling process initiated during the Late Huacaloma Phase, in order to produce a stepped platform. Once completed, this pyramid-platform measured 109 m by 81 m, and its exterior walls were decorated with clay murals painted in six colors. Judging from fragments recovered at the base of the walls, serpents and felines were among the themes represented.[18] Stone-lined canals and stone buildings were located on the terraces, and a broad central stairway led from one level to the next until the summit was reached. During the last phase of Initial Period construction, this staircase was roofed over with large stone slabs and its interior walls were plastered with a thick layer of clay. The result was a subterranean stairway that led from the base of the stepped platform to the uppermost of the three terraces. Residential areas seem to have occupied the flat land surrounding the Huacaloma mound, and a trench located to the east of the main mound revealed a series of superimposed houses dating to the Early and Late Huacaloma periods.

Huacaloma is one of the smallest of the ten late Initial Period sites located in the Cajamarca Valley. The largest are Layzón and Agua Tapada, a pair of sites built on opposite sides of a narrow gorge at 3,200 m. These may have been the regional centers of a settlement system that included smaller sites such as Huacaloma. Excavations at Layzón indicate that its Late Huacaloma period complex consisted of a six-tier stepped pyramid constructed by carving the volcanic tuff bedrock or building terrace walls of cut stone blocks of the same material. Elaborate curvilinear symbols were engraved on the face of the lowest terrace next to the central staircase. As at Pacopampa and Huacaloma, subterranean stone-lined canals were found on the summit and terraces of Layzón.[19]

Layzón and Agua Tapada may have been integrated into a single ceremonial system organized around the famous Cumbemayo Canal. This pre-Hispanic

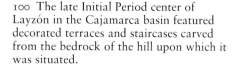

100 The late Initial Period center of Layzón in the Cajamarca basin featured decorated terraces and staircases carved from the bedrock of the hill upon which it was situated.

101 The 9-km long Cumbemayo canal on the slopes above Cajamarca takes runoff from the Pacific drainage and diverts it across the continental divide into the Atlantic drainage. The first section is carved into bedrock and adorned with late Initial Period iconography which, along with its irregular course, suggests that the purpose of the hydraulic system was not purely utilitarian.

hydraulic project has long been recognized as extraordinary because it took waters from the Pacific drainage and diverted them by artificial means to the Atlantic watershed. Running for 9 km, the first 850-m stretch of the canal system was carved into bedrock, often in an elaborate zig-zag path not justified by engineering considerations alone. The curvilinear petroglyphs that decorate some of the canal walls led Tello to propose that the Cumbemayo system was originally built in "Chavín" times. Since the rock carvings recently uncovered on the Layzón terrace walls are very similar to those at Cumbemayo, the canal (or at least its upper section) can at last be dated with some confidence to the late Initial Period.[20]

The Cumbemayo Canal begins at 3,555 m, at the foot of Cerro Cumbe, as an open canal measuring 35–50 cm in width and 30–65 cm in depth. When it reaches the hill on which Agua Tapada is located, the canal goes underground only to reemerge again in spring-like fashion from the earth. At this critical point the canal divides, with one branch running along the southern edge of Agua Tapada and the other running along the southern side of the Layzón site. The two branches join together again just below the two centers and flow towards the valley floor as a single canal.

Scholars have repeatedly concluded that this hydraulic system cannot be explained solely in terms of subsistence agriculture. Shorter canals from the headwaters of the tributaries of the Cajamarca River would have been sufficient for this, considering the ample rainfall in the area. Instead, the Cumbemayo Canal appears to have been built primarily for cult activities related to rainfall and fertility. In fact, the locations of the two major centers, Agua Tapada and Layzón, may have been partially due to their proximity to the canal and the symbolic significance of these spots in the sacred geography of the valley.[21]

In trying to understand the beliefs lying behind constructions such as the Cumbemayo Canal or, for that matter, the elaborate hydraulic systems at sites like Pacopampa, Layzón or, as we will see later, Chavín de Huántar, it is worth considering certain 16th-century Inca concepts concerning water and fertility. According to this cosmological model, the ocean is the primary source of all

102 One of the most remarkable sculptures discovered on the summit at Kuntur Wasi was a free-standing stone pillar carved in a local style with different images on its two main faces; *c.* 1.85 m high. While its precise age is still uncertain, its iconography represents the expression of a local religious tradition.

Opposite

103–106 A shaft tomb was excavated at Cerro Blanco that included an abundance of grave goods including: (*top*) a Cupisnique-style stirrup-spouted bottle, height 24.5 cm; (*center above*) a bowl with red and cream geometric designs, probably from the eastern slopes of the Andes (diameter 14.5 cm); (*center below*) a short-necked bird effigy jar in an unknown style, 11 cm high; and (*bottom*) a small *Spondylus* shell carving with perforations on the reverse to attach it to cloth (2 cm in length).

water, and this water is circulated by a network of underground ducts from the sea to the mountain peaks. The occasional springs appearing from the earth even in the desert or rocky highland outcrops come out of this subterranean system. Rainbows transfer the water from the high mountain peaks to the sky so that it can be made available to the fields and canals and, eventually, to the rivers which return the waters to the sea. Out of this native model grew beliefs concerning the sanctity of peaks, glacial lakes, and springs. Rituals were carried out at these critical spots to guarantee the smooth functioning of this system, and shells from the Pacific shores were sometimes offered to "feed" or propitiate the supernatural forces involved. The Incas performed rituals in which liquid offerings were poured into earth shrines or *ushnus* and, in some cases, into specially built ritual canals. The origination of these ideas is unknown, and how Inca ideas differed from their antecedents is unclear, but late pre-Hispanic expressions of Andean ideology at least offer a starting point for trying to comprehend otherwise anomalous constructions such as the Cumbemayo Canal. Certain related beliefs still exist today in some highland areas, over 450 years after the Spanish Conquest.[22]

Kuntur Wasi. Just across the continental divide from Cajamarca, in the headwaters of the Jequetepeque River, is the site of Kuntur Wasi. At 2,200 m, the site enjoys abundant seasonal precipitation, and rain-fed agriculture still flourishes in the area. The architectural complex was built by transforming the natural peak of La Copa into a quadrangular stepped platform-pyramid with four terraces and a leveled summit covering 13 hectares. Access between the different terrace levels was by way of a massive 11-m wide cut stone staircase in the center of the northern side of the complex. A sunken plaza, measuring 24 m on a side, was built atop the summit for public gatherings. It was decorated with clay murals painted in white, red, orange, and black pigments. Adjacent to it was a stone platform whose original height exceeded 2 m and which may have supported temple buildings. Additional sunken courtyards, platforms, and other structures existed elsewhere on the summit, although the central plaza and stone platform were probably the principal constructions. A subterranean stone-lined canal system cut in the bedrock drains the summit, running unseen beneath the architectural features, and dates from the earliest building phase at the site.

Kuntur Wasi was built during the late Initial Period, and subsequent modifications during the Early Horizon respected its original layout and main architectural elements. Its closest cultural ties were with the coeval populations of Cajamarca, and the ceramics recovered are similar to those of the Late Huacaloma Phase. Links with the coastal populations living in the middle and lower Jequetepeque were weaker, although materials were imported from or related to the Cupisnique, such as stirrup-spouted bottles with graphite paint.[23]

Although Kuntur Wasi is impressive from an architectural perspective, it is best known for the stone sculpture found on its summit. The first examples of it were discovered in 1945 by Tello's collaborator, Rebeca Carrión Cachot, and additional pieces were uncovered in 1989 by the University of Tokyo expedition led by Yoshio Onuki.[24] Some of the carvings resemble Early Horizon sculptures from Chavín de Huántar, but others are distinctively local in theme and style. Some or all of these pieces may date to the late Initial Period, and four large free-standing monoliths carved in the round are particularly noteworthy for their idiosyncratic features. These monoliths were set into the floor or ground judging from the large undecorated sections below the carving.[25]

One sculpture discovered on the summit of the temple is carved with two different anthropomorphic images. On one side is an image that represents a supernatural with a wrinkled face, flared nose, and downturned mouth with squared interlocking fangs. Its left eye is shown as a profile snake, while its right eye appears as a profile feline face; the result is an asymmetric frontal visage reminiscent of some Cupisnique pottery representations. The figure holds a trophy head in its taloned hands and the four appendages running from its mouth may represent a stream of blood. The strangeness of this image is completed by its cross-legged stance and upturned clawed feet. On the other side of the sculpture was an equally unsettling image with goggle-like eyes and a fanged agnathic (jawless) mouth out of which issue serpents. The figure ominously holds a large spear in its hands. Like the other supernatural, it wears a loincloth, bracelets, and anklets. A second monolith shows an image of an anthropomorphic skeletal figure with crossed fangs and prominent ribs, while a third depicts a crouching monkey.[26]

A small Initial Period center has been found only 2 km away from Kuntur Wasi on a low crest above the modern town of San Pablo. This site, called Cerro Blanco, was established before Kuntur Wasi some time during the early or middle Initial Period, locally called the La Conga period. This period is characterized by ceramics similar to the Early Huacaloma pottery of Cajamarca, and a radiocarbon measurement associated with these materials yielded a date of 1730 BC. The subsequent occupation has ceramics most similar to Late Huacaloma and Pacopampa Pacopampa, and three radiocarbon measurements from these strata averaged 1089 BC.[27] Although this occupation is probably contemporary with the construction of Kuntur Wasi, its pottery assemblage differed from this nearby major center.

Perhaps the most interesting discovery at Cerro Blanco was a 2-m deep shaft tomb cut through strata with La Conga materials. The shaft was extended horizontally to form a narrow burial chamber, where a body covered with red pigment was interred along with seven pottery vessels, none of which were local in style. Judging from the ceramics, the tomb dates to the late Initial Period. One of the grave goods is a late Initial Period Cupisnique-style bottle with its characteristic trapezoidal stirrup and flared spout. Other pieces, like the pedestal-based bowl (compotera), probably came from far northern coastal areas (e.g. Piura). The source of other vessels, like the bird effigy jar illustrated here, is much more difficult to determine. One particularly unusual bowl is decorated with red and cream geometric designs in post-fire paint, and may have been produced by groups on the eastern slopes of the Andes. The buried individual wore a necklace of lapis lazuli beads (probably from what is now northern Chile), and a bead pectoral of Ecuadorian *Spondylus* shell, lapis lazuli, and turquoise-like stone. A carved *Spondylus* pendant of a frontal face was carved in a northern Peruvian style despite its exotic material.[28] Like the materials recovered from the late Initial Period refuse at Kuntur Wasi and Pacopampa, this tomb confirms that long-distance exchange networks were well established in the northern highlands during the Initial Period. The appearance of these items as grave goods suggests the nascent ability of individuals in the highlands to concentrate exotic materials as a form of personal wealth.

Zaña and the Lambayeque headwaters. Explorations and limited excavations in the upper reaches of the Zaña and Lambayeque suggest that the setting of Kuntur Wasi and Cerro Blanco is not unusual. Comparable centers exist in the highland portions of several other northern coastal valleys. In the upper Zaña, for example, eight complexes with monumental architecture have been dated to the Initial Period. None have been investigated in depth but at least one of them, the mound of Macuaco, was initially established during the Late Preceramic and continued as a local center after the adoption of pottery. As in the upper Jequetepeque, the sites in Zaña are generally located on the crest of low hills or ridges above the valley floor, and their most conspicuous feature visible today is the stone terracing which gives a quadrangular shape to these natural features.

Remnants of a tropical montane forest habitat still exist today in the Zaña drainage, wedged between the irrigated *yunga* environment of the mid-valley and the rain-fed *quechua* agricultural lands of the upper valley. Archaeologist Tom Dillehay and ethnohistorian Patricia Netherly believe that this wooded environment may have been more extensive in the past and that it could have provided the coast with tropical resources, such as chonta wood, usually associated with the eastern lowlands or the rainforests of the Ecuadorian coast. Several of the Initial Period centers were located within the forest habitat or at what is now the transition between this zone and the highland agricultural zone, at approximately 2,600 m. The large tiered mound of El Palmo, located at 2,200 m, is currently covered with dense secondary forest. Two of the largest sites in Zaña – La Toma and Uscundal – are located in the transitional zone and, like Layzón and Agua Tapada, face each other across a deep escarpment. The main platform mound at La Toma measures 180 m on a side, and 10–12 m in height.[29]

An even more extensive archaeological complex was investigated by Walter Alva in 1978 in the headwaters of the Chancay River in the Lambayeque drainage, just north of Zaña. Known as Poro-Poro or Udima, this complex comprises at least five concentrations of monumental architecture dispersed over an area of 8 sq. km.[30] It is likely that not all of these are contemporary, but most appear to be early in date. The one sector studied thus far revealed a terraced quadrangular mound fronting a semi-subterranean rectangular plaza. The plaza's construction was exceptional in its use of finely dressed, cut and polished dark stone blocks. A set of massive ashlars, each 2.6 m in height, flanked the broad stone staircase leading from the deeply sunken plaza to the terraced platform mound. On the summit archaeologists discovered a deposit of offerings which included 12 ceramic vessels and 2 stone vessels, all apparently dating from the late Initial Period. Like the burial goods at Cerro Blanco, this votive offering

107 Isometric reconstruction of the fine masonry architecture at Poro Poro in the upper Zaña Valley. Note the presence of the pecked stone "altar" in the lower left-hand corner.

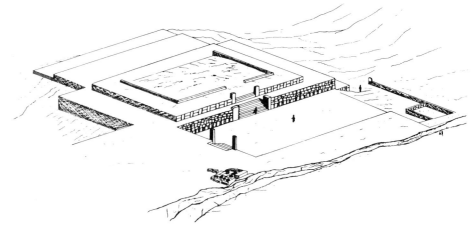

appears to have been composed mainly or solely of items brought from other sites in the highlands, coast, and eastern slopes. The local pottery from Poro-Poro is said to be related to late Initial Period ceramic assemblages from Pacopampa, Kuntur Wasi, and Huacaloma.

Besides the fine masonry plaza, staircase, and platform walls, there is also a cut-stone closed subterranean canal system, accessible by a central perforation in a large polished stone block. Among the distinctive elements of the Poro-Poro public architecture are huge stone blocks from which circular depressions and steps have been hewn. These features have tentatively been interpreted as altars, but their function and date remain largely a matter of speculation at this point.

The quality of the stonework at Poro-Poro rivals that of Chavín de Huántar and later Tiahuanaco. Like some of the early masonry at Pacopampa, La Galgada, Huaricoto, and Cerro Sechín, the platform walls at Poro-Poro were built by alternating large vertical blocks with vertical rows of smaller stones. The material for these constructions came from a quarry bordering the site. Studies there revealed that the stone was partitioned into the desired size by cutting channels into the quarried blocks; once the approximate form was obtained, the stone was shaped by pecking with chert hammerstones, and then polished with abrasives.[31]

Not all of the northern highlands show the same degree of population density or socioeconomic development during the Initial Period. A vast area has yet to show any evidence of large settlements or public architecture for the second millennium BC. While major early sites may be buried beneath natural overburden or later cultural deposits, it is nevertheless difficult to discount completely the results of several systematic studies of this region, all of which have reached the same conclusion.

There is evidence in Huamachuco of a plain ceramic style apparently dating to the Initial Period which is associated with a few small sites. This pottery, used to define the Mamorco Phase, features simple convex-curved bowls, neckless ollas, and necked jars with rims thickened on their exterior. The vessels were often covered with overall red slip, or occasionally decorated with a band of red slip or a simple horizontal line of punctations, around the vessel mouth or on the neckless ollas. This pottery never had more than a local distribution.[32] Additional surveys and excavations by the Polish Scientific Expedition in the upper reaches of the Chicama drainage, and the provinces of the Otuzco and Santiago de Chuco, have failed to encounter any evidence of an occupation belonging to sedentary agriculturalists prior to the Early Horizon.[33] The situation appears to be in stark contrast to that of highland Cajamarca to the north and Ancash to the south, and these differences suggest a pattern of uneven development in the northern highlands during the Initial Period.

Unequal development in the highlands of Huamachuco and Otuzco

As noted in Chapter 3, a series of geographical factors favored interaction between the lowland peoples of the Amazonian drainage and those of the highlands and the coast in the lands now comprising northernmost Peru. The mountains in this region are lower than those further south and the highlands are narrower, so the distance between the coastal plain, the intermontane valleys,

The eastern slopes and beyond

and the tropical forest is relatively short. Finally, heavily forested tributaries of the Marañon and Huallaga rivers protrude deeply into the highland region, offering natural corridors into the Amazonian heartland. The Initial Period groups living along the lower eastern slopes at the transition between the rugged Andes and the vast eastern lowlands appear to have played a crucial role in linking the economies of the highlands and the tropical rainforest. Unfortunately, the high altitude rainforests (*ceja de selva*) which cover the eastern flanks of the Andes remain for the most part *terra incognita* for archaeologists. Nevertheless, research has been carried out in several areas of the eastern slopes and adjacent lowlands, and the results have been fascinating.

First of all, no Initial Period sites with monumental architecture have been discovered in the *ceja de selva* or the adjacent tropical forest, even in those areas which have been surveyed, such as Bagua or the Abiseo National Park.[34] Nor have archaeologists found large sites which could conceivably have contained monumental public architecture of perishable materials. This suggests that Initial Period population density was lower here than in the highland valleys or coast, and that the level of sociopolitical integration was less developed. On the other hand, there is compelling evidence that groups in these zones were in contact with coastal and highland societies during the late Initial Period.

Cueva Manachaki. One of the natural routes east into the tropical lowlands is via the Montecristo Valley, a tributary of the Huallaga located to the east of the Marañon. This valley leads down from the moist *páramo* tundra into thick low cloud forest and ultimately into the eastern lowlands. In 1988, a University of Colorado project carried out investigations in the Manachaqui River, a tributary of the Montecristo. Test excavations focused on a concentration of glacial boulders on the edge of the *páramo*, just above the beginning of the cloud forest. The overhangs of some of the enormous stones would have provided convenient short-term protection in an area which receives precipitation throughout the year. One of these rockshelters, dubbed Cueva Manachaki, yielded a thick deposit of Initial Period pottery above Preceramic layers. The earliest of this pottery consists of thin, strongly carinated bowls, whose closest parallels are with the Valdivia style of Ecuador and Pandanche A material from the Pacopampa area. The later Initial Period material includes numerous modes of decoration known from the northern highland valleys, including incised appliqué bands and zoned punctation. These materials suggest that the Montecristo Valley route into the cloud forest and tropical lowlands was being used by highland peoples during the Initial Period, even though no major settlements were established there.[35]

Bagua. The most intensively investigated area of the lower eastern slopes is the zone of Bagua Chica and Bagua Grande, located at the foot of the Andes along the Utcubamba River. Situated at 522 m, only a short distance from where the Utcubamba drains into the Marañon, this area receives relatively little precipitation (600–800 mm yearly) because of a rain shadow produced by the local topography. Since 1969, Peruvian archaeologists Ruth Shady and Hermilio Rosas have located some 20 sites in this area, several of which were subsequently tested.[36] Evidence of Initial Period settlement occurs near watercourses, on natural or artificial mounds high enough to avoid the annual inundation of the valley floor. All the sites with early occupation are small, and the characteristic pattern of settlement appears to be one of dispersed villages, each comprising 5 to 25 families. The local subsistence system today, and possibly in the past, focuses on manioc, maize, and sweet potatoes. Faunal remains recovered from late Initial Period contexts document the consumption of various kinds of wild game, particularly deer, as well as land snails, frogs, and fresh-water crab.

The Bagua area was described by 16th-century Spanish chroniclers as a gateway into the eastern lowlands, a place frequented by travelers from the southern Ecuadorian highlands, the intermontane valleys of Peru and distant parts of the tropical forest. Judging from archaeological evidence recovered at the sites of Alenya and El Salado, the Bagua area was fully participating in a panregional system of communication by the late Initial Period, if not earlier. At Bagua Grande, pottery was discovered at the bottom of the archaeological deposit that resembled the earliest known ceramics from Pandanche and Huacaloma. This material was associated with the predominant Bagua style pottery, which is a much more elaborate ceramic style comprising simple bowls and necked jars, and lacking the neckless olla so pervasive in the highlands and coast. The Bagua style features three principal modes of decoration: incised motifs with zones painted in white and black on top of an overall red slip; overall white slip with incised patterns; and vertical red bands painted on an unslipped surface. The distinctive Bagua style ceramics have been found over a wide area, including the Initial Period cemeteries of Jequetepeque, sites in the Huánuco area, and most frequently at Pacopampa.[37]

A large quantity of late Initial Period pottery from Pacopampa was recovered from sites in Bagua, and links to groups from the southern Ecuadorian highlands were also strong, as evidenced by similarities in their ceramic styles. Thus, during the second millennium BC, Bagua lay at the crossroads of several overlapping spheres of interaction. Its economic and cultural relations with the northern highlands and coast of Peru, particularly the public center at Pacopampa, were close, but ties were also maintained with the adjacent eastern lowlands and the Ecuadorian highlands of Loja and Cuenca. Through contact with groups at sites such as Bagua, highland and coastal societies could have gained access to the vast array of goods from the rainforest.

The durability of pottery lends itself to archaeological study, but the goods probably sought from Bagua were largely perishable and consequently remain elusive. In early colonial times, the main items of exchange from the eastern slopes and tropical forest were colorful bird feathers, medicinal plants, tropical woods like chonta, vegetable dyes, animal skins, cotton, fruit, honey, parrots, and monkeys. The coca leaf, which grows at altitudes of between 500 m and 1,500 m along the eastern slopes, was also produced for exchange.[38] It is likely that some or all of these items comprised the heart of the Initial Period trade with the peoples of the Bagua area. The exotic pottery recovered at Bagua is best considered as an index of these complex pan-regional relationships, rather than their driving force. One important inference that can be drawn from Bagua's early assemblages is that the Initial Period occupants of the area had a distinctive culture, and do not represent a temporary or permanent colony from the highlands.

The Upper Huallaga and the Callejón de Huaylas

The Huallaga and the Callejón de Huaylas were the heartland of the Kotosh Religious Tradition during the Late Preceramic, and continued to be an important locus of early highland developments during the Initial Period. Many of the old religious centers survived and flourished, and the tradition of building free-standing chambers for making burnt offerings was maintained at several of them, including La Galgada, Huaricoto, and Shillacoto. Although the scale of the highland public constructions never approached that of the contemporary Initial Period monumental architecture on the coast, these small community temples remained the single most important centralizing institution for Initial Period societies in this region.

One of the most impressive Initial Period buildings of the Kotosh Religious Tradition was unearthed in 1967 at the site of Shillacoto (1,920 m) near the confluence of the Huallaga River and its tributary, the Higueras. Waira-jirca pottery was found in the central firepit and on the upper section of the ritual chamber's split-level floor. Built of large dressed stone blocks, this early Initial Period construction is five times the size of the largest of the Mito temple buildings at Kotosh.[39]

No intact late Initial Period temple structure has yet been unearthed at either Shillacoto or Kotosh, and it is therefore unknown whether the Kotosh Religious Tradition continued to survive in the Upper Huallaga. At Kotosh, the building believed to have been a late Initial Period temple was almost totally destroyed by later construction activity. A dedicatory offering of three headless bodies was found beneath its floor.[40]

Several early Initial Period circular ritual chambers similar to their local precursors have been documented at La Galgada. The main focal point of religious activity was on the pyramid summit, where there was an unenclosed firepit in the middle of a two-level court, surrounded on three sides by a low platform and open on the side facing the central stairway and plaza below. With the Initial Period remodeling of the pyramid, the ritual hearth was shifted to a public stage, and its ceremonies would have been visible to an audience far larger than those able to fit into the relatively modest ritual chambers. In the final construction stages at La Galgada, the traditional asymmetric arrangement of multiple ritual chambers on top of the platform was abandoned in favor of a more symmetric ground plan with a strong centerline bisecting the single dominant firepit. This architectural shift has been interpreted as a material expression of the changing patterns of governance, perhaps the subordination of pluralistic authority to a single recognized leadership hierarchy.[41]

It should not be presumed, however, that similar changes transpired throughout this region of the highlands. The longest architectural sequence documented for an early religious center is from Huaricoto in the central Callejón de Huaylas. During the Initial Period, this site featured numerous small ritual chambers with central firepits on top of a low platform sustained by narrow stone terraces. The superstructures of these small buildings often had only a low stone footing to support walls of perishable materials. The buildings varied in form and size, and there is no evidence of increasing architectural standardization or centralization of the overall layout.

Unlike the Initial Period constructions at Shillacoto and La Galgada, none of the Huaricoto ritual chambers are large enough to be considered a "corporate" construction; all could have been built by a large family. Nevertheless, the public

108 The largest known example of a ceremonial chamber of the Kotosh Religious Tradition is from the site of Shillacoto in the Upper Huallaga drainage. Constructed during the early Initial Period, this chamber featured a split-level floor and a central firepit with a stone-lined flue.

109 A small ceremonial chamber of the Kotosh Religious Tradition built at Huaricoto during the late Initial Period.

110 A modeled monkey face is represented on this late Initial Period bowl or mask from Shillacoto. Modeled in reddish-brown clay, the eyes and head of the monkey were covered with graphite painting, and the zones surrounding the eyes were colored with bright yellow post-fire resin paint.

setting of these buildings is clear, and group labor must have been used to create the retaining walls encasing the mound on whose summit the ritual chambers were built. Despite shared beliefs and rituals, the variability and small scale of the asymmetrically arranged chambers at Huaricoto suggest that considerable differences in social structure existed between the peoples of the central Callejón de Huaylas and those of the Tablachaca or Upper Huallaga.[42]

As during the Late Preceramic, the nature of the religious ideology lying behind the Kotosh Religious Tradition is difficult to reconstruct. The presence of coastal shell and transparent quartz flakes in the firepits at Huaricoto suggests that the rites may have been designed to ensure adequate rains and fertility. The figurative iconography on the Initial Period pottery of the Upper Huallaga sheds additional light on the belief system. The most common images are of tropical lowland animals, specifically felines, capuchin and spider monkeys, spectacled owls, and snakes. These representations were drawn from the wild and inspiration for them came from outside the habitat in which Shillacoto and Kotosh are located. Analysis of the faunal remains from the two sites confirms that these animals, native to the cloud forest, did not play any role in daily subsistence. Instead, they must have constituted culturally meaningful symbols or metaphors. It is noteworthy that, in contrast to the animal symbols of the coast, these representations do not emphasize ferocity; there is no exaggerated treatment of fangs, teeth, and claws.[43]

This does not necessarily imply, however, that these highland societies were less violent than their coastal neighbors. A recurrent theme in Waira-jirca and Kotosh style pottery is the naturalistic depiction of human heads, probably representing "trophies" fashioned from decapitated heads. One such trophy head was discovered in a small stone cist at Kotosh. A Kotosh period bottle from a tomb at Shillacoto depicts a modeled face with eyes and mouth closed; the liquid in it would have been poured from its elongated spout, which was

111,112 An undisturbed subterranean stone tomb at Shillacoto, dating to the late Initial Period, yielded an unusual quantity of grave goods, including six ceramic vessels. One of these (*left*) was adorned with a naturalistic depiction of a human head which, judging from its closed eyes, may have corresponded to a severed "trophy" head. Another (*right*) was incised with geometric designs. Both *c.* 13.2 cm high.

113 A votive offering was made at the foot of the main staircase of La Galgada during the Initial Period that included shell disks wrapped in cotton textiles. They were carved in various styles; one provides an antecedent for the later Chavín style, while another seems to be derived from the local Late Preceramic style. Diameters 3.28–3.75 cm.

modeled as hair, as though one was drinking from the head itself. This artistic conceit appears to imitate reality, since a shallow cup carved from a fire-hardened human cranium was recovered in Initial Period layers at Shillacoto.[44]

Although the ritual significance of highland trophy heads has obvious parallels at Cerro Sechín, the continued construction of ritual chambers with firepits as the central feature of public architecture indicates enduring differences in beliefs between the highlands and coast. There were likewise substantial differences in their treatment of the dead, most clearly expressed in the substantial investment of labor for the construction of burial chambers and in the goods buried with the dead. At both Shillacoto and La Galgada, elaborate stone tombs were built during the Initial Period and a rich assortment of grave goods was included with the deceased. Since relatively few undisturbed tombs have been excavated thus far, it is difficult to know whether or not these elaborate tombs were a function of greater social differentiation in the highlands, or reflected beliefs concerning death that differed from the coast; of course, these two possibilities are not incompatible.

One of the most impressive tombs known from the Upper Huallaga was built at Shillacoto during the early Initial Period. It is an overground rectangular stone construction measuring 3.7 m by 3.2 m, and 2 m in height. The interior was plastered with white clay and the lower portion of the room was painted red. The tomb had been disturbed, but the remains of at least seven individuals had been buried in it. Some of the grave goods escaped the looters, including a T-shaped stone ax, a semicircular jet mirror, and two Waira-jirca pottery fragments representing monkeys.[45]

At La Galgada, several disturbed early Initial Period tombs were documented. These "gallery" tombs were constructed outside the mound's revetment walls or in between the revetment walls of two sequential building stages, rather than in old ritual chambers. The typical Initial Period tomb was built of massive parallel stone walls roofed by flat wall-to-wall slabs to form a short, narrow passageway leading to a small dark chamber. One of the final tombs measured 7.3 × 6.5 m and had a height of 4.8 m. Cut stones of up to 1 m in length were used in its walls. The labor involved in constructing these tombs rivaled that expended in the construction of the ritual chambers.[46]

Almost all the funerary buildings at La Galgada show evidence of multiple burials in which men, women, and children of all ages were interred together. A minimum of 27 individuals, for example, had been buried in one tomb. Individuals were buried in both flexed sitting positions and extended on their backs. Despite the disturbance of all the Initial Period tombs, archaeologists have found remnants of decorated textiles, bone pins inlaid with turquoise, necklaces of Pacific shell, and other grave goods. In one tomb there were unique imported items, including a drilled amber pendant, a foreign ceramic vessel decorated with bicephallic snakes, and a meteorite fragment. All the Initial Period tombs yet encountered at La Galgada have been impressive. The labor invested in their construction, their collective nature, and the wealth of their grave goods contrast vividly with the simple pit graves of Initial Period coastal centers.[47]

Excavations at Shillacoto revealed one of the few undisturbed late Initial Period tombs in the Upper Huallaga. This Kotosh period burial was fully subterranean, and had been built by adding walls of cut stone to an already existing curved Waira-jirca wall to form a chamber. A single body was discovered inside, along with 6 complete ceramic vessels, 2 jet mirrors, 4 chipped projectile points, 1 stone figurine (similar to ones made at Cardal), 1 stone vessel, 2 objects of coastal shell, and 5 bone objects, several of which may have been imported from the Chavín de Huántar area.[48] The wealth of this single burial has no documented parallel, although it is rivaled by interments known from Cerro Blanco and Poro-Poro. It is probably significant that rich burials like those described for Shillacoto and La Galgada may not be present in or near the public architecture at smaller sites. For example, no Initial Period burials were encountered at Huaricoto despite extensive excavation.

As on the coast, some of the most valuable items discovered in the highlands occur in dedicatory offerings on public architecture rather than in burials. For example, a tropical forest monkey was found buried on its side in the platform foundation on the pyramid summit at La Galgada, and a cache of precious items was found buried at the foot of the central staircase of the main mound. Wrapped in a cotton cloth, this offering consisted of 124 biconically drilled beads of gray stone, blue stone, and crystal, 5 crystals of iron pyrite, 2 chunks of turquoise, several carved shell disks, and 2 small turquoise and shell mosaics.[49] Analysis of the cloth yielded a radiocarbon measurement of 1621 BC. These carved shells and mosaics are particularly important because of their iconography. One white shell disk depicts bird heads in a style reminiscent of the local Preceramic; the eyes of the birds had been inlaid with red and green stone. Another shows fanged monsters in a style related to the complex iconography of Garagay, Huaca de los Reyes, and Chavín de Huántar; this carving is on Ecuadorian *Spondylus* shell inlaid with red pigment and greenstone. A third shell disk portrays raptorial birds in a style intermediate between the two other disks. Finally, there are cut shell fragments which form a frontal monstrous face, related to the Chavinoid iconography of later times. This early Initial Period cache embodies the transition from the rather formal, schematic Preceramic art style to the more baroque and evocative style of the Chavinoid imagery of the late Initial Period at sites such as Garagay and Caballo Muerto. The early date of this cache does not, however, imply that the Chavín style developed at La Galgada; on the contrary, these images are made on exotic materials in a style found nowhere else at the site. There is no evidence that they were carved locally and it seems more likely that they had been brought to the site from some coastal center.

The high frequency of exotics in the dedicatory offerings and burials at La Galgada and the Upper Huallaga sites, reinforces the impression that long-distance trade was an important element in some highland economies. The imported items found at La Galgada are paralleled in the Upper Huallaga sites by the discovery of parrot bone and Early Shakimu pottery imported from the tropical forest, as well as Pacific mussels and anthracite mirrors. The local pottery styles at Kotosh and Shillacoto show influences from the coast, tropical forest, and other highland areas.[50] In general, major centers in this highland region seem more cosmopolitan than the more massive but somewhat parochial coastal centers, and they are a far cry from the isolated pastoral groups of the Mantaro. The continued viability of sites such as Shillacoto, Kotosh, Huaricoto, and La Galgada during the Initial Period may be due, in part, to their excellent location with respect to natural routes of transportation.

114,115 Among the rich grave goods found at Shillacoto were two bone artifacts carved in a foreign style; they carry the religious imagery of Chavín de Huántar's Old Temple, and they may have been brought from that religious center. The artifacts – shown here from two angles – were highly polished, and the incised designs were filled with a black charcoal-like pigment for greater contrast.

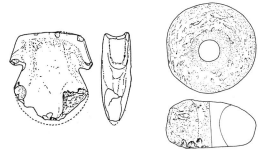

116,117 Among the most common agricultural tools in highland areas such as the Upper Huallaga were the T-shaped ax, most likely used for felling trees, and perforated and polished cobbles that probably served as clod-breakers and/or digging stick weights. The examples here were found in early Initial Period contexts at Kotosh in the Huanuco area.

While trade in exotics may have been of some importance, the economic foundation of Initial Period societies in this part of the highlands appears to have been a combination of farming and hunting. At La Galgada, squash, beans, avocado, and other domesticated cultigens, including a maize cob, were recovered in Initial Period contexts, thanks to the arid conditions. At higher elevations in the Callejón de Huaylas and the Upper Huallaga, evidence for agriculture comes mainly from the artifactual assemblage. There are pecked ring-shaped stones with a central hole, believed to have been used as clod-breakers and/or digging stick weights, and polished ground stone axes with a T-shape form to facilitate hafting. Similar ground-stone axes were still being used by Amazonian farmers to clear the rainforest at the beginning of the 20th century.[51]

Although camelid herding was developed on the Junin *puna* long before the Initial Period, analysis of faunal assemblages from intermontane valley settlements like Kotosh and Huaricoto indicates that wild game continued to be the principal source of meat, at least during the early Initial Period. Analysis of the Waira-jirca Period animal bones at Kotosh revealed that deer outnumbered camelid 3 to 1, and many of the camelids present were guanaco or vicuña. Deer continued to be eaten more often than camelids during the late Initial Period at Kotosh, but the difference narrowed, presumably because of the gradual integration into the economy of domesticated llamas. The same pattern of animal utilization is mirrored in the faunal remains of Huaricoto. Throughout the Initial Period, guinea pigs were a relatively common food, at least at public centers such as Kotosh, where they constituted 16–22 percent of the animals consumed, though actually comprising less than 1 percent of the total animal protein.[52]

The pattern of highland settlement in upper portions of the Huallaga and the Santa valleys remains poorly understood. Nevertheless, it is evident that large sites are often found on the valley floor rather than on the steep slopes or in the open grasslands, and that the overall population levels were high, particularly when compared to the Huamachuco-Otuzco area or the central highlands. In the Huallaga basin, there is a profusion of Initial Period settlements. One unpublished survey located approximately 70 Formative sites, most of them with Initial Period occupation. Besides Shillacoto and Kotosh, the University of Tokyo expedition also discovered early and late Initial Period public constructions at Waira-jirca, 20 km downstream from Kotosh.[53]

There was likewise a substantial Initial Period population in the highland portion of the Santa basin. La Galgada is only one of a host of Initial Period sites on both banks of the Tablachaca River, and a major Initial Period center, La Pampa (1,788 m), has been identified on the Manta River, which is another tributary of the Santa. There are eight large mounds at La Pampa, one of which primarily dates to the early Initial Period. Excavations at another mound at the site revealed a series of contiguous small rooms on a large platform associated with the local early Initial Period ceramic style called Yesopampa. The use of these rooms is unknown, though it was presumably public in nature. What if any relation the public architecture at La Pampa has to the Kotosh Religious Tradition remains to be determined.[54]

In the Callejón de Huaylas, there are numerous early mounds similar in size and location to Huaricoto. Such mounds are visible at almost every juncture of the Santa with a small tributary, and at sites such as Uchuccoto Initial Period sherds can be found eroding from the mounds. Unfortunately, the character of these sites is unknown. The much larger mounds of Chupacoto near Huaylas and Tumshucayco near Caraz probably have significant Initial Period constructions buried beneath later occupations. Local residents near Chupacoto encountered two stone sculptures with a strong resemblance to the carvings from Cerro Sechín. The use of stone sculptures at Chupacoto raises the possibility that some groups in the Callejón de Huaylas may have broken with the Kotosh Tradition during the Initial Period and adopted a religious ideology more like that of contemporary societies on the coast.[55]

Less ambiguous influence of coastal religious traditions on Initial Period highland groups exists for the Callejón de Conchucos, a series of fertile valleys to the east of the Callejón de Huaylas on the other side of the continental divide, in which Chavín de Huántar is located. The Initial Period developments at this famous site will be considered in more detail in the next chapter.

Many of the large highland sites discussed in this section are located at relatively low elevations (ie. below 3,000 m) and this has led Japanese scholar, Yoshio Onuki, to propose that highland agriculturalists of the Initial Period favored the lower intermontane valley lands, particularly those in the *yunga* environment.[56] Unfortunately, a problem in evaluating this idea and in studying Initial Period highland settlement systems in general is that many occupations of this age are covered by later deposits. For example a deeply buried Initial Period village was uncovered at Piruru (3,800 m). It consisted of small circular houses of stone and wattle-and-daub.[57] At this point, it is impossible to predict how many other Initial Period villages and public centers lie beneath later occupations, particularly in the heavily occupied *quechua* and *suni* zones favored by later prehistoric cultures.

Moreover, it remains uncertain what proportion of the total supporting population actually lived at the highland centers with public architecture on the valley bottoms. Highland farmers dependent primarily on rainfall must exploit a wide range of production zones to provide a balanced and varied diet. Consequently, in many highland areas today and at various times in the past, populations are dispersed over the landscape in homesteads, hamlets, and small villages. Groups are drawn together sporadically in larger centers on the valley floors, usually only for short periods, at times of public or religious celebrations, and for the acquisition of exotic goods. It is possible that Initial Period societies in this area may likewise have had a dispersed settlement pattern with only a small proportion living full-time at major centers like Shillacoto. Whether any population was present throughout the year at small shrines such as Huaricoto remains to be determined.

One conclusion that does seem well established is that the groups in these intermontane valleys were culturally diverse and organized into a multitude of small-scale locally independent societies. The non-hierarchical settlement pattern consisting of equivalent closely spaced centers implies this, as does the variety of coeval cultural patterns. For example, studies of the ceramic styles in the upper Santa and Huallaga drainages have documented the existence of numerous discrete styles during both the early and late Initial Periods. In the early Initial Period the Yesopampa style at La Pampa featured brushing and narrow bands of appliqué fillets with depressions, while the Toril style at Huaricoto favored thick appliqué lugs with incisions, and Kotosh utilized an enormous decorative repertoire, particularly bands of zoned hatching. These local styles continued to evolve in different directions during the late Initial Period, so that by the time zoned hatching was adopted at Huaricoto, it had already lost its popularity in the Huallaga, where new techniques such as post-fire painting in graphite had come into vogue.[58] Similar contrasts appear to have existed in house forms and other aspects of material culture.

The central highlands

The intermontane valleys and open grasslands of the central highlands were inhabited by societies very different from those of their coastal neighbors and highland neighbors to the north, both in terms of the economy and their level of sociocultural integration. Monumental architecture has not been discovered, nor is there evidence of large nucleated centers. On the contrary, populations throughout the region appear to be light and dispersed. Investigators were surprised to find that the only abundant evidence of Initial Period occupation occurs above 3,800 m in the *puna* environment, rather than in the deep highland valleys.

The largest valley in the central highlands is the Mantaro, which extends for over 100 km. Today, as in Inca times, it is the demographic core of this region and it has consequently been the object of intensive archaeological exploration. A systematic survey of the upper Mantaro, in which the modern cities of Tarma and Jauja are located, documented 160 pre-Hispanic sites. Remarkably, the only site apparently occupied during the Initial Period is Ataura (3,400 m), a 2-hectare site on a terrace above the valley floor. Its earliest cultural layer appears to date to the late Initial Period, and its ceramics share stylistic features with pottery assemblages from Lurín and Chillon, including small stamped circles, zoned punctation, and wide incisions. This early occupation at Ataura is poorly understood because it is buried by Early Horizon strata.[59] In the same valley further south, surveys of the Huancayo area have revealed only one other small Initial Period site, Pirwapukio. The earliest ceramics from Pirwapukio are dissimilar to those at Ataura, and probably have more in common with materials from the south-central highlands.[60]

The absence of early Initial Period occupation in the Mantaro Valley and the tiny population during the late Initial Period are difficult to explain, particularly when one considers the substantial populations existing at the same time in more northern highland valleys. It is possible to speculate that the greater aridity and more frequent frosts of the Mantaro Valley made it less attractive to early agriculturalists than these other areas, but clearly additional research is needed. By way of contrast, the vast well-watered grasslands high above the Mantaro supported a significant population of pastoralists throughout the Initial Period.

One survey in the San Pedro de Cajas area located 15 early ceramic sites in small caves and rockshelters. A dozen of these were situated between 4,200 m and 4,400 m and two others were at even higher elevations. These spots would have been selected for their proximity to sources of permanent water and good pastureland. Many of the caves had been used by Preceramic populations, and considerable cultural continuity existed between the Initial Period herders and their hunter-gatherer predecessors.[61]

One of these sites, Telarmachay (4,420 m), has been completely excavated by a team led by French scholar Danièle Lavallée.[62] This rockshelter is 14 m wide and only 2.5 m deep, and it is unlikely that such cramped quarters could have housed more than a single family or other small group. During the Initial Period, there was little effort to modify the cave. Two hearths were used near the mouth of the rockshelter, one apparently for cooking with ceramic vessels and another for baking with earth and heated stones. The latter technique, called *pachamanca*, is still popular in the highlands today. In front of the cave are the remains of a prehistoric corral and, judging from the faunal remains, the inhabitants of Telarmachay were camelid herders. Unlike the situation at sites like Kotosh, the overwhelming majority of the bone remains (89 percent) belonged to llamas and alpacas. Many of these animals were newborn, their deaths probably the result of diseases spread in the corrals where they were enclosed at night. Domesticated camelids give birth between December and April when pasture is plentiful and frosts are rare, and Telarmachay may have been occupied only seasonally each summer by transhumant pastoralists.[63]

The sheer quantity of animal bones recovered at Telarmachay is much greater than would be expected, even if the site was permanently occupied. It has been argued, therefore, that the meat and other animal products produced there may have been intended for consumption elsewhere. Many of the stone and bone tools at Telarmachay were apparently used to prepare hides. Projectile points are even more common in Initial Period levels than in Preceramic strata, constituting 55 percent of the lithic assemblage. However, wear pattern analysis indicates that many were used for cutting and it has been suggested that these "points" were actually part of the butchery kit. This conclusion is consistent with the scarcity of hunted animals in the refuse; the locally available taruca deer constitutes a mere 6 percent of the bones, and vicuña only about 2 percent.[64]

During their stay in the *puna* caves, the pastoralists took advantage of the wild resources, gathering seeds and roots and occasionally hunting viscachas, deer, and birds for a change of diet. The results of botanical analyses at Telarmachay have yet to be published, but a study of the Initial Period plant remains at the nearby cave of Pachamachay (4,300 m) indicated a vegetable diet very similar to that consumed by the local Preceramic people. It consisted of the seeds of chenopodium and amaranthus, the fruits of the opuntia cactus, green rushes, and other wild plants. No newly introduced domesticated cultigens were present despite the numerous grinding stones for food preparation. All the plants eaten could have been gathered within 5 km of the cave.[65]

The situation in the San Pedro de Cajas area is typical of the Junín *puna* and the entire high tableland where the Mantaro originates. There is evidence of Initial Period occupations at hundreds of high-altitude caves, but the small groups that stayed at these spots were probably connected with villages and hamlets at slightly lower elevations where herding could be supplemented by lacustrian and perhaps horticultural products. The pioneer of archaeological research in the *puna*, Ramiro Matos, discovered four early village sites along the shores of Lake Junín (4,100 m): Ondores, Warmipukio, Pari-Coral, and Sacra-Familia. At least two, and perhaps all, of these were occupied during the Initial Period. None of these sites are larger than 3 hectares and none have yielded evidence of public constructions. Limited excavations have unearthed the remains of rustic circular stone houses and corrals. Pari-Coral is comprised of several dispersed patio groups, each consisting of four to six buildings around an open central space. A fifth small Initial Period settlement was established 4 km from Lake Junin next to the natural salt springs of San Blas, and presumably provided the Junin area with a local alternative to ocean salt.

The high-altitude herders of Junin used crude neckless globular cooking pots and, more rarely, simple open bowls. Decoration on pottery is infrequent and usually consists of incised bands of zoned punctation on the exterior of the pots. The dating of the earliest pottery in this remote area is nearly the same as that on the coast: the early ceramic strata at San Blas and Huargo near La Union yielded measurements of 2288 BC and 1908 BC respectively. At Telarmachay, a radiocarbon measurement of 1840 BC was produced by a sample from the second Initial Period layer; the lowest ceramic-bearing stratum has yet to be dated.[66]

The relationship of these *puna* dwellers to the valley settlements and the more distant coastal centers does not appear to have been a close one. In later times, these groups of herders played an active role in moving goods between the tropical forest, highland valleys, and coast, and more extensive investigation of open village sites may show that such activities were already underway during the Initial Period. However, the absence of major centers of public constructions during this period points to a relatively simple kin-based society, independent of and very different from their coastal neighbors.

The same general pattern of settlement also characterizes more southern sections of the Mantaro drainage. The Ayacucho Valley, formed by one of the southern tributaries of the Mantaro, was the focus of intensive research by the Ayacucho-Huanta Archaeological Botanical Project from 1969 to 1972.[67] The region was systematically surveyed and excavations were carried out in all the ecological zones. These investigations revealed evidence of high-elevation settlements used seasonally by semi-nomadic llama pastoralists during the Initial Period. These herders were apparently linked to small villages where tubers and other high-altitude crops were grown. A small number of hamlets existed at lower elevations where, judging from the macro-botanical analysis, agriculturalists grew beans, squash, gourds, lucuma, and probably quinoa, and supplemented their diet by hunting animals and collecting wild plants. However, the evidence available suggests that most of the Initial Period population in Ayacucho was centered in the higher elevations near the grasslands, and that agriculture merely supplemented a basically pastoral economy. Despite the availability of the appropriate technology and cultigens, intensive agriculture in the valley remained a relatively unattractive alternative for most people.

The notable absence of public architecture and art throughout the central highlands during the Initial Period can be understood as a function of the dominant economic strategy, and ultimately as a product of decisions about the best way to exploit the environment. The pasturelands of this region are particularly extensive and rich and, as we saw in Chapter 2, the shift from a hunting and gathering regime specializing in wild camelids to a herding and farming strategy focusing on domesticated camelids and tubers, appears already to have taken place by the Late Preceramic. The success of the herding/high-altitude farming strategy in this rugged environment accounts for its persistence into the Initial Period. At the same time, dependence on these high-altitude resources may have constrained the rate of population growth, due both to the semi-nomadic lifestyle and to the limited carrying capacity of *puna* herding when it is not complemented (through exchange or reciprocity) by valley agricultural systems. The comparatively low population density of the central highlands was a major reason for the relatively low level of sociopolitical integration that characterized this region during the Initial Period. Moreover, the greater aridity and frequent frosts of the Mantaro Valley probably made agriculture in this zone a less attractive alternative to pastoralism and high-altitude cultivation than in the northern highlands, where rainfall was more plentiful, frosts were rare, and camelid herding was not yet a viable option.

While the peoples of the central highlands differed culturally and organizationally from their more advanced neighbors to the north and west, they were in touch through trade. Raw materials from the central highlands occasionally appear in the large public centers of the coast during the Initial Period, and it was through such exchange networks that these small-scale groups acquired some exotics as well. Obsidian from the south-central highland source of Quispisisa in the Huancavelica region has been discovered in small quantities at centers such as Garagay, Cardal, and the earliest occupation at Chavín de Huántar; and red cinnabar powder, probably from deposits near Huancavelica, has been found covering the dead at Cupisnique cemeteries on the north coast.[68]

The beginnings of gold metallurgy

While peripheral to the development of early Andean civilization, at least one of the innovations in the central highlands ultimately had a significant impact on the more northern cultures. The first evidence of metallurgy appeared unexpectedly during excavations at Waywaka, a small Initial Period village in the south-central highlands of Andahuaylas. Dozens of tiny sheets of thin gold foil were recovered in association with early Muyu Moqo style ceramics that date to between 1900 and 1450 BC. Nine of the pieces of hammered gold were found in a burial clutched in the hands of an adult male along with tiny lapis lazuli beads, and another piece of gold had been placed in the mouth of the dead man. The subsequent discovery of a metal worker's kit indicates that the precious metal was actually produced at Waywaka. It is possible that bits of gold collected from river beds or other deposits were hammered into these delicate sheets. The tools used in this process were a mushroom-shaped anvil of fine-grained green porphyry and a series of three small polished stone hammers differing in weight and hardness.[69]

No other discoveries of gold foil or precious metal artifacts have been made at Initial Period sites in the central Andes and apparently the technology did not spread or develop further for nearly a millennium. This pattern of early experimentation in gold sheet production at Waywaka is analogous to the somewhat later Initial Period production of hammered copper sheet on the central coast, discussed in the previous chapter. The Waywaka find is important because it shows that, perhaps because of its color, shine, or some other quality, gold had already been singled out as a substance of special significance by early Andean peoples.

118 Reconstruction of the way in which the hammers and anvils discovered at Waywaka might have been used to produce the tiny sheets of hammered gold foil during the Initial Period.

5

The Early Ceremonial Center of Chavín de Huántar

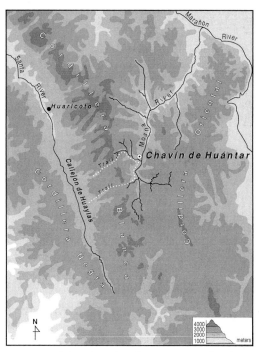

119 Map showing the terrain of Chavín de Huántar and the routes across the glaciated Cordillera Blanca.

Chavín de Huántar appears to have been founded during the late Initial Period, *c.* 900 BC. The large temple, which is the most conspicuous testimony of this early occupation, differs from the public buildings of the highland Kotosh Religious Tradition in layout, architectural elements, and masonry. The distinctive stone sculptures which adorned its walls and galleries were emblematic of its position as an independent center of highland culture, which rivaled the grandeur of large northern highland centers such as Pacopampa or Kuntur Wasi or coastal centers like Huaca de los Reyes and Garagay. Although Chavín de Huántar was by no means the largest of these late Initial Period centers, I believe it was probably the most beautiful and almost certainly the most unusual.

No one knows the meaning of the word Chavín, but Chavín de Huántar is only one of several towns so named. Tello thought the term could come from the Carib word *chavi* for feline or tiger, while Luis Lumbreras suggests a derivation from the Quechua term *chawpin* meaning "in the center," a word which comes close to summing up the site's cosmological significance.[1] Neither etymology is convincing from a linguistic perspective and for most scholars the problem remains unresolved.

Chavín de Huántar is located at the base of the eastern slopes of the Cordillera Blanca at an elevation of 3,150 m. The site occupies the bottomland adjacent to where the deeply entrenched Huachecsa River flows into the broader Mosna. Below Chavín, the Mosna River merges with the Huari River to form the Pukcha, which in turn empties into the Marañón, one of the principal tributaries of the Amazon. The trip down to the *ceja de selva* environment along the Marañon is a treacherous one, taking up to six days on foot. The journey to the arid Pacific coast is no less difficult, since it requires crossing the Cordillera Blanca into the Callejón de Huaylas and then traveling over the Cordillera Negra into one of the coastal valleys between Pativilca and Casma. This trip also takes about six days, so Chavín de Huántar is roughly midway between the coastal plain and the tropical forest.

The terrain surrounding Chavín de Huántar is well-suited to a mixed agricultural system of high-altitude farming and camelid herding. There is abundant precipitation (annual average 856 mm) which presently supports rainfall agriculture on the valley slopes. Supplementary water from the glacial lakes and snowcapped peaks of the Cordillera Blanca is used to irrigate the narrow valley floor. However, seasonal frosts make it difficult to grow more than one crop per year, even with irrigation, and above 3,800 m the freezing temperatures preclude the cultivation of crops except in a few sheltered spots. Fortunately, the natural grasslands between 3,800 m and 4,800 m provide a rich habitat for camelids, deer, and other wild game. Within a 10 km radius of Chavín de Huántar, roughly 36 percent of the land is currently devoted to herding, while 35 percent is dedicated to the production of high-altitude tubers (potatoes, oca, ullucu, mashua), native grains (quinoa, achis), lupines (tarwi), and crops introduced after the Spanish Conquest (barley, wheat, peas). Only 4 percent of the land is suitable for growing maize, fruit, and other irrigated crops popular in lower intermontane valleys. Irrigation is largely confined to the valley floor and has probably never been more than secondary importance to the local subsistence economy. The three major production zones of Chavín de Huántar are compressed into a small area, and it is only a two or three hour walk from the narrow valley floor to the broad expanses of the *puna*.[2] This topography facilitated the integration of a broad range of agricultural activities into a nearly self-sufficient subsistence system during the late Initial Period and Early Horizon.

The Chavín de Huántar area is attractive from an agricultural perspective, but it is not really exceptional. Similar settings exist elsewhere in Ancash and Huanuco, many of which have larger tracts of farmland and better soil. Thus the productive characteristics of Chavín de Huántar do not in themselves explain the construction of a particularly impressive late Initial Period public center. Nor are there mineral deposits or other rare natural resources near by which might have stimulated these developments.

On the other hand, few locations are better situated than Chavín de Huántar in relation to natural routes of transportation. The Cordillera Blanca runs parallel to the coastline, forming the continental divide, and this 180-km long span presents a formidable barrier to movement. Almost all of it is glaciated and there are only ten snow-free passes across it. These narrow passes have elevations of 4,700–4,850 m, while the surrounding peaks commonly exceed 5,700 m. Two of the southernmost passes, Raria and Cahuish, are on alternate branches of a route leading down the Mosna from its headwaters. A third pass, Yanashayash, is on another route leading into the central Mosna from Olleros, in the southern Callejón de Huaylas. There are no other direct routes between the Mosna Valley and the Callejón de Huaylas. Chavín de Huántar was established at the juncture of these two routes and it provides a natural gateway into the rich intermontane valleys collectively referred to as the Callejón de Conchucos and ultimately into the vast Amazonian lowlands further east.

Coca, chili pepper, salt, dried fish, and other items must have been of importance for the late Initial Period inhabitants of Chavín de Huántar, but they could not be locally produced. Their acquisition would have been greatly facilitated by Chavín's strategic location along these natural corridors of trade. Moreover, even a small population would have been able to control commerce. This could have been done either at the northern edge of Chavín de Huántar where the valley floor constricts to a width of only a few hundred meters, or next to the temple at the Huachecsa River crossing, which is impassable most of the year. Thus, the early settlement of Chavín de Huántar was in an excellent position to gain access to exchange networks linking distant production zones, and to profit by regulating or controlling the use of these routes by other groups.

The location of Chavín de Huántar can also be interpreted as a response to ideological as well as economic considerations. For example, in traditional Quechua communities the juncture of two rivers or two trails is referred to by the term *tinkuy*.[3] In its broadest sense, this term refers to the harmonious meeting of opposing forces. It is possible that the positioning of Chavín de Huántar may have expressed its association with the principles of balance and prosperity.

The large size of the earliest public constructions at Chavín de Huántar implies the existence of a sizable local population during the late Initial Period. Thus far, investigations on the valley floor surrounding the temple area have revealed only a small settlement probably consisting of fewer than 500 people. On the other hand, there is evidence for dispersed coeval villages and small hamlets, like Pójoc and Waman Wain, scattered in the *quechua* and *suni* zones around Chavín.[4] It appears that Chavín de Huántar began as a public center constructed by and for the surrounding rural population. The temple would have provided a central focus for integrating this local population into a single cohesive society, and the temple authorities undoubtedly influenced the social and economic relations of these groups through the manipulation of religious beliefs. Indeed, the role of priests as intermediaries with the supernatural realm was probably not incompatible with their pivotal position in more secular affairs. For example, the temple leadership was in a favorable position to enter into exchange relationships with analogous centers in distant areas in order to acquire exotic goods for local distribution. Some of these goods, such as the distinctive pink *Spondylus* shell from Ecuador, were impossible for individual farmers to acquire, and the temple's success in this regard may have been perceived as a validation of their sacred authority, as well as a boon from a practical standpoint. The importance of religious ideology as an organizing principle in Initial Period societies has been emphasized by numerous scholars; and many of the unusual features of the Chavín de Huántar temple become more intelligible if we accept the proposition that fear and awe of the supernatural, combined with social sanctions based on religious ideology, produced a degree of coercion later achieved by institutionalized force.

The Old Temple

The monumental constructions of Chavín de Huántar display a complex pattern of additions and renovations. Based on observations of abutting walls, superimposition of features, and changes in architectural style and building technique, it is possible to distinguish between the original late Initial Period architectural complex, referred to as the Old Temple, and the subsequent Early Horizon remodelings of the complex, sometimes referred to collectively as the New Temple. The Old Temple is associated with *in situ* sculpture (which has not fallen or been reused), whose style has been designated as Phase AB by John Rowe.[5]

The focus of the late Initial Period temple at Chavín de Huántar was a U-shaped pyramidal platform enclosing a sunken circular courtyard. For descriptive purposes, the main building can be divided into the north wing, which measures 45 m by 75 m, the central wing, 29 × 44 m, and the south wing, 35 × 71 m. As these measurements indicate, the original U was probably asymmetric, with the north wing slightly larger than its southern counterpart. The central wing rises 11 m above ground level and is lower than the northern

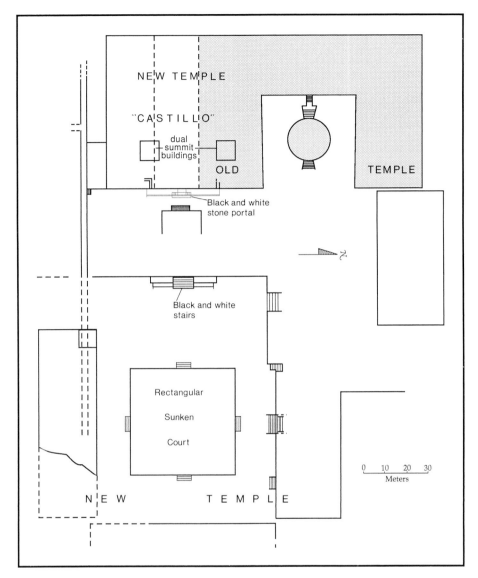

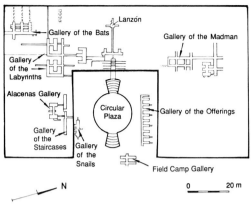

120 The Old Temple (*above*) and some of its interior gallery complexes, and (*left*) a simplified outline showing its relationship to the much larger New Temple (see Chapter 6).

wing which is 14 m high, and the southern wing which reaches 16 m in height at its summit.[6] The structure is freestanding and its exterior face inclines slightly inward, perhaps to maximize the stability of the interior fill. The facade of this massive stone construction would have towered above the heads of all visitors.

The trails along the Mosna and Huachecsa rivers lead directly to the Chavín de Huántar monumental complex, but these paths channel visitors to the western, southern or northern faces of the temple, where there are no visible entrances. Thus, a seemingly impenetrable four-story high wall of cut stone decorated with monstrous heads and elaborately carved cornices would have been the first sight encountered by a visitor arriving at Chavín de Huántar.

The exterior walls of the Old Temple were built of alternating rows of thick and thin horizontal blocks of granite, sandstone, and limestone. The slabs of fieldstone were placed vertically and horizontally between the larger stones to reinforce the clay mortar binding the walls. Approximately 10 m above the

121 Larger-than-life sculpted heads projected from upper portions of the temple walls, seemingly in defiance of gravity. The monstrous tenoned head illustrated here is the only one that remains *in situ*. Height 83 cm.

ground hung a series of anthropomorphic and zoomorphic stone heads, frequently displaying contorted expressions, nasal extrusions, and fangs. These sculptures were distributed along the upper wall in a horizontal row at intervals of roughly 3 m, and probably encircled the entire Old Temple. They were carved at a scale more than double that of human heads, and their individual weight would have sometimes exceeded half a ton. Nevertheless, they gave the appearance of being suspended high in the air without means of support. This optical illusion was produced by a relatively simple building technique: on the back of the sculpted heads are undecorated rectangular projections called tenons, about 70 cm long, which were inserted into a hole in the masonry facing. The pressure from the wall above the tenons countered the weight of the sculpted portions protruding from the parament.[7]

The upper section of the Old Temple is badly damaged, but it appears that a row of ashlars carved on their underside and outer edge were similarly inserted into the parament as a cornice. Like the tenoned heads, they had a plain portion which fitted into the building and supported the salient sculpture. None of these cornice stones was encountered *in situ*, but most scholars believe they were placed about a meter above the tenoned heads. They are frequently recovered at the foot of the temple walls along with the tenoned heads, apparently having fallen when the upper edge of the Old Temple collapsed.[8]

The U-shaped pyramidal platform of the Old Temple opens to the east towards the Mosna River and the rising sun. It faces away from the areas of habitation, roads and the other elements of the secular world. Measurements taken by Gary Urton, an expert on the archaeoastronomy of the Andes, indicate that the buildings were not laid out in relation to the cardinal directions as some earlier investigators believed, but instead have an orientation of 103°31', more than 13 degrees clockwise of due east. This may be related to celestial phenomena. Urton observes, for example, that the axis on the west (283°28') is remarkably near the azimuth of the setting of the Pleiades around the time of its construction (283°41'), if one postulates the use of a hypothetical flat horizon such as that used by native groups like the Hopi. If the actual horizon of Chavín de Huántar was utilized, the most likely correlation is with the setting of the nadir or anti-zenith sun (280°35').[9]

The Mosna River, which is 12 m wide, defines the eastern limit of the ceremonial architecture and, like virtually all highland and coastal rivers, it is not navigable. Thus, the layout of the Old Temple effectively ruled out a direct approach to the area of sacred activity. After their first exposure to the temple's impenetrable facade, worshipers would have had to walk around the truncated pyramid down to the low-lying western bank of the Mosna, and then ascend a series of low stone-faced platforms. From these terraces, the open end of the U-shaped temple would have been visible against the backdrop of the Huachecsa River and the Cordillera Blanca, including the traditionally sacred mountain of Huantsán.[10]

Ceremonial architecture, like the Old Temple, is both a frame or stage for religious rituals and a physical expression of the ideology itself, a sort of cosmological model. Earlier in this volume, I referred to William Isbell's interpretation of the U as a metaphor for the mediation of dual opposing forces, represented by the right and left wings. Donald Lathrap has further suggested that this form was conceived as a way of focusing sacred energy in order to

122 An inset staircase of cut stone blocks leads from the Circular Plaza to an open landing on the eastern face of the Old Temple. Note the small stone-lined drainage canal that runs under the staircase and beneath the paved floor of the plaza.

control it for the benefit of the center's adherents. The flux of this energy between the sky and the underworld can be envisioned as a vertical axis, or an *axis mundi*, passing through the center of the Old Temple.[11] If this interpretation is correct, the space enclosed within the U and the center of the central wing would probably have been loci of particular importance.

The Circular Plaza

For decades, the enclosed area within the U appeared to be an open square court, some 40 m on a side. However, in 1972 a project directed by Luis Lumbreras discovered a circular plaza set into the middle of the square court.[12] The plaza floor is sunk 2.5 m below the court surface and wedge-shaped staircases provide access to this semi-subterranean feature from the east and the west. With a diameter of only 21 m, the plaza could not have comfortably held more than 550 people, and was probably designed for even fewer.

The stonework of the Circular Plaza is much finer than that of the adjacent platforms. The plaza's interior facing consists of carefully cut and polished stone

123 The Circular Plaza was decorated with a stone frieze depicting a procession of mythical figures and jaguars moving towards the central staircase. Two of the figures blow shell trumpets (known as *pututu* or *huayllaqquepa*).

arranged in nine courses. Two thin horizontal slabs alternate with single rows of larger rectangular slabs. This retaining or revetment wall supports the stone and earth rubble fill that makes up the core of the surrounding square court. Most of the wall was undecorated, but carved slabs were unearthed alongside the two staircases. A 10-cm high step or plinth rings the interior of the plaza wall. The floor of the plaza was paved with a patchwork of irregular light yellowish slabs bisected by a strip of black slabs which delineates the east–west axis of Old Temple and connects the two staircases of the plaza. An impression of a large fossilized gastropod was included in the floor. The conspicuous inclusion of this particularly large fossil must have been intentional, especially since fossilized remains of this kind are not found locally.[13]

The eastern stairway of the Plaza was flanked by sculptures of four profile felines – two on the small horizontal rectangular slabs in the lower wall and two on the larger vertical rectangular slabs above them. The main concentration of stone carvings was found next to the western staircase at the foot of the Old Temple. The northwest quadrant of the Circular Plaza was completely excavated by Lumbreras and 13 profile representations of jaguars from the lower course of rectangular slabs were recovered. These slabs were carved in identical pairs and it is likely that there were originally seven pairs of these felines on each side of the staircase. In both quadrants, the jaguars were arranged as if in procession towards the main staircase.

Above the row of profile felines is an analogous row of larger vertical rectangular slabs representing pairs of anthropomorphic figures dressed in elaborate costumes. Like the row of jaguars, the anthropomorphic figures likewise appear to have been carved in duplicated pairs and they are shown facing, or perhaps marching towards, the white granite stairway of the Old Temple. On one sculpture, an individual wears ear pendants and a crown-like headdress with a jaguar tail hanging from it. He carries a shield and blows a *Strombus* shell trumpet or *pututu*. The *pututu* is a traditional Andean instrument still played in Cuzco and other parts of the southern highlands at the beginning and end of public ceremonies. In another carving, a fanged individual grasps a ribbed staff or club. In modern Quechua communities of the southern highlands, the staff is the principal emblem of authority. The staff represented in the Plaza sculpture closely resembles a stalk of San Pedro, a columnar cactus whose flower blooms in the night. Its stalk has a high content of mescaline, an active alkaloid which produces hallucinations, and a potent brew made from San Pedro is used in evening curing sessions by traditional folk healers of the Peruvian north coast.[14]

The Old Temple appears to be built of large cut stone blocks. In reality, the platform consists mainly of earth and rock fill. The cut masonry facing conceals this unexceptional core, while serving as a retaining wall for the unstable mass. The paucity of windows and doorways in the finished stone parament underscores the impression of stark solidity presented by the Old Temple. In actuality, the pyramidal platforms of this complex are honey-combed with a maze of narrow passageways, subterranean chambers, ventilation ducts, and canals. Tello estimated that these hollow interior features make up a quarter of the building's volume.[15] Underground passageways and chambers are found on three sides of the Circular Plaza beneath the floor of the rectangular court, and numerous unseen stone-lined canals run beneath the court and plaza, eventually draining into the Mosna River.

The galleries

The subterranean passageway-chamber complexes, referred to as galleries, are one of the most unusual features of the Chavín de Huántar temple. In general, the passageways and rooms are narrow, rarely more than 1.1 m in width. They are roofed with flat rectangular slabs, measuring 1.5–3.0 m in length, 50–100 cm in width, and 40–60 cm in thickness. The roofing slabs usually rested on top of the walls, but in a few galleries they were supported by stones projecting from the upper walls. The galleries were generally built of rough, horizontally coursed walls and packed earth floors.[16] They vary in height and width but can be walked through comfortably in single file. They were definitely not designed to accommodate large groups of people. Most galleries include several floor levels connected to each other by short stairways.

There is no source of natural lighting within the subterranean passageways, and though grease or resin torches could have been used, the frequent right-angle turns and changes in floor level would have reduced the effectiveness of artificial lighting. The result of this unusual design is a maze-like ambience in which the visitor cannot relate to the world outside the temple, or even to the passageways through which one has entered. The intention seems to have been to create a sense of confusion and disorientation in which the individual is severed from the outside world. Only a fraction of the gallery system has been explored: much of it is inaccessible because of collapsed walls and roof beams, while other parts were buried by the 1945 landslide or intentionally sealed in antiquity.

The most important of the passageway complexes in the Old Temple is the Lanzón Gallery. It is located in the center of the central wing of the U and is today

124 The lower register of the Circular Plaza frieze features seven matching pairs of jaguars on each side of the western staircase.

125 The upper register features matching pairs of mythical figures, including this fanged anthropomorphic individual with claws. The figure holds a staff resembling stalks of the mescaline-bearing San Pedro cactus.

126,127 (*Below*) The supreme deity of Chavín de Huántar was represented in a large stone idol known today as the Lanzón, kept deep in the interior galleries of the Old Temple. (*Right*) The Lanzón constitutes an *axis mundi* with its upper section set into the roof of a cruciform chamber and its base deeply embedded in the floor.

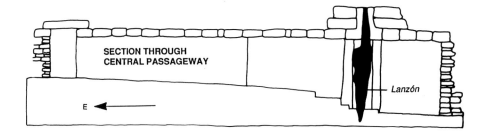

SECTION THROUGH
CENTRAL PASSAGEWAY

E ←

Lanzón

reached by a doorway to the south of the central staircase. This was not the original entrance and it is probable that the entrance to this gallery, like the better preserved ones, would have been hidden from the eyes of the visitors in the Circular Plaza below, perhaps leading down from the roof. At present, one enters into a wide passageway or vestibule parallel to the exterior parament. Two small cells are symmetrically arranged at its northwest and southwest extremes. Branching off from the middle of the vestibule and directly behind the central staircase is a long passageway (11.9 m in length) which is so narrow that it can only be traversed single file. It leads back into a cruciform chamber, 1.8 × 1.8 m; three short passageways radiate from its western, southern, and northern sides, and the long passageway enters at its eastern extreme. On the walls of the chamber are projecting stones from which torches or ritual paraphernalia could have been hung. The niches in these walls could have been used for offerings or for temporary storage of ritual items. The roof of this unique central room is formed by two rows of slabs supported by projections from the wall. The resulting crude corbeled arch permits a room height of 3.5 m, almost double the norm at Chavín de Huántar.

In the center of the chamber is a carved granite shaft with a notched upper section. This 4.53-m tall stone is carved with the image of a fanged anthropomorphic deity. Its top was fitted into a space in the gallery ceiling and braced by cut roofing slabs, while the pointed base was set deeply into the floor of the chamber.[17] Placed in this position when the Old Temple was built, its incorporation into the structure of the building prevented its removal from this original context. The sculpture's location at the center of the central wing of the Old Temple, along with its size, artistry, and iconography all indicate that this was the principal cult image of the Old Temple.

Julio C. Tello called this sculpture the Lanzón because of its lance-like shape. However, the use of the name here does not imply our acceptance of this unlikely analogy. Alternatively, it has been suggested that the unusual form of the Lanzón is based on the Andean foot-plow (*chaki taklla*), the basic agricultural tool of the highlands.[18] Whatever its original significance, the sculpting of notched shafts or prismatic stones was reserved for the most sacred religious images at Chavín de Huántar (and also among the early pre-Hispanic cultures of the southern highlands).

The Lanzón faces east along the axis of the Old Temple. Its right arm is raised with open palm of the hand exposed, and its left arm is lowered with the back of the hand visible. This pose eloquently expresses the role of the deity as a mediator of opposites, a personification of the principle of balance and order. The association of the Lanzón deity with the concept of centrality is expressed by its location at the center of a cruciform gallery, and is iconographically reinforced by four ropes or guilloches rising from the base of the sculpture. The Lanzón's penetration of the roof and floor of the gallery can likewise be seen as symbolic of its role as an axis or conduit connecting the heavens, earth, and the underworld. This *axis mundi* concept is further indicated by a vertical guilloche that runs up the back of the Lanzón, from floor to ceiling.

A vertical channel leads down from the top of the sculpture into a cruciform design with a central depression on the top of the deity's head. This configuration mirrors the layout of the Lanzón Gallery and, for that matter, the Circular Plaza. In this light, it is not surprising that the depression is centrally located on the top of the notched portion of the granite shaft making even more explicit the vertical axis and its centrality within the horizontal plane.[19] A complementary functional interpretation by Tello was that the blood of sacrificed victims was poured from the gallery above into the channel, and that it ran down the sculpture into the circular depression and eventually over the cult image.[20]

Tello's investigations actually revealed a gallery (Gallery VIII) directly above the Lanzón Gallery. Its layout was a somewhat simplified version of the cruciform gallery below it. No other cruciform galleries are known at Chavín de Huántar nor are there other instances of the superposition of similar gallery complexes. Tello suggested that Gallery VIII was designed for activities related to the Lanzón Gallery. In fact, the top of the Lanzón could be reached by removing a single slab in Gallery VIII so it would have been feasible to make offerings to the Lanzón. On the floor of the central chamber of Gallery VIII directly above the Lanzón, Tello recovered a perforated human finger bone which had been carved with a Chavín motif; this discovery reinforced his belief in the integral relationship between the two cruciform galleries.[21] More recently, Thomas Patterson proposed that an oracle may have been associated with the Lanzón and that divinations made from the central room of the gallery above would have seemed to emanate from the Lanzón itself.[22] Ethnohistoric accounts of Chavín de Huántar suggest that its temple functioned as an oracular center long after it had fallen into disrepair, and oracles are known to have played a central role in Andean ceremonial centers throughout Peru in Inca and pre-Inca times. Thus Patterson's suggestion is plausible, though impossible to prove, especially since Gallery VIII was destroyed by the 1945 landslide.

To the south of the Lanzón Gallery is the Gallery of the Labyrinths (Galería de los Laberintos); the two complexes may have been interconnected before the eastern parament of the Old Temple collapsed. Presently, three stairs lead down into a wide vestibule with small cells at its extremities and center. A narrow staircase leads upwards out of the central cell and into a complex series of passageways, two of which end in relatively large chambers (2 m × 5 m). Like the coeval Lanzón Gallery, the stone utilized is coarse and mortar is abundant. The ceiling is supported by projecting stones in the passageways and chambers, but there is no sculpture or other indication of activities carried out.

In the south wing of the Old Temple a number of distinctive interior rooms and passageways have been located and mapped. The Gallery of the Staircases (Galería de las Escalinatas) consists of a small vestibule leading to two stone staircases, one of which has some 21 stairs leading up through the interior of the central building onto the flat summit of the Old Temple. Remnants of the original plaster still cover its walls, and several coats of yellow, red, and white

128 An engraved human finger bone (71 mm long) was found in the gallery directly above the Lanzón; the incised motif is of a supernatural with avian attributes.

129 The interior gallery complexes of the Old Temple, such as the Gallery of the Labyrinths depicted here, consist mainly of a maze of narrow passageways and small chambers.

130 It is probable that some or all of the bottles found in the Gallery of the Offerings were used to contain maize beer, and one of them was actually decorated with a partially peeled ear of maize. This vessel, decorated in the Puca Urqo style, was probably brought to Chavín de Huántar from somewhere in the Cajamarca region.

131 The technology and style of the Mosna pottery recovered from the Gallery of the Offerings is dissimilar from the local ceramics, and pottery of this kind was probably produced somewhere in the highlands further north.

paint testify to numerous renovations. Layers of fine clay and fragments of pigment are frequently found collapsed on gallery floors elsewhere and it is likely that other interior passageways and rooms were finished in a similar manner.[23]

The Alacenas Gallery is located only a few meters from the Gallery of the Staircases and it consists of a simple arrangement of two rooms connected by a short passageway. The rooms have a distinctive series of large deep vertical niches called *alacenas* – hence the gallery's name. Entry into this gallery would have originally been by way of a stairway on the south, but today it can be reached only through a vertical airshaft. Test pits in the rooms of this gallery uncovered objects that may have been left as offerings. The Gallery of the Bats (Galería de los Murciélagos), in the southwest corner of the Old Temple is composed of a long passageway with three narrow lateral cells on the west and one on the north. Its stonework resembles that of the other galleries but, like those in the north wing of the Old Temple, it has not been the focus of any investigations. Today it provides a home for a large group of the winged nocturnal mammals from which it takes its name.[24]

Three galleries were discovered below the surface of the rectangular court of the Old Temple by Marino Gonzales: the Gallery of the Offerings (Galería de las Ofrendas), the Gallery of the Snails (Galería de los Cararoles), and the Field Camp Gallery (Galería del Campamento). Though these galleries are subterranean, they are nevertheless on the same level as the Circular Plaza.

The Gallery of the Offerings, located to the north of the Circular Plaza, is the most intensively studied of any gallery in Chavín de Huántar. Excavated in 1966 and 1967, it produced an abundance of beautiful objects without equal at other early sites in Peru. The gallery consists of a straight passageway 24.6 m long and 0.9 m wide, running east to west. It was originally entered from the north by a short staircase descending from the court of the Old Temple. Nine rectangular cells are spaced along the north side of the gallery.[25] In the middle of the main passageway was a human skull surrounded by a circle of 40 milk-teeth. The skull came from a middle-aged woman, perhaps 30 to 40 years old.[26]

On the floor of the passageway and cells were the remains of some 800 broken pots. It was originally believed that these vessels had been ritually smashed but a later study of the distribution of the fragments convinced Lumbreras that they had been unintentionally broken and scattered during the reutilization of the Gallery centuries later. The ceramics had apparently been filled with food, since the bones of camelids, deer, guinea pigs, and fish were found together with the pottery fragments. The bottles originally may have been filled with *chicha* beer and one of them has an incised decoration of an ear of maize. Mussel shells from the Peruvian shoreline and cut fragments of *Spondylus* from the Ecuadorian coast were also recovered.[27]

Mixed with the abundant food waste were 233 human bones. Like the other faunal remains, most are burnt and fragmented. The bones of at least 21 children, juveniles, and adults were identified and the full spectrum of body parts appears to be represented. The calcination, fragmentation, and context of these bones raises the possibility of ritual cannibalism, although supporting studies of cut marks and other features have yet to be reported. The frequency of human bones in the gallery (6.6 percent) was *not* paralleled in the refuse deposits of the Chavín de Huántar settlement, which are entirely lacking in such remains.[28]

The pottery found in the Gallery of the Offerings constitutes a unique assemblage.[29] Most of the vessels do not closely resemble the pottery recovered elsewhere in the Old Temple or in the coeval settlement surrounding the ritual precinct. Instead, they appear to have been brought to Chavín de Huántar from other regions. Lumbreras has divided the pottery from the gallery into four main stylistic groups: Chavín, Raku, Wacheqsa, and Mosna. Other yet unpublished styles have also been noted, called Pukcha and Puca Orqo.

The Raku pottery is characterized by dark-gray stirrup-spouted bottles decorated with thin superficial incisions made in relatively dry paste. The trapezoidal form of the stirrup, the decorative technique, and the motifs represented are typical of Cupisnique pottery and Raku pottery is particularly similar to the ceramics from the Barbacoa cemetery in the Chicama Valley. It is likely, therefore, that the delicate Raku ceramics were brought to Chavín de Huántar from the north coast, a journey of approximately 300 km.

Wacheqsa pottery is usually red-slipped and frequently displays incised designs filled with silver-black graphite paint. The stirrups are rounded rather than trapezoidal. The Wacheqsa style also resembles pottery from the north coast of Peru and similar ceramics were referred to as Cupisnique Transitorio by Rafael Larco. Luis Watanabe recovered similar pottery during his excavations at Herederos Chica, a mound in the Moche Valley site of Caballo Muerto.

The Mosna pottery style is characterized by single-necked bottles and jars with concave-curving necks. The oxidized orange surface of these vessels was painted with red designs before firing. The lip of the vessel is also frequently painted with a red band. These traits and the painted toothless serpentine motifs on the bottles were totally alien to the Chavín de Huántar area, but they were more common at centers in the northern highlands, particularly Huacaloma and Kuntur Wasi in Cajamarca. It is likely, therefore, that the Mosna pottery was brought to Chavín de Huántar from a highland area over 200 km away.

The final major stylistic component in the Gallery of the Offerings was the Chavín or Ofrendas style, characterized by monochrome bowls and single-necked bottles.[30] These pieces are finely polished and elaborately decorated with

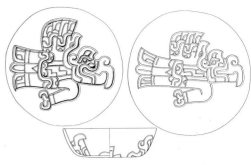

132 Some of the vessels discovered in the Gallery of the Offerings were decorated with birds and felines similar to the representations on the stone sculpture of the Old Temple. For example, on the lustrous blackware bowl shown above, a supernatural with avian attributes was incised on both the interior and exterior of the vessel. Diameter 21 cm.

133 This Ofrendas-style bottle from the Gallery of the Offerings achieves an elegant esthetic effect by surrounding highly polished undecorated zones with unpolished areas that have been heavily textured by "dentate rocker stamping" (a technique produced by rocking a small serrated sea shell back and forth to form a series of wave-like designs).

134 A bottle in the Chavín-Qotopukyo style from the Gallery of the Offerings depicting an anthropomorphic supernatural with severed heads hanging from his waist.

135 Many of the bowls and bottles from the Gallery of the Offerings show a mythical figure referred to by Luis Lumbreras as the Ofrendas Monster. The design illustrated here is taken from the exterior of a highly polished incised blackware bowl.

curvilinear incisions and surface texturing such as plain rocker-stamping, dentate rocker-stamping, punctations, and hemispherical depressions. The bowls are unusual because they were decorated either on the interior and exterior walls or on the exterior and bottom of the vessel. Some of the designs on the bowls and bottles show felines and raptorial birds similar to those on the Chavín sculpture of the Old Temple, and many of these secondary elements have close parallels in the Tello Obelisk, a second shaft-like sculpture of a deity (see below). The most common motif, sometimes referred to as the "Ofrendas Monster," is a profile head with eccentric eyes and multiple fangs. It is not represented in the iconography of the Chavín stone sculpture but it does bear a resemblance to the figure represented on the polychrome friezes of the atrium at Garagay. Perhaps the Ofrendas-style pottery comes from one of the poorly known central coast valleys of Chancay, Huarmey, or Pativilca, but further petrographic and stylistic studies will be needed before any firm conclusions are reached.[31]

The materials in the Gallery of the Offerings were apparently segregated according to their use. The first cell held bottles, the third cell bowls and plates, the sixth cell had a preponderance of globular jars, and the ninth cell contained carved stone objects, including a plate shaped like a fish and a mortar in the form of a bear. Peruvian archaeologist Jorge Silva has suggested that the gallery was designed to store temple paraphernalia, and the materials recovered by Luis Lumbreras and Hernán Amat may represent items broken during storage and abandoned when it fell into disuse.[32] If this were the case, the skull and children's teeth might have been left as part of a ritual marking the end of the gallery's original use. The proximity to the Circular Plaza and the ease of access to the rooms in the gallery are compatible with the storage hypothesis, although they do not preclude other alternatives, such as one which would view the objects and food as part of a ritual offering or series of ritual offerings. The varied materials found in the Gallery of the Offerings provide a glimpse of the temple's capacity to obtain exotics from a vast area. It suggests the existence of reciprocal relations and gift exchange between the diverse religious centers of the late Initial Period. Evidence for this extensive sphere of religious and social interaction has already been discussed in the preceding chapter for other highland sites like Pacopampa, Poro-Poro, and Cerro Blanco.

The Gallery of the Snails is located to the south of the Circular Plaza and it runs parallel to its northern counterpart, the Gallery of the Offerings. Its central corridor is 7 m long and 1.1 m wide, and only three lateral cells have been found along its south side. Excavation was limited to a few test pits, but these yielded a large number of *Strombus* shell fragments which had been cut into irregular geometric shapes. The *Strombus* is a very large warm-water gastropod which, like the shell of the *Spondylus princeps*, would have had to be imported to Chavín de Huántar from waters off the southern Ecuadorian coast. Since several of the sculptures of the Circular Plaza show figures blowing *Strombus* shell trumpets, it is not surprising to recover evidence of the worked shell. Small blue-green sodalite beads and Pacific mussels were also found, but pottery and animal bones were conspicuous in their absence.[33]

Ventilation and drainage. Besides creating interior environments, the construction of gallery complexes inside the platforms and courts of the temple had structural advantages. The stone passages and chambers acted as internal retaining walls for the clay and stone fill. The grid formed by the parallel and perpendicular gallery walls bore the stress that would otherwise have been concentrated on the masonry parament.

The subterranean galleries lacked windows and had to be supplied constantly with fresh air. This problem was solved by constructing hundreds of air ducts linking the galleries to each other and ultimately to the atmosphere outside. The ducts are stone-lined and rectangular in cross-section. They run both horizontally and vertically connecting otherwise unrelated gallery complexes. The largest of the ducts measures 70 cm by 70 cm in cross-section but most are only half that size. It is possible to crawl through some of the larger ventilation shafts and a number of previously unknown galleries have been discovered in this manner. The ventilation ducts brought all the passages and chambers of the Old Temple together into a single system of air circulation whose outlets were in the masonry facing of the parament and the roof of the pyramid. The interior of the Old Temple remains cool at all times, protected from the sharp diurnal changes outside by thick layers of fill and masonry. The thermal difference between the two environments generated a continual flow of fresh air throughout the subterranean galleries.

Drainage of the Old Temple presented an even more serious engineering problem. The rainy season in Chavín de Huántar lasts from five to eight months each year, and the semi-subterranean plaza and flat-topped pyramid of clay and fieldstone are simply maladapted to this climate. The structural integrity of the ruins is currently threatened by surface erosion and filtration, with the subterranean galleries being particularly vulnerable. Yet archaeological investigations prove that the Old Temple did function successfully for many centuries, so these problems must have been effectively overcome. A study undertaken by Julio Bustamante and Enrique Crousillat at the National University of Engineering in Peru concluded that drainage was accomplished through a multifaceted strategy which prevented the filtration of water through the buildings and platforms and carried precipitation to the Mosna River via a system of stone-lined tubes or canals.[34]

The first line of defense against precipitation was to create an impermeable exterior surface for the temple. This was achieved through the use of stone in the facing of the Old Temple and the paving of the Circular Plaza, and with a thick layer of burnt clay on the summit of the Old Temple. A second line of defense existed inside the buildings where horizontal layers of stone and unbaked clay were alternated with layers in which the stones were oriented at right angles.

These measures were effective because they were coupled with a tiered hydraulic system designed to drain water rapidly away from the temple complex before significant filtration could occur. The entire drainage system has yet to be explored but 924 m of conduits draining an area of 35,000 sq. m have been mapped thus far. Over half of these served the Old Temple. Unseen canals run over the Lanzón and then under the central staircase and Circular Plaza, eventually draining into the River Mosna. The hydraulic network frequently differs from the standard orientation of the buildings, galleries, interior rooms, and airducts. Many conduits run obliquely through or below these features and some have a sinuous course alien to the visible grid-like pattern dominant at the site.

136 Some of the major drainage canals at Chavín de Huántar were lined with walls of unmodified river boulders.

The water conduits are always rectangular in cross-section and lined with stone and slate to minimize seepage. Some canals display stonework comparable in quality to the passages and chambers they drain, but most, especially the larger collector canals, are crudely built and some even utilize unmodified river boulders. Besides the differences in orientation and construction, larger conduits can be distinguished from galleries by the slope of their floor and by the presence of vertical and inclined conduits feeding into them. Before this was recognized, several of the major water conduits were incorrectly designated as galleries. The dimensions of the water conduits vary considerably, apparently in response to a number of variables (e.g. slope and total flow). Nevertheless, most superficial canals and subterranean feeder canals are small, usually measuring no more than 30–40 cm on a side, and lacked paved floors because they were used only to channel water over short distances. The principal canals frequently measure up to 60–70 cm on a side, and on rare occasions over 1 m.

The canal system was designed to ensure that water drained away quickly, and a simulation study has shown that the late Initial Period drainage system of Chavín de Huántar could accommodate even the most severe local conditions, when 65 mm of rain can fall in a single day and 75 percent of that in a 4-hour period. It is significant that the smaller conduits remain in excellent repair, showing neither evidence of damage from wear or sediment deposits left from loads dropped within them. The floors of the subterranean conduits with steep grades were generally stepped in order to slow the flow of the water. This technique is crucial for reducing wear on the canals and for controlling water at peak flow. Inclined slabs were suspended above the bottom of vertical conduits in order to stop the water from falling directly into the canal system with a potentially damaging force. Curved walls were employed only at points of radical direction change where the water flow might have caused damage. Surprisingly, there are few instances in which changes or repairs were made after the system was completed. Since most of this system would have been inaccessible once it went into operation, its construction presupposed a sophisticated empirical knowledge of hydraulic engineering as well as the construction skills to actually build the drainage system.

The function of the galleries. It can be argued that the combination of the ventilation and drainage systems was created to produce an environment within the galleries suitable for storage. Storage of perishables, for example, requires a relatively low temperature, constant humidity, and good air circulation. The conditions in the subterranean chambers would have been well-suited for preserving tribute or offerings brought to the religious center. In later pre-Hispanic times, large warehouses constituted an important component of temple complexes. At the central coast center of Pachacamac, for example, depositories held cloth, ceremonial paraphernalia, agricultural produce, and gifts from pilgrims; these goods were brought from Pachacamac's hinterland and the more distant areas where branch shrines had been established. Based on archaeological remains, we have suggested that the Gallery of the Offerings and the Gallery of the Snails may have functioned as storage chambers for ritual paraphernalia. Other galleries differ significantly from these two in layout and presumably served other functions. The Lanzón Gallery, for example, provided a special environment for subterranean religious rites.

A number of scholars have suggested that some galleries may have been used to house priests or initiates, perhaps along the lines of cells in medieval monasteries. Unfortunately, it is difficult to evaluate this hypothesis, especially if we assume that daily food preparation and consumption was carried on outside the cells. While the absence of interior lighting would seem to rule out normal domestic activities, it does not preclude the use of these unusual environments as temporary or permanent habitations by small numbers of individuals involved in temple activities.

Convent-like institutions called *acllawasi* were maintained in Inca times, and ethnographic accounts of other native American groups like the Kogi of highland Colombia indicate that such institutions may have been more common in indigenous South America than generally realized.[35] The Kogi cloister priestly initiates for up to 18 years in isolated religious centers in the mountains behind the villages. During these years, the novices lead a strictly nocturnal life and are forbidden to leave their windowless houses during the daytime. The Kogi believe that these future sun-priests acquire the gift of visions and knowing all things, no matter how far away they might be, precisely because they were raised in darkness. The regimen of these initiates consists of a program of fasting, ingestion of hallucinogens, religious instruction, and nocturnal ritual activity. We cannot rule out *a priori* the idea that chambers within the Old Temple served a function analogous to the ritual houses of Kogi initiates. Nevertheless, the emphasis in most galleries on long passageways rather than chambers would not, on the face of it, seem to be well-suited for this purpose.

In the opinion of Luis Lumbreras, the profusion of air ducts and water conduits exceeds practical needs and their presence requires an explanation above and beyond maintenance considerations.[36] He proposes that the sound of water draining through the Old Temple would have been distorted and amplified by the ducts and galleries, and that the resulting sound would have been projected onto the plazas and terraces below. He suggests that much of the Chavín infrastructure was designed and built to create these acoustic effects, whose mysterious source would have been known only to the temple priests. As an experiment, Lumbreras poured 200 liters of water into the conduits that ran under the central staircase. The noise made by the water rushing through stone-lined canals, over steps and around right-angled corners was surprisingly loud, and closer to the sound of pulsating applause than flowing water. Within the Old Temple, these sounds would resonate in the empty passageways and chambers and be amplified by the galleries. He speculates that the air ducts could have been opened and closed like the valves of a trumpet to modulate the sound.

In order for such a system to operate during the dry season, water would have to be channeled up to the roof of the Old Temple from an intake on the Huachecsa River. One point along the Huachecsa half a kilometer upstream is 2 m higher than the temple summit and theoretically water could have reached the roof without mechanical devices. There is, however, no evidence of such a canal intake, nor of the connector canal leading from the Huachecsa or the vertical water conduit which would have carried the water to the temple summit. More research needs to be done on the Lumbreras hypothesis, but even if some of it proves to be without basis, the vision of the Old Temple as a thunderous building has considerable merit and it helps us to understand the measures adopted to validate the Old Temple as a center of supernatural power and authority.

As we have seen, the Old Temple may have been the most conspicuous feature on the landscape, but it was also the least accessible. Profound mystery was designed into the complex, as the absence of doorways and staircases on the three sides facing the approach of visitors illustrates. The sight of religious functionaries emerging from the unseen galleries at the summit shrine of the ostensibly impenetrable pyramid must have had a powerful impact on the viewers.

The Andean concept of religious architecture as a focus of potentially dangerous supernatural forces is alien to modern Judeo-Christian thought, but was widely held in much of the ancient world. It may be profitable to consider the observations made by the Spanish in 1534 at the thriving ceremonial center of Pachacamac. According to their eyewitness accounts, Pachacamac was filled with pilgrims from throughout Peru. Admittance was restricted to nobles, priests, and pilgrims and, in order to enter the lower plaza of the temple, it was necessary to fast for 20 days, and to move to the upper plaza a year long fast was required. Fasting in late pre-Hispanic Peru consisted of abstinence from salt, chili pepper, and sexual intercourse. The emperor Thupa Inca, who had conquered the central coast and claimed to be of divine ancestry, was forced to fast for 40 days before consulting the Pachacamac oracle, and even then this was done through a priest of the cult. The principal idol of Pachacamac, a wooden statue, was guarded in a windowless room on the summit of a terraced pyramid. Only temple priests were allowed to ascend the structure and consult the oracle on behalf of the fasting pilgrims. A cloth veil hung in front of the wooden idol so that even the priests could not gaze on the principal cult image. Questions concerning the weather, harvest, health, and warfare were put before the oracle and the answers, vocalized by one of the priests, were communicated to the petitioners below, along with demands for offerings and tribute. Failure to comply with the mandates of Pachacamac were believed to lead to earthquakes and other natural disasters.[37]

As at Pachacamac, most visitors to the Old Temple of Chavín de Huántar probably got no further than the open plazas and terraces. The focus of their religious experience would have been the ceremonies that occurred below and those conducted on top of the temple that were visible from a distance. The rituals are lost to us, but fragments of the myths which supported their beliefs and rituals are shown on the sculptures decorating the exterior facade of the temple architecture. These remains are the most direct link with this extinct ideological system, as well as being among the greatest works of art produced in ancient South America.

Chavín sculpture

The sculpture of the Old Temple consists almost exclusively of ashlars carved in flat relief, tenoned heads sculpted in the round, and elegantly crafted mortars. The carved ashlars and tenoned heads were set into the walls of the temple as architectural ornamentation; the mortars were portable ceremonial items. The shaft-like Lanzón and Tello Obelisk are exceptional in not belonging to these three groups and their form sets them apart as particularly sacred images.

White granite and black limestone was most frequently used for sculptures, although these materials had to be quarried at geological deposits outside Chavín de Huántar. The sandstone and quartzite available in local outcrops was

137 The large granite blocks leaning against the eastern wall of the Old Temple were carved with elaborate images of supernatural birds. They were probably originally set flush against the lower section of the wall as a decorative frieze.

less frequently utilized. In the case of the white granite, the closest known sources lie in the upper reaches of the Cordillera Blanca near Yanashayash, 18 km to the west of Chavín de Huántar, or near Cahuish, 15 km south. Outcrops of black limestone are found near Pójoc, 2 km west of Chavín, and there are still vestiges of ancient quarrying activity there. Most of the large prestigious sculpture, such as the Lanzón, is made of granite, the hardest of the available stones. Its transport must have been a major undertaking since draft animals and wheeled vehicles were lacking and stones like that used for the Lanzón weigh more than 2 tons.

Part of the attraction of Chavín sculpture for the modern viewer is the skill with which it was designed and executed. Though the Chavín carvings were produced with a simple neolithic technology, their quality rivals that of classical Greece and it was not surpassed by later Peruvian cultures. Since metal tools were unknown during the Initial Period and Early Horizon, percussion and pecking with particularly hard stones and gradual abrasion with sand and water must have been used to shape the sculptures. Great care was devoted to polishing the carvings. Some of the granite carvings have flat lustrous surfaces which could have been achieved only by polishing with a series of graded abrasives, perhaps beginning with a coarse riverine sand and gradually advancing to fine eolian sand. Only these portions of the sculptures seen by the public were finely finished. The edges and back of the ashlars and the shafts of the tenoned heads were left rough, thereby saving the artisans considerable labor.

The ashlars were decorated with narrow incisions carved at right angles into the prepared flat surface. Small depressions were sometimes added to represent pupils or other elements. The incisions and depressions were superficial, usually only 2–4 mm deep, and the complex motifs they form seem to almost float on the even surface of the stones. On some sculptures, such as those ringing the Circular Plaza, the main figure was surrounded by a plain recessed background and framed by an undecorated band.

The preponderance of two-dimensional sculpture was by choice, since a mastery of carving in the round is evidenced by the modeled stone tenoned heads. Even the naturalistically sculpted heads frequently have supplementary details incised into them using the same technique seen on the ashlar sculptures. The execution of the Lanzón differs from other Chavín sculpture because it employs bas-relief carving. Although the design is laid out as if on a flat surface, it is subtly modeled to emphasize the features of the great image. Carving in the round, bas-relief, and incised designs all coexisted in fully evolved form at the Old Temple.

The Chavín style

The style of Chavín de Huántar sculpture is so distinctive that it has served since Tello's time as the primary basis for identifying Chavín culture and its influence outside the site. The Chavín style is fundamentally representational, but the conventions employed by the temple artists intentionally mystified natural forms. To begin with, the main figures were reduced to a series of simple curves, straight lines, and scrolls. Wild animals and other creatures were invariably shown in rigid formalized poses and only their essential details were included. Tello referred to this process as idealization.

Chavín conventions obscure the idealized figure with an abundance of smaller elements which do not correspond directly to its observable parts. Some of these elements were added as metaphorical substitutes for body parts, a practice that Tello described as elimination and substitution. For example, snakes were used in place of the whiskers of the cornice jaguar and the hair of the Lanzón. Visual metaphors were also carved along significant axes or at important junctures of the figures. For example, a continuous mouth band of interlocking canines is shown in place of the vertebral column of the cayman, and a similar mouth band is featured in place of the wing bones of the supernatural avians. An even more common use of visual metaphor is the addition of fanged agnathic (jawless) mouths or faces at transition points in figures. In the cornice jaguar, for example, agnathic faces appear at the juncture of the paws with the legs, the tail with the body, and the ear with the head. Archaeologist John Rowe has suggested that since the tail emerges from one of those fanged agnathic mouths, it acts as a substitute for a tongue. There is no difference between the width or depth of the incisions used to create the main figures and those used for the metaphorical secondary motifs, and the extraneous eyes, teeth, and other elements of these visual metaphors overwhelm the principal image.[38]

Rowe has compared Chavín visual metaphors to the literary metaphors employed in Old Norse poetry. In these epic narratives, comparisons were made by direct substitution in order to create poems which were unintelligible without prior knowledge of the imagery or the story being related. These substitutions, called kennings, provided a field for artistic virtuosity and permitted limitless variations on a small number of themes. Chavín "kennings" likewise offered the artist the potential of non-repetitive elaboration of a limited thematic repertoire.[39] However, unlike Old Norse poetry, the range of metaphors utilized at Chavín de Huántar was quite restricted. A more fundamental difference is that Old Norse kennings were stylistic conceits, whereas the Chavín kennings were highly charged multivalent religious symbols. Perhaps a better analogy is the metaphorical substitutes characteristically used in the speech of Kogi religious specialists. Ethnographer Gerardo Reichel-Dolmatoff writes:

> He [the Kogi novice] acquires the faculty of seeing behind the exterior appearances of things and perceiving their true nature. The concept of *aluna*, translated here as "inner reality," tells him that mountains are houses, that animals are people, that roots are snakes and he learns that this manipulation of symbols and signs is not a simple matter of one-to-one translation, but that there exist different levels of interpretation and complex chains of associations. The Kogi says: "There are two ways of looking at things; you may, when seeing a snake, say 'This is a snake,' but you may also say: 'This is a rope I am seeing, or a root, arrow, a winding trail'." Now, from the knowledge of these chains of associations that represent, in essence, equivalences, he acquires a sense of balance, and when he has achieved this balance, he is ready to become a priest.[40]

For the uninitiated, the visual confusion created by the metaphorical substitutions at Chavín de Huántar is compounded by a series of other distinctive artistic conventions. A particularly unusual practice is followed in many zoomorphic representations. The profile face of the animal is shown in a standardized fashion with flared nostrils, a grimacing face, bared fangs, and upward-looking pupils. Some scholars believe this face to be feline, although it lacks features such as whiskers or upright ears. A signifier of animal identity is appended to the front of these faces, almost like a mask. For example, beaks are juxtaposed on "feline" faces to represent raptorial birds.

Another distinctive aspect of the Chavín style was its architectural conception of design.[41] A representation, no matter how complex, was treated as a composite of autonomous units drawn from a finite repertoire of elements. Modular design units were combined and repeated to form complex motifs in an almost mechanical fashion. Several investigators have suggested that this process, along with the regularity of the repeated elements, may reflect the use of stencils or templates. Repetition of almost identical elements in different contexts within a single larger representation produces an almost hypnotic pattern and distracts from the recognition of the principal figure. In the case of the frontal depiction of the raptorial bird (ill. 138), for instance, the same agnathic fanged mouth appears 20 times as a kenning on the wings and tail feathers. This complex image is actually composed of only a dozen basic design elements.[42]

138 Drawing of a sculpture depicting a supernatural crested eagle with its wings extended. The sculpture once decorated the eastern frontice of the Old Temple.

The density of figurative elaboration in Chavín art was increased still further by what art historian George Kubler refers to as anatropic organization, the practice of designing elements which can be rotated 180 degrees and still be visually meaningful.[43] The inverted orientation generally reveals images not intelligible previously, as in the detail taken from the Tello Obelisk (ill. 139). In other examples, such as the headdress element of the Lanzón, the upright and inverted designs are the same. In either case, the use of anatropic design requires extra eyes, noses, and other details which are meaningless when viewed under normal circumstances, and add further to the perceptual confusion.

Yet another popular Chavín convention is the depiction of two adjacent profile faces in such a way that they can also be visualized as a third face frontally represented. The creation of visual tension is inherent in this practice because of

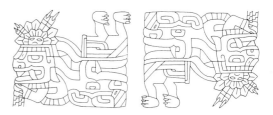

139 An example of anatropic design taken from the Tello Obelisk. When the sculpture was in place, the viewer would have seen the image on the left.

the difficulty of simultaneously recognizing both the profile and frontal images. The sharing of an outline by two separate wholes – each with a shape of its own – its disturbing, and this visual phenomenon has been termed contour rivalry by perceptual psychologists.[44] It is widespread at Chavín de Huántar, and is also an intrinsic feature of anatropic elements and kennings.

Art historian Esther Pasztory has observed that communication systems such as art are not generally meant to be equally comprehensible by every member of a society. They are used to separate as well as unite.[45] The Chavín conventions produce an esoteric art style which is intentionally inaccessible to the casual viewer and uninitiated, but which would have been comprehensible to those individuals privy to the religious mysteries of the cult.

Two final conventions of Chavín art which require mention are modular width and bilateral symmetry. Modular width refers to the organizing of designs in relation to an imagined framework of parallel horizontal bands of equal width, almost as if the representation was being laid out on graph paper. This practice is consistent with the Chavín canon of rough bilateral symmetry in relation to a vertical axis. The designs strive towards an overall sense of balance, as in the case of the Lanzón, rather than exact symmetry by the mechanical replication of detail.[46] Some sculptures, such as the profile jaguars from the Circular Plaza, may not appear to conform to this convention, but it should be remembered that these carved slabs were elements in a larger wall frieze which was bilaterally symmetric in relation to the staircase of the Old Temple.

Our admiration for the Chavín style should not allow us to forget that it was primarily a vehicle to embue worldly matter with a transcendent message belonging to the religious system. An aura of profound moral seriousness suffused the creations and probably influenced the technical and artistic aspects of production. Although we are ignorant of details of this creative process, the Spanish chronicler Cristobal de Molina does provide a description of the creation of a much later pre-Hispanic idol – the image of the solar deity housed in the temple of Coricancha in Cuzco. According to Molina, the Inca Pachacuti was said to have glimpsed a slab of rock crystal falling into a spring and inside the crystal he saw a form with a monstrous head from which rays emanated like the sun. The figure had intertwined snakes emerging from below its arms and the head of a feline between its legs, and another on its shoulders. It wore earspools and a crown like that used by the Inca. This vision was a turning point in the career of Inca Pachacuti, and he ordered artists to produce a statue exactly like the image he had seen in the crystal. This is the one that stood in the temple of Coricancha.[47]

The decoration of the Chavín de Huántar temple likewise chronicles the sacred symbols in which are stored the meaning of their belief system and the way in which the cosmos operates. Religion, ancient or modern, pre-Hispanic or Old World, invariably fuses metaphysics and ethics. It defines the way in which humans ought to behave and carries with it the potential for coercion by giving the dominant set of social values an appearance of objectivity, even inevitability. It is interesting in this light that the sculptures at Chavín represent static supernatural images. There is little narrative or historical content. Missing are the royal portraits, the epic scenes of royal births or military victories. In fact, most of the Chavín figures are monstrous, both in the sense of being terrifying and in the sense of combining features which do not occur together in nature. No background is provided for these images and consequently they seem situated outside the mundane world and historical time. The stone sculptures appear to represent the supernatural realm and its articulation with this world through shamanistic transformation and as expressed in creation myths.

Chronology of sculpture

In 1962, John Rowe proposed a relative chronology for the stone sculptures at Chavín de Huántar. He argued that the structural association of the Lanzón with the Old Temple implied that it was among the oldest sculptures known from the site. He used its style as the basis for defining the earliest phase of the Chavín sculptural style, which he referred to as AB. With the discovery of carved slabs in the Circular Plaza, it is now possible to distinguish between Phase A sculptures such as the Lanzón or the cornice shown in ill. 142 and Phase B sculptures like those in the Circular Plaza. In the Rowe sequence, the Tello Obelisk was used to define Phase C. The Obelisk was found near the surface in the southwest corner of the rectangular plaza, one of the less ancient portions of the site. Its original location is unknown and there is no architectural or stratigraphic evidence to help determine its age. None of the tenoned heads are executed in the style of the Tello Obelisk and only few sculptures resemble it. Its closest ties are with some of the pottery from the Gallery of the Offerings and with the adobe frieze of the late Initial Period temple at Garagay.

Though these resemblances suggest an early date for the Obelisk, they do not shed light on its age relative to the sculptures associated with the Old Temple. The intermediate chronological placement of the Tello Obelisk was originally based on parallels with the earliest phases of the Ocucaje pottery sequence of the Ica Valley on the southern coast of Peru. Unfortunately, these phases of the Paracas sequence have not been substantiated by archaeological associations, and their validity is in doubt. Donald Lathrap suggested that the Tello Obelisk is older than the Lanzón and may actually have been brought to Chavín de Huántar from another site.[48] Additional data are needed for a definitive resolution of the problem but, whatever its origin, the Tello Obelisk was probably used at Chavín de Huántar while the Old Temple was the focus of activity.

The Lanzón

As noted earlier, the Lanzón seems to represent the principal deity of the Old Temple, and the carving of the image on a notched shaft identifies it as a cult object rather than a piece of architectural decoration. The deity depicted by the Lanzón is strongly anthropomorphic. Its arms, ears, legs, and the five-digit hands with opposing thumbs are those of a human. The deity wears ear pendants, bracelets, anklets, a short skirt with tabs sewn along the bottom edge, and an ornamental collar or tippet. Although no primary or secondary sexual characteristics are shown, this dress suggests that its dominant aspect is male.

There are, of course, non-human elements shown on the Lanzón which have been interpreted as representing its supernatural powers. The large upper incisors or fangs that emerge from the upturned or snarling mouth of the deity are particularly noteworthy. Traditionally, scholars have argued that these

140 The iconography of the Lanzón, clearly seen in this rollout of the idol, offers one of the oldest and most eloquent representations of Chavín de Huántar's supreme deity. See also ill. 126.

fangs express the feline qualities of the Chavín deity. However, prominent fangs are common among other carnivorous animals: the prominent curved incisors of the howler monkey, the fearsome protruding teeth of the cayman, the deadly fangs of the anaconda, and even the small but sharp teeth of the vampire bat could all have served as inspiration for the Lanzón. Donald Lathrap has suggested that the representation of upper incisors rather than crossed fangs like those seen on the jaguars of the Circular Plaza may indeed express other than feline associations. Or the fangs could have simply represented special strength and ferocity, serving as a generalized indicator of supernatural character. The eyebrows and hair of the Lanzón are shown as swirling snakes and its headdress consists of a column of fanged feline heads. A horizontal band of similar heads adorns the skirt of the deity, and the ends of the skirt's ties are likewise shown as snakes. Directly above the nose of the supernatural is the face of a small fanged animal possibly representing a vampire bat.

The Lanzón's placement in the middle of the axis of the Old Temple graphically expresses the centrality of this supernatural within the religious ideology. The absence of its representation on smaller sculptures of the Old Temple and the restricted access into the Gallery of the Lanzón bespeak an inaccessible, powerful, and dangerous god. Its upturned mouth, enlarged upper canines and elongated sharpened nails on its hands and feet dispel any doubt about its ferocity. Yet the pose of the deity seems to depict him in the process of preserving the balance of the cosmos. The reconciliation of opposites and the maintenance of cosmic harmony were probably believed to hold the key to the stability of Chavín society, as well as the continued fertility of crops and animals.

The German ethnographer Otto Zerries has noted that belief in a supreme being who coexisted with lesser supernaturals was widespread in aboriginal South America, and that in a majority of cases such primary deities were associated with celestial phenomena, such as lightning.[49] This generalization was true in much of Peru at the time of the Spanish Conquest and John Rowe has speculated that the Lanzón too may be a sky god of some kind. Julio C. Tello, on the other hand, identified the Lanzón with Wira-Kocha, the creator god worshiped by the Incas.[50]

The Tello Obelisk

Of the zoomorphic representations, only the supernatural cayman shown on the Tello Obelisk appears to have come close to the Lanzón deity in importance. Like the Lanzón, the Tello Obelisk is a prismatic granite shaft with a notched upper section. It is smaller than the Lanzón, 2.52 m tall and 0.32 m wide. Its edges are faceted to form four flat sides and its lower section is not tapered. Sculpted on it in bas-relief are two profile representations of a hybrid monster dominated by cayman attributes. The two representations so closely resemble each other in outline and detail that Tello concluded that they were dual aspects of a single deity rather than two separate supernaturals.[51]

Caymans, specifically black caymans, are the dominant aquatic predators of the tropical forest and grow up to 6 m in length. They are abundant in the riverine floodplains of the Amazon and its tributaries. For the most part caymans subsist on large quantities of fish, but they occasionally consume an unlucky human or other large mammal. Perhaps the most diagnostic feature of the cayman on the Tello Obelisk is its mouth. A cayman's upper row of teeth are visible even when its mouth is closed. The Tello Obelisk also represents the supernatural with distinctive "flame eyebrows," which probably correspond to the distinctive tubercles or heavy brow ridges that appear above the eyes of all crocodilians. The naturalistic treatment of the legs – flexed as though floating or swimming – is also noteworthy, as is the realistic open cayman foot. This position is characteristic of the cayman; among the Suya people of Mato Grosso the cayman is called "the controller of the still waters" because it lies motionless in the water without creating ripples, though its arms are extended and its hands are open. From this position of apparent repose caymans will suddenly charge at lightning speed onto the nearby bank grasping some victim in its jaws and dragging it back into the water.[52]

Not all the features of the supernatural on the Tello Obelisk are drawn from the cayman, however. The tail is clearly not crocodilian, but instead resembles the tail feathers of an eagle or hawk, perhaps suggesting the supernatural's capacity for flight.[53]

The two cayman representations (A and B) of the Tello Obelisk are shown covered with small figures. This unique juxtaposition of autonomous secondary elements supplements the kennings and other stylistic conventions described earlier in this chapter. Another unusual feature of the Tello Obelisk is the prominence of plants. The flora in question are schematic, but several have been identified by Donald Lathrap as domesticated plants. For example, emerging from the penis of Cayman A is a plant which appears to be manioc, judging from the palmate leaves and the eyes on the branches; and manioc tubers may be extruding from the nose and mouth of the fanged face appended to Cayman A's rear leg. From an isolated head within the animal appears a plant resembling achira (*Canna edulis*), and from its rear claws drop geometric symbols which Tello identified as peanuts. Cayman B has the fruit and flowers of chili peppers grasped in its rear claws, while the flowers and fruit of the bottle gourd appear from a secondary fanged face on its back. Lathrap observed that Cayman A is associated with vegetatively propagated root crops and legumes whose economically valuable portions are found below ground, while the plants found on Cayman B are seed crops valued for their overground fruits.[54]

This dichotomy led Donald Lathrap to suggest that Cayman A represents the Cayman of the Underworld and Cayman B the Cayman of the Sky. Consistent with this interpretation is the raptorial bird in front of the mouth of Cayman B and the *Spondylus* shell (the spiny oyster gathered at the bottom of the deep waters of the Ecuadorian coast) in front of Cayman A. In Lathrap's opinion, the Tello Obelisk appears to represent the dual aspects of the Great Cayman and its role as bestower of domestic plants to mankind. Tello similarly speculated in his early writings that the two images of the Obelisk were dual opposites, one representing the rainy season and vegetative growth and the other representing the harvest and the dry season. At the same time, the sculpture reiterates a host of dual oppositions familiar to students of South American mythology: animal–plant, wild–domestic, above–below, seed–root, and so forth.[55]

Myths explaining the origins of food crops, similar to the one illustrated on the Tello Obelisk, are still told among groups of the South American lowlands. For example, among the Trio of Surinam there is a myth in which the culture hero, Pereperawa, caught a fish that transformed itself into a woman. When the

A   B

141 The Tello Obelisk appears to depict an important origin myth concerning the role of a pair of mythical caymans in the introduction of manioc and other lowland domesticates. Rollout drawing.

142 Along with the jaguar, the crested eagle and the serpent were the most common themes in Chavín art. Jaguar and serpent images were carved on the side and broad face of this Old Temple cornice, which was later relocated in the corner of the New Temple.

woman found that Pereperawa and his village were subsisting on the pith of wild reeds, she convinced her father, a giant alligator, to come to the village bringing a range of domesticated foods including corn, sweet potatoes, and cashews; manioc, the most important of the crops, was carried on the penis of the giant alligator. She collected these food crops and gave them to Pereperawa, thereby introducing agriculture.[56]

Secondary supernaturals

The Lanzón and the Tello Obelisk are, of course, exceptional. The majority of the sculptures at Chavín de Huántar are dedicated to lesser supernaturals. Most prominent of these is a raptorial bird with a powerful recurved beak, massive feet with long talons, and a tuft of feathers on its head. These avian supernaturals are carved on the large granite slabs decorating the lower exterior walls of the Old Temple. Tello originally identified these birds as condors, the birds of prey which soar above the intermontane valleys of the highlands. However, condors lack strongly recurved beaks and massive taloned feet because they feed off dead animals, and their heads lack feathers because they must reach deep within decaying carcasses. Instead, the Chavín sculptures clearly represent eagles, and the specific treatment of the feathers, beak, cere, and nostrils of these eagles suggests that they were most likely based on the harpy eagle (*Harpia harpyja*), a crested predator which feeds on monkeys in the Amazonian lowlands.[57]

143 Sculpture of the head of a raptorial bird (probably a harpy eagle) from Chavín de Huántar.

The harpy eagle is the dominant avian in the tropical forest, and one of the world's largest raptors. It has strong solar associations in Amazonian cosmology, and is frequently described as a guardian or attendant of the sun. On iconographic grounds alone, Rowe independently suggested that the Chavín raptorial birds were attendants and messengers of a celestial deity, rather than deities themselves. Another monkey-eating crested eagle, the Black-and-Chestnut Eagle (*Oroaetus isidori*), is found in the *ceja de selva* and could also have inspired the Chavín representation, though the harpy eagle conforms more closely to the details of the sculptures. The habitat and behavior of these two species overlap, and some indigenous groups in northwest Amazonia use the same term for both birds.[58] Neither of these crested eagles occurs naturally in the highlands or coast of Peru.

Chavín religion was initially described by Tello as a cult dedicated to the feline, and the Chavín art style was defined by the pervasiveness of feline attributes. This perspective has been considerably modified by more recent iconographic research. The feline certainly played an important role in Chavín cosmology, but never rivaled the god of the Lanzón or the Great Cayman in prestige.

The felines depicted on the sculptures of the Old Temple have pelage markings typical of jaguars rather than the monochrome gray-brown puma native to the highlands. The variety of crosses, petals, concentric circles, and other idealized forms on the body of the felines, and the generally realistic ears, whiskers, and body shape suggest a first-hand knowledge of the animal. The jaguar has an unusually wide distribution, and rare instances of jaguars have been reported in the Peruvian highlands and coast. However, the core of its habitat is the tropical forest of the eastern slopes and Amazonian lowlands. This powerful, swift, and ferocious animal is the largest carnivore in the American tropics.

The jaguar is both a threat and a competitor to hunters in the rainforest. Its thunderous roar and its nocturnal stalking along watercourses all add to its potential as a symbol with several meanings. Throughout lowland South America, religious leaders claim they can transform themselves into jaguars in order to communicate with celestial forces and mediate with the supernatural sphere on behalf of human society. As we will see, the religious leaders of Chavín de Huántar likewise believed the jaguar to be their natural alter ego. The role of the jaguar as mediator is graphically represented on the Tello Obelisk, where it is shown between the Cayman of the Sky and the Cayman of the Underworld.[59]

The fourth and final animal with an important role in the art of the Old Temple is the snake. It usually appears as a secondary element in larger figures, but on at least one early cornice is represented autonomously with an undulating body and a protruding tongue. One scholar was convinced that the Chavín snakes represented germinating powers and fertilizing waters, which is why they appear as frequent attributes of other supernaturals.[60] Some scholars believe that the Chavín snake is an anaconda, another dominant predator of the Andean riverine systems. This plausible suggestion is consistent with the identification of the other Chavín animals as large tropical forest predators and would explain the bullseye markings on the cornice snake. In any case, it is significant that snakes do not figure among the major fauna of the Chavín de Huántar area. In contrast, they are a ubiquitous and dangerous component of tropical lowland ecology.

Tropical forest symbols in Chavín art

This brief review of Chavín religious art raises a question that has haunted archaeologists since Tello. Why are the major animals represented in Chavín religious art drawn from outside the local highland environment? As we have seen, the entire cast of animals appears to have been derived from the floodplains of Amazonia or, at the very least, from cloud forests and rainforests of the mid and lower eastern slopes of the Andes. Although counter-arguments can be made, the dominance of the jaguar, snake, crested-eagle, and cayman in the iconography leads one to conclude that the myths forming the basis of the Chavín religious system had their origin east of the Andes. These animals still play a prominent role in the mythology and ritual symbolism among dozens of modern tribes of lowland South America.[61]

The intimate knowledge that lowland peoples possess of these predators leads to their repeated appearance as symbols. Drawn from real life experiences, these multivalent symbols are woven together to form comprehensive and coherent cosmologies. This same process occurs in the highlands as well as the lowlands but, as would be expected, colonial and modern Quechua myths of the high Andes feature fauna which are familiar locally, such as the llama, deer, condor, fox, and hummingbird. These animals are conspicuously absent in Chavín art.

The intrusive character of Chavín religious imagery is also reflected in the crops carried by the Great Cayman: manioc, bottle gourd, achira, hot peppers, and possibly peanuts. These are lowland crops and none of them can be successfully cultivated at or near Chavín de Huántar. Yet the fact that they are carried by the cayman suggests that the origin myth depicted is from the tropical forest. Analogous aboriginal myths were recorded in the highlands by the Spanish chroniclers, but these explain the origin of the potato, oca, ulluco, and other cultigens of local economic and ritual importance, not the lowland cultigens.[62]

It would be incorrect to assert that Chavín iconography exclusively represents Amazonian fauna and flora. The shells of the *Strombus* and *Spondylus* on the Tello Obelisk are unambiguous evidence of coastal input. Likewise, the San Pedro cactus, depicted in the Circular Plaza, can be found growing near the site of the Old Temple and in other highland and coastal valleys. Nevertheless, these and other isolated secondary motifs do not negate the basic conclusion that Chavín religious cosmology is dominated by fauna and flora from tropical forest habitats.[63]

How can we explain the depiction of lowland animals and plants on the sculpture of Chavín de Huántar, 3,150 m above sea level? Three alternatives come to mind: 1) the climate was radically warmer and more humid during the late Initial Period; 2) the Old Temple was built by migrants (or their descendants) from the tropical forest; and 3) highland religious leaders at Chavín de Huántar were in direct contact with Amazonian cultures and chose to adopt aspects of their exotic religious ideology. The first of these alternatives can be eliminated on the basis of paleoclimatic studies in Peru and the identification of animal bones recovered in excavations at Chavín de Huántar.

The second explanation was originally advanced by Tello, but its most persuasive advocate is Donald Lathrap, who has argued that the ancestors of the builders of the Old Temple were forced to migrate from the floodplains of the Amazon or Orinoco basins by population pressure.[64] In Lathrap's opinion, the tropical-forest animals and plants shown on Chavín art recall the hearth of Chavín civilization and pay homage to the subsistence system originally responsible for the success of the Chavín elite. But, as John Rowe once remarked, myth is not history, and the use of Chavín art to generate a hypothetical historical sequence is a questionable procedure. Moreover, the resulting model is undermined by the lack of Amazonian influence on the earliest ceramics known from Chavín de Huántar.

Urabarriu-phase pottery contemporary with the Old Temple shares numerous features with early highland and coastal ceramic styles, but holds little in common with the Late Tutishcainyo or other Initial Period styles of the tropical forest. If the Urabarriu-phase settlers had descended from migrant lowland groups, their pottery style would be expected to display a direct relationship with the ceramic tradition of the earlier group. But the Urabarriu style appears instead to be a conscious pooling of earlier ceramic traditions from surrounding and more distant areas in the highlands and coast.

Urabarriu ceramics are well made, but not particularly attractive or distinctive.[65] Pottery was fired in an oxidation atmosphere and the resulting wares were either reddish or dark brown. The most common vessels were globular neckless pots, often slipped with red pigment but rarely decorated. Their ubiquity, and the carbon frequently caked on them, suggest that they were the main cooking pots and, perhaps, storage vessels. Plain jars with constricted concave-curved necks and shallow open bowls also occur. These simple utilitarian forms were also widespread in much of the central and northern coast and highlands during the late Initial Period.

Bottles were the best-made and most frequently decorated class of Urabarriu vessels. These were serving vessels, probably for corn beer, and their exterior decoration was meant to be viewed in public contexts within the household. The chambers of single-necked or stirrup-spouted bottles were adorned with a surprisingly large range of surface texture techniques including rocker-stamping, dentate rocker-stamping, dentate impression, six types of punctation, two types of modeling, appliqué nubbins, and appliqué tiers. Curvilinear incisions delineated geometric and mythological motifs, and design registers. Differences in surface luster were used to create or reinforce decorative effects. The Urabarriu bottles have particularly strong parallels in the late Initial Period assemblages of central coast sites such as Ancón, and north central coast sites such as Las Haldas. Incised cups, sometimes with carinated bases, have stylistic ties with the highland Kotosh style of Huánuco. Other cups were decorated with a type of incision and post-fire paint reminiscent of the Pacopampa style from the northern highlands. The result is a cosmopolitan style of a highland community whose social identity was intimately tied to its economic and social interaction with non-local coastal and highland groups. It is difficult to reconcile this stylistic patterning with the Tello-Lathrap hypothesis of tropical forest origins.

The subsistence strategy utilized by the original inhabitants of Chavín de Huántar was developed in the Peruvian highlands over 1,000 years before Chavín de Huántar was founded and, as we saw in Chapter 2, highly organized populations of considerable size occupied the intermontane valleys near Chavín de Huántar by the Late Preceramic period, if not before. It is consequently unlikely that a tropical forest group was either directly or indirectly responsible for the distinctive high-altitude mixed agricultural system that supported Chavín de Huántar or for the establishment of the Old Temple.

The third theory, which proposes that elements of Amazonian cosmology were brought to Chavín de Huántar and promoted by the leaders of the Old Temple, is the most plausible of the hypotheses. Commodity exchange between the tropical forest, highlands, and coast stretches back to the Late Preceramic, and the proximity of Chavín de Huántar to the Marañon River leaves little doubt that its inhabitants had some contact with the lowland zones. We can speculate that Chavín's religious leaders justified the promotion of alien symbols by claiming that the exotic lowland groups had esoteric knowledge unusually effective in controlling supernatural forces. In contrast to the examples of emulation usually cited by archaeologists, this would be a case in which a more "complex" society adopted features from a more egalitarian society, perhaps because the latter was viewed as having closer ties to original sources of wisdom and supernatural power.

There are accounts in the ethnographic literature of shamans making long journeys to acquire supernatural wisdom and power, frequently crossing ethnic and ecological boundaries in the process. Modern highland and coastal shamans and healers often travel to the tropical forest, which is viewed as a potent source of sacred knowledge, medicinal plants, and other ritual paraphernalia. The Jivaro and Achuara shamans of the *ceja*, for example, regularly make pilgrimages of hundreds of kilometers to contact religious leaders of the Canelos Quichua in order to obtain esoteric knowledge and invisible magic darts.[66] The attraction of alien religious cults is likewise a well-known phenomenon in Western history, and we have only to recall the success of Egyptian cults in the late Roman Empire to provide an analogue.

The existence of tropical forest elements in Chavín religious art meshes well with the eclectic nature of the Old Temple's religious architecture. As noted, this building complex has little in common with the local highland temples which preceded it at Huaricoto or Kotosh. Instead, the Old Temple seems a combination of elements drawn mainly from coastal antecedents. The U-shaped monumental platform, for example, is apparently based on the architectural patterns of the central coast, while the small, semi-subterranean Circular Plaza fronting the central complex appears to be modeled on the layout of the north-central coast centers. The concept of decorating the exteriors of ceremonial buildings with bas-relief and modeled public art also has antecedents in the clay friezes of the central and north coast. Cerro Sechín in Casma remains the only fully documented pre-Chavín center which employed abundant stone sculpture in decorating its exterior walls. Chavín de Huántar probably drew upon this and other yet undiscovered sites in its use of sculptural embellishment.

It is noteworthy that the Old Temple's elaborate hydraulic system similarly draws upon the technological tradition of the coast, where irrigation was an essential feature by the beginning of the early Initial Period. Likewise, the flat rooftop of the Old Temple almost certainly derives from coastal antecedents, since this design is fundamentally incompatible with the heavy rains typical of the highlands. The subterranean galleries do not have known parallels at Initial Period coastal centers and they may be a variation on the underground gallery tombs of La Galgada or other similar sites. Nevertheless, we can generalize that the Old Temple is a creative synthesis of architectural elements drawn mainly from the Pacific coast.

Our analysis of Chavín art and architecture leads to the conclusion that the Chavín cult was created by fusing exotic tropical forest and coastal elements to forge a unique local highland religion. The end product was a cosmopolitan ideology consonant with Chavín de Huántar's position at the crossroads of long-distance trade routes linking the highlands with the coast and eastern lowlands. The Old Temple was the physical expression and embodiment of the coalescence of these diverse regional traditions.

One important feature of Chavín ideology was the belief that its priests could transform themselves into jaguars in order to contact and affect the behavior of supernatural forces. Hallucinogenic snuffs and beverages apparently catalyzed these changes, and their consumption was an integral part of the rituals of the Old Temple. Through the professional manipulation of drug dosage and the altered-state experience, the supernatural can be made to appear empirically verifiable. The central role of psychotropic substances at Chavín is amply documented by its graphic representation on the sculptures; these depictions can be interpreted as providing the mythical antecedent and divine charter for the use of these substances and, ultimately, for the religious authority of temple priests.[67]

The role of hallucinogenic snuffs in shamanistic transformation is clearly expressed in the tenoned heads which gazed outwards from the parament of the Old Temple.[68] A typological analysis of these individual sculptures suggests that they represent different stages in the drug-induced metamorphosis of the religious leaders (or their mythical prototypes) into their jaguar or crested-eagle alter egos. One set of these sculptures represents naturalistic anthropomorphic faces with almond-shaped eyes, bulbous noses, and closed mouths; their most distinctive features are an unusual hair arrangement – often a sort of top knot – and a wrinkled face, as if they were experiencing the onset of nausea. A second group of tenoned heads portray strongly contorted anthropomorphic faces, gaping round eyes, and mucus dripping from their nostrils, either slightly or in long flowing streams; the features and hairstyle suggest that the same group of individuals is being shown. The depiction of nasal discharges in prominent public contexts is alien to Western religious traditions, but its significance becomes clear from accounts of hallucinogenic snuff use among lowland South American Indians. The 17th-century friar Pedro Simon offered the following first-hand characterization of the Muisca of Colombia:

> they take these powders and put them in their noses and which, because they are pungent, make the mucus flow until it hangs down to the mouth, which they observe in the mirror, and when it runs straight down it is a good sign . . .[69]

The flow of mucus is caused by the irritation of the nasal membrane by potent psychotropic substances, and it is the most conspicuous external index of an altered mental state. Facial contortions and bulging eyes are likewise characteristic of these physiological changes.

A third group of tenoned heads combines anthropomorphic features, such as head and ear shape, with large fangs and other non-human features. In the fourth and final group of tenoned heads, the visage is totally transmuted into a feline, a raptorial bird, or a hybrid of the two. It is possible to arrange the tenoned heads into a series in which the phases of this process are linked together by the continuity of certain traits. For example, one of the grimacing tenoned heads has one almond-shaped eye and one bulging eye; another the head of the jaguar with mucus still hanging from its nose.[70]

The inference that snuff was actually consumed in ritual contexts is supported by the recovery of elaborately sculpted stone mortars from Chavín and nearby sites such as Olayán and Matibamba. The quality of the carving and polishing, and the small size of the depressions in the mortars rules out their use for

Hallucinogens and Chavín ritual

144 The tenoned head of a mythical priest almost fully transformed into a feline state; the strands of mucus running down from the nostrils signal the involvement of hallucinogenic snuff in this process. Height 63 cm.

145 A ceremonial mortar in the form of a jaguar from Chavín de Huántar, possibly used to process hallucinogenic snuff. Length 33 cm.

146 A bird-shaped ceremonial mortar from Matibamba, a small site 20 km downriver from Chavín de Huántar. Length 37 cm.

147–155 A selection of sculptured heads once tenoned into the upper walls of the temple at Chavín de Huántar. These heads are ordered in a sequence that illustrates the shamanic transformation from priest to feline or other animal intermediary (eagle or monkey).

grinding grain. They would have been ideal for preparing psychotropic snuff from vilca seeds or epena. Bone trays, spatulas, miniature spoons, and tubes have also been found in Chavín associations. Similar objects, but without known provenance, are engraved with Chavín iconography. These artifacts closely resemble the snuffing paraphernalia used by late pre-Hispanic cultures and modern South American indigenous groups.[71]

In the light of the foregoing discussion, it is worthwhile returning to the stone frieze in the Circular Plaza. The anthropomorphic figure holding the stalk of the psychotropic San Pedro cactus has prominent fangs and feline paws. In the same row of carved slabs are a pair of anthropomorphic figures with almond-shaped eyes and bulbous noses, reminiscent of the first group of tenoned heads; the jaguar tails hanging from their headdresses are likewise suggestive of shamanistic transformation. The register of sculptures beneath the anthropomorphic figures consists of paired representations of jaguars with the taloned feet of the eagle. The similarity in the size, pairing, and arrangement of these two rows of sculptures implies that they are intimately connected. The flying jaguars of the lower register may represent the anthropomorphic figures in their fully transformed state. Could the two rows of sculpture be depicting the prototypes of Chavín religious authorities in their two different, but complementary states: one as religious functionaries conducting rituals for pilgrims at the temple, the other as flying jaguar-priests mediating with the supernatural?

Both the explicit representation of the San Pedro cactus, usually consumed as a beverage, and the indirect evidence of hallucinogenic snuffs on Phase AB sculpture make it likely that diverse hallucinogens were being used at the Old Temple. As we have already noted, the active ingredient of San Pedro is mescaline, which has a different and usually less radical effect than tryptamine derivatives, the active principal in epena and vilca. The modern Jivaro utilize several hallucinogens, but the strongest of these is consumed only by religious specialists.

Unlike the San Pedro cactus, which grows locally around Chavín, the plants most commonly used to produce snuff come from the tropical rainforest. The seeds ground to make vilca snuff store well and are easily transported; they have traditionally figured prominently in jungle-highland trade.[72]

Who built the Old Temple? What kind of highland society was capable of producing surpluses and labor sufficient for the maintenance of a public complex of hitherto unprecedented scale in this region? The answer to these questions are to be found in the 6 hectares of coeval Urabarriu-phase residential area near the Old Temple. Unfortunately, very little of this zone has been excavated and much of it has already been destroyed by modern constructions. Nevertheless, some information is available.[73] The ancient settlement area is located in two discontiguous areas: a southern locus of approximately 5 hectares surrounding the Old Temple and a northern locus of approximately 1 hectare. It is unlikely that more than 500 people lived in the two areas. The residential zone nearest the Old Temple extended to the banks of the Huachecsa River. Part of the sector nearest the monumental architecture was probably occupied by the people responsible for the religious activities and the construction and maintenance of the buildings. In 1974, excavations directed by the University of San Marcos

The Urabarriu-phase settlement

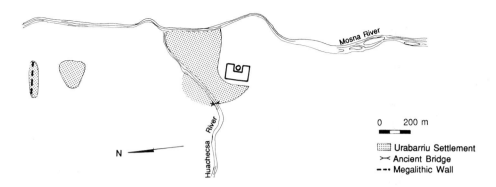

156 The location of the Urabarriu-phase settlement associated with the Old Temple.

157 The bridge across the Huachecsa River photographed here in 1934 linked two sections of Chavín's ancient settlement. It was destroyed by a landslide in 1945.

unearthed small rustic rectangular buildings, perhaps houses, along the southern bank of the river, and near by they encountered Urabarriu-phase refuse including sherds of the Kotosh style from Huánuco.[74] In 1976, I encountered Urabarriu domestic refuse near the northern bank of the Huachecsa.

From the outset, inhabitants of Chavín lived on both sides of the Huachecsa and this implies the existence of a bridge, since the river is wide and deep. During the rainy season it is filled with torrential waters draining from the slopes of the Cordillera Blanca, and it is impassable for most of the year. Remarkably, the bridge built over the Huachecsa during Chavín times actually survived until 1945. The cut and dressed granite masonry utilized in the bridge identifies it with the Chavín culture rather than with later occupations. Moreover, the engineering principles employed are closely related to those used in building the temple galleries and canals.

The Chavín bridge, known locally as the *rumi-chaka*, was located 110 m north of the Old Temple, in a spot where the Huachecsa narrows to only 7 m in width.[75] It was built entirely of stone and consisted of a lower course of four parallel rectangular beams which supported an upper course of smaller granite ashlars. The total weight of the bridge superstructure must have exceeded 20 tons. Like the ceilings of the underground galleries, the bridge rested upon cornice-like slabs projecting from megalithic walls at the edges of the river banks. The massive retaining walls were part of the overall canalization of the lower Huachecsa River during Chavín times. The conversion of the Huachecsa into a stone-lined channel was essential to the stability of the bridge and the protection of the adjacent ancient settlement from gradual erosion and flooding. The Chavín cantilever bridge was 665 cm long and 285 cm wide and, before its destruction by a massive landslide, it sustained thousands of years of camelid caravans, packtrains of mules, and finally truck transport. Even today all commerce moving through the Mosna Valley must cross the Huachecsa on a makeshift wooden bridge. The construction and maintenance of the *rumi-chaka*, or perhaps earlier bridges, must have been of strategic importance to the Urabarriu settlement and the leaders of the Old Temple.

A small community of perhaps 50–100 inhabitants lived 0.5 km to the north of the Old Temple. These people were involved in farming, herding, and hunting. Basic tools for daily production, such as clod-breakers, were recovered from their refuse. Clod-breakers – typical pre-Hispanic Andean agricultural implements – were used to break up soil during planting and could also serve as digging stick weights. They were manufactured by pecking and drilling local river cobbles. Ground and polished T-shaped axes were also used by these farmers, perhaps for obtaining firewood and lumber to build their houses.[76] Most of the other agricultural tools, like digging sticks, were probably made of perishable materials.

Urabarriu-phase diet

Plant preservation is poor at Chavín de Huántar and there is limited direct evidence about what was being grown. From the Urabarriu refuse came a single carbonized kernel of *Confite chavinense*, a Peruvian popcorn. We have already noted that although maize thrives on the valley floor, it is not well-adapted to the higher valley slopes which surround the site. We would not, therefore, expect maize to have been a staple of these early residents. A recent study was undertaken by the author with Nikolaas van der Merwe of the stable carbon isotope ratios of human bone found in the northern Urabarriu phase settlement, in order to determine the relative amount of maize in the diet. This C_{13}/C_{12} ratio directly reflects the consumption of C_3 plants such as potatoes, relative to the quantity of C_4 plants, like maize. The four Urabarriu skeletons analyzed all showed a preponderance of C_3 foods; maize, the only C_4 crop in the Andes, constituted about 18 percent of the diet. It is likely therefore that, even in Urabarriu times, potatoes and other high-altitude tubers formed the basis of the Chavín subsistence economy.[77]

The Urabarriu valley residents were also actively involved in hunting and herding on the high *puna* above Chavín de Huántar. Over 54 percent of the animal bones from the Urabarriu garbage came from camelids, and these large herbivores provided most of the animal protein for the late Initial Period agriculturalists. But were these animals llamas or alpacas being herded on the *puna*, or wild guanaco or vicuña being hunted on the *puna* and valley slopes? As noted in earlier chapters, there are technical difficulties in identifying the particular species of camelids, but the quantitative studies of zooarchaeologist George Miller suggest that the Urabarriu people definitely availed themselves of two different species of camelids. One group consists of large animals which can be identified with some confidence as llamas. The other somewhat more frequent group is made up of smaller camelids which Miller believes are vicuñas. The exploitation of wild camelids, such as vicuñas, by the Urabarriu farmers is consistent with other evidence for hunting. Deer bones, including the antlers from white-tailed deer, constitute over 10 percent of the animal remains, and bones of smaller game – including the viscacha, skunk, and small birds – are also found. Relatively small-scale excavations in the northern Urabarriu sector unearthed no less than 25 chipped stone points, 3 ground-stone points, and 1 bone point. All these artifacts could have been used as dart projectile points by atlatl-wielding hunters. The llamas and wild game were brought back to Chavín de Huántar where the animals were finally butchered and consumed. Guinea pigs and dogs were kept by Urabarriu villagers, although the remains from these household domesticates are infrequent in refuse.[78]

Craft production

Inhabitants of the northern Urabarriu sector were also involved in part-time craft production. The importance of textile manufacture at Chavín de Huántar

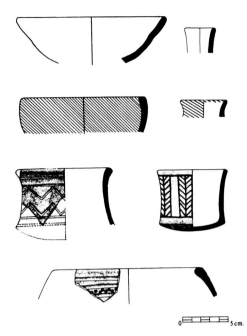

158 The pottery style of the Urabarriu phase shares features with other late Initial Period ceramic assemblages in the highlands and coast, including Kotosh, Pacopampa, and Las Haldas.

159 Quartzite and chert projectile points found in refuse of the Urabarriu phase, along with abundant remains of deer and wild camelids. Heights (left to right) 46, 40, and 31 mm.

is documented by the presence of polished bone weaving implements and fine bone needles. Coarse wool sheared from their llama herds, and perhaps finer vicuña wool, would have provided a convenient source of fiber for cloth. It is likely that the wool was spun locally, perhaps using spindle whorls of perishable materials such as wood or maize cobs.

Members of the Urabarriu community also used the bones of slaughtered llamas and deer to make tools and ornaments, including the weaving implements mentioned above. The production process was a simple one. The bone was usually polished first, and then sawn laterally with a thin stone flake or fine-edged tool in order to remove the ends. The resultant cylinders were then cut or split to arrive at the rough form before the final shaping and, in the case of beads and needles, drilling. The large numbers of sawn bone ends and partially completed tools recovered from the Urabarriu garbage testify to the variety of worked bone items produced by Urabarriu artisans.

As we have seen, evidence for local food and craft production suggests a largely self-sufficient community. It is noteworthy that most of the projectile points and crude stone unifaces were made of quartzite, slate, and other stone found immediately around Chavín de Huántar, or of chert and related fine-grained stones from the Cordillera Blanca. Similarly, beads and other emblems of personal status were made exclusively of locally available bone, rather than imported raw materials. On the other hand, imported items are interspersed with the daily refuse of these early farmers. For instance, there are fragments of an incised Cupisnique bottle which had been brought from the north coast of Peru, and several fragments of incised bichrome bottles, probably brought from the central coast. There are also a few small flakes of obsidian from geological sources in the south-central highlands. These and other items suggest involvement with the commerce passing through Chavín de Huántar, either directly or through the mediation of the Temple.

Two of the sawn-off bones discarded in the Urabarriu refuse came from large felines, either pumas or jaguars, and it is possible that inhabitants occasionally manufactured ritual paraphernalia from special materials for the ceremonies of the Old Temple or for exchange with pilgrims and other outsiders. While most of the locally produced wool textiles, bone tools, and ornaments were probably consumed by the residents of Chavín de Huántar, some may have been exchanged for exotic materials being conveyed along the Mosna Valley trade route.[79]

The northern wall

The northern Urabarriu-phase residential area is located 150 m south of a monumental wall and causeway constructed during Urabarriu times. Unlike the ceremonial constructions, this wall consists mainly of unworked boulders of glacial origin. Many weigh almost a ton and measure over 2 m in height and over 1 m in width and thickness. A line of these stones runs east–west for at least 110 m; the spaces between are filled with smaller stones. This wall merges with an even higher stone causeway built of fieldstone retaining walls and gravel fill. The total visible length of this barrier is some 160 m, but its unseen western extreme is buried under soil eroded from the steep outcrop which overlooks it. On the east, the causeway was bordered by the entrenched channel of the Mosna. The wall

160 Although it is only partially visible today, a large megalithic wall was built across the Mosna Valley to the north of the Urabarriu settlement, possibly to control movement along this natural route of communication.

seems to have been designed to block movement along the valley floor, and thus to control the flow of goods and people along the Mosna trade route and restrict access of llama caravans into the Chavín de Huántar area. Excavations revealed a small amount of Urabarriu-phase garbage inside the wall. An underground gallery, like those of the Old Temple, runs perpendicular to the wall and could have been used to store tribute and/or gifts collected there. Future investigations are needed to test this possibility.

Perhaps this wall was built by the leaders of the Old Temple to establish their authority over a trade route whose antiquity was greater than the ceremonial center itself. One additional activity of occupants of the northern residential area may have been to guard and maintain the megalithic wall. The latter suggestion would explain why this small community was located near the wall, rather than next to the Old Temple or closer to the higher elevation fields and herds being exploited daily.

Based on the available data, it would appear that the resources supporting the Old Temple were twofold: surplus of a mixed agricultural system supplemented by hunting, and gifts and/or tribute from the trade route through the Mosna. The basis of both sources of the Old Temple's wealth existed prior to its construction and thus the critical question is not what the sources of support were, but rather how it became possible to extract the surplus and tribute, and to channel the incoming goods and labor towards the construction of monumental buildings and maintenance of this cult center. The answer to this question would seem to lie in the ephemeral realm of ideology and its power to unify a weakly linked interregional social system without physical coercion.

The emergence of a religious leadership responsible for the new cult of the Old Temple with its alien rites and symbols bespeaks a new order, one in which the multitude of small rural communities surrendered a portion of their agricultural produce and leisure time for ends not directly associated with individual or

161 Rural versions of Chavín religious art were present in the small villages above Chavín de Huántar, and suggest the presence of Chavín shrines at these sites. This rustic version of a jaguar carved on a sandstone block comes from the site of Waman Wain. Height 33 cm.

162 One cornice stone depicts elaborately costumed figures with knives and trumpets.

163 A supernatural anthropomorphic figure carrying a bleeding decapitated head, recovered from the small site of Yurayacu located 5 km downriver from Chavín de Huántar. Height 51 cm.

lineage interests. The discovery of elaborate Chavín sculptures in these isolated villages suggests the degree to which religious beliefs and rituals were the catalysts in this transformation.

The absence of elaborate elite burials and the lack of historical themes in the public art may reflect the initial inability of the Old Temple's hieratic authorities to transform their collective power and prestige as mediators in the social and supernatural realms into personal wealth and individual power. Instead, they used the surplus collected to reinforce their corporate authority and further promote the cult's success through larger constructions, more elaborate public rituals, dressed and polished stonework, great sculpture on exotic stones, and other labor-intensive public works. The end product was a sacred center which transcended the mundane world in which Initial Period agriculturalists and herders labored.

Self interest on the part of the villagers, including the desire to gain access to temple resources, and shared religious beliefs may have been sufficient to unify the local social system and permit the pooling of its resources, but this factor was not apparently sufficient to establish the right of the Old Temple authorities to control the Mosna trade route. It is difficult to study the megalithic wall to the north of Chavín de Huántar without concluding that the threat of physical coercion must have existed to prevent outside groups accustomed to using this natural path from breaching the stone barrier.

A related observation is that lances and shields are depicted on the sculptures of the Circular Plaza, and realistic trophy heads are shown hanging from the waist of a Lanzón-like supernatural on one of the Ofrendas bottles. Other sculptures from Chavín de Huántar and neighboring sites graphically show knife-, club-, sling- and atlatl-wielding priests and bleeding trophy heads.[80] It seems likely that these sculptures were intended to express the authority of the earthly representatives of the fierce Lanzón deity and Great Cayman to organize *ad hoc* raiding parties and to defend the temple center and trade route from outside groups.

The Old Temple of Chavín de Huántar represented an innovation in the sociocultural patterns of the Callejón de Conchucos and the neighboring Callejón de Huaylas, but comparable centers already existed further to the north in the highlands at Kuntur Wasi and Pacopampa, as well as along the entire central and north coast. Available radiocarbon measurements from the northern Urabarriu habitation area and the Gallery of the Offerings indicate that the construction of the Old Temple and the occupation of the area around it probably did not begin much before the 10th century BC.[81] Therefore, the Old Temple would seem to be one of the *last* major Initial Period cult centers to be constructed, rather than one of the earliest as Tello believed. This conclusion is consistent with the unusually synthetic character of the architecture and art. The Old Temple can be seen as a latecomer, eclectically selecting elements from successful religious complexes elsewhere. Even the specific institutional mechanisms which permitted the Old Temple to organize labor and extract surplus may have been modeled after innovations made in these older centers.

The Proto-Urban Center of Chavín de Huántar

Unlike many of the early public centers on the coast, Chavín de Huántar continued to thrive during the Early Horizon. The remodeled and expanded cult center, called the New Temple, was among the most impressive ceremonial complexes in Peru. Even more interesting from an anthropological perspective was the corresponding growth of the surrounding community into a large settlement. Though the evidence is fragmentary, it is possible to piece together the evolution of Chavín de Huántar from its origins as a local ceremonial center during the Initial Period to a proto-urban center during the Early Horizon.

The Urabarriu phase, during which the Old Temple was built, is estimated to have lasted from 1000 BC to 500 BC on the basis of radiocarbon measurements associated with Urabarriu refuse and exotic materials from the Gallery of the Offerings (see Appendix). The Urabarriu phase was followed by the Chakinani phase and the Janabarriu phase, both of which fall within the Early Horizon and are contemporary with the New Temple. Only two radiocarbon measurements are available for the Chakinani phase: 408 BC and 400 BC, and its duration is tentatively estimated as 500–400 BC. The absolute dating of the final phase of the Chavín culture, the Janabarriu phase, remains problematic but it probably lasted from around 400 to 200 BC, bracketed between the Chakinani phase and the Huarás culture.[1]

Chronology

Following the Urabarriu phase, the northern settlement area of Chavín de Huántar was abandoned and the entire population gathered into a single nucleated community on both sides of the Huachecsa River. The Chakinani phase site covers approximately 15 hectares, an area twice that of the preceding phase and several times larger than the surrounding villages; but it is unlikely to have contained more than 1,000 residents.[2] The change that occurred in the relationship between what had once been two closely related communities, separated by half a kilometer, may be as significant as the absolute increase in village size. It is tempting to see this new configuration as a reflection of the rising power and prestige of the temple leadership, as well as the increasing economic opportunities provided by the flourishing New Temple. The concentration of population around the ritual core during the Chakinani phase is a transitional stage in the growth of Chavín de Huántar.

The Chakinani-phase settlement

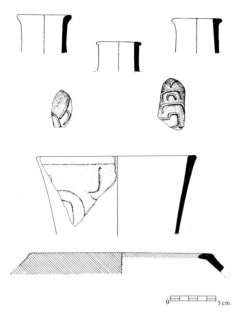

164 A selection of Chakinani-phase bottles, bowls, and cooking vessel fragments.

Ceramic style

The domestic pottery of the Chakinani phase is considerably more refined and elaborate than that recovered from the Urabarriu habitation area.[3] Although superb pottery was produced prior to the Chakinani phase, as illustrated by some of the materials in the Gallery of the Offerings, it was rarely encountered in the refuse. In contrast, fragments of finely finished and decorated classic Chavín bowls and bottles abound in the Chakinani phase habitation refuse on the slopes above the New Temple. Many serving vessels have even black surfaces polished to a high luster never surpassed at Chavín de Huántar, while others were completely covered with a graphite wash to create a silvery mirror-like surface. Complex curvilinear designs displaced simple geometric motifs as the preferred decoration for local household pottery.

The most carefully crafted class of vessel was the bottle, perhaps because it was used for chicha beer in domestic rituals and social occasions. Its characteristic form during the Chakinani phase was the stirrup-spouted bottle, rather than the single-necked bottle, and elaborate incised designs often cover the stirrup as well as the bottle chamber. The craftsmanship of Chakinani pottery bespeaks a prosperous community requiring a quality of products unknown in simple rural villages. Moreover, the pervasiveness of religious symbols on everyday pottery manifests the profound connection between the settlement and the temple, and also suggests the degree to which the religious ideology of this center structured daily life, probably including the subsistence activities of the populace.

Economy

In late prehistoric times, and even in many modern highland communities, the building and annual cleaning of canals is intertwined with cyclical rituals of fertility and ancestor worship. These "mundane" activities of hydraulic maintenance are scheduled in accordance with the religious calendar and carried out in conjunction with ritual offerings, feasting, music, and dance. At Chavín de Huántar, the temple authorities might well have been responsible for designing the canals and organizing labor for their building and upkeep. The scale of the canal system and the technical knowledge needed for its construction makes other alternatives unlikely. The hydraulic system at Chavín de Huántar extends well beyond the ritual precinct. Numerous canals have been found in the ancient settlement area and may have served to irrigate household gardens. The full extent of the canal system is unknown but there is a large canal surrounded by open fields located 3 km to the north of Chavín de Huántar near the modern hamlet of Machgas. This canal was virtually identical in construction to the principal canals of the temple area, and a fragment of a Chakinani-phase bowl was found on its floor.[4]

The economy of the Chakinani-phase settlement appears to have been increasingly tied to opportunities created by the temple, and the community was correspondingly less involved in producing all of its own food. Faunal analysis has provided some of the best evidence of this shift away from self-sufficiency.[5] Wild animals were still an important source of animal protein during the Urabarriu phase, but they became economically insignificant during Chakinani times. For example, the viscacha (a large burrowing rodent reminiscent of a

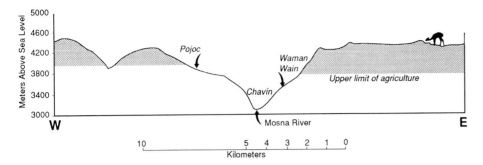

165 Integrating the vast *puna* pasturelands into the local subsistence system was an important element in the expansion of the Chavín de Huántar economy during the Early Horizon.

rabbit) no longer appears with any frequency in the refuse, and previously common deer remains constitute only 2 percent of the identifiable bones. Camelids make up 95 percent of the Chakinani faunal assemblage, and the majority of these appear to be llamas. The change in the faunal assemblage between the Urabarriu and Chakinani phases thus reflects the transition from an economic strategy of mixed herding and hunting to one of specialized llama breeding.

A closer look at the Chakinani camelid bones reveals that this transformation also brought a profound alteration in meat production. The frequency of camelid crania and feet bones in the Chakinani and Janabarriu faunal assemblages is unnaturally low, displaying a skewed representation of skeletal parts not observed for the Urabarriu phase. The most plausible explanation is inspired by ethnographic observations of modern high-altitude pastoralist-farmers in southern Peru. In these communities, animals are slaughtered at the onset of the cold season (usually May) when pastures begin to become scarce and animals are vulnerable to frosts. The alternation of nightly winter frosts and the hot midday sun is then used to dehydrate the butchered meat and convert it into *ch'arki*, a dried meat product which can be conserved for years. Most of this *ch'arki* is exchanged with farmers living at lower elevations for agricultural goods such as maize, and other goods not available locally, such as salt or manufactured items. Animal feet and heads are not considered suitable for making *ch'arki* and are therefore consumed locally by the herders; these body parts rarely reach the valley settlements. In contrast, bones from the torso, meaty forelimbs, and hindlimbs remain embedded in the *ch'arki* and are eventually disposed of far from where the animal was herded and butchered.[6]

If the skewed bone representation of the Chakinani and Janabarriu phases reflects this "*ch'arki* effect," it would imply that Chavín de Huántar had begun to depend on high-altitude communities such as Pójoc for their meat, itself no longer primarily responsible for meat production. This, of course, is consistent with the near absence of projectile points (presumed to be hunting implements), and the scarcity of wild game in the valley floor refuse. The strengthening of religious, as well as economic, links between the valley floor residents and the villagers adjacent to the *puna* pastureland during the Urabarriu phase mentioned in the last chapter apparently paved the way for the integration of the two settlements into a single socioeconomic system during the Chakinani phase.

This deepening relationship would have facilitated the acquisition of cargo animals for the long-distance transport of goods, as well as helping to ensure the safe passage of pilgrims and commerce across the desolate open stretches of the

166 Early Horizon villages such as Waman Wain were frequently located along ridges near the boundary between the upper limits of agriculture and the beginning of *puna* pasturelands.

puna and the narrow high-altitude passes of the surrounding mountain ranges. Some sense of the benefits to the valley residents from this relationship can be gleaned from the abundance of exotic foods in the Chakinani-phase refuse. Shell fragments of Pacific clams, mussels, and scallops, and bones from at least three kinds of marine fish are conspicuous indicators of the increased flow of goods between the coast and highlands. The presence in Chavín de Huántar's domestic refuse of obsidian flakes from Quispisisa in Huancavelica in the south-central highlands and fragments of "Mosna" pottery from the northern highlands implies the existence of an analogous long-distance movement of goods through the highlands. The way in which these goods reached the households is still poorly understood. It is conceivable that they were acquired by the temple authorities and redistributed to the local inhabitants. But whatever the mechanisms, it is clear that these exotic items were distributed throughout the society rather than being concentrated within the temple precinct. In fact, Pacific shells, obsidian, and even *Spondylus* have been recovered in Early Horizon contexts in the small villages above Chavín de Huántar.[7]

The Janabarriu settlement

The population of Chavín de Huántar continued to grow during the Janabarriu phase until the site covered approximately 42 hectares of the western banks of the Mosna. The residences were dispersed, but the total population may have approached 2,000–3,000 people. This was an extremely large settlement, one of the largest in Peru during the Early Horizon. The monumental constructions still lay at the core of the site, but they constituted less than 12 percent of its total area. By this time, the settlement was some 20 times larger than the villages and hamlets which supported it.[8]

Dwellings covered the level land around the temple, and in order to gain additional land for habitation the lower slopes of the valley were terraced. One of the few excavations of such a terrace revealed an offering of guinea pigs and

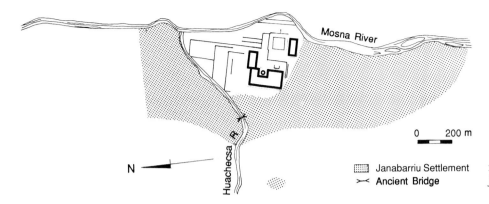

Mosna River

0   200 m

N

Huachecsa R.

▦ Janabarriu Settlement
⤬ Ancient Bridge

167 Map showing the extent of the Janabarriu-phase settlement.

Spondylus shell beneath the platform floor and the base of the retaining wall. The guinea pigs were probably eaten in feasts marking the beginning and end of this Janabarriu phase construction. (Indeed, the fatty succulent meat of the guinea pig is still a common holiday dish in most of the central Andes. Despite its small size, it is generally divided among three or four people, although special guests are occasionally served a half or an entire animal, while low status individuals or children may be given only the feet or head.) Since the remains of a minimum of 40 guinea pigs were recovered from the offerings of the Janabarriu platform and only a small section of the structure was excavated, it is likely that a very large group was involved in the feasting, and presumably in the actual construction of the terrace. The presence of *Spondylus* shell, a preferred offering to the Andean gods, points to the role of religious ritual in the organization of collective labor for what are often considered secular objectives.[9]

The expansion of the settlement during the Janabarriu phase reflects the success and development of the earlier Chavín de Huántar economy. In the agricultural realm, for example, C_{12}/C_{13} analyses (Chapter 5) suggest that maize consumption increased only slightly, if at all, and that C_3 crops such as potatoes remained the basis of the diet. Similarly, llamas continued to provide around 95 percent of the meat consumed. As in the preceding phase, this meat was mostly imported as *ch'arki* and it is safe to assume that the division of labor between the high-altitude pastoralist-farmers and the more urban residents of Chavín de Huántar continued to be a basic feature of the economy.[10]

There is considerable cultural continuity between the Janabarriu phase and the preceding phases. Everyday items such as bone needles and awls, ground stone axes, chipped or polished stone points and knives, and even ground stone anthracite mirrors display only minor differences between the Urabarriu and Janabarriu phases.[11] One of the rare additions to the household toolkit is the rocker grinder. This consists of a heavy stone with a curved lower edge, sometimes shaped by pecking and polishing, which was used to grind grain and other foods. Rocked back and forth on a flat stone base, these stones used gravity rather than human strength to pulverize, and consequently saved countless hours of hard labor. The efficiency of this device is still evident in highland Peru where daily grinding is often done by children or the elderly (rather than by adult women as in Mesoamerica, where the mano and metate are still used). Rocker-grinders were found in Janabarriu contexts in Chavín de Huántar and in the nearby coeval village of Pójoc.[12]

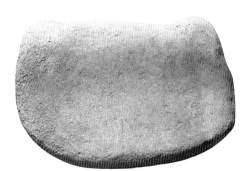

168 A rocker-grinder with carved handles that was uncovered in a Janabarriu-phase building at the high-altitude village of Pojoc. Width 38 cm.

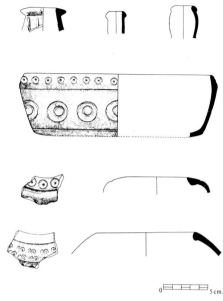

169 A selection of Janabarriu-phase bottles, bowls, and cooking vessel fragments.

Ceramics

Perhaps the best evidence of cultural continuity at Chavín de Huántar comes from the domestic pottery.[13] Most Janabarriu pottery, like that of the preceding phase, is either blackened by superficial reduction or covered with pre-fire red hematite slip. The black or red monochrome surfaces are decorated by a host of surface texturing techniques such as rocker-stamping, dentate rocker-stamping, rouletting, combing, appliqué nubbins, and so forth. Highly polished lustrous zones are often contrasted with adjacent mat zones to heighten the visibility of these patterns. The form, technology, finishing, and decorative techniques are almost all derived from Chakinani antecedents.

There are, however, some features of the Janabarriu ceramic assemblage which are distinctive, and therefore particularly useful for dating. Probably the most diagnostic feature of Janabarriu pottery is the frequency of designs made by stamps and seals. Circles, circle-dots, S's, and other stylized designs extracted from religious iconography are impressed in rows on the exteriors of bowls, cooking pots, plates, and cups. This labor-saving device exceeded the popularity of more complex incised motifs on all vessels except the highly prized stirrup-spouted bottles. One wonders whether the increased use of seals might not be in response to greater demand for Chavín de Huántar pottery from beyond the immediate area. Exterior beveling of bowl rims also sharply increases in popularity as does the exterior thickening of rims by adding an extra ridge of clay to form a flange. The latter practice, first introduced on Chakinani-phase bottle spouts, is extended to cups and bowls during the Janabarriu phase, and on bottles these exterior flanges are often rounded into a phallic shape.

Other products

Exotic items, both utilitarian and sumptuary, increased in volume and variety and it is difficult to avoid the conclusion that the growth of Chavín de Huántar was intimately tied to a boom in long-distance exchange, as well as to the pan-regional drawing power of the temple. The penetration of exotic materials into the local economy is exemplified by the role of obsidian. The closest source is 470 km to the south at Quispisisa, a journey which would take a llama caravan approximately a month each way. Alternative materials such as quartzite are locally available, and chert, which was indeed used for some tools, can be acquired within a two-day trip. Nevertheless, obsidian was by far the most frequent lithic material recovered from Janabarriu-phase refuse and literally hundreds of flakes were recovered from small test pits. Many of these flakes show remnants of the original stone surface, indicating that the obsidian was imported as nodules and fashioned into tools at Chavín de Huántar.

Obsidian flakes were found in all parts of the site, regardless of household status.[14] Similarly, the same kinds of domestic pottery, bone needles, small unifaces, and anthracite mirrors were recovered from different sectors of the settlement. Polished stone earspool fragments, made of chlorite, are also found throughout the habitation area.[15] From the large diameter of these artifacts (40–52 mm) we can infer that they were worn by adults. These beautifully carved ear ornaments may have been ceremonially presented at the transition to adulthood as they were in some later pre-Hispanic cultures of Peru (and are to this day in parts of the Amazonian rainforest). These elements of material culture shared by the entire settlement, however, are only part of the picture: there were also striking economic and social *differences* within Janabarriu-phase society.

Differentiation in Janabarriu society

Excavation in the Janabarriu settlement has been limited in scope, but it has been demonstrated that craft activities were carried out in the habitation area, and that households may have specialized in producing particular classes of artifacts for exchange. For example, 200 m to the east of the temple, 53 *Spondylus* fragments were recovered, the majority of which were by-products of the manufacture of beads and pendants. Unmodified *Spondylus* shell was apparently brought to Chavín de Huántar from Ecuador, and was then transformed into ornaments for local use or perhaps for exchange with visitors from communities lacking the socioeconomic power to acquire this highly valued raw material.[16]

Further from the temple on the north side of the Huachecsa River in sector A, a lithic assemblage was recovered which includes large unifaces, ground stone knives, and stone perforators or gravers. These tools are absent from other parts of the settlement. The production of goods from perishable materials, such as hide, appears to have been a distinctive feature of sector A's household economy, just as *Spondylus*-working may have been in sector D. How many types of craft activities were carried out in the settlement? Did these activities supplement or replace agricultural labor by these household groups? We cannot yet answer these questions, but the information at hand is sufficient to conclude that a range of craft activities was carried out in the residential areas, and that the production of certain kinds of goods was restricted to particular parts of the site. These observations from outside the temple precinct are consistent with traditional suggestions of craft specialization at Chavín de Huántar based on the quality of the stone sculpture, the sophistication of the hydraulic system, and other features in the center which seem to imply the existence of artists and engineers working on the temple.

Did the existence of full- or part-time occupational specialization at Chavín de Huántar during the Early Horizon lead to an unequal concentration of economic wealth and the emergence of unambiguous social stratification? Once again, the sample is small but many separate lines of evidence point to the conclusion that households in different sectors did not have equal access to the same resources. This suggests that social stratification had set in by the Janabarriu phase.

A comparison of the refuse from sectors A and D illustrates this. The remains of Pacific fish and shellfish are much more common in the refuse of sector D than in sector A, as is the presence of foreign pottery. Likewise, the only known example of gold jewelry from a Janabarriu-phase context derives from sector D. If the rectangular dwellings of these two sectors are considered, we find that both utilize locally available undressed stone and clay mortar, rather than the cut and polished granite and black limestone of the temple. Nevertheless, evidence exists in sector D for houses with tall stone walls and niches, while in sector A there is evidence only of stone foundations, the buildings presumably made of adobe or other perishable materials.[17]

A final indication of incipient class differences between the households in sectors A and D comes from a comparison of the meat consumed in the two sectors. In both areas, llamas constitute the prime source of meat, but in sector D, 80 percent of the llamas eaten were 3 years old or less, while in sector A, 65 percent were over 3 years old and 60 percent were over 4. In short, it would appear that while the residents of sector D were dining on the meat of tender young llamas, the people in sector A were consuming tough animals which had reached the end of their lives as productive cargo animals.[18]

The preceding overview of the Janabarriu-phase settlement suggests a society undergoing the initial stages of urbanization and the social transformations often associated with it. The society's increasing differentiation would have reinforced the role of the religious authorities to act as mediators between the residents of Chavín de Huántar, the rural peasantry, and the outsiders drawn to the temple for religious and economic reasons. Evidence from Mesoamerica and the Old World might suggest that the concentration of power in the hands of these authorities would lead to the emergence of a highly visible ruling class which reinforced its authority creating public art glorifying the ruling elite. It has become apparent, however, that no such scenario took place at Chavín de Huántar. On the contrary, the temple authorities continued to remain hidden behind the mysterious images of the Chavín supernaturals.

Perhaps leadership at the site continued to be exercised by a priestly organization rather than by individual families. If this were the case, the absence of historical imagery could be understood as a reflection of the corporate and sacerdotal nature of authority. The fundamental justification of such a society would continue to derive from claims of sacred knowledge and supernatural support rather than the deeds of historical figures. With these concerns in mind, it is interesting to focus again on the public art and ceremonial architecture of Chavín de Huántar, and to consider how it was modified during the Janabarriu phase while the surrounding settlement was undergoing the profound socio-economic transformation just described.

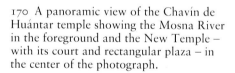

170 A panoramic view of the Chavín de Huántar temple showing the Mosna River in the foreground and the New Temple – with its court and rectangular plaza – in the center of the photograph.

Sculpture

The enlargement of the ceremonial precinct required the production of a multitude of new sculptures. As in the Old Temple, most of the carvings were set in the exterior walls as cornices, tenons and, most frequently, ornamental facing. The style of the New Temple carvings forms a continuum with that of the Old Temple.

The sculptural style of the New Temple has been divided into two phases: D and EF. Phase D is defined on the basis of the carved columns flanking the Black and White Portal of the New Temple. The large carved lintel which spanned the columns, and the series of sculptures from the small court or patio directly in front of the Portal, form a single stylistic unit which is anchored architecturally to the southern expansion of the central pyramid. The Raimondi Stone (see below) serves as the basis for Phase EF.[19] Its placement at the end of the sequence was originally due to its distinctive style and its similarity to the Phase D sculptures as opposed to the Phase AB or C carvings. This seriational argument is now supported by the *in situ* discovery by Marino Gonzales of columns carved in a style related to the Raimondi Stone.[20] These columns were designed to flank the so-called Monumental Stairway leading down to the rectangular plaza, but at least one was never completed. Judging from their location at the site, the columns cannot be earlier than the Black and White Portal, but they could be contemporary or later. The unfinished state of one of the columns suggests that

The New Temple

172 An unfinished column with Chavín designs, found next to the staircase leading down to the rectangular plaza at Chavín de Huántar.

173 The eastern facade of the New Temple and its Black and White Portal.

174 Fragment of a sculpture illustrating the late Chavín tendency towards rectilinearity and modular width. Height 87 cm.

175 Sculpture of the supreme deity (53 cm high) that decorated the patio of the New Temple. The deity holds a *Strombus* shell in its right hand and a *Spondylus* shell in its left, a metaphor for its role in balancing the male and female forces of the universe. See also ill. 183.

the carving of this sculpture was halted by the events leading to the abandonment of the temple. Significantly, it is in EF style, reinforcing the final portion of Rowe's sculptural seriation.

For the most part, the changes in the sculptural style of the New Temple are in degree rather than kind. Both phases (D and EF) display the full range of Chavín conventions: kennings, anatropic design, dual profiles, bilateral symmetry, and modular width. As the use of these conventions intensified, the resulting images became more sophisticated and complex. The price of this stylistic extravagance was the loss of some of the original strength of the earlier Chavín images.

The evolution of the Chavín style from the Lanzón to the columns of the Black and White Portal, and finally to the Raimondi Stone constitutes what the anthropologist Alfred Kroeber called "a style cycle."[21] Such cycles begin with the relatively simple and evolve into sophisticated and complex styles until the point of diminishing returns is reached. This should not, however, distract from the significance of the fact that the conventions already evident in the Lanzón continued to serve as the basis for the art of the New Temple.

Perhaps the most distinctive element of Phase D style is the use of angular mouths, eyes, and eyebrows. The use of kennings proliferates, sometimes almost overshadowing the principal themes. Phase EF sculptures emphasize modular width in their design, and pieces like the Raimondi Stone look almost as if they were produced on grid paper or, probably more to the point, on a weaver's loom. The loss of naturalistic detail is especially evident in secondary elements, such as snake heads, where the nose and sometimes even the mouth are omitted.

The thematic content in the sacred images of the New Temple does not seem to differ significantly from that of the Old Temple. The main deity is represented on a small bas-relief sculpture recovered in the rubble of the patio of the New Temple, and the anthropomorphic figure shown is the same as the one carved on the Lanzón five centuries earlier. The deity is shown frontally with its enlarged upper canines and upturned snarling mouth. As before, the supernatural is elaborately arrayed in bracelets, anklets, and a pair of circular ear pendants, with braided serpents growing from its head. Its stance differs from that of the Lanzón, but it still conveys the same message: the power to mediate and maintain harmony. The deity holds a *Strombus* shell in its right hand and a *Spondylus* in its left.

In ancient Andean ritual, these two shells formed a symbolic dyad with the *Strombus*, associated with male forces, and the reddish *Spondylus*, representing female forces. This symbolism was maintained by the 20th-century Kogi priests of Colombia and a variant of it still exists in the fertility rituals of the Peruvian highlands.[22] Since both of these mollusks are native to coastal Ecuador, the choice of this dyad indirectly alludes to the temple's ability to acquire non-local materials, including the exotic shells and other ritual paraphernalia considered essential for appeasing the appetites of the deities and maintaining fertility.

The Raimondi Stone depicts the same anthropomorphic deity, but in the highly stylized EF style. The finely executed carving was carried out on a large highly polished granite ashlar, measuring 1.98 m in height, 74 cm in width and 17 cm in thickness. The figure of the deity shown full face occupies only the lower third of the sculpture. Elaborate staffs held in each hand still convey the message of balance and authority, but the deity's distinctive earspools and hairstyle have been sacrificed to give freer rein to the late Chavín artistic conventions. Nearly

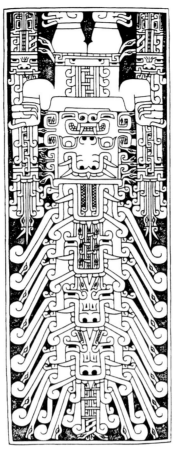

176 The Raimondi Stone is one of the final representations of the supreme deity in Chavín art. Besides the pronounced anatropic organization (which can be seen in the inverted image on the right), there is also a heavy reliance on the use of modular width as a convention. Height 1.95 m.

two-thirds of the carving is devoted to a stylized depiction of the deity's headdress. Repeating scrolls on recurved rays emanate from its sides and the inverted feline faces that adorn it.

The secondary supernaturals of the New Temple show the same continuity with the belief system of the Old Temple. As in the past, crested eagles and hawks with their wings fully opened decorate the base of the pyramid and snakes continue to pervade the art style. Jaguars are less common, but several late Chavín jaguar representations on cornices and ashlars are known including one with emanating recurved rays like those of the Raimondi Stone. Monstrous caymans still held a special place in the supernatural pantheon, and one decorates the lintel carved to span the Monumental Staircase. As in the Old Temple, the tenoned heads emphasize themes of shamanic transformation and evidence for the ritual use of hallucinogenic drugs is as strong in the New Temple as it was in the Old.

As we have seen, complementary opposition remained at the heart of Chavín cosmology. The carved columns of the Black and White Portal illustrate the way in which this theme was expressed in the iconography of public constructions. The Portal consists of a short two-color stairway flanked by cylindrical andesite columns and massive stone jambs. Each column depicts an anthropomorphized, staff-bearing bird of prey that may have been attendants of the principal deity. The two columns were arranged symmetrically in relation to the central axis of a

177 Jaguars continued to be depicted in the art of the New Temple, as seen in this photograph of a late Chavín cornice.

178,179 The two columns of the Black and White Portal were carved with contrasting images of supernatural birds: (*left*) a supernatural crested eagle with female attributes and water associations, and (*right*) a male supernatural hawk with sky associations.

180 The sculptures decorating the small court of the New Temple depicted a wide range of supernatural figures, such as this anthropomorphized monkey (or priest impersonator) holding a serpent staff in one hand and a *Strombus* shell trumpet in the other.

181 A miniature tenoned head, 27 cm long, with a San Pedro cactus growing from its eye.

bi-color staircase. The bird on the northern column displays a zig-zag eye-band that identifies the hawk; the avian of the southern column is a crested eagle, perhaps the harpy eagle.[23] A host of other differences in position and detail distinguish these superficially similar images from one another. The most striking of these differences is in the metaphorical representation of the genitals. On the northern column, the agnathic face at the juncture of the upper and lower body displays a prominent central fang, which can be interpreted as phallic; the nostrils probably correspond to the testicles. The crested eagle of the southern column has a double profile treatment of the waist, and a vertically oriented set of teeth which seem to be a pre-Columbian expression of what Freud called the "vagina dentata" theme.[24] These complex avian representations completely enveloped the cylindrical columns and are consequently unintelligible to the viewer. Modern scholars make use of rubbings to understand their content, but to most ancient visitors the images must have remained as inaccessible as the interior galleries of the temple.

The columns and adjacent jambs of the Black and White Portal supported a two-piece lintel that spanned almost 10 m. It depicts alternating pairs of crested eagles and hawks in procession towards an imaginary line in the center of the lintel. This arrangement is fundamentally the same as that of the jaguars in the Old Temple's Circular Plaza, but the theme of duality is further emphasized by carving half of the lintel in white granite and half in black limestone.[25]

It would be difficult to argue for any significant change in the religious ideology of the New Temple solely from the content of the sculptures. Rare depictions of *Spondylus* and fish appear on the ceiling slabs of one interior chamber, the Chamber of the Ornamental Beams (Celda de las Vigas Ornamentales), but these have antecedents on the Tello Obelisk.[26] Moreover, the association of ocean elements with interior rooms and galleries had already been established in the Old Temple by the offerings in the Gallery of the Snails. Three carved ashlars from the patio of the New Temple are more innovative. One shows an anthropomorphized howler monkey blowing a *Strombus* shell trumpet, another depicts a viscacha, and a third represents either a bat or a butterfly.[27] Could this apparent proliferation of secondary supernaturals have consciously or unconsciously reflected the increasing heterogeneity of Chavín society?

Architecture

The continuity in religious cosmology was also mirrored in the architecture of the New Temple. Like the sculpture, the architecture embodies and expresses the religious ideology, though perhaps in more subtle ways. Virtually all the architectural designs present in the Old Temple are reproduced in the New Temple, including cut and polished ashlars, cornices, tenoned heads, truncated platforms, sunken plazas, and subterranean passageways. The building technology, including the hydraulic and ventilation systems, also remains unchanged. Consequently, the renovation and expansion of the ceremonial center during the Early Horizon do not imply radical changes in ideology.

During the Early Horizon, the southern wing of the Old Temple doubled in size. The massive truncated pyramid was enlarged in two stages on its southern edge. The sections added are identifiable from vertical seams still visible on the eastern and western faces of the temple and from minor modifications in the masonry style of the temple walls. In the second and final extension, the cutting and polishing of the blocks shows greater skill than in the earlier construction stages. Nevertheless, the orientation of the pyramids, interior galleries, and plazas of the Old and New Temple are the same.

On the summit of the enlarged southern wing of the temple was a 2-m high square platform on top of which were a matching pair of two-room buildings of cut and dressed stone.[28] These constructions, and the flat roof surface around them, would have been visible from the plazas and terraces to the east, and were probably a focus of ceremonial activity. Access to the rooftop is through a maze of subterranean passages and stairways. No central staircase exists in the New Temple and thus its summit appeared even less accessible than in the Old Temple. Two rectangular openings with short stairways are located 6 m above ground level, which would have allowed the priests to emerge mysteriously from the core of the pyramid to conduct rituals without having to descend to the open plaza. There is no evidence that these "reverse balconies" were ever connected to the Black and White Portal below.

The arrangement of paired summit buildings and dual inset balconies indicates the establishment of a second axis of ceremonial organization, bisecting the enlarged southern wing and running parallel to that of the Old Temple. This ritual axis is made explicit in the decoration of the New Temple. The Black and White Portal is located precisely at the center of the New Temple's eastern parament and immediately in front of it is a square semisubterranean patio or court, 20 m wide. A short stone stairway leads down into the patio from the Portal. The sides of the patio were faced with finely cut and polished stones, and decorated with a host of small rectangular sculptures, some of which have already been described. From the patio, a second black-and-white stairway, called the Monumental Staircase, provides access to the principal plaza of the New Temple. This rectangular plaza measures 105 m by 85 m, and encloses a still lower square sunken court measuring 50 m on a side. The scale of the plaza and the size of the stones in the staircases leading into it surpass anything known from the Old Temple.

In the southwest corner of the lowest plaza's upper level there is a 10-ton limestone slab whose upper surface has been pecked to form seven circular depressions. It has been dubbed the Altar of Choque Chinchay because the

182–184 Three of the carved slabs which adorned the New Temple, portraying a butterfly or bat (*top*), the supreme deity (*center*), and a viscacha (*bottom*).

177

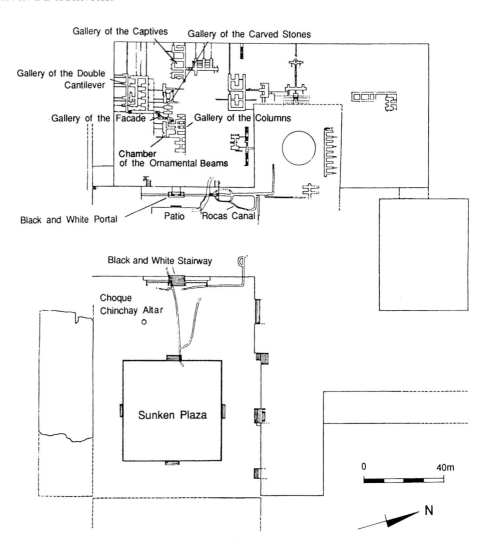

185 Map showing the New Temple and its gallery complexes.

186 An offering of a Janabarriu-phase bottle was found in the New Temple's rectangular plaza.

distribution of the depressions resembles the cluster of seven stars visible to the naked eye that was known in the Old World as the Pleiades. In modern times, Quechua farmers in Cuzco observe this star cluster which is sometimes called the Collca (i.e. store house). According to ethnographer Gary Urton, the star clusters in the Collca constellation are the main astronomical observations used to schedule the planting of crops and predict the outcome of the harvest.[29]

The rectangular plaza is flanked by a low platform on the north and a small truncated platform on the south, recreating the general configuration of a U. This does not mean, however, that this new complex replaced the original temple.[30] In fact, the Old Temple and Circular Plaza seem to have continued to function during the Early Horizon, and an elaborate stairway leads out of the northwest corner of the rectangular plaza in the direction of the Old Temple. However, the new rectangular plaza could easily have held over 1,500 people and must have relieved pressure on the Old Temple facilities from the growing numbers of pilgrims.

The cylindrical columns and sunken rectangular plazas of the New Temple are unknown in the Old Temple, but they have numerous antecedents in the late

Initial Period architecture of the north coast at sites such as Huaca de los Reyes, Purulén, and Huaca Lucía. Similarly, the Altar of the Choque Chinchay resembles the pecked stone "altars" of the late Initial Period northern highlands site of Poro-Poro in the headwaters of Zaña. The northern architectural features seem to appear at the same time as such iconographic elements as the angled mouth, which also have long histories at Initial Period centers in the north. The apparent incorporation of exotic architectural and artistic elements, even at the height of Chavín de Huántar's popularity can be interpreted as part of its continuing effort to create a cosmopolitan style through synthesis – a style which was unique to Chavín de Huántar, but not entirely foreign to most of its visitors.

A supplicant at the New Temple would descend to the edge of the Mosna and then, if permitted, ascend through a series of defined open areas. Each new environment is higher and presumably more sacred than the previous one. In this light, it is understandable why the large lower rectangular plaza is unpaved and its walls are made of undecorated ashlars with variable size and polishing, while the upper patio features sculptures and finely polished ashlars of standardized size and quality. The upper environments are also smaller in size and entry into them may have been restricted to the select, as at Pachacamac.

Additional gallery complexes were built within the New Temple which, like the accompanying canals and ventilation shafts, were connected to the pre-existing subterranean features of the Old Temple. Each gallery of the New Temple has distinctive features. The Gallery of the Columns is the best-known complex within the first temple extension, and is so-named for the engaged cylindrical columns of clay and stone in the walls of two small rectangular chambers. This complex originally included the Chamber of the Ornamental Beams, which is an unusually large room measuring 8 m in length. Like other interior chambers, its ceiling consists of parallel rectangular stone slabs, but uniquely two of its beams are sculpted. The carving on one depicts four *Spondylus* shells, and on the other is a fanged fish surrounded by crosses and circle-cross motifs. Remnants of red, green, and blue pigment remain on these sheltered carvings, which suggests that at one time they were painted in bright polychrome colors.[31] The sculptures decorating the outside of the temple may have also once been painted.

A series of long passageways and stairways lead from the Gallery of the Columns to a gallery with finely dressed ashlars, at the southern limit of the first building extension. According to Luis Lumbreras and Hernán Amat, this gallery functioned as the entrance into the temple before the second extension was

187 A portion of the supernatural with cayman attributes carved on the cornice decorating the entryway into the rectangular plaza.

188 Carvings of fish and *Spondylus* shells appear on the roof of the Chamber of the Ornamental Beams, reinforcing the strong water associations of several of the subterranean gallery complexes.

189 Some of the passageways and chambers inside the New Temple, such as the Gallery of the Facade, were constructed from cut stone blocks.

added, and they consequently called it the Gallery of the Facade (Galería de la Portada). Another subterranean complex in the first extension also utilizes dressed ashlars, but it consists of two levels of rectangular chambers connected by a stairway; these are collectively known as the Gallery of the Carved Stones (Galería de las Piedras Labradas). Further to the west is the Gallery of the Captives (Galería de los Cautivos), whose name derives from wild speculation that prisoners may have been tied to the short stone shafts which jut out from the walls. Its L-shaped chambers are unique. As in the Gallery of the Columns, the stonework in the Gallery of the Captives is coarse and was probably once covered in clay plaster.[32]

The growth and prosperity of Chavín de Huántar had its basis in three inter-related developments: the expansion of long-distance trade, the panregional popularity of its temple cult, and the integration of specialized llama herding into the local agricultural system. Religious ideology served as a catalyst in this process as it provided the rationale first for linking the rural communities to the valley floor center, and then for establishing ties with more distant regions previously unrelated to Chavín de Huántar. In societies based on ideologies of kinship and reciprocal exchange like those of the Initial Period, new religious beliefs can provide the energy and direction necessary to overcome the fears and antagonisms produced by long-standing provincialism, and the internal tensions among groups provoked by incipient stratification.

While long-distance exchange existed prior to the establishment of Chavín de Huántar, the scale and variety of items exchanged was limited, especially compared to that of the Early Horizon. Long-distance movement of bulk goods in the Andes required a constant supply of llamas as pack animals, and the unfettered use of open grasslands through which trade routes could pass. The consolidation of a socioeconomic system which included both the valley dwellers and the high-altitude pastoralist-farmers was thus a critical step. The resulting availability to valley residents of llama meat in the form of *ch'arki* was only one advantage of this relationship.

The details of Chavín cosmology remain unknown, but like all religions it must have consisted of a code of values as well as a cosmology. In expansive cults, like that of Chavín, this code encourages a broadening of identity to include people beyond the local group. This ideology may well be expressed in the themes of the resolution of opposites and the maintenance of harmony and balance that pervade Chavín iconography, and in the inclusion of artistic and architectural elements drawn from a broad spectrum of earlier cultures. Such universalist values help to create an environment in which interregional social and economic contact is increasingly feasible and in which long-distance exchange flourishes.

But how was the temple able to extract tribute and influence the daily decisions of society? In order to answer this question it is necessary to consider the general conception of *huacas* in late pre-Hispanic Peru and their relationship to the larger socioeconomic order. The *huaca* was a sacred place or object which was considered a source of power and prosperity. It was necessary to feed and care for a *huaca*, much as one would a sacred ancestor, and in return it would ensure abundant rains and ample harvests. Thus, offerings of tribute were conceived as part of an ongoing reciprocal relationship with the larger supernatural force, and the labor and goods expended in support of the *huaca* were therefore no less relevant to community welfare than the cleaning of canals. It was the responsibility of all communities to provide public labor to maintain the *huacas*, but the largest *huacas* also had specialized priests as well as full-time servants from the supporting communities.

Disasters and illness were believed to stem from the actions of individuals, and the *huacas* were consulted to determine what deeds might have been responsible and how balance could be restored. Acts of adultery or incest, for example, might be identified as the cause of a drought or a sudden frost affecting an entire community. The priests were responsible for interpreting the answers of the *huacas* and making the required offerings, and through this role they had considerable power in controlling group behavior and resolving internal disputes. The *huacas* were consulted and offerings were made at all important events including journeys, illnesses, deaths, as well as at critical junctures in the agricultural cycle. Not surprisingly, the largest *huacas* in late pre-Hispanic times had rich storehouses well stocked with food, coca, and textiles received as tribute from worshipers drawn from many ethnic groups and ecological zones. On special occasions, these different groups were expected to participate together without conflict in drinking, dancing, feasting, and competitive games such as racing; uncontrolled violence would have provoked the wrath of the deity and risked the welfare of the group. Thus, the temple rituals served to bridge intergroup hostilities and heal any conflicts which had developed from them.

As with these later *huacas*, the wealth of the Chavín de Huántar temple was probably based in part on tribute in the form of offerings from supplicants and travelers. The collection of this income became easier as the supernatural power and efficacy of the religious center was recognized across a broader area. This acceptance probably accounts for the decrease in the depiction of trophy heads and weapons in the religious art of the New Temple, and also explains why the massive wall to the north of Chavín de Huántar was not maintained after the Urabarriu phase.

The new social environment at Chavín de Huántar permitted the concentration of several thousand people in a single settlement surrounding the temple, in what begins to approach an urban setting. Many of them, no doubt, were still engaged in agriculture, but some were part-time artisans and others probably provided services for visitors. The differential involvement of these people in activities unrelated to subsistence-oriented or kin-oriented production led to class formation and, in all likelihood, to the emergence of the state. The incipient state organization of this Early Horizon society was probably a fragile institution with very limited powers over production and distribution of goods. Its basis was the collection of tribute in the form of gifts, and its main source of authority came from supernatural claims rather than coercive power. Behind the terrifying visages of the Chavín supernaturals and the awe-inspiring elements of Chavín monumental architecture lay a group of religious leaders attempting to cope with new and complex kinds of class and inter-group conflicts with the relatively weak governing tools inherited from simpler Initial Period times.

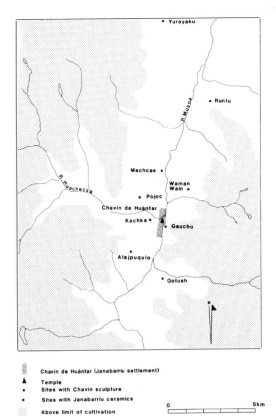

Chavín de Huántar (Janabarriu settlement)
▲ Temple
● Sites with Chavín sculpture
● Sites with Janabarriu ceramics
░ Above limit of cultivation

0   5km

190 Map showing the small sites constituting the local socioeconomic system of Chavín de Huántar.

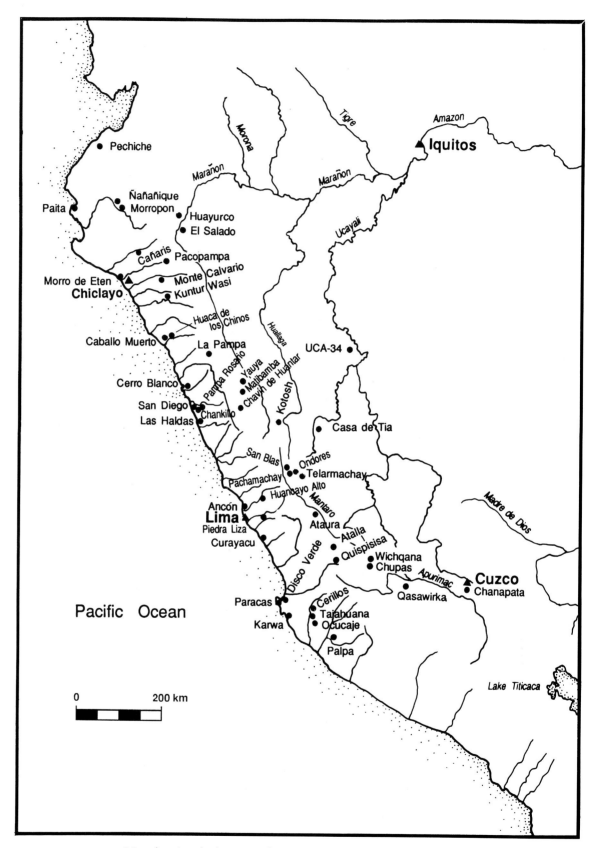

Pacific Ocean

Pechiche

Paita

Ñañañique
Morropon

Marañon

Huayurco
El Salado

Cañaris Pacopampa

Morro de Eten
Chiclayo Monte Calvario
Kuntur Wasi

Huaca de
los Chinos

Caballo Muerto La Pampa

Cerro Blanco Pampa Rosario Yauya
Majibamba
Chavín de Huántar

San Diego
Las Haldas Chankillo

Kotosh

San Blas

Pachamachay Ondores
Telarmachay

Huancayo Alto

Ancón
Lima
Piedra Liza
Curayacu

Disco Verde Maniaro

Ataura

Atalla
Quispisisa

Paracas

Karwa Cerrillos
Tajahuana
Ocucaje

Palpa

Wichqana
Chupas

Qasawirka

Morona

Tigre

Amazon

Iquitos

Marañon

Ucayali

Huallaga

UCA-34

Casa de Tia

Madre de Dios

Apurimac

Cuzco
Chanapata

Lake Titicaca

0   200 km

191 Map showing the location of Early Horizon sites discussed in Chapter 7.

The Florescence and Collapse
of Chavín Civilization

The uninterrupted development that Chavín de Huántar experienced during the late Initial Period and Early Horizon resembles a smooth pathway towards sociocultural complexity. The processes responsible for this were produced in part by forces outside the center and its surrounding hinterland. In the last chapter, I proposed that an increase in interregional exchange and tribute in the form of gifts to the religious center contributed to this transformation. If this was the case, the wealth that initially fueled the emergence of social differentiation would have come from the selective appropriation of non-local resources rather than from local agricultural goods. In order to better understand the changes, therefore, it is necessary to shift from a narrow focus on Chavín de Huántar back to a broader pan-regional perspective. From this wider approach emerges a very different pattern which contradicts the impression of gradualistic evolutionary development at Chavín de Huántar.

In many portions of the central and northern Peruvian coast, radical disruptions occurred at the beginning of the first millennium B C. The widespread collapse of most major coastal centers just prior to the Early Horizon presents something of a paradox, since the developments of this period have traditionally been described as occurring within the context of cultural growth and florescence, rather than being products of a time of troubles. These contradictory perceptions result from contrasting approaches to the archaeological record: one emphasizing the style and technology of artifacts as the basis for understanding prehistoric culture, the other focusing on the monumentality, areal extent, and distribution of ancient sites as an expression of prehistoric sociopolitical organization.

What struck Julio C. Tello and many later scholars as remarkable about the cultures of the Early Horizon was the quality of the religious art, the sophisticated and innovative technologies used to produce it, and the unprecedented degree of homogeneity that characterized the assemblages from previously unrelated regions. The similarities between the art and artifacts of a broad area led scholars to argue for the existence of a stylistic horizon, the earliest of Peru's three pre-Hispanic horizon styles. This phenomenon, called the Chavín horizon after the site, was seen as a useful tool in linking the myriad local and regional sequences to each other. More importantly, it was assumed to indicate a profound socioeconomic and ideological change affecting much of ancient Peru.

Unfortunately, the original formulation of the Chavín horizon by Tello,

Alfred Kroeber, Gordon Willey, and others mistakenly included Initial Period sites such as Moxeke, thereby hampering an understanding of chronology and cultural processes. After these misunderstandings have been corrected, however, there still remains a core of materials that support the existence of a Chavín horizon that lasted two or three centuries (c. 500–250 BC) during the Early Horizon. Without considering the significance of this pattern, we will not be able to understand how or why the societies of the Early Horizon differed from their Initial Period forerunners.

The spread of Chavín elements across the central Andes appeared on the heels of the collapse of many early coastal social formations. Out of this turbulence new cultural patterns emerged, including the artistic and technological achievements for which Chavín civilization is famous. An unprecedented amount of contact began to occur between distant and previously unrelated groups, entailing hitherto unknown degrees of shared ideas and technology, as well as the actual movement of goods and people. Thus, the Chavín horizon can be viewed as a forerunner of later attempts to forge a single Andean civilization out of the staggering diversity of local cultures. Before looking at the nature of Chavín civilization and possible explanations for its appearance, we will examine some of the evidence for the preceding crisis on the coast.

Crisis on the coast

By approximately 900 BC, the coastal societies responsible for some of the New World's earliest monumental architecture had begun to disintegrate, and by 700 BC few of them continued to function as they had during the Initial Period. For over a millennium, the agricultural groups on the central and north-central coast had prospered and their populations increased, while the pyramids and plaza complexes in the center of their settlements grew incrementally in size until they reached enormous proportions. The labor donated periodically to their construction and maintenance helped define community identity, and the incremental growth of these structures was, in a sense, the physical expression of community coherence and well-being. The continuous use of these centers also expressed social and ideological continuity with the ancestors. While centers were occasionally abandoned during the Initial Period, they were usually replaced by nearby complexes that were similar in concept, design, and construction technique.[1] Changes of this kind can be interpreted as relocations, perhaps due to such factors as the constructions of new canals. More common than these relocations was the creation of new centers to house the growing population, without the abandonment of old ones – such was the case of the founding of Cardal, possibly by a splinter group from the older center of Mina Perdida, located only 5 km away.[2]

The changes that occurred between 900 and 700 BC were very different. On the central coast, new construction ceased at the U-shaped complexes in the lower valleys. In Lurín, where investigation has been extensive, there is clear evidence that building was halted at both Cardal and Mina Perdida at the end of the Initial Period and the sites were subsequently abandoned. At Cardal, the community did not complete the construction of a matching pair of causewayed plazas, and never buried the final atrium complex and central staircase following the traditional practice of ritual entombment.

It remains unclear what happened to the populations that had supported the major public complexes of the central coast. No new centers with or without monumental architecture were established in the lower valleys during the Early Horizon, nor has evidence of a large rural population for this time period been recorded. Nevertheless, it is conceivable that public activity and construction at the centers could have been stopped without the depopulation of the dispersed and archaeologically difficult to detect homesteads of valley farmers. Alternatively, the people of the lower valley could have migrated upvalley to locations that were more defensible and/or closer to the sources of irrigation waters. In the Lurín Valley, a site known as Piedra Liza (or Malpaso) apparently flourished in the narrow mid-valley sector following the abandonment of the lower valley centers, but it does not fully replicate the U-shaped format. Thus, the evidence from Lurín suggests a disruption in the cultural patterning of the people that lived in the lower valley, with the possibility of some associated depopulation of the zone.

Judging from the available data, the situation in the Lurín Valley was typical of the central coast as a whole: Garagay in Rimac and San Humberto in Chillón also ceased to be major public centers around the same time as Cardal and Mina Perdida.[3] Despite the fact that the most extensive tracts of irrigable land are located in the lower valleys, these zones appear to have been only thinly inhabited during the first half of the Early Horizon. The focus of settlement may have shifted upvalley; unfortunately, this area remains little studied by archaeologists. Small shoreline settlements apparently escaped the disruption so evident at the inland centers. At maritime villages like Curayacu and Ancón, the inhabitants continued to fish and gather mollusks, some of which they exchanged for agricultural products with inland farmers.

The Early Horizon settlement pattern just described for the central coast has some striking parallels and a few differences with that on the north-central coast. The rupture at the end of the Initial Period is particularly well-documented on the north-central coast for the Casma Valley. New constructions and renovations of old structures apparently ceased between 900 and 800 BC at the centers of the lower valley including Taukachi-Konkan, Huerequeque, Sechín Bajo, and apparently Sechín Alto. At Taukachi-Konkan, for example, there are mounds that never received the intended stone facing and summit constructions that were never completed.[4]

The most dramatic illustration of abandonment comes from the public buildings of Las Haldas on the shoreline south of Casma. When archaeologists excavated the central staircase, they found that construction had been halted while finishing the steps. Plastering had been completed on only half of the stairs and wooden survey stakes and cotton cord used to lay out this feature had been left in place. Following the cessation of construction, the zone of public architecture was reoccupied after a hiatus by simple villagers who built crude houses on top of the circular court, and threw their garbage on what once had been the central staircase to the pyramid summit. No new public architecture was initiated by these fisherfolk.[5] An analogous Early Horizon reoccupation seems to have occurred at Sechín Alto after its public center fell into disuse. Pallka, located 35 km inland in the mid-valley section of the Casma River, was one of the few major centers that continued to flourish after the Initial Period.[6]

In contrast to the central coast, large Early Horizon centers were established in the lower valley of Casma. However, the architecture at these sites was radically

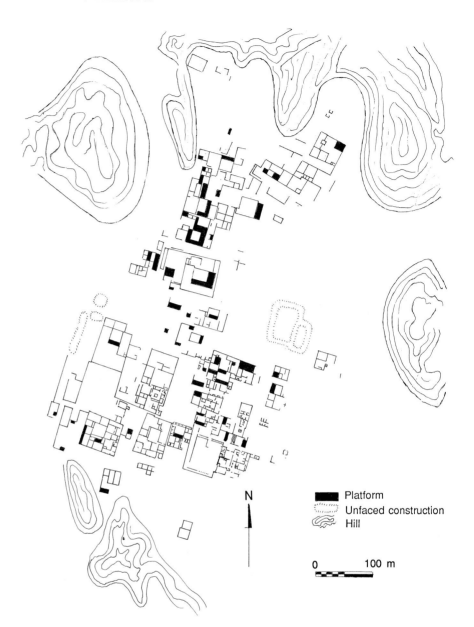

192 The Early Horizon site of San Diego in the Casma Valley lacked the emphasis on ceremonial architecture and public space that characterized local Initial Period centers of comparable size and importance.

Platform
Unfaced construction
Hill

0   100 m

different from those of the Initial Period. The sites of Pampa Rosario and San Diego were both founded during the Early Horizon and large populations appear to have resided at these settlements, which covered 40 and 50 hectares respectively. Like the Janabarriu-phase settlement at Chavín de Huántar, the permanent population at these sites probably numbered in the thousands. However, Pampa Rosario and San Diego lacked massive pyramid-plaza complexes and instead feature a sprawling multitude of small mounds surrounded by interconnecting rooms, corridors, and courtyards. At Pampa Rosario, a low narrow platform 1–3 m high located on the edge of the site has been tentatively identified as a possible focus of the community, but whether or not this was the case there is little evidence of massive labor being appropriated for public ends.[7]

Casma's neighboring valleys likewise lacked major pyramid complexes during the first part of the Early Horizon and, like the valleys of the central coast, there are few traces of occupation in the lower valley between 600 and 250 BC. In Nepeña, dense populations were living in small sites in the middle and upper sections of the drainage during the Early Horizon. Most of these settlements were built on flattened hilltops or ridges in naturally defensible locations. Occasionally, they were bordered by terraces or stone walls, but more frequently public architecture was confined to a few rectangular buildings of coarse fieldstone. Most of the domestic buildings were probably constructed of perishable materials such as wattle and daub. One site in the upper valley, Virahuanca Alto, did feature a stone-faced platform mound but it was a mere 2 m in height. Only one of the Nepeña sites, Caylán, equals the size of Pampa Rosario. It is located at the beginning of the middle valley at the foot of the mountain slopes; unfortunately its dating remains problematic, although its complex arrangement of rooms, corridors, and courts does resemble that of the nearby Casma centers like San Diego.[8]

The coastal section of the Santa drainage is one of the most intensively surveyed valleys of Peru. Site reconnaissance there detected 54 sites from the first portion of the Early Horizon (called the Cayhuamarca period in Santa). Small habitation sites averaging 2 hectares in area were the most common type of site and few probably had populations greater than 200. Most of these villages were located in the middle and upper valley on defensible hillside slopes and ridges, usually between 25 and 50 m above the valley floor. Archaeologist David Wilson has grouped the Early Horizon sites into four clusters, supposedly corresponding to tiny "polities" of some sort, but the absence of clear-cut centers in each of these clusters leaves open the alternative possibility of even smaller acephalous social units lacking a supra-village level of political integration. Several platform mounds in the middle and upper valley have been suggested as possible ceremonial centers, but their chronological placement remains uncertain.[9]

Interspersed with Santa's rather undifferentiated rural population were some 21 hilltop forts or citadels stretched over around 40 km of the middle and upper valley. Although some may have also served as habitation centers, the location and design of the sites indicate that their primary function was to provide the dispersed population with a refuge against attack. The identification of these constructions as citadels is based in part on their placement in high, remote spots. While these positions enhance defensibility, they also increase the problem of acquiring daily water and managing the agricultural lands below. All the citadels possess architectural features that can best be understood in terms of strategic functions. They generally have one or more massive stone enclosure walls encircling them, ranging from 1 to 2 m in height. Parapets or bastions often protrude from the corners or sides of the outer walls, allowing the defenders to engage the enemy with slings and slingstones from a high, well-protected position. Massive stone buttresses reinforced the defensive walls, and entrances into the citadels were few in number and narrow enough to be closed in an emergency. In some cases, dry moats were dug on the sides that were most accessible, and stone bulwarks were added adjacent to the trenches in order to make them still more formidable.[10]

Early Horizon citadels have been found on both sides of the Santa and its tributaries, and similar complexes, albeit in smaller numbers, were built at

193 One of the 21 citadels believed to have been built in the lower and middle Santa Valley during the Cayhuamarca period. This structure incorporates such defensive features as bastions, buttresses, and baffled entrances.

194 An aerial photograph of Chankillo in the Casma Valley, one of the best-known Early Horizon fortresses.

roughly the same time in the Casma and Nepeña valleys. Probably the best-known fortress of this period is Chankillo in Casma.[11] The citadels on the north-central coast are the first convincing indication of intersocietal warfare, as opposed to occasional small-scale raiding. It is significant that the construction of these fortresses in Nepeña and Santa was roughly contemporaneous with a shift in the settlement pattern to less vulnerable locations, away from the valley floor. It is important to emphasize, however, that hilltop citadels apparently did not appear outside the north-central coast until post-Chavín times. Judging from the sheer number and location of the citadels of the north-central coast, the hostilities may have been between the small-scale groups within these valleys rather than with more distant groups in the highlands or elsewhere on the coast. Nevertheless, these complexes are a dramatic index of the insecurity produced in some areas by the disintegration of Initial Period social formations. In fact, the hilltop forts were the single most significant products of public labor in this region during the Early Horizon.

The situation along the north coast is not well understood, but the limited information available meshes well with that already presented for the central and north-central coast. The settlement pattern in Virú resembles that in Santa, but without the impressive forts. Further north, where Initial Period monumental architecture had been common, few if any major Early Horizon sites are known in the lower valleys. Most of the early centers in the lower and middle valleys, including Huaca de los Reyes and Herederos Chica at Caballo Muerto, Purulén, and Huaca Lucía, were abandoned at the end of the Initial Period.[12]

Huaca de la Cruz and Huaca Guavalito at Caballo Muerto in Moche's valley neck may date to the Early Horizon, but both are relatively small constructions built by modifying natural hillslopes in order to make them appear imposing without a major investment of manpower. Huaca de los Chinos is one of the few major Early Horizon centers with public architecture known from this region. It is located in the middle section of the Moche Valley, 15 km upstream from Caballo Muerto.[13]

195 Early Horizon villages in the Virú Valley such as the one depicted here were frequently located on defensible ridges. Public architecture was limited to a few low platforms at these small settlements.

An intensive survey of the mid-Jequetepeque drainage referred to in Chapter 3 revealed a dense Initial Period occupation, but very little evidence of settlement during the Early Horizon. Although exquisite Early Horizon pottery from Jequetepeque, Zaña, and Lambayeque appears in museum collections, most of these pieces come from looted cemeteries. A few Early Horizon burials have been documented in Lambayeque along the shoreline at Morro de Eten and in the mid-valley sector at Chongoyape, but knowledge of Early Horizon settlement patterns in Lambayeque or the neighboring valleys is still rudimentary.[14]

In summary, the abandonment of large-scale public constructions in the lower valleys along the coast at the end of the Initial Period can be interpreted as indicative of a serious crisis for many, if not all, of the small-scale societies in this region. Inasmuch as the ceremonial architecture provided a setting for community rituals and the design of these centers can be interpreted as expressing aspects of religious cosmology, the failure to maintain these centers or reproduce them elsewhere implies a profound cultural change. If the legitimacy of a center's cosmology was called into question, so too would the non-coercive authority of the leaders associated with this sacred knowledge. Ultimately, this would have undermined the very basis of the social relations that underlay the productive systems, and the functioning of these societies as viable units. With the loss of protection provided by the old social order and the disintegration of intergroup alliances, the population in most valleys splintered into smaller units and apparently sought more secure locations for their settlements, away from the vulnerable bottomlands of the lower valley and closer to the source of irrigation water that was critical for their crops.

What factors could have produced such cataclysmic changes? The evidence available does not permit a satisfactory answer to this question, but it is worth considering some of the possibilities. The internal contradictions within Initial Period societies probably played some role in their decline. In Chapter 3 we argued that these societies were only weakly differentiated, with leaders who were unable to convert their authority, based on sacred knowledge, into coercive power and individual wealth. Attempts to bring about changes in the political and economic order probably occurred more than once, especially when coastal leaders were exposed to the incipient economic stratification that began to appear in the highlands during the Initial Period. The problem these leaders faced was how to accomplish this without coming into conflict with the ideology that they represented. The placement of a small number of houses and tombs on the pyramid summit during the final episode at Cardal may represent an unsuccessful attempt to lay the basis for such changes by more closely associating the community leaders with divine authority and power.

While inescapable structural problems may have provided the ultimate reason behind the decline of these centers, external factors may have precipitated the collapse. Shelia and Thomas Pozorski, for example, posit a highland invasion as the proximate cause for the changes in Casma.[15] At present this argument remains unconvincing, because there is no plausible motive for nor evidence of an invasion. Thus far, there is no indication of massive destruction, violent death, or a change in biological population. Moreover, the invasion hypothesis for Casma would not explain why transformations apparently occurred in valleys throughout the coast at roughly the same time.

Peru is a land of natural catastrophes and, as we have seen, archaeologists

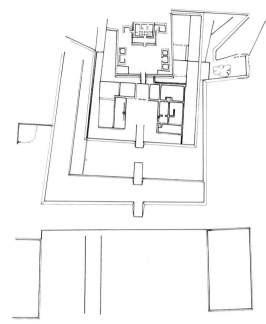

196 Huaca de los Chinos in the mid-valley zone of Moche continued the architectural traditions of the Initial Period, including the use of colonnades on the summit of flat-topped pyramids.

197,198 Early Horizon stirrup-spouted bottles in the Chavín style looted from cemeteries on the north coast, probably in Jequetepeque or Zaña.

frequently seek explanatory recourse in the climatic and tectonic forces to which this territory is subject. Somewhat uneven evidence does exist on the north coast for floods, a massive tidal wave and a climatic downturn that resulted in severe erosion of the topsoil.[16] But these are estimated to have occurred around 500 BC, long after the Initial Period centers had gone into decline. Thus, while these problems may have deepened the existing crisis along the coast during the Early Horizon, they cannot be viewed as producing it.

Whatever the causes, these changes in coastal society had ramifications affecting the entire central Andean region. Not only did the demographic focus shift away from the littoral towards the upper valleys, but many coastal groups reacted by increasing the intensity of reciprocal transactions and economic interdependency with the adjacent highlands. Some groups also appear to have sought from the highlands a religious ideology better equipped for dealing with social and economic upheaval, thereby facilitating the spread of the Chavín cult beyond the confines of the Mosna drainage. The possible onset of environmental difficulties during the mid-Early Horizon would only have intensified these trends. Following this scenario, the articulation between the various coastal and highland regions produced a new and much broader sphere of interaction, one which transcended the narrow framework of localized social units.

Prosperity in the highlands

The prosperity of Chavín de Huántar during the Early Horizon (described in Chapter 6) was far from unique. It was paralleled at other major centers in the northern and central highlands. Some, like Pacopampa, reached their maximum extent with large resident populations. At this and other major highland centers public architecture continued to be erected, often incorporating elements similar to those at Chavín de Huántar. For example, on the summit of Pacopampa, a massive rectangular semi-subterranean plaza was built using cut and polished stone, and its central staircase was flanked by cylindrical stone columns. Carved columns and lintels, blocks carved in low relief, and sculpture in the round adorned the Early Horizon temple, sometimes showing motifs reminiscent of the

199 A sunken rectangular plaza of cut stone was built on the summit of Pacopampa during the Early Horizon. It shares many features with the New Temple at Chavín de Huántar.

Chavín de Huántar center. Among the more memorable examples of public stone sculpture is a granite stela carved in the form of a fanged supernatural and a pair of large, three-dimensional jaguars.[17]

At Kuntur Wasi the broad summit of the terraced hill was completely transformed by arranging three platforms around a sunken rectangular plaza, thereby achieving a U-shaped layout. The size of the Kuntur Wasi site and the amount of its public construction appear to have peaked during the Early Horizon. The staircases of the central plaza were decorated with stone carvings in a variant of the Chavín style. Two pairs of these stairway sculptures with frontal fanged faces are known – one set carved in white stone, the other in red.[18]

Medium-sized highland centers such as Kotosh and La Pampa also witnessed massive new constructions. According to Seiichi Izumi, the Early Horizon temple at Kotosh surpassed the earlier constructions in scale and quality. At La Pampa, the three major public architectural complexes date to the first portion of the Early Horizon. These monumental constructions have little in common with the small rustic Initial Period buildings uncovered there during the 1975 excavations. They feature U-shaped layouts around sunken plazas of dressed stone. Even at the small religious center of Huaricoto in the Callejón de Huaylas, the population broke with their local building tradition and constructed a sunken circular plaza, which could have served as a central focus for public rituals and other activities. This plaza included a dressed stone plinth and appears to have been modeled on the Chavín de Huántar prototype.[19]

The continued occupation of these and other highland centers, and the ongoing maintenance and enlargement of their public architecture, points both to social continuity and economic prosperity. The contrast with the coastal situation could not be more striking. Apparently, the ability to mobilize the public for community ends remained undiminished. Moreover, there was no shift of the highland centers to more defensible locations on ridgetops, nor is there any evidence of hilltop forts or other features that would suggest the importance of armed conflict.

The increasing similarity between public complexes of different regional centers in the highlands is just one symbol of the increasing ties between them. The expression of this emerging set of relationships in the public architecture is particularly significant, because it reflects conscious decisions by community leaders to modify local building conventions so that their centers would share features with groups of different cultural backgrounds.

The resemblance between the ceremonial architecture of these different highland centers during the Early Horizon might also be interpreted as expressing some degree of convergence in the religious ideology and rituals of these different groups. This possibility is of particular interest in light of the wide distribution of Chavín-style religious art at these and other settlements. It was this highly sophisticated religious art, rather than the architecture or other elements, that has served as the basis for defining the Chavín horizon.

200 A Chavinoid stone sculpture incorporated into the Early Horizon sunken plaza on the summit of Kuntur Wasi in the upper Jequetepeque Valley. Double-profile composition and anatropic organization were employed in this image.

A functional interpretation of the Chavín horizon

There is a longstanding consensus that the Chavín horizon style is the symbolic expression of a religious ideology, and that the Chavín horizon resulted from the diffusion of what may be referred to as the Chavín cult. Rafael Larco Hoyle pioneered this mode of interpretation, and even in his early writings he insisted that a set of beliefs centering around the feline spread over a wide area, profoundly influenced the diverse peoples who embraced this ideology. According to him, these populations expressed their new religion through their art and the erection of temples.[20] Wendell Bennett's explanation of the distribution of the Chavín style was similar to Larco Hoyle's, and Gordon Willey's "functional" analysis of the Chavín horizon style also concluded that the diffusion can be explained most easily as the peaceful spread of religious concepts autonomously manipulated by individual communities. Even Tello's disciple, Rebeca Carrión Cachot argued that the "Chavín empire" was religious, not political, and that this religion spread a homogeneous art style and a standardized set of rites over zones dissimilar in culture and environment.[21] This viewpoint has continued to be accepted in the following decades.

Unfortunately, non-Andean concepts have frequently been introduced into discussions of the spread of Chavín ideology, including the very Western model of proselytizing missionaries converting an ever-widening number of groups at the expense of local cults. Alana Cordy-Collins, a specialist in pre-Columbian iconography, has even suggested that the Chavín painted textiles found on the south coast may have served as a kind of catechism, communicating the message of Chavín ideology to the peoples beyond the Chavín heartland.[22] While the Chavín cult may have been an expansive religious movement, its organization probably bore little resemblance to the "world religions" of the Old World, such as Christianity or Islam.

Ethnographers working among certain tribes and chiefdoms of Africa have documented the importance and widespread occurrence of religious phenomena which are more far-reaching than the parochial cults of the community, but less inclusive than world religions. Sometimes referred to as regional cults, these are often spread over thousands of kilometers and incorporate groups differing in language, culture, and natural resources.[23] The scale and configuration of these regional cults are comparable to the Chavín cult, and a closer look at this general phenomenon is warranted. In her study of the local cults and regional prophet cults of Zambia, ethnographer Elizabeth Colson makes the following general observation:

> No cult which primarily functions to serve the particular interests of a territorial community on a regular basis can serve a general public unless it radically alters its practice and its constituency: a cult serving a wider constituency on an ad hoc basis may well serve the special purposes of local communities. The two [regional and local cults] can co-exist and reinforce each other. The cult with universal claims then serves as a further court of appeals when a local cult does not satisfy its adherents . . . This was true in ancient Greece where each small city state had its own cult, associated with its fate as a human community but delegations went to consult the Oracle of Delphi, or perhaps Dodona, which served the entire classical world for many centuries.[24]

Local cults emphasize the exclusive domain, boundedness, and stability. They are intimately tied to the land and the local system, and their rituals often have a politico-jural focus. Regional cults, on the other hand, transcend political and ethnic boundaries, their ideology and rituals fostering universalism and openness. Each regional cult has its own distinctive idiom, but they are similar in their formal and hierarchic organizational structure, which maintains officials with the authority to legitimize branches of the cult and limit deviance in local congregations. Regional cults also usually resemble each other in their doctrines of universality, theism, and moral responsibility; in order to survive and spread, they must stress values of peacefulness based on recognition of the transcendent interest of the macrocosm irrespective of longstanding differences, hostilities, and competition between local communities. The right of free movement across communal borders by religious functionaries and pilgrims is a basic feature of the "ritual fields" generated by regional cults, and ultimately these "middle-range" organizations provide networks for the flow of goods, services, information, and people. The potential contradictions and conflicts created by the inter-penetration of regional and local cults are often resolved by mutual affirmation and acceptance. Frequently, local cults acknowledge the legitimacy of the regional cult, and even become formally affiliated with it, without necessarily modifying their own ideology or rituals.[25]

The Pachacamac model for Andean regional cults

Several examples of late pre-Hispanic regional cults from the Andes are known from colonial accounts. The best-known of these is Pachacamac and a number of scholars believe its organization may have been related to that of the Chavín cult.[26] The historical evidence of this 16th-century ceremonial network illustrates the way in which religious networks could be organized in an Andean manner, consistent with distinctively Andean concepts of community, reciprocity, taxation, and kinship.[27]

The center of the Pachacamac cult was a large ceremonial complex of the same name at the mouth of the Lurín River. It featured an oracle located in a chamber at the summit of one of the large adobe platforms, but access to the oracle was restricted to specialists of the cult. There were also open plazas, where pilgrims fasted and participated in public ceremonies. The Pachacamac cult provided oracular predictions, favorable intervention with the elements, protection against disease, and, presumably, specialized knowledge concerning auspicious times for planting and harvesting. Divine sanctions, including earthquakes and crop destruction, were thought to result from antagonizing the god of Pachacamac.

A community interested in establishing a branch shrine had to petition Pachacamac and demonstrate its ability and willingness to support cult activities. If the request was accepted, a resident priest was supplied from Pachacamac to the new branch and, in return, the supporting community set aside agricultural land and/or pasture for the cult and provided public labor for farming and herding. Lands assigned to the cult were worked before the lands alloted to the local elite or community members, and all segments of society were expected, at least symbolically, to donate labor.[28] A portion of the produce from the fields or herds supported the local branch of the cult, while the rest was sent as tribute to the principal ceremonial complex. Large quantities of cotton, corn, dried fish, llamas, and guinea pigs were brought to Pachacamac, as were scarce raw materials (e.g. gold) and manufactured goods (e.g. fine cloth).

By the time of the Spanish Conquest, Pachacamac had developed a network of shrines spanning the range of production zones. A branch oracle was established in the middle of the Rimac Valley, and the first leaves of the coca harvest from that area were brought to Pachacamac before the local community was permitted to chew them. Other secondary cult centers were located near the high-altitude pastures of llamas and alpacas, and also on the eastern slopes of the Andes. Branch oracles were reported from valleys throughout the coast of Peru and tribute was said to have been brought to Pachacamac from Ecuador. Peruvian historian María Rostworowski has described the ceremonial network of the Pachacamac regional cult as an archipelago of religious centers, stretching vertically across the diverse ecological zones of central Peru and horizontally along the central and northern Peruvian coast. The cult cut across a patchwork quilt of ethnicities and languages, forming a system parallel to and partially independent of the regional and national levels of political organization. The groups within this religious archipelago were linked ideologically by their shared belief in the oracle of Pachacamac, and their sense of supra-local and supra-national identity was expressed and reinforced through annual pilgrimages to Pachacamac.[29]

The branches of the Pachacamac cult were conceptualized as the wives, siblings, or children of Pachacamac, and each oracle had his or her own name and origin myth. The kinship said to exist between the secondary cult centers and the primary center underscored the reciprocal obligations between them, and joined the culturally diverse communities supporting these oracles into a single ideological family.

The Pachacamac cult resembles many African regional cults in its multi-ethnic character, its maintenance of a formal and hierarchical organization, its funneling of tribute from branch centers into a primary center, and its binding together of a wide-ranging ritual field through pilgrimage. While it also shares these traits with some of the well-known proselytizing religions of the Old World, it more closely parallels African regional cults in its emphasis on oracles and its compatibility with older local cults. The "multiplication" of individualized but related branch oracles using the metaphor of kinship is perhaps the most distinctive aspect of this Andean regional cult.[30] It is noteworthy that there is no historical evidence for the use of aggressive missionaries as a means of spreading the religious ideology of Pachacamac. The role of missionaries would be difficult, if not impossible, to identify archaeologically, and debate concerning their presence or absence in prehistory only blurs the broader issue of regional religious networks.

The dearth of investigation at Early Horizon ceremonial centers inhibits a critical evaluation of the degree to which the Pachacamac regional cult provides a viable model for the much older religious institutions of the Early Horizon. The major sociopolitical changes which occurred between the Early and Late Horizon make it likely that the model will have to be modified on the basis of future fieldwork. On the other hand, some aspects of it do appear to be consistent with the extant archaeological record.

If the growth of the Pachacamac cult did parallel that of older Andean religions, we can assume that some local ceremonial centers of the Early Horizon would have continued to function, even if they lay within the sphere of the Chavín cult. Huaricoto, in the Callejón de Huaylas, may be an example of this pattern. As we saw in Chapters 2 and 4, ritual activity at Huaricoto centered around the burning of offerings in small specialized chambers, a practice typical

201 The dual ritual chambers at Huaricoto, built during the Early Horizon for the incineration of ritual offerings, indicate that the Kotosh Religious Tradition continued without interruption in some northern highland societies, even at the apogee of the Chavín cult.

of the Late Preceramic centers of the Kotosh Religious Tradition. There is archaeological evidence for the continuation of these religious ceremonies at Huaricoto throughout the Initial Period and Early Horizon, and material evidence left from the rituals indicates that some version of traditional local ceremonies persisted even at the apogee of the Chavín cult. In fact, the largest and most elaborate of the ritual chambers at Huaricoto was built during the Early Horizon. Nevertheless, the impact of the Chavín cult was clearly felt by the worshipers at Huaricoto and some degree of syncretism, or at the very least accepted complementarity, between the two religious cults is evidenced by the discovery in the ritual precinct of Huaricoto of a carved spatula depicting the main Chavín deity of the Lanzón and elaborate pottery decorated with Chavín designs. If the Chavín cult had spread at the *expense* of older cults, replacing the earlier religious systems with the new ideology, this pattern should have been evident in the Callejón de Huaylas, which is situated between the Callejón de Conchucos (in which Chavín de Huántar is located) and the coast.[31]

As we have seen, many of the most important Early Horizon sites had already emerged as regional centers during the late Initial Period and, in that capacity, they were the focus of religious activity dedicated to patron gods associated with their particular territorial interests. The diffusion to these sites of the Chavín cult during the Early Horizon may have implied no more than the addition of a branch oracle of Chavín alongside the local temple, just as later the Incas established a branch of the sun cult alongside the Pachacamac oracle without disrupting the latter's activities.

Ideological flexibility and the Chavín cult

Karwa. The discovery which most clearly illuminates the distinctive regional organization of the Chavín cult was made illegally by looters at the site of Karwa. The Karwa cemetery lies 8 km south of the Paracas Necropolis and its location was noted by Tello in 1927, but the site did not attract the attention of archaeologists until 1970 when *huaqueros* (looters) uncovered a large rectangular tomb which differed in shape, size, and construction from the surrounding interments. The unusual tomb reportedly contained the bodies of several individuals and an abundance of grave goods. Over 200 fragments of decorated cloth were recovered from the tomb, along with Paracas ceramics dated to the early phases of the Ocucaje sequence (*c.* 400–200 BC). A small number of sherds said to have been associated with the Chavín textiles of Karwa are currently stored at the Museo Amano in Lima. These fragments are closely related in form and decoration to the Janabarriu-phase ceramics of Chavín de Huántar.[32]

Most of the textiles from the Karwa tomb were not decorated according to the local Paracas tradition. Instead, vivid depictions of the symbols of Chavín de Huántar were painted in red-orange, tan, brown, olive-green(?), and blue pigments; on some pieces, a resist technique was used to form white motifs on a colored field. The textiles were made of loosely woven cotton thread and were painted in the style of Phase D Chavín de Huántar sculptures.

Individual Karwa design elements, such as eyes and ears, have counterparts in the sculpture from Chavín de Huántar, and the painting adheres to Chavín compositional canons, including kenning, approximate bilateral symmetry, anatropic organization, and double-profile composition. All of these complex

202 This bone spatula with Chavín-style carving was recovered near the Early Horizon ritual chambers at Huaricoto.

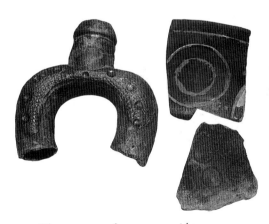

203 These pottery fragments, said to come from the "Chavín" tomb at Karwa, share many features with the Janabarriu-phase ceramics from Chavín de Huántar. Width of stirrup spout 8 cm.

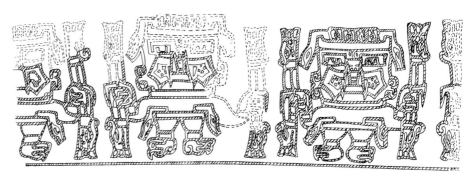

204 The Karwa textiles were decorated by painting the repeated image of the supreme deity (or Staff God) in typical late Chavín stylistic conventions on white cotton cloth.

205 Chavín motifs such as this crested eagle were often represented on the locally produced Paracas style ceramics.

206 Chavín themes were also used on the south coast to decorate pyroengraved gourds. Note the kenning of the feline's tail as a snake. Diameter 15.9 cm.

and somewhat idiosyncratic artistic conventions are followed at Karwa in an orthodox Chavín de Huántar manner.

As already noted, the iconographic content of the Karwa textiles is closely linked to that of the Chavín de Huántar sculptures. The common subsidiary supernaturals at Chavín are felines or raptorial birds shown in profile, and examples of both appear on the Karwa textiles, in borders surrounding the primary figure. Chavín's principal deity (usually shown holding staffs as on the Raimondi Stone), or a supernatural resembling it, was the most frequent primary figure on the Karwa textiles, a fact consistent with Rowe's reconstruction of the Phase D Chavín de Huántar pantheon. As many as 25 such representations appear in the Karwa collection studied by Alana Cordy-Collins, and at least 23 more occur on other textiles from the same tomb.

The other of Chavín de Huántar's principal deities, the supernatural with cayman attributes, was represented only on a few major stone sculptures at the highland center, but nevertheless appears as the main motif on at least three of the Karwa textiles. As in Chavín de Huántar, it was sometimes shown using the "flayed pelt convention" in which the supernatural was split down the middle so that mirror images were formed by its sides. One of the cayman representations from Karwa is particularly reminiscent of the Yauya Stela, the famous granite sculpture found on the eastern slopes above the Marañon River.[33]

The content and style of the Karwa textiles leave little doubt that a variant of Chavín's religious ideology existed on the south coast during the middle of the Early Horizon. Despite the 530 km separating the two sites, the complex body of information which constituted Chavín ideology appears to have been transmitted intact, without simplification or unintended distortion. Furthermore, the replication of Chavín motifs on locally produced pottery and pyroengraved gourds provides additional indication of the Chavín cult's successful penetration into local coastal society.

If the branches of the Chavín cult were integrated with local cults in the same fashion as those of the Pachacamac cult, we would not expect them to have been smaller versions of Chavín de Huántar, since each one would have been dedicated to a wife or child of the main deity. This organization may help to explain some of the anomalous elements in the iconography of the Karwa textiles. Several iconographic themes at this site were absent from the Chavín de Huántar sculpture. Among the most important of these was the frequent representation of the deity with the staffs as female, with breasts kenned as eyes and vagina kenned as a vertically oriented set of teeth and crossed fangs.

Since the specification of female gender and the floral associations (see below) are alien to the representations of the main deity at Chavín de Huántar, it is plausible that a local female supernatural is being represented. Perhaps, drawing upon the Pachacamac model, these textiles depict the wife, sister, or the daughter of the Chavín de Huántar Staff God. An analogous interpretation could be applied to the distinctive female supernatural carved on a monolith from the northern highland center of Pacopampa.[34] An alternative to this interpretation, proposed by Cordy-Collins, is that the principal supernatural at Chavín de Huántar had both male and female aspects, and the Staff Goddess of Karwa (as Patricia Lyon suggested she be called) represented the female component of its dual identity.[35]

The Karwa Staff Goddess was sometimes shown with cotton bolls emerging from her headdress and staffs, and it has plausibly been suggested that she was the patron and/or donor of cotton, the quintessential coastal cultigen. Unprecedented zoomorphized representations of the cotton plant and stylized cotton bolls also occur as repetitive motifs on several other of the textiles.[36]

The Karwa textiles were not simply painted copies of the Chavín de Huántar sculpture. Rows of conventionalized eyes, concentric circles, S's, and double-profile snake heads were used as borders at Karwa which never appeared on Chavín sculpture.[37] The circular format and the use of these repetitive symbols on many of the Karwa textiles could represent a coastal variation of the highland style or, alternatively, could mirror the yet unknown textile style from Chavín de Huántar. Rayed circles, also unknown from Chavín de Huántar, were shown on the Karwa textiles as minor elements in between secondary supernaturals and, in one instance, this symbol appeared prominently on the torso of the Staff Goddess. This motif has tentatively been identified as a sliced section of the hallucinogenic San Pedro cactus; painted representations of more naturalistic cacti, also interpreted as San Pedro, appear on another Karwa fabric. Although the San Pedro cactus was occasionally depicted on sculptures at the Chavín de Huántar temple, it was not a frequent theme; and though the Tello Obelisk depicted the cayman as the donor of manioc, the bottle gourd, capiscum pepper, and other cultigens, it did not represent the San Pedro cactus or, for that matter,

207 The main deity worshiped at Karwa during the Early Horizon (depicted here on painted cotton cloth) appears to have been a female supernatural with strong floral associations; this deity may have been thought of as a wife, sister, or daughter of Chavín de Huántar's supreme deity.

208 (*Above*) Many of the Karwa textiles feature circular arrangements of Chavín themes, as in this image.

209 (*Far left*) A cloth fragment painted with the image of a cayman's torso in late Chavín style, said to have been found in the Callango section of the Ica Valley.

210 (*Left*) This Chavín textile (reputedly from a deep tomb in the Chincha Valley) utilized the technique of wrapping individual or groups of warp threads with colored cotton to form vertical and diagonal lines with areas of colored infill.

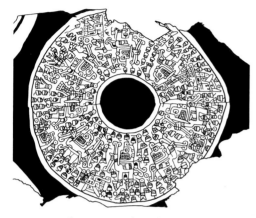

211 A large painted Early Horizon cotton textile from Samaca in the lower Ica Valley; it depicts a complex mythical scene alien to Chavín de Huántar and Chavín horizon sites outside the south coast.

212 Free-standing stone sculpture from Pacopampa representing a female supernatural with *vagina dentata* and other Chavín-related features.

cotton.[38] Whatever explanation is provided for the significant differences between the iconography of Chavín de Huántar and Karwa, the contrasts bear testimony to the flexibility of the Chavín cult.

Some of the large decorated Karwa textiles may have been used as mummy-wrappings, as looters claim, but their original function remains uncertain. It is possible that they once decorated the walls of a Chavín shrine somewhere in Paracas or Ica before they were finally interred. In the dry climate of the coast, textile hangings would be a practical alternative to adobe sculpture or other media. One painted textile from Karwa is calculated to have been 4.2 m wide by 2.7 m high. This textile would have had a total surface area roughly eight times that of the Raimondi Stone, and many of the other textiles are comparable in size to stone and clay sculptures of the Initial Period and Early Horizon.

The Karwa tomb has no known parallel on the south coast, but the Chavín-style painted textiles that were extracted from it are not unique. Two textiles painted with Chavín motifs appeared on the antiquities market in 1960 and were said to have come from the Callango section of the Ica Valley; the style and technology of these pieces are almost identical to those from Karwa. A similar textile was reported to have been looted from a deep tomb 15 km inland from the coast of Chincha. This piece features a late Chavín motif painted in yellow, white, rose, and brown, but it differed in construction technique from most of the Karwa textiles.[39]

More recently, other painted textiles related to those of Karwa were looted from the site of Samaca in the lower Ica Valley.[40] One of these cloths features a repeated Chavín-style face, while another shows an elaborate mythical procession of individuals holding bones and fish surrounded by hummingbirds and flowers. Like some of the Karwa pieces, the latter cloth commemorates mythical events apparently unknown at Chavín de Huántar and points to the richness of the local elements within the Chavín cult along the south coast.

At present, the Chavín horizon style can be documented unevenly on the coast from Ica to Lambayeque and in the highlands from Huánuco to Pacopampa. The themes represented on Chavín horizon objects are conspicuously lacking in explicit political content. Unlike Olmec art, the Chavín style does not portray historical personages, scenes of conquest and submission, or the explicit confirmation of royal authority by supernaturals. The unworldly concerns of Chavín iconography are likewise in sharp contrast with the significant sociopolitical content present on the later Peruvian art of the Early Intermediate Period.

Evidence from the north. In the northern highlands, where textiles and pyroengraved gourds have little chance of survival, stone sculptures provide prima facie evidence of the spread of the Chavín cult. Chavín-related sculptures have been known for several decades from the sites of Kuntur Wasi and Pacopampa. The Chavinoid sculptures at both sites utilized a style similar to that of the final phases of the sculptural sequence at Chavín de Huántar, but their size and certain design elements indicate that they were produced locally.

In 1990, during the course of ethnographic research in the Canaris district of the upper Lambayeque-La Leche drainage (*c.* 2,500 m), anthropologist James Vreeland stumbled upon further examples of Chavín-related sculptures. He found a matched pair of carved columns, similar in concept to those from the portal of the New Temple of Chavín de Huántar and most comparable in style to the Chavín horizon carvings from the summit of Kuntur Wasi.[41]

Finely carved stone sculpture corresponding to the Chavín horizon is virtually unknown from the lower and middle sections of the coastal valleys. This pattern is particularly intriguing now that the presence of pre-Chavín stone sculpture has been established at sites such as Cerro Sechín and Moxeke. On the other hand, Early Horizon petroglyphs have been widely encountered throughout the coast and some were executed in styles reminiscent of more sophisticated stone sculpture. If a relatively loose definition is used, the southernmost example of Chavín horizon stone carving known at present is a petroglyph from Chichictarra in the Palpa Valley of the Nazca drainage.[42]

In the upper reaches of the Zaña Valley, explorations encountered paintings and petroglyphs on the cliffs of Monte Calvario, near the site of Poro-Poro. One painting showed a Staff God in yellow, white, green, and brown. There were at least 17 paintings, including depictions of felines, birds, and an anthropomorphic figure resembling the main Chavín god, but lacking staffs.[43]

Monumental examples of the Chavín horizon style have rarely been encountered along the coastal plain but, as Tello vividly demonstrated at Nepeña and Casma in the 1930s, apparently insignificant adobe mounds frequently incorporate decorated adobe Initial Period and Early Horizon temples. The unique friezes covering the shrine of Cerro Blanco in Nepeña remain the earliest evidence for the appearance of the Chavín horizon style on the coast. The portion of this relatively small site that was cleared by Tello appears to have been a shrine in the form of a giant sculpted Chavín supernatural with feline, avian and ophidian attributes. Judging from the pottery and iconography its use may have been short-lived, the site perhaps abandoned after

213 This petroglyph from Chichictarra in the Nazca drainage is idiosyncratic in style and theme but it may be the southernmost example of an Early Horizon stone carving with Chavín influence.

214 The elaborate petroglyphs from Monte Calvario near Poro-Poro were carved with themes from Chavín iconography, such as the staff-wielding supernatural above.

215 A small Early Horizon construction at Cerro Blanco in the Nepeña Valley was completely covered with incised and modeled Chavín-style decoration that had been painted red, white, greenish-yellow, orange, pink, and black. Discovered in 1928 and excavated by Tello in 1933, this photograph was taken when the site was reopened in 1958.

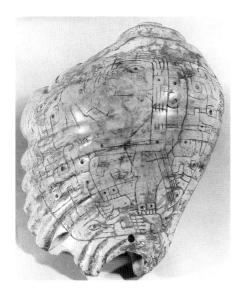

216 Shell trumpets played a central role in Chavín ritual, and a complete example of a heavily decorated trumpet made from Ecuadorian *Strombus* shell was encountered near Chiclayo in the Lambayeque drainage. Length 23.5 cm.

217 Carved stone mortars and pestles in the form of jaguars, birds, and serpents were important ceremonial paraphernalia in the Chavín cult. The example above comes from the site of Pacopampa.

Religion, innovation, and diffusion

the beginning of the Early Horizon. Another possible center of the Chavín cult may have existed in what became the Cooperativa Casa Grande in the Chicama Valley. This now destroyed site had painted adobe columns, one of which displays a bird motif reminiscent of the decoration on the columns of the Black and White Portal at Chavín de Huántar.[44]

Ceremonial paraphernalia. Portable objects bearing Chavín iconography have been recovered throughout the coast and highlands. Many of these objects, judging from their form and decoration, appear to have functioned in ceremonial contexts as ritual paraphernalia or as part of the costumes of officiants.[45] One of the best known of these items is the so-called Pickman Strombus, first described by Tello in his early synthesis of Chavín civilization. This conch-shell trumpet was discovered in the 1930s during construction on the Chiclayo air base in the Lambayeque drainage. The large *Strombus galeatus* shell had been transformed into a musical instrument by cutting off its apex, and a hole had been drilled in the shell so that it could be hung by a cord. The surface was covered with fine incisions showing an anthropomorphic figure in the process of blowing a conch shell trumpet. A profusion of Chavín-style snakes and fanged agnathic faces were shown emanating from the instrument, as though expressing the trumpet's power of communication with the supernatural realm. As Tello suggested, the Pickman Strombus was probably a ceremonial trumpet (*pututu* or *huayllaquepa*), used in public rituals like those represented in the sculptures of Chavín de Huántar's Old Temple.

Several classes of portable items are believed to have been involved in the preparation and ingestion of hallucinogens. Among the most beautiful of these are elaborately carved mortars, too small to have been used for grinding corn or other staples. It has been suggested that these mortars are the forerunners of the *vilcanas* of the 16th century. According to the 16th-century Spanish chronicler Cristóbal de Albornoz, *vilcanas* were small stone or hard wood mortars carved in animal forms and used by sorcerers to grind *vilca*, a hallucinogenic snuff. Perhaps the finest examples of these Chavín mortars are the pair collected by Larco Hoyle at Pacopampa: one mortar was carved in the form of a raptorial bird, the other a feline, while the two pestles were serpent-shaped.[46]

Chavín themes also adorned bone tubes, bone and metal spatulas, and small spoons that were probably designed for inhaling snuff. Like the small mortars, these items were decorated with representations of wild animals that are associated in South America with shamanistic transformation. It is possible that some of the elaborate pottery with Chavín motifs may have also been used in ritual eating and drinking, and votive offerings. Residue and contextual studies will be critical in evaluating the functions of all of these artifacts.

This review of the evidence for the Chavín horizon style reveals that it consisted of a small number of items, most of which are probably related to the rituals of the Chavín cult. While this evidence supports the empirical reality of a Chavín horizon style, it was not the only, or even the dominant, iconographic style at most sites in central and northern Peru during the Early Horizon.

The broader significance of the Chavín horizon in Andean prehistory may be better appreciated if the focus is temporarily shifted from the spread of a horizon style to other, ostensibly unrelated, spheres of human activity such as technology. Studies of material culture and ancient technology generally have lagged behind those of style, but recent investigations have yielded results which, in a sense, support Tello's insistence on the concept of a multifaceted Chavín civilization. In both metallurgy and textile production, numerous innovations appear suddenly and diffuse over an extensive area, laying the basis for later regional technological developments. The introduction and diffusion of this new technology appears to have been intimately involved with the spread of the Chavín cult.

Textile expert William Conklin has proposed that cloth production was truly revolutionized during the Chavín horizon by a host of new techniques and materials first utilized as carriers of the Chavín designs. In fact, a series of inventions was promulgated whose influence obliterated most of the older textile traditions in the coastal areas, and which became the foundation for later Peruvian textile evolution. These textile innovations included: (1) the use of camelid hair in cotton textiles; (2) textile painting; (3) supplemental disconti-nuous warps, including various types of tapestry; (4) the dying of camelid hair; (5) warp wrapping; and (6) negative or "resist" painting techniques (i.e. tie-dye and batik). Judging from the existing collections of Early Horizon textiles from the south, central, and north coast, there are few regional distinctions in these textile techniques or in their associated art styles.[47]

Technological advances of a comparable magnitude also occurred in metallurgy at roughly the same time. Only small sheets of hammered gold and copper are known from the Initial Period, but during the Early Horizon large objects of forged and annealed gold and silver with complex Chavín-style motifs were produced by a number of techniques which have no known antecedents. According to Heather Lechtman, the production of three-dimensional forms by metallurgically joining pieces of preshaped metal sheet is one of the important traditions in Peruvian metallurgy, and it appears for the first time during the Early Horizon. Soldering, sweat welding, repoussé decoration, and the creation of silver-gold alloys were all utilized in the production of Chavín-style objects. Analysis of the solder in a gold artifact from Chavín de Huántar revealed that its melting point was 70° lower than the pieces of metal being joined, due to a higher proportion of copper in the predominantly gold-silver alloy. An understanding of alloying and soldering, as well as the ability to control temperature, is implied by a metallurgical join of this kind.[48] Furthermore, gold artifacts have been excavated or looted from a large part of the region under Chavín influence. This contrasts with the isolated example of Initial Period gold-working in Andahuay-las, which was limited to the production of small hammered gold sheets. How can we explain this sudden advance in the development and distribution of gold-oriented metallurgy during the Chavín horizon? Lechtman writes:

> It may be that in the Central Andes gold was used earlier than any other metal and that its prominence in the archaeological record during the period of spread and influence of the Chavín cult . . . reflects a religious and ceremonial bias of the cult for the metal . . . My feeling is that gold may have had special symbolic significance for the cult and that certain religious values or doctrine were expressed through its use.[49]

Both Conklin and Lechtman propose a link between the Chavín cult and the

218 A piece of cotton tapestry decorated with a crested eagle excavated by Gordon Willey in the Supe Valley.

219 This small snuff spoon was fashioned out of sheets of gold and silver foil that had been hammered into form and soldered together to create one of the first three-dimensional metal objects known from the Andes. A priest or mythical figure is shown blowing a trumpet and a crested eagle is embossed on his back. This piece (11.1 cm long) was said to have been found at Chavín de Huántar.

introduction of new technology. But what is the nature of this link? Like all religions, the Chavín cult was faced with the paradox of trying to describe the undescribable and to evoke an unworldly experience, while relying on materials, techniques, and symbols drawn from the mundane environment. All religious art is based ultimately on analogy and metaphor, but Chavín artists made this principle the cornerstone of their style, spinning visual metaphors into a web so complex that many find the end product incomprehensible. Yet even modern viewers find that the best of Chavín art succeeds in evoking the sensation of being in the presence of something extraordinary. Alfred Kroeber considered the artistry of Chavín to be the pinnacle of prehistoric South American art, and it is thought to have been the work of full-time specialists who could dedicate themselves to developing an artistic style capable of communicating the power of Chavín religious ideology.[50]

The materials used as the medium of this religious art style may also have been expected to convey the sensation of the "wholly other" to the viewer. This objective could have stimulated the sudden burst of invention which provided artisans with new media (such as three-dimensional metal objects), and innovative ways of transforming old media into new (such as the brightly painted polychrome textiles). Most of these Early Horizon technological innovations did not produce any clearcut saving of energy. On the contrary, labor surpluses would have been required for these technologies to exist. However, the inventions did provide the means of manufacturing objects which were immediately distinguishable from other items and therefore especially suitable and effective as symbols or emblems of religious authority. The images in polished granite or breastplates in hammered gold must have been awe-inspiring when viewed by those unfamiliar with the new technology.

The ability of a cult to convey or evoke religious awe through artistic or technological devices would have helped to validate its sacred propositions and the authority of its representatives. The success of the Chavín cult and the extension of its ritual field into new zones would have produced additional resources and increased the demand for religious paraphernalia. In this view, the maintenance of full- or part-time artisans could have been motivated by pragmatic as well as theological considerations, and the "early great art style" of Chavín may have contributed actively to the success of the Chavín cult and the prestige of the leaders associated with it.[51]

The network established by the spread of the cult permitted contact between distant zones and would have facilitated the sharing and borrowing of innovations, allowing a more rapid accumulation of technology than would have been possible if these regions had remained isolated from each other. The nucleated proto-urban towns of the Early Horizon, such as those that grew up around the religious centers of Chavín de Huántar, Pallka, and Pacopampa provided a better matrix for scientific and artistic development than does a dispersed settlement pattern. The increasing social differentiation in these communities and the consequent demand for material indicators of hierarchical social status would also have helped to fuel the development of new technologies.

While metallurgy and other technologies associated with the cult and the emerging regional elites underwent a radical transformation, most subsistence technologies remained unchanged and surprisingly rudimentary when con-

220 A gold pectoral decorated with Chavín designs, said to be from Chavín de Huántar. The face in the central cartouche has been made with a champlevé technique while the guilloche or ornamental braid encircling the vessel was produced by embossing. Holes were cut in the pectoral so that it could be hung. Diameter 12.3 cm.

221 A Chavín feline, 10.4 cm in length, cut from gold sheet metal and embossed according to classic Chavín conventions. Judging from its perforations, it was probably designed to be sewn on to cloth.

trasted with the much lauded "high" achievements of Chavín civilization. People still fished with hooks made from shell or cactus spine, and they continued to farm with digging sticks and pecked stone clod-breakers. As in the Late Preceramic and Initial Period, they lit their fires by placing tinder on a wooden stick with shallow depressions and rotating another stick on top of the tinder until enough friction was produced to light it. Although ground slate points did gain in popularity in many communities of the coast and highlands, coarsely worked cobbles and flakes continued to be the most common stone tools.[52]

At the crux of understanding the Chavín horizon is the way in which disparate Early Horizon societies became interconnected and how these linkages were forged and maintained. The Chavín cult and the ideological and social ties generated by its expansion provided one of the most important articulating mechanisms. Correlated with the growth of this religious archipelago was the emergence of stratified societies with elites that wielded real economic and political power. As noted, some incipient stratification was already evident in the highlands during the Initial Period, but it was during the Early Horizon that there appears the first clear evidence of economic inequality and the amassing of personal wealth in both highland and coastal societies. It is possible that regional leaders, appreciating that egalitarian norms were embedded in the fabric of localized ideologies, intentionally encouraged the adoption of the Chavín cult in order to justify circumventing the long-standing social conventions prohibiting the unequal appropriation of goods for personal gain. Significantly, many of the portable examples of Chavín religious art have been discovered in the rich burials of the upper social stratum. It is likely that these individuals used the ideology of the Chavín cult to legitimize and naturalize their wealth and positions of authority; indeed, the iconography of the cult frequently appears on jewelry and garments that these people wore. The physical association of these people with exotic materials and innovative technologies would have helped to symbolize their separation from the rest of the population.

The number of these elite individuals appears to have been very small, as would be expected. Of the multitude of Early Horizon graves that have been excavated or looted, we know of fewer than a dozen that included significant concentrations of precious metals and other valuables. Most individuals continued to be buried in shallow pits, wrapped in simple cotton cloth and accompanied only by the mundane tools they had used in everyday life. In order to give some sense of the socioeconomic stratification that emerged during the Chavín horizon, we will review the evidence from some of these rare tombs of the regional elites. One such tomb discovered at Karwa on the south coast has already been mentioned. Most of the other elite tombs of the Chavín horizon have been found in northern Peru and the valuables included as grave goods are usually precious metal objects rather than fine textiles.

Actually, the existence of elaborate Early Horizon tombs first came to light on the north coast in 1928 or 1929, when Alejandro and Antonio Galloso discovered a rich burial containing artifacts decorated with images similar to those on the sculpture at Chavín de Huántar. These brothers had been enlarging a water reservoir near the town of Chongoyape in the upper reaches of the Lambayeque

Social stratification and the Chavín cult

222,223 (*Left*) A gold crown (23.5 cm high) embossed with the image of the supreme deity of the Chavín cult, found in a cache or tomb at Chongoyape in the Lambayeque drainage. (*Right*) One of the three gold crowns uncovered at Chongoyape shows a highly conventionalized representation which, although reminiscent of Chavín designs, cannot be identified with confidence. Height 18.7 cm.

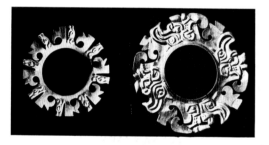

224 Two examples of the decorated gold earspools found together in the Chongoyape cache; judging from its small size, the one on the left (5.4 cm in diameter) may have been used by the deceased individual during his youth.

225 Gold tweezers, 4.4 cm long, found with the crowns and earspools at Chongoyape. In Inca times, similar tweezers were used by men to remove unwanted facial hair.

drainage when they encountered an undisturbed burial of three individuals associated with evidence of burning and numerous grave goods. The inventory of the burial was impressive. It included a gold headband, 66 hollow gold beads, 2 pottery beads encased in gold, 19 gold snail shells, 2 large gold ornaments or gorgets, 3 gold finger rings, 4 gold pins, a gold and silver pin, a small greenstone disk, a small stone spoon, a stone bowl, 2 stirrup-spouted bottles, a red plate, a polished stone mirror fragment (probably made of anthracite), 4 shades of cinnabar pigment, and a piece of gold sheet. Judging from these grave goods, it is likely that the principal individual in the tomb was female. She was apparently buried wearing a golden headdress, and her neck would have been draped in several gold bead necklaces, perhaps ending in large golden pendants; her cloak and/or hair would have been held in place by pins of precious metal. The pottery vessels and plate found with her would have been appropriate for offering corn beer and food, and the small stone spoon would have been suited for inhaling snuff, perhaps hallucinogenic.[53]

Around the same time as the discovery of the Chongoyape tomb, a group of young boys discovered another cache of gold at the bottom of a damaged irrigation ditch on the Hacienda Almendral near Chongoyape. Unfortunately, not all of the items from it were documented but the following were apparently recovered from a single tomb: 3 tall crowns, a gold headband, 7 decorated gold earspools, 4 undecorated gold earspools, and a pair of gold tweezers. In late pre-Hispanic times, earspools were characteristic features of male dress and tweezers were used by men to remove facial hair. It is thus reasonable to suggest that these items may have come from the tomb of a prominent male. It is also noteworthy that the diameters of the earspools can be arranged to form a series with the smallest having a diameter of 5.4 cm, to the largest which measures 6.9 cm. Archaeologist Samuel Lothrop, who provided the first detailed description of the Chongoyape materials, suggested that these may have been made for a single individual whose earlobes became larger and more distended as he grew older (and the weight of these enormous ear ornaments took their toll). The largest set was undecorated and may have still been in production when the owner died. If the smaller earplugs were given to him during his youth, it is probable that his status was inherited rather than achieved later in life through personal accomplishment.[54]

The materials in both of the Chongoyape caches appear to be evidence of individual wealth since they were items of personal adornment and use, and were buried with the deceased rather than returned to the community at the time of death. The burial of the materials prevented them from circulating and thus kept them scarce, while at the same time emphasized their association with the deceased. Most of the items would have constituted highly visible items of status when worn and, in later pre-Hispanic times, these elements of dress (head ornaments, earspools, pins, etc) were favored markers of elite status. The precious metal jewelry in these Chavín horizon tombs represents the conspicuous consumption of labor and expertise.

Judging from the style of the pottery and the iconography of the metal artifacts, the two tombs from Chongoyape were roughly coeval with the Janabarriu phase at Chavín de Huántar. Additional elite tombs from the same period were also encountered during Rebeca Carrión Cachot's 1946 excavations on the southern slopes at Kuntur Wasi, in the headwaters of the Jequetepeque.

She and Pablo Carrera discovered the tomb of what was interpreted as a high-ranking individual associated with a "Chavín" style pottery vessel. The deceased wore 2 necklaces, 1 of bone beads with semi-precious stones and 6 gold discs embossed with snakes, and the other made of small gold sheets, 4 of which were shaped as *Strombus* shells. A small gold sphere and turquoise beads were also found in the grave.[55]

Investigations were reinitiated at Kuntur Wasi in 1989 under the direction of Yoshio Onuki. On the summit of the site, intruding into an earlier platform, the team unearthed a series of four shaft tombs averaging 2.3 m in depth, each containing the skeleton of a single individual. The dead were seated in a sealed chamber at the bottom of these tombs. A layer of cinnabar was found covering the floors of the burial chambers. One of the richer tombs belonged to an elderly male. Two pottery bottles and a cup had been placed next to him, and an elaborate gold crown, a decorated gold plaque, a pair of polished gold ear-spools, and 2 shell pendants accompanied him in death. He also had 3 trumpets of Ecuadorian *Strombus* shell, one of which was engraved in a manner similar to the Pickman Strombus. In the neighboring tomb, a badly preserved skeleton was found associated with a gold crown, 3 gold pectorals, and 2 pottery vessels. In a third tomb, the grave goods left with an elderly female consisted of a pottery bottle and 2 cups, a pendant of gold and silver, and a carved stone cup. The floor of her burial was covered with some 7,000 stone and shell beads, which may have once been part of a beaded garment of some sort.[56] Judging from the ceramics and other artifacts, these tombs – like those at Chongoyape – were roughly coeval with the Janabarriu phase at Chavín de Huántar.

Unlike the Chongoyape tombs, the recent Kuntur Wasi finds can be located in the context of the Early Horizon settlement. The high-status individuals at this site were deliberately buried on the temple summit in the center of the religious architecture, underlining the symbolic link between leadership, divine sanction, and sacred knowledge. The contents of the deep and richly furnished burials from Kuntur Wasi and Chongoyape sharply contrast with the burials known from Late Preceramic and Initial Period sites. They also differ fundamentally from common mid-Early Horizon tombs known from the coast and highlands at such sites as Morro de Eten and Pacopampa. Most interments of this period were shallow burials with rarely more than one or two pieces of pottery, and sometimes lacking grave goods entirely; gold and silver jewelry is rare or entirely absent.[57]

In some burials, unusual types of grave goods suggest special statuses for some of the dead individuals, while not implying that this differentiation was expressed by sharp differences in personal wealth. A particularly interesting instance of this is in the case of religious specialists. One individual buried on the terraces at Pacopampa was unique in having a quartz crystal placed in his mouth, and archaeologists have suggested that he may have been personally involved in religious rituals since quartz crystals were an important element of ceremonial paraphernalia in the ancient Americas. Nevertheless, only a single pattern burnished bowl accompanied the deceased into the afterlife. Another individual, also identified as a shaman or curer, was excavated at Morro de Eten. This elderly male, roughly 60 years of age, was buried with a carved rattle of deer bone inserted into his right leg. Analysis of the skeleton suggests that a cavity in the leg has been formed by the pointed end of the rattle while the individual was still

226 A gold crown discovered on the summit of Kuntur Wasi in the shaft tomb of an elderly elite male. While dating to the Chavín horizon, the style and theme of this crown draws on the Cupisnique tradition of the north coast. Height 18 cm.

227 At Kuntur Wasi, another individual was found buried with a gold crown (13.5 cm high) decorated with classic Chavín motifs, as well as a gold pectoral, three shell trumpets, and other rare items.

228 Chavín iconography was used on items of adornment as well as precious metal jewelry. The carved bone pendant seen here is from Pacopampa (length 8.5 cm).

alive and that the ritual instrument had been carried by the shaman in this natural pouch. Near the shaman's head were two bone spatulas, perhaps used for inhalation of hallucinogens, as well as an anthracite mirror. Although elaborate pottery and small gold beads and pendants are known from the Morro de Eten cemetery, none had been included in the shaman's grave. The relative simplicity of the vast majority of burials during the Chavín horizon, even in the case of possible ritual specialists, lends weight to the conclusion that richly furnished tombs like those at Kuntur Wasi were the interments of elite members of a stratified society.

While grave goods have much to tell us about differential patterns of consumption and the unequal distribution of wealth in past societies, the inclusion of these objects was ultimately an aspect of the funerary rituals which were intended to convey public messages to the living. Consequently, they do not always mirror the social realities of the past. In order to compensate for this, it is necessary to use independent sources of information to evaluate whether burial materials accurately reflect the lifeways of the communities in question.

Such evidence is not yet available for Chongoyape or Kuntur Wasi, but in the previous chapter we summarized evidence from the settlement of Chavín de Huántar which indicated that a stratified society had appeared there by the Early Horizon. Living adjacent to the public architecture, the elite did not apparently engage in the same productive activities as others, and were able to maintain a pattern of consumption that was qualitatively better than that of their less prosperous neighbors in the settlement and those people living in the rural hinterland. The only piece of gold ever found in a non-burial context at Chavín was associated with the houses of this elite group. It was a very tiny fragment of gold jewelry that had probably been broken off during use or storage and swept out with the rest of the household refuse. A large collection of gold crowns, breastplates, and other objects of precious metals similar to those from Chongoyape were said to have been looted from the site; these materials may have come from the tomb of one of Chavín's leaders.[58]

On the basis of the Chavín de Huántar evidence, our view that the rich burials from Chongoyape, Kuntur Wasi and elsewhere reflect social inequality would seem to be plausible, as does the symbolic association of precious metals with the social elite. Indeed, the public burial of these individuals with an abundance of objects difficult to obtain and produce must have carried with it a message about the power and authority of the elite group.

The sculptural representations of mythical personages (or their priestly impersonators) in Chavín de Huántar's Circular Plaza show them wearing distinctive crowns, elaborate ear ornaments, pectorals and, in some cases, blowing the *Strombus* shell trumpet. The appearance of analogous paraphernalia in the interments of actual individuals bespeaks the religious or mythical basis of their authority. As already noted, the gold and silver objects worn by these elite individuals were covered with religious iconography, much of which resembles the sculpture from Chavín de Huántar in style and the themes represented. For example, one of the Chongoyape crowns depicts a supernatural bearing two staffs – a representation strongly reminiscent of the figure on the Raimondi Stone. The gold headband from the same cache shows the monstrous fusion of the feline and serpent common on Chavín sculpture, and the earspools too are covered with bands of snakes and felines. The style of these pieces fits well with John Rowe's final sculptural phase (EF) and most of the popular Chavín conventions are employed, including kenning, double-face profiles, and anatropic design.

While many of the motifs on the Chongoyape and Kuntur Wasi gold were variants of the Chavín style, others show links with the Cupisnique artistic tradition of the north coast. One of the Chongoyape graves included a naturalistic gold image of a crab (a creature unknown on Chavín de Huántar sculpture), and one of the recently discovered Kuntur Wasi crowns features human heads dangling within two braided bands.[59] The local themes in the metalwork as in the textiles from Karwa, should not be underestimated. Nonetheless, the strong links with the iconography of Chavín de Huántar still justify positing the association of these regional leaders with the Chavín cult.

The cultural diversity indicated throughout this volume is intimately linked with the ecological diversity of the central Andes and longstanding differences in basic systems of subsistence. Although all the major cultigens and domesticated animals had been introduced to the highlands and coast before the Early Horizon, this did not result in a pattern of homogeneous agricultural villages throughout the Chavín sphere of influence. On the contrary, recent archaeological investigations have revealed that several strategies of subsistence coexisted during the Early Horizon.

In the highlands a minimum of four distinct subsistence systems can be identified for the Early Horizon: (1) a system of mixed agriculture emphasizing high-altitude crops and llama-herding; (2) an agricultural system focusing on irrigated crops of the *quechua* and *temple* zone, e.g. maize; (3) a pastoral system based on the herding of camelids supplemented by hunting and gathering wild plants; (4) a system based on herding and seasonal cultivation.

The subsistence system at Chavín de Huántar, discussed in the last chapter, exemplifies the first of these types. Investigations in the Pacopampa area of northern Cajamarca provide an illustration of the second. Pacopampa – the largest site in the region – and two small sites were located within the *quechua* zone, which is best suited for intensive maize agriculture. Carbonized remains of maize and beans were recovered at Pacopampa, Pandanche and nine other small coeval sites were situated near by within the lower temple zone. The steep slopes of the *temple* are most appropriate for manioc cultivation using a swidden technique. Despite repeated exploration, no Early Horizon sites have been located above the *quechua* zone. The paucity of high-altitude settlements suggests that potatoes, quinoa, and other high Andean crops were no more than minor components within the local subsistence system. Similarly, there is little evidence that the patches of *páramo* pastureland were being intensively exploited and, judging from the refuse, llamas seem to have played a relatively small role in the local diet, although llama meat as well as venison was eaten on occasion.[60]

The third type of highland subsistence, based on pastoralism, was well established in the central highlands by the Initial Period, as we saw in Chapter 4. Investigations on the *puna* of Junin, Pasco, and Huanuco have revealed hundreds of caves (of altitudes of up to 4,600 m) which continued to be used by herders during the Early Horizon. In some cases, Early Horizon *puna* dwellers

Subsistence diversity during the Chavín horizon

resided in caves with no previous occupational history. Analysis of the faunal remains from these caves shows a preponderance of domesticated camelids, and archaeologists have in some cases located the nearby rustic stone corrals that were built to hold the llamas and/or alpaca herds.[61] The diet of the herders continued to emphasize wild seeds, roots, and rushes rather than domestic cultigens.[62] These herders probably had ties with small open village sites on the *puna* like those located on the shores of Lake Junin. These villages, which had been established in the Initial Period, never exceeded 3 hectares in size and were composed of dispersed semi-subterranean circular houses with adjoining corrals.[63]

At a distance of 15 km from Lake Junin, the natural salt springs of San Blas were exploited during the Early Horizon, as they had been for over 1,000 years. During the Initial Period and Early Horizon, the salt was extracted by evaporating saline water in cooking pots, and thus the quantity of ceramics discarded at San Blas can be seen as a reflection of the volume of salt production. Judging from the sharp increase in ceramic waste in the Early Horizon strata, it can be inferred that the exploitation of this rare highland source of salt increased dramatically during Chavín times.[64]

The fourth type of highland subsistence, based on a combination of seasonal horticulture and herding, appears to have characterized the intermontane valleys in the Mantaro drainage of the central highlands. Archaeologist David Browman maintains that a seasonally transhumant semi-nomadic lifeway was maintained in the Mantaro throughout the Early Horizon. In the northern part of the valley, the only major sites located thus far are Ataura and Huarisca. Both were agricultural settlements located on small rivers suitable for irrigation. Ataura, the most extensively investigated of the sites in this area, covers only 3 hectares, which is the equivalent of some of the secondary sites in the Chavín de Huántar or Pacopampa areas. Flotation of refuse from the residential sector of Ataura yielded squash, beans, achira, chili peppers, peanuts, cotton, and possibly maize.

Further down the Mantaro Valley the Early Horizon villages of Cochachongos and Pirwapukio were located along permanent springs, and a number of very small sites have been found in the *quechua* zone of the southern Mantaro. Wet-season agriculture could have been carried out at these valley sites as a supplement to the pastoral activities on the vast *puna* above the valley.[65]

Despite extensive survey, no Early Horizon public architecture of monumental scale is known from the Mantaro. Some small public or non-residential constructions were recorded at Ataura and the poorly-known site of the Muruhuay near Tarma. The latter site is located in a sheltered ravine rather than in the open valley. The paucity of large-scale Early Horizon ceremonial centers in the Mantaro drainage was paralleled in the Ayacucho area. Small centers of ritual activity in Ayacucho, such as Wichqana and Chupas, were occupied throughout the last millennium BC, but the modest corporate architecture known from these two sites dates to the end of the Early Horizon, and consequently postdates centers like Pacopampa or Chavín de Huántar.[66]

The Early Horizon subsistence system on the coast was probably less varied than in the highlands. Generally speaking, it was an intensive agricultural system dependent on irrigation. Although Early Horizon canals have rarely survived, the settlement patterns which occur throughout the coast can best be explained by postulating a widespread system of runoff canals. Maize, beans, sweet potatoes, manioc, squash, peanuts, avocado, and many types of fruit were included in the varied coastal diet, which has been amply documented from the well-preserved botanical remains of coastal refuse deposits. Perhaps the most conspicuous change in the refuse is the increase in the quantity of maize compared to other cultigens.[67] Small settlements along the shore supplied fish and mollusks to inland agricultural sites, and abundant shell remains were recovered at the inland villages of Huancayo Alto, in the Chillón Valley, and Cerrillos in the Ica Valley. As we have seen, this interdependency between littoral stations and agricultural villages predates the Early Horizon. Llamas provided a major supplementary source of meat for the middle and upper portions of coastal valleys, but not for the coastal plain, where sea mammals were still a significant source of protein.[68]

Although the general configuration of coastal subsistence systems was similar during the Early Horizon, differences did arise from the uneven distribution of rainfall, prime agricultural land, and microenvironments. The relative importance of coastal microenvironments during the Early Horizon is only beginning to be appreciated. One of the few excavations of an Early Horizon site in the *chaupi yunga* occurred at the small site of Huancayo Alto. A group of Early Horizon stone structures (interpreted as store houses) were uncovered there. These buildings contained the remains of coca leaves and maize cobs, thereby providing circumstantial evidence concerning the early use of this habitat for the cultivation of coca and other crops requiring an especially mild climate, and the possible role of *chaupi yunga* communities like Huancayo Alto in producing these goods for exchange. Other coastal microenvironments, such as the montane evergreen forests of the north coast or the *lomas* vegetation of the central coast, also offered potentially significant but unequally distributed resources.

A pattern of uneven development emerged from this range of subsistence strategies. The two agricultural subsistence strategies developed in the northern highland areas supported large dense populations, and the corporate constructions erected during the Early Horizon by such groups bear testimony to the productivity of these economies. The pastoral and seasonal horticultural economies of the central highlands supported a smaller and more dispersed population. As a consequence, there was a north–south division in social, economic, and political development during the Early Horizon. An analogous pattern of uneven development may be perceived if archaeological evidence from the north and central coast are contrasted with the south coast. Clearly heterogeneity rather than homogeneity continued to characterize the Andes during the Early Horizon, whether the focus is on economic, demographic, religious, or other aspects of culture and society.

229 Maize appears to have gained increasing importance as a food crop on the coast during the Early Horizon. The remains of maize cobs and other plant parts shown here come from the excavations at San Diego in the Casma Valley.

Interregional exchange and the Chavín horizon

Before the widespread adoption of the llama as a beast of burden, the effort needed to transport goods over the harsh Andean terrain limited the range and intensity of interregional economic interaction, as did the danger of passing through the patchwork of politically independent and potentially hostile small-scale societies that occupied much of the landscape. Even after the llama was introduced, market exchange was not well developed in the pre-Hispanic central

Andes, and standardized currency was never employed. Exchange transactions usually involved reciprocity and redistribution, whereby locally available goods from one area were exchanged with communities in another where these items were scarce or absent. These exchanges were often deeply embedded in social relationships and the arrangements underlying such transfers were diverse. Nevertheless, as seen in the preceding chapters, interregional exchange did occur during the Late Preceramic and Initial Period, particularly between peoples living in adjacent and ecologically complementary zones.

It was only during the Chavín horizon that domesticated camelids became commonplace outside their natural habitats on the high pasturelands. Prior to this time, they were rare on the coast and in the *páramo* highlands north of Chavín de Huántar. In these areas, llamas first begin to appear with frequency in refuse dating to the Early Horizon, as has been documented at sites such as Cerrillos, Ancón, Morro de Eten, and Pacopampa. This shift is probably due to the adoption of llamas as pack animals by non-*puna* dwellers, and the maintenance of small herds for long-distance llama caravans or more localized transport. A byproduct of this change would be the annual culling of herds and the consequent appearance of domesticated camelid meat in the diet, providing an attractive alternative to marine products or wild game. Whether additional dried camelid meat (*ch'arki*) was traded with coastal areas where natural pasture was scarce remains to be determined.[69]

The advantages of domesticated llamas for interregional exchange were considerable. A llama can carry 20–60 kg for 15–20 km per day and, because llamas follow a lead animal, a single driver can control 10–30 animals. On long trips llamas acquire their own fodder and water from the local environment. Although llamas are native to the *puna*, they are not biologically constrained from traversing the coast and highland valleys as long as sufficient pasture or some alternative (such as maize fodder) is available. Thus, it would have been possible for a hypothetical llama caravan of 50 animals to carry over 2 metric tons of goods per day without requiring more than two or three herders or any supplementary investment besides these people's provisions. The spread of domesticated camelids during the Chavín horizon was probably stimulated by the newly favorable conditions for trade among the agricultural groups of the intermontane valleys and coast. Once the cargo animals became widely available, their efficacy may have in turn further encouraged a broadening in the range of items being exchanged and the distances over which they could be transported. With llama caravans, it would have been feasible even to exchange cultigens and other bulk items.[70]

Whether in the desert or the mountains, the construction of formal roads would have had practical advantages, particularly once llama caravans were in use. Evidence of prehistoric highway systems are almost always elusive, but in a pioneering study, University of California archaeologist Colleen Beck demonstrated that a system of well-constructed intrasite and intervalley roads did exist along the north coast during the Early Horizon. Major Early Horizon roads connected the Virú, Moche, and Chicama valleys, and sites such as Huaca de los Chinos may have been intentionally positioned to monitor the movement of travelers along this highway system. The simplest sections of the road system varied from 1–11 m in width and had been made by clearing the roadbed of debris and forming stone lines to mark the sides. In other portions of the system, the roadbeds were cleared and graded, sometimes reaching 24 m in width. High stone walls were added along the sides in critical sections, thereby controlling as well as facilitating travel. Beck's study concluded that Early Horizon roads were nearly as complex as those built by much later pre-Hispanic cultures in the Andes.[71]

During the Chavín horizon, the amount of interregional exchange rose sharply and the regions involved in this panregional network of reciprocal transactions increased to unprecedented dimensions. In some cases, the social ties underlying these exchanges may have originally been forged by the spread of the Chavín cult; in other instances, exchange links between communities may have served as channels for the spread of Chavín religious ideology and the technological innovations associated with it. There may have been other situations in which groups became involved in this expanding exchange network without adopting the Chavín cult. Whatever the case, several regional spheres of interaction that had existed during the late Initial Period interlocked to form a single panregional network of economic interaction during the Chavín horizon. Although it could be said that Chavín de Huántar had a position of *primus inter pares*, because of the interregional prestige of its temple, there was no politically or economically dominant center in the system. On the contrary, the sphere of interaction was multifocal and included a host of roughly equivalent regional centers, each continuing to serve as the center of more limited social systems.

At its zenith during the mid-Early Horizon, this field of interaction extended unevenly from Pacopampa in the far northern highlands of Cajamarca to Jargam Pata de Huamanga in Ayacucho, a linear distance of approximately 950 km. Many of the communities living on the adjacent coast and western slopes were drawn into this economic field, as were those located along the eastern slopes. However, not all groups within these geographic limits participated to the same degree in the developments, and some groups seem to have resisted incorporation.

The kinds of goods being exchanged were diverse. Some were valuable lightweight items sought by local elites for their personal consumption or for use in religious rituals. Exotic pottery, particularly bottles and bowls used in entertaining, was traded over great distances despite the fragility of these items. Dried fish, coastal shell, semi-precious stones such as chrysacola, vermilion pigment (cinnabar), wool, fine textiles, and precious metals were among the prestige goods exchanged between regional elites. From the periphery of this supraregional network, the leaders of these communities acquired lapis lazuli from sources in Moquegua or the Atacama Desert of northern Chile, and *Spondylus* and *Strombus* shell from the deep waters off the Ecuadorian littoral.

Other naturally rare items, such as obsidian, were widely exchanged but not used exclusively by the elite. Unfortunately, studies of long-distance exchange are few and limited in scope. Obsidian is one of the few materials investigated thus far and the results indicate that the procurement of obsidian from Quispisisa in the south-central highlands became widespread during the Chavín horizon. Flakes of this volcanic glass have been found at Kotosh, Ancón, Huaricoto, and even at Pacopampa, the northernmost center of the Chavín horizon. At Chavín de Huántar, 450 km north of Quispisisa, obsidian replaced the locally available chert as the primary lithic material during the Early Horizon.[72]

230 Janabarriu-related ceramics from the salt mine at San Blas in the Junín *puna*.

The intermontane valleys of the highlands are separated by substantial expanses of high-altitude pastureland, and these *puna* environments were natural corridors for the movement of goods by llama caravans. As we have seen, the dispersed populations occupying these areas subsisted primarily on the basis of camelid herding, sometimes with supplementary horticultural activities on the adjacent upper slopes. As a result of the expansion of long-distance exchange, these previously isolated groups held a strategic position because of their control of large herds and the *puna*, and they were soon incorporated into the sociocultural and economic changes that were occurring. Even at Pachamachay in Junín, one of the temporary cave shelters of these herders, there are flakes of imported obsidian and other evidence of involvement with outside groups.[73]

The emergence of complex societies and supraregional economic systems during the Chavín horizon had a particularly powerful impact on the less developed societies in the south-central highlands. This region has yielded only sparse evidence of occupation during the Initial Period, even in those areas intensively surveyed and excavated by the Ayacucho-Huanta Archaeological-Botanical Project, directed by Richard MacNeish. Nevertheless, the south-central highlands were the principal source for two important commodities: cinnabar and obsidian. Cinnabar or mercuric sulphide becomes the vivid red colorant vermilion when ground into powder, and it is easily distinguishable from its alternatives, the more common hematite or red ocher pigments. Cinnabar had strong religious associations during the Early Horizon, and it was frequently applied to the surface of jewelry and employed in burial rituals. The deposit at Huancavelica is the only major cinnabar source in the central Andes and there is archaeological and ethnohistoric evidence of its use in pre-Hispanic times.[74] Deposits of obsidian are somewhat more common – there were about a dozen that were used extensively in pre-Hispanic Peru – but Quispisisa near Castrovirreyna is the northernmost of these deposits, and it was the main source of obsidian for the societies of the Chavín horizon.

As we have indicated, the south-central highlands were inhabited by agriculturalists and herders dispersed in small villages and hamlets, with little if any overarching political organization. The expansion of the exchange network during the Early Horizon and the demand for products from this zone apparently served as a catalyst for the emergence of a more centralized mode of political and economic organization in this region. The site of Atalla, located at 3,850 m near the modern town of Huancavelica, was one focus of these developments. Situated at the upper limit of agriculture adjacent to the vast high plains, Atalla was the highest of all the major Early Horizon centers. Its position suggests the importance of *puna* resources to its economy. On the uppermost part of Atalla's mound, the local population built a massive rectangular construction of quarried and selected stones. Surrounding the public architecture were circular dwellings and burial chambers.[75]

While Atalla is not comparable in scale or sophistication to Chavín de Huántar or Pacopampa, its construction would have required the cooperation of many family units, and fundamental changes in the socioeconomic organization of the society must have therefore occurred. The appearance of local leaders associated with a central place would have greatly facilitated the steady procurement of goods from this region by the more advanced societies to the north. Located very near the cinnabar sources, and only 20 km from Quispisisa,

Atalla could have served as the regional ceremonial and trade center at which local goods for exchange were collected and contacts with representatives of outside groups were established.

Ataura, a much smaller site in the Mantaro drainage, and sites such as Wichqana and Osno Era in the Ayacucho Basin, may have developed for similar reasons, although none of these sites have as yet yielded evidence of even small monumental constructions contemporary with the Chavín horizon. However, excavations at Ataura have produced substantial evidence that goods were obtained from the lowlands to the east and the coastline to the west. In summary, the appearance of regional centers in the central highlands appears to be a local response to stimulus from the panregional sphere of interaction associated with the centers of the Chavín horizon.[76]

Ceramic style and changing cultural identity

In the foregoing discussions, it has been suggested that the Chavín horizon was not produced by political expansion, but instead resulted from the extension of a shared cosmology made visible in ritual objects, and from the growth of a complex web of socioeconomic links made manifest in the surge of interregional exchange. These circumstances allowed more contact with neighboring and distant societies, whether it was for pilgrims who passed safely through the lands of alien ethnic groups to visit distant shrines or for vulnerable llama caravans that crossed the open *puna* or narrow mountain passes far beyond their home territory. Although this *Pax Chavinensis* was conspicuously absent on the north-central coast, in other areas it made possible the creation of new social ties and an unprecedented sharing of information about technology and other aspects of culture. But one must now ask whether the changes described were primarily limited to a few elite members of these diverse societies, or whether the cultural impact was more profound.

The abundant information that exists on ceramic styles during the Early Horizon is directly relevant to this question since, with some exceptions, pottery was locally produced and most of it was employed at the household level. Thus, the style of ceramics can be interpreted as expressing popular tastes, which in turn are active expressions of individual and group identity. The plasticity of the ceramic medium offers the possibility of an almost infinite variety of forms and decorative attributes, particularly in the hands of skilled potters. As we have seen, the presence of dozens of easily recognizable ceramic styles during the late Initial Period vividly expressed the close link between cultural identity and the small-scale social groups that characterized this period. The new panregional economic and religious phenomena of the Early Horizon would not have transformed this pattern unless they also provoked a fundamental change at the household level. The continued popularity of local ceramic traditions in some regions of the Inca empire illustrates this point.

Ethnographic studies of material culture suggest that it is not a quantitative increase in interaction or the mere exposure to new stylistic ideas that produces marked stylistic change, but rather decisions about the way in which alien ceramic attributes can be manipulated to express changing cultural identity vis-à-vis other households or groups. Thus pottery styles can be used to reinforce cultural boundaries or, when convenient, to blur preexisting divisions in order to express an ideology of complementarity rather than competition and conflict.[77]

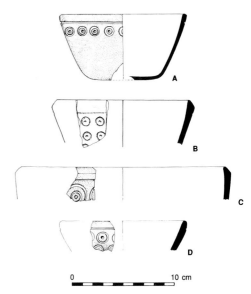

231 A comparison of decorated bowls from selected sites that participated in the Chavín horizon: (a) Pacopampa in the northern highlands, (b) Chavín de Huántar, (c) Ancón on the central coast, and (d) Atalla in the south central highlands.

232 As a result of Pacopampa's integration into the Chavín sphere of interaction, stirrup-spouted bottles such as this were occasionally produced, although the vessel form never became popular in the area.

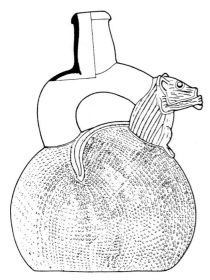

233 An Early Horizon stirrup-spouted bottle from the cemetery at Morro de Eten on the shores of the Lambayeque drainage. 19 cm high.

It is particularly significant, therefore, that the Chavín horizon was marked by the increased similarity of pottery assemblages, even among groups that shared few if any antecedent cultural and historical links. In fact, there is probably more panregional similarity in the pottery assemblages of this time than in any period before or after. First noted by Julio C. Tello, this pattern has been documented conclusively by modern research. It is now evident that the interregional similarities between ceramic assemblages were the result of intentional choices to produce and use pottery with forms and designs resembling rather than contrasting with those of other contemporary groups.

A constellation of ceramic traits diffused throughout much of the Peruvian coast and highlands during the Early Horizon. These elements included: distinctive shapes such as the neckless cooking pot with thickened rim, carinated shallow bowls with flat bottoms, and the stirrup-spouted bottle with exterior thickening of the spout lip; decorative conventions such as rows of repetitive circles with central dots, concentric circles, S's and others; dark monochrome surfaces in which lustrous undecorated zones contrast with textured unpolished zones; decoration made by broad incisions in leather-hard paste; a broad spectrum of decorative texturing techniques, including rocker-stamping, dentate rocker-stamping, dentate impressions, appliqué nubbins, and combing; and such functional features as pouring lips on bowls. This complex of attributes is best known from Chavín de Huántar, where it is characteristic of the Janabarriu phase. However, it should not be assumed that the potters provisioning these sundry centers and villages were directly imitating the pottery of Chavín de Huántar itself, but rather that the potters of many different regions were drawing inspiration from the same set of attributes, whose historical origins were diverse and complex.

These new traits were usually combined with features retained from the local late Initial Period style. In each area, the outcome of this mixture of local and foreign features was a cosmopolitan style that expressed a desire for a broader, less parochial sense of cultural identity without relinquishing all the features emblematic of local culture.[78] The diffusion of Janabarriu-related ceramic traits can be considered in more detail using examples taken from near the northern and southern limits of their distribution: Pacopampa, Morro de Eten, Ayacucho, and Ica.

At Pacopampa, the Chavín style of the Early Horizon was characterized by stamped circles, concentric circles, circles with central dots, S's, and crescent-shaped eyes. These motifs partly replaced the earlier incised geometric and figurative designs of the Pacopampa Pacopampa phase, but in some cases they were integrated with earlier decorative motifs in combinations which never appeared at Chavín de Huántar. The Pacopampa-Chavín phase was also typified by broad lustrous incisions rather than the mat and irregular incisions of the previous phase, which were usually made in dry paste. On the other hand, many Pacopampa-Chavín bowls had carved rims and interior pattern burnishing, techniques retained from the local ceramic tradition. Although stirrup-spouted bottles, neckless ollas, graphite-filled incisions, and various surface-texturing techniques were introduced in the Pacopampa-Chavín phase, they remained unpopular. The Pacopampa-Chavín style was, quite simply, an independent style which synthesized extraneous motifs, decorative techniques, and vessel forms with the local ceramic tradition.[79]

A burial ground at Morro de Eten, on the Pacific littoral of the Lambayeque drainage, offers one of the best-documented Early Horizon assemblages from the far north coast; these materials are closely related to those found in the Chongoyape tomb in the upper portion of the same valley. The bottles, bowls, and neckless cooking pots recovered at this site incorporate many of the styles and forms of the Chavín-related constellation already described. These elements occur in conjunction with traits typical of the late Initial Period Cupisnique style. For example, the stirrup-spouted bottles were sometimes decorated with naturalistically modeled animal representations. On one, a mouse-like rodent is shown eating. Both the naturalism and the thematic content of such pieces were derived from the earlier north-coast ceramic tradition, but the vessel form (lip shape, spout form, stirrup curvature etc.) was shared with other Chavín-related assemblages, including Janabarriu. One of the more popular vessels at Morro de Eten was a strap-handled deep bowl or *tazón* reminiscent of a chamber-pot. This form had local Cupisnique antecedents and was popular further to the north, but it was rare or absent at Chavín de Huántar and more southern sites.[80]

On the south coast of Peru, intrusive Janabarriu-like traits were similarly combined with non-Chavín features to produce the distinctive local style known as Paracas. As noted earlier, phases 3–5 of the Ocucaje sequence for Paracas pottery had marked similarities to the Janabarriu phase of Chavín de Huántar. However, zoned polychrome resin painting and resist painting remained more common decorative techniques in the Ica Valley than the Chavín-related rows of stamped or incised concentric circles, which also occur. Although stirrup-spouted bottles with convex curved spouts were produced, they seem to be less frequent than the double-spout and bridge bottles, which can be traced to the Initial Period styles of the south coast. Many of the heavily decorated bowls and bottles in the early Paracas style incorporate Chavín themes and symbols, but the heavy emphasis on modular width in the composition is a local characteristic, as are most of the forms and decorative techniques.[81]

It would seem that a wide range of Peruvian cultures in the mid-Early Horizon chose to modify their traditional ceramic styles in order to emulate more closely the pottery of groups beyond their territory. In a sense, this pattern constitutes a horizon phenomenon analogous to that described for the Chavín art style or the technology of textiles. Unlike these, however, the changes in ceramics were initiated at the household level rather than by a centralized religious authority or the local elite.

It can be suggested that the emergence of these Chavinoid pottery styles in some, but not all, cases was intertwined with the adoption of a more universalist ideology, and reflected a desire to manifest this sense of supra-group identity. Throughout the Chavín horizon utilitarian ceramics were decorated with simplified Chavín elements (S's, concentric circles), which were also used in Chavín religious art. Relatively elaborate Chavín religious themes appeared in many regions, including on early Paracas and late Cupisnique bowls and bottles. Whether or not shifts in religious ideology were always involved, the new pottery styles were an unequivocal expression in a changing ideology of group identity. Although the move towards a broader, more universal cultural identity was striking, it sometimes may have been more of an ideal than a fully realized social reality. Whatever the case, this new world view produced significant departures from the cultural patterns of the Initial Period.

234 A single spout-and-bridge bottle from the Ica Valley on the south coast. Although the resin-painted vessel is thoroughly local in form and technology, it is decorated with a Chavinoid face and several circle-dot elements. Height 13.3 cm.

235,236 These two Janabarriu-related stirrup-spouted bottles were found on the north coast and depict (*left*) a Chavín-style jaguar and (*right*) a Chavín-style crested eagle.

237 Slip-painted bottle (32 cm high) from a tomb in the Zaña Valley, portraying the Chavín supreme deity in a yet unknown Early Horizon style from northern Peru.

The northern frontiers of Chavín civilization

Many groups resisted being incorporated into the religious and economic networks that bound Chavín civilization together. To the north, east, and south there was a frontier zone beyond which Chavín civilization had little impact other than providing a market for small quantities of exotic raw materials. Within the broad frontier zone, Chavín-related cultures and non-Chavín cultures interacted in a dynamic manner.

The northernmost groups actively participating in the Chavín horizon were those occupying the Lambayeque-La Leche drainage on the coast, and the Pacopampa area in the upper Chotano Valley in the highlands. To the north of this area was the frontier zone occupied by poorly known groups that had some limited contact with Chavín-related cultures and may have played an active role in acquiring goods from the north for eventual consumption by groups of the Chavín horizon. As in the Initial Period, this frontier zone begins with the Sechura Desert, a 225-km expanse where water was scarce and agriculture was not possible. While coastal valleys throughout Peru are separated by stretches of desert, these average only 35 km. Not surprisingly, the Sechura Desert region had little human occupation, with the exception of some small fishing communities along the Pacific shoreline. While the Sechura Desert was by no means impassable in prehistoric times, it did provide an obstacle to communication or, from another perspective, a convenient buffer zone between potentially hostile groups.

The public center at Cerro Ñañañique (in Piura's mid-valley sector) was abandoned at the beginning of the Chavín horizon, but further upvalley, materials with some Janabarriu-related features have been recovered at Morropón, including the famous stirrup-spouted bottle highlighted by Tello. It is possible that groups in the upper Piura drainage played a role as intermediaries between Chavín civilization and the Ecuadorian and tropical forest cultures beyond its limits. Further to the north, the Pechiche culture of Tumbes and a related culture in the lower Arenillas were coeval with the Chavín horizon, but show little evidence of direct cultural or commercial contact with it. No mid-Early Horizon occupation of the Chira-Catamayo Valley has been discovered

238 (*Above left*) This bottle from Morropón in the Piura drainage exhibits surface decoration (dentate rocker-stamping and modeled nubbins) typical of Janabarriu-related styles, but the motifs incised on the lower chamber were apparently of local inspiration.

239 (*Above right*) The contact between the northernmost groups in the Chavín sphere of interaction and the societies of the adjacent frontier zone is evident from this Early Horizon bottle, probably produced in the Piura drainage, but found at a cemetery in the Zaña Valley.

240 (*Right*) The Pechiche ceramics of the Tumbes area share few characteristics with assemblages from sites within the Chavín sphere of interaction.

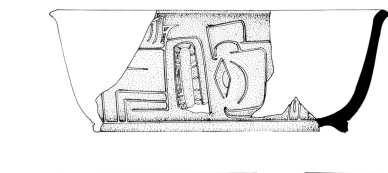

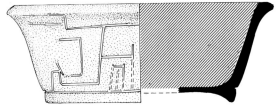

thus far, and the entire far north coast of Peru appears to have been very lightly inhabited during the centuries of the Chavín horizon.[82]

Tello interpreted the Formative cultures of southern Ecuador, particularly those of the Cuenca basin, as manifestations of the Chavín phenomenon, but contemporary research has shown that this was not the case. The cultures contemporary with the Chavín horizon, Chorrera on the coast and the Chorrera-related Pirincay-phase culture in the highlands, shared few features with Chavín-related cultures to the south. Most of the similarities that do exist, such as the use of ceramic seals and stirrup-spouted vessels, can be understood as part of a shared legacy from the preceding period. Thus, the evidence available suggests that at the height of Chavín civilization, direct contact with the cultures of southern Ecuador may actually have decreased. There is no published evidence of Chavín ceramics, metals, or other items being acquired or emulated in the north, nor is there any indication that the Chavín cult made any inroads into the area. Despite a fairly large sample of decorated Chorrera ceramics, no evidence of Chavín iconography has been encountered.[83]

The impression that movement across the frontier zone was limited during the mid-Early Horizon was reinforced by a trace element study of the obsidian artifacts recovered in association with Chavín horizon ceramics at the site of Pacopampa. Volcanic glass of excellent quality occurs naturally at the Mullumica and Yanaurco-Quiscatola deposits in the Cayambe region southeast of Quito. This obsidian was exploited throughout the first millennium BC, and artifactual obsidian has been recovered from Pirincay and coastal Chorrera sites in southern Ecuador, albeit in small quantities. Pacopampa was situated approximately 1,000 km south of the two major Ecuadorian obsidian sources and 1,325 km north of the closest major Peruvian obsidian deposit – the Quispisisa source in Huancavelica. Thus the Ecuadorian sources were several hundred kilometers closer, as well as being more accessible in terms of the intervening terrain. Nevertheless, laboratory analyses indicate that all the Pacopampa obsidian had been brought from the Quispisisa source. Such a pattern would be difficult to understand without positing the existence of a frontier. While *Spondylus* and *Strombus* shells native to the Ecuadorian shoreline continued to be obtained from across the frontier, items existing within the Chavín sphere of interaction were procured internally, even when greater distances were involved.[84]

Chorrera culture and its highland counterpart were fundamentally different from the cultures of the Chavín horizon. Large centers with public architecture were lacking. Irrigation agriculture was of minimal importance because of the abundant and reliable precipitation. The use of llamas for food or as pack animals was still unknown. Furthermore, the peoples of southern Ecuador were unfamiliar with the rocker-grinder, the production of gold and silver objects, and a host of features characteristic of Chavín civilization.[85]

The tropical forest

In Chapter 4, the impact of the tropical forest on the emergence of Chavín civilization was discussed. However, despite the importance of Amazonian groups in creating the conditions for these developments, it appears that these cultures never became fully incorporated into the Chavín sphere of interaction, and their relationships with the highlands may have diminished in intensity during the Chavín horizon. For example, as noted earlier, the tropical forest peoples of the lowland Bagua area – located near the juncture of the Utcubamba River with the Marañon – imported large quantities of incised pottery from Pacopampa during the late Initial Period. Bagua's own distinctive incised polychrome ceramics were widely sought-after by groups in the northern highlands and coast, and may have even been emulated by highland groups in the Catamayo area. During the mid-Early Horizon, the people of Bagua began to produce a new pottery style called El Salado which, besides painted pottery, also included monochrome pottery and the use of red post-fire paint in incisions. Small quantities of these ceramics have been found at Morro de Eten and Pacopampa. However, Bagua's primary cultural and economic orientation shifted eastward towards the Amazon and the Orinoco basins. In fact, the excavator of the Bagua sites, archaeologist Ruth Shady, attributes many of the innovative features in the El Salado phase to influences from cultures of the Venezuelan Saladoid Tradition of the Orinoco drainage.[86]

Nevertheless, the communities near the ecotone between the eastern slopes and the lowlands continued to play an important role in mediating contact between highlands and *selva*, and some communities appear to have developed specialized craft industries to more fully participate in the panregional network of interaction that flourished during the Early Horizon. Particularly informative were the results of the 1961 excavations at Huayurco by one of Tello's protegés, Pedro Rojas Ponce. Huayurco is located within the zone of dense cloud forest at the confluence of the Tabaconas River with the Chinchipe River, a tributary of the Marañon. In historic and late prehistoric times, this area was controlled by lowland groups culturally and economically tied to the tropical forest. Separated from the vast floodplains of the eastern lowlands by two impassable rapids (*pongos*), the Pongo de Chinchipe and the Pongo de Manseriche, as well as 38 areas of turbulence between these rapids, this eastern slope was integrated into the extensive system of lowland riverine trade by footpaths leading to the lands below the *pongos*. Huayurco had cultural and economic ties to the Early Horizon communities in the Bagua area.

In his excavations, Rojas discovered ten complete polished stone vessels. Most were shallow undecorated plates with simple convex-curved walls and a rounded base. They are made from a variety of stones, ranging from opaque limestone to a translucent veined onyx. A pair of deep bowls with straight sides and flat bases were adorned with stylized curvilinear serpents. A fragment from a unique vessel has a howler monkey sculpted in high relief. Most of the complete pieces appear to have been placed in burials, but the recovery of an additional 130 stone plate fragments and a group of polishers suitable for working stone, led Rojas to conclude that the earliest inhabitants of Huayurco produced stone vessels for exchange, and furthermore that some of the lapidary plates found at sites in the eastern lowlands, northern highlands and coast may have been acquired directly or indirectly from Huayurco. This hypothesis has yet to be confirmed by petrological studies of the vessels and the local geological deposits, but it is particularly plausible in light of two *Strombus* shell trumpets imported from the Ecuadorian littoral that were found in the Huayurco burials. Ruth Shady believes that the fragments of stone vessels discovered in her excavations in Bagua came from the Huayurco workshops. Also present was a finely polished

241 The discovery of shell trumpets, fine pottery, and beautifully made stone bowls in the Early Horizon burials at Huayurco (in the dense *ceja de selva* zone of the eastern slopes) suggests substantial involvement of lowland communities in the Chavín sphere of interaction.

242 The quantity of complete and fragmented stone vessels recovered at Huayurco suggests that this Early Horizon community was producing such items for exchange with other groups.

ceramic black-ware necked bottle, and a necklace of marine shell beads and carved mother-of-pearl pendants in the form of fish. Clearly, this small Early Horizon community on the eastern slopes was an active participant in an extensive sphere of interregional exchange, and was in a position to acquire high quality goods of exotic origin. Communities in the *ceja de selva*, such as Huayurco, may have begun to engage in part-time craft activity to supplement the existing trade in lowland natural resources to the highlands and coast.

Further south, the tropical forest groups adjacent to the central highlands produced the Shakimu style pottery and its variants. Donald Lathrap first discovered these ceramics at the Shipibo village of San Francisco de Yarinacocha in the Ucayali Valley, but similar materials were subsequently encountered in the Huallaga and in the Alto Pachitea.[87] The Shakimu style evolved out of the earlier Tutishcainyo style, although Lathrap attributes the popularity of Shakimu's lustrous flat-bottomed open bowls and elaborate excised motifs to Chavín influence. If any connection exists between Shakimu and coeval highlands styles, it is minor indeed, and certainly not comparable to the ties linking coastal and highland Janabarriu-related assemblages. While imported ceramics from numerous cultures of the coast and highlands have been recovered from Chavín de Huántar, no Shakimu or other tropical forest style has been identified thus far. Of course, importation of perishable items like colored feathers, medicinal plants, and perhaps hallucinogenic snuff from the eastern lowlands may have occurred. Sites with Chavín-related objects have been reported from the eastern slopes of the Andes since Tello's 1919 expedition, but most of this zone remains *terra incognita* for archaeologists. Archaeologists have yet to excavate a single Early Horizon site in the forested eastern slopes and narrow canyons adjacent to the Marañon and Huallaga that probably comprised the eastern frontier zone of Chavín civilization.[88]

Along the broad floodplains of the tropical forest at the foot of the Andes, water transport was basic to subsistence and the wide distribution of Shakimu ceramics suggests considerable movement along the river systems of the upper Amazon during the mid-Early Horizon. Shakimu pottery is found more commonly than any of the previous lowland styles, and some scholars believe that lowland populations were larger than those during the Initial Period. At the same time, there is still no evidence of large population centers or public constructions for this period within the tropical forest of the upper Amazon. The pattern of Early Horizon settlement appears to have been one of scattered small sedentary villages with a riverine orientation.[89]

Judging from the northern and eastern limits, it would appear that Chavín civilization was adopted primarily by those regions that already possessed permanently functioning centers prior to the Early Horizon. Only along its southern edge in areas such as Ayacucho, Huancavelica, and Ica did the Chavín horizon incorporate groups that had been organized at lower levels of sociocultural integration.

The southern highlands

Yet even in the southern highlands and coast, Chavín civilization affected far less territory than Tello had originally thought. To the south of Huancavelica and Ayacucho are the high intermontane valleys and *puna* of Apurimac and Cuzco.

243 One of the finest examples of Chavín sculpture was recorded by Tello in the highland town of Yauya, not far from the Marañon. The large granite carving represents a supernatural with cayman attributes. Length 1.65 m.

Archaeologists have finally begun to chronicle the Early Horizon cultures of these areas, and it would appear that they were not involved in the Chavín horizon. The Qasawirka cultures in Apurimac and the Chanapata culture in the Cuzco basin were characterized by prosperous sedentary villages employing mixed strategies of high-altitude farming and camelid-herding. They maintained ties with each other, and also had strong links with the altiplano groups of the Lake Titicaca basin. Neither the Waywaka nor Chanapata cultures appear to have been strongly influenced by what was going on in the north.[90]

Like the groups of southern Ecuador and the tropical forest, societies in the southern highlands remained culturally and economically independent and relatively self-sufficient. This does not imply that they were necessarily unaware of the changes to the north or that the frontier separating them from these Chavín-related groups was sealed. The presence at Chavín de Huántar of small quantities of the kind of obsidian popular in Cuzco and Andahuaylas may be the result of occasional visitors from the south.

Nonetheless, the Early Horizon groups in Cuzco had much stronger ties with the complex societies developing around Lake Titicaca than with those in the Chavín sphere of interaction. There is increasing evidence that during the Early Horizon an independent process of sociocultural transformation was occurring among the groups living around Lake Titicaca at elevations of over 3,800 m. According to archaeologists Karen and Sergio Chavez, temple complexes had been established in this region by 600 BC that were characterized by brightly painted storage buildings situated on low platforms surrounding a sunken central court. These public constructions were decorated with a distinctive style of stone sculpture known as the Yaya Mama style, whose supernatural images were unrelated to those of Chavín art. Frogs or toads, heads with rayed appendages, checkered crosses, raised circles, and serpents were common themes. The ceremonies conducted at the public centers involved specialized ritual paraphernalia such as ceremonial burners and heavily decorated ceramic trumpets. Examples of Yaya Mama sculpture have been discovered in numerous altiplano sites and the religious system it represented appears to have linked groups around the Lake, including those using different ceramic styles. The best known of these early altiplano centers is Chiripa on the southern shores of Lake Titicaca. Many of the same iconographic and architectural elements occur later in the Pucara (c. 200 BC–AD 200) and Tiahuanaco (AD 300–1200) cultures, with the Yaya Mama Religious Tradition, rather than Chavín civilization, appearing to have provided the cultural matrix out of which these later altiplano cultures developed.[91]

244 A sculpted slab belonging to the Yaya Mama style found at the site of Chiripa in Bolivia. Height 53 cm.

Some concluding thoughts on Chavín civilization

On the basis of the evidence now available, most archaeologists would acknowledge that civilization had appeared in the central Andes by the mid-Early Horizon (c. 400 BC). The centers of the Chavín horizon rivaled the classical Greek *polis* in size and beauty. With their massive public structures of finely cut-and-polished masonry decorated with detailed stone sculptures, these settlements were the product of a complex society which was differentiated along lines of both social status and productive activities. The artistic quality and technological sophistication of Chavín metallurgy, textile arts, and ceramics strongly imply the existence of part- or full-time specialist artisans; and the abstract knowledge necessary to successfully design the irrigation and drainage systems, and to produce the soldered three-dimensional gold and silver objects, certainly approximate the kind of scientific knowledge that scholars such as Gordon Childe used as one of the defining features of civilization. As in the Old World and Mesoamerica, the appearance of civilization in the central Andes was the cultural expression of a basic socioeconomic transformation – the emergence of complex societies.

For many contemporary scholars, particularly those outside Peru, the fundamental question raised by the appearance of pristine civilization in Peru is whether the basic causes or factors responsible for its emergence were the same as those involved in the four or five other cases in world history. Various general hypotheses have been advanced to explain the appearance of authochthonous civilizations but, until recently, there was insufficient information to determine if any of these hypotheses could account for the beginnings of Andean civilization. While research on Chavín and its antecedents is still in its infancy, the broad outlines of this historical process are now visible and a preliminary consideration of some popular (and not so popular) explanatory models is now feasible.

There are those scholars who consider it unlikely that civilizations appeared independently several times in different parts of the globe. In fact, one of the oldest explanations for Andean civilization was to attribute its origin to stimulus from other civilizations. At the beginning of the century, Max Uhle, arguably the "father of Peruvian archaeology," suggested that visits of Maya seafarers from Mesoamerica could have been the critical factor in the appearance of Peruvian civilization. And in the early 1960s, attempts were again made to link the appearance of Chavín civilization with Mesoamerican contacts. Interaction with China or Polynesia has also been proposed.[92]

Such diffusionary hypotheses were more plausible when Chavín civilization was believed to have appeared suddenly without local antecedents. However, as the coastal, highland, and tropical forest sources of Chavín civilization have become better understood, attempts to attribute Andean civilization to outside stimuli lose whatever plausibility they may have once had. As we have seen, many of the specific elements of Chavín civilization can be traced back over 1,000 years to the cultures of the Late Preceramic and early Initial Period. Furthermore, the refinement of New World chronologies has revealed that many of the supposed contacts could not have occurred since the cultures in question were not contemporary with each other. Features once posited as being derived from Mesoamerica, such as pyramid construction, are now known to have emerged in the central Andes centuries before their appearance in Mesoamerica.

Despite the exponential growth in research, archaeologists in Peru have yet to discover one unambiguous example of an object from Mesoamerica or any other area outside western South America. Like Egypt and the Indus Valley in the Old World, the civilizations of Peru and Mesoamerica appear to have developed without direct interaction. They may have known of each other through mutual contacts with the Machalilla and Chorrera cultures of coastal Ecuador, but besides a few shared cultural features (e.g. stirrup-spouted bottles and napkin-ring earspools) these indirect ties appear to have had little impact on the larger processes of cultural development. Moreover, it now appears that it was the Ecuadorian rather than Mesoamerican cultures that may have served as the "donor" for some of the shared features. Contacts with more distant areas such as Polynesia and China still remain a remote possibility but, even if such contacts occurred, it is unlikely that they ever modified the basic trajectory of pre-Hispanic cultural development, and even less likely that they had anything to do with the appearance of Chavín civilization. For these reasons, there is widespread consensus among archaeologists that Andean civilization developed *in situ* without any significant input from other autochthonous civilizations. There is considerably less agreement, however, on the factors responsible for its development.

Many anthropologists presume that the causes of pristine civilization should be sought in the nature and structure of the basic productive systems. One of the most resilient of such hypotheses was that proposed by historian Karl Wittfogel. He argued that in areas where irrigation agriculture was essential, bureaucracies were required to coordinate and direct the functioning of the canal systems. This position ultimately gave the administrators the power to control and exploit the farming population, thus producing social stratification and the centralized state.[93] Underlying Wittfogel's model was the assumption that irrigation agriculture in arid lands such as coastal Peru and Egypt was necessarily dependent on large canal systems beyond the administrative capacity of small-scale agrarian communities.

The archaeological research summarized in this volume confirms that irrigation was indeed critical to the development of Andean civilization. But the irrigation systems employed in the central Andes were small gravity canals which required no mechanical devices or elaborate bureaucracy. In most areas, local topography and scarce water resources severely limited the expansion of these hydraulic systems, even after the development of large centralized states. Historical documents have revealed that expanded versions of Initial Period and Early Horizon canals continued to be administered and maintained at the community level during later pre-Hispanic and colonial times. Even in the kingdom of Chimor and the Inca empire, authorities left all but a few canals in community hands.[94] Thus, there was no need for the permanent bureaucracy central to the Wittfogel hypothesis.

Nevertheless, irrigation was a precondition for the agricultural development of virtually all coastal valleys and, to a lesser extent, some highland valleys like Ayacucho. It was an important factor in the development of Andean civilization because it permitted the expansion of agricultural lands and, as a consequence, the growth and maintenance of dense human populations capable of sustaining a civilization. Completion of a canal was beyond the capacity of a single family and its construction was by necessity a community venture. Until recently, participation in canal construction and maintenance served to define the membership of many highland and coastal indigenous communities.

The communal character of early Initial Period cultures on the coast, reflected in their creation of public buildings and plazas at the center of their settlements, must have been reinforced by the need to jointly maintain and protect the canals upon which survival depended. In this sense, irrigation agriculture can be seen as one of the factors shaping the particular cultural form of Chavín civilization. But it was not its cause. Anthropologists Julian Steward and Louis Faron argued in their discussion of the development of Peruvian civilization that it was the surplus produced by irrigation agriculture that enabled political, military, and religious specialists to appear, thus resulting in stratification and the state.[95] As we have seen, irrigation farming had been practiced along the coast for over 1,000 years prior to Chavín civilization without leading to stratification of this kind. And when this socioeconomic transformation finally occurred, it first took place in northern highland areas, at centers such as Chavín de Huántar and Kuntur Wasi, where irrigation agriculture was of only secondary importance.

Alternatively, some scholars have suggested that the introduction of especially productive cultigens could have precipitated the emergence of Chavín civilization. For example, Donald Collier, Alfred Kidder II, and others posited a link between Chavín civilization and the introduction of high-yield varieties of maize and squash from Mesoamerica. Such attempts to portray the development of Chavín civilization as the result of a "green revolution" have not been confirmed by recent research. Indeed it is now known that the full range of food crops had been known for centuries, and in some cases millennia, prior to the Chavín horizon. While maize increased in importance in some parts of the coast during the Early Horizon, it remained a secondary food crop in the Chavín heartland.[96]

One of the most influential attempts to delineate regularities in the evolution of cultural complexity was Leslie White's hypothesis that sociocultural level was ultimately determined by the amount of energy that could be captured and utilized by a culture. According to this theory, technology is the key to understanding the growth and development of cultural complexity;[97] so if this theory held true, we would expect to find basic technological innovations in energy production and utilization underlying the emergence of Chavín civilization. However, while many revolutionary techniques did appear, most were unrelated to the acquisition or harnessing of energy. On the contrary, most innovations actually consumed large amounts of energy in order to create effective emblems of transcendent religious concepts and elite status. The tools utilized by the peoples of the Chavín horizon were little different from those of the Late Preceramic and Initial Period. The underlying differences between the cultures of the Initial Period and Early Horizon are primarily socioeconomic and ideological, not technological. (One conspicuous exception to this generalization is in the realm of transportation and meat acquisition. In many areas, the substitution of llamas for humans as pack animals and domesticated camelid meat for venison and other wild game, was a departure from earlier patterns and would have produced gains in the energy available to the societies living beyond the high pasturelands. However, this can be interpreted as a consequence rather than a cause of the Chavín horizon.)

Population pressure on resources is another variable that has been used to explain the appearance of civilization on a worldwide basis. There are scholars who see population growth as an independent variable that forces societies to adopt increasingly intensive subsistence strategies in order to accommodate the growing population and, as a consequence, develop increasingly complex patterns of social differentiation and political organization. Some investigators have argued more specifically that pressures resulting from population growth caused conflicts over critical scarce resources, and that fundamental changes in sociopolitical organization were required to ensure social harmony in the face of these chronic difficulties. Others argue that such competition produced a dominant exploitative class and ultimately its institutionalized apparatus, the state.[98]

Population growth is difficult to study archaeologically, especially in such areas as Peru where floods, landslides, earthquakes, and other natural disasters affect site survival and visibility. Problems are particularly severe for more ancient archaeological sites since these have been exposed to destructive forces for a greater length of time. Despite these difficulties, some archaeologists have attempted to address questions of demographic growth on the basis of comprehensive archaeological surveys. In such studies site numbers and sizes are converted directly into population estimates. Thus far, the pattern that appears in several valleys is that population increased during the Late Preceramic and Initial Period. Whether or not demographic growth continued during the Chavín horizon is more uncertain. Perhaps the key observation in these studies is that population levels immediately prior to the Chavín horizon were much lower than in late Andean prehistory. Considering the technology and cultigens already available, it would seem that the Early Horizon populations on the coast and in the highlands were well below the maximum size that could be sustained comfortably in their territories; the problems caused by demographic pressure should not, therefore, have been a major concern.

One of the features of the central Andes that has parallels in other areas of autochthonous civilization is that severe constraints existed on human societies due to the uneven distribution of resources. This was particularly marked once relatively large sedentary populations became established. The role that topography and circumscribed resources may have played in the origin of Andean civilization was appreciated by Pedro Cieza de León, an itinerant Spanish soldier who traveled through much of the central Andes, including the Chavín de Huántar area, shortly after the collapse of the Inca empire in the sixteenth century. In a remarkable passage written in 1550, Cieza prefigures the writings of most contemporary theoreticians as he attempts to explain why the native peoples of northern South America lacked the stratification and state government found in the central Andes:

All the Indians subject to the jurisdiction of Popayán [Colombia], have always been, and are, without lords . . . They are lazy, slothful, and above all loathe serving, and being subject, which is sufficient cause for them to distrust being under foreigners and in their service . . . But there is another much greater cause, which is that all these provinces and regions are very fertile, and on both sides there are dense mountain forests, canebrake and other brush. As the Spaniards close in on them, they burn the houses in which they live, which are of wood and straw, and remove themselves a league or two from there or go as far as they want, and in three or four days they make a house, and in as many more they sow the amount of maize they want, and they harvest it in four months. And if there also they are hunted, they leave that place and go on or go back, and wherever they go or are they find food and fertile land ready and available to give them fruit. For this reason they serve when they want, and war or peace is in their hands, and they never lack food. Those of Perú serve well and are submissive, because they are more intelligent than these others, and because all were made subject by the Inca kings, to whom they gave tribute, serving them always. They were born in that condition; and if they did not want to serve, necessity forced them to it, because the land of Perú is all waste, full of mountains and sierras and snow fields. If they left their towns and valleys to go to these deserts they could not live. The land gives no fruit, nor is there any place that does so other than their own valleys and provinces; so that in order not to die to the last man, they have to serve and not abandon their lands . . .'[99]

This idea was more fully developed four centuries later by Robert Carneiro, an ethnographer of the tropical forest. He reasoned that when population growth takes place in regions with environmental circumscription, the first response is to engage in agricultural intensification, such as building canals and terraces. Assuming that population continues to grow, conflict and warfare would eventually arise over scarce resources. When one group emerged victorious, the subjugated population dependent upon the agricultural infrastructure would have no choice but to remain as a newly formed lower class or as slaves in the communities of the dominant group. The state would then emerge as a byproduct of the class stratification and the new administrative needs resulting from the conquests. This hypothesis, first proposed in 1970, used the Andean case to support the argument.[100]

While this model presents a plausible scenario, its emphasis on the role of warfare within a constricted environment appears to be at odds with the circumstances and chronology in which complexity initially appeared in the central Andes. As has been shown, complex societies emerged within a context of increased interaction and economic interdependency. In contrast to later settlement patterns in the Andes, the centers of Chavín civilization were not fortified, nor were they located in defensible locations. While there *is* evidence for warfare during the mid-Early Horizon, it appears to be confined to peripheral societies that were probably less, not more, complex than the societies incorporated within the Chavín sphere of interaction. Processes like those described by Carneiro may have been important later in Peruvian prehistory, but they cannot be accepted as an explanation of the initial evolution of complexity.

Setting aside warfare and population pressure on resources, it is still possible that the circumscribed character of the central Andes may help to explain the appearance of early civilization. Warfare is not the only form of coercion. If a subgroup within a small-scale, weakly differentiated society on the coast or highlands claimed economic and social prerogatives previously absent, and could implement these privileges through their association with supernatural forces and their exchange links with comparable subgroups elsewhere, the other households might have found themselves in a situation comparable to the one posited by Cieza: either accept the new asymmetric socioeconomic arrangement or risk perishing in unsettled areas where no infrastructure exists. While community fission or revolt would have been possible, the inherent difficulties and dangers involved may have made these less attractive alternatives than they would have been in the less restricted environments of the north. The threat of excluding resisting families from water management systems on the coast or from communally controlled intermontane valley farmland in the highlands could have been powerful tools of social control. The obvious alternative, flight to the *puna* grasslands in the highlands or the intervalley wasteland on the coast, would have been a daunting prospect for a family of farmers.

Judging from the evidence available, the stratification process may have begun in the highlands, and the association of the incipient elites with large quantities of imported goods suggests that control of long-distance exchange by these leaders may have been an important tool in their attempt to manipulate and modify the earlier socioeconomic system. Tribute offered to regional ceremonial centers from travelers and pilgrims may have been a major source of wealth and authority for the newly emerging elites. Religious ideology likewise seems to have played a critical role in promoting and legitimizing these profound transformations. In the coastal valleys, where the economies appear to have been somewhat more self-sufficient and exchange somewhat less important, the process of stratification may have accelerated as a result of the articulation of these coastal groups with their highland neighbors, and the adoption of the panregional religious ideology associated with them.

The emergence of complex societies in the central Andes is an important subject, yet its study implicitly emphasizes the social rather than the cultural order. While Chavín civilization does appear to represent a very early example of complex society, it is quite distinct in character from the earliest complex societies in Mesopotamia or Mesoamerica, just as Tawantinsuyu, the Inca empire, was fundamentally unlike the Aztec empire or the imperial realm of the Hapsburgs. Indeed, one of the most striking features of Chavín civilization is how distinctively Andean it is in character.

As we have seen, most of the basic features of pre-Hispanic Andean culture were already present during the Chavín horizon. Among these cultural elements are an emphasis on public labour and its expression in monumental constructions, the role of dual principles in conceptualizing the cosmos and human society, the privileged position of textiles as the most prominent and highly developed art form, the identification of finely cut masonry as the hallmark of high-status public architecture, the symbolic linking of precious metals with divine principles, and the related association of the elite with gold and silver objects. These typically Andean cultural notions are paralleled by the presence of equally basic and distinctive Andean behavioral patterns, including processing of grain with a rocker grinder; a dual subsistence basis of irrigation agriculture supplemented by marine exploitation and high-altitude agriculture supplemented by camelid herding; long-distance foot travel along roads with goods transported by llamas; cultivation with simple stone and wooden tools that emphasized improvements in the infrastructure (terraces, canals, etc.) rather than mechanical improvements or animal energy, and so forth. It was through the manipulation and subtle transformation of these core cultural elements that wealth was accumulated and power was contested over the subsequent two millennia in the Andes, and it is these same features that modern anthropologists highlight when they attempt to identify the distinctive character of Andean civilization.

Of course, the idea that Chavín civilization had provided the cultural matrix for all later Andean civilizations was first proposed by Julio C. Tello, and it was this concept that he expressed metaphorically when he described Chavín as the trunk of an enormous tree out of which grew a dense and tangled three-dimensional network of later cultures that were its branches and twigs.[101] While some of the features associated with Chavín civilization had existed earlier, the pooling and reworking of ideas and their spread during the Chavín horizon led to the creation of the shared cultural consciousness in the central Andes that was Chavín's most enduring legacy.

The image of Chavín civilization forging cultural unity from the multitude of regional cultural traditions continues to hold a special place in the education of modern Peruvians, since it serves as a historical legitimation of their attempt to create a single nation, despite the conflicting interests of the diverse social and cultural groups incorporated within it. As Tello understood, the idea that communities throughout the Peruvian highlands, coast, and, to a lesser degree, the tropical forest had been linked together 2,500 years ago by their culture, economy and religion, makes modern attempts to build a nation state seem less arbitrary, no matter how different the historical circumstances or motivations. Moreover, the growing understanding of Chavín civilization and its multiple antecedents provides compelling evidence of the autochthonous cultural achievements and genius of the native Andean peoples, long before the empire of the Incas and the Spanish invasion.

8

Epilogue

Some time in the third century BC, the Chavín sphere of interaction began to disintegrate. A social upheaval occurred in many of the Early Horizon centers throughout central and northern Peru and, in many cases, construction of public architecture was abruptly halted and never completed. Some sites were completely abandoned while in others the ceremonial architecture was leveled to make way for agglutinated villages.

At Chavín de Huántar, for example, a small village was built over the Circular Plaza, and some of the stone carvings were incorporated in the house walls. Elsewhere on the site sculptures collapsed forward in the rubble of decaying public architecture. Similar patterns have been recorded at Kotosh, Huaricoto, Kuntur Wasi, Pacopampa, and other sites. In all these cases, the traditional use of space was suddenly shifted from public gatherings and religious rituals to mundane domestic activities. With this transformation, a cultural pattern was broken that had existed for centuries and, in some cases, millennia.

The changes in site function were usually paralleled by radical modifications in the culture. These changes are particularly evident in local pottery styles. The related assemblages of lustrous black or red incised monochrome ceramics that characterized the Chavín horizon disappeared and were replaced by a plethora of distinctive local styles, usually unlike the Chavín-related assemblages in form and decoration. These new styles expressed both a rejection of the Chavín culture and the increasingly balkanised culture of post-Chavín times. Moreover, the pattern is frequently one of stylistic disruption and replacement, rather than of gradual evolution. Whether this process occurred in a matter of years, decades, or even a century or more remains an open question.

The social instability underlying these changes can be seen unambiguously in the archaeological record. The construction of hilltop fortresses became widespread for the first time in both coastal and highlands valleys. In the tiny Virú Valley, for example, defensive architecture was unknown during the Chavín horizon, but during the subsequent one or two centuries no fewer than six hilltop forts were built. In some fortified sites in Virú, there were small pyramids and houses inside the defensive walls. After a survey of Andean militarism in the northern highlands, Canadian archaeologists John and Teresa Topic concluded that the earliest highland fortified sites had been built during this same period (i.e. 200–0 BC).[1]

This trend towards militarization was not apparently limited to northern Peru. Similar constructions have been found along the central and south coast.

Considering the proliferation of military architecture, it is not surprising that the immediately post-Chavín (i.e. Salinar) cemetery at Puémape differed notably from the earlier Cupisnique burial ground since a large number of buried individuals had missing heads or limbs. It would appear that raiding became widespread and that for the first time in Andean prehistory the threat of intergroup conflict became a significant consideration in the allocation of public labor and the organization of societies. As a consequence of the violence and the breakdown of alliances between groups, long-distance travel declined. Inter-regional trade in items such as obsidian and cinnabar dropped off sharply, although more limited regional networks of exchange and interaction between neighboring valleys continued to be maintained.[2]

In some respects, the sociopolitical disintegration and reorganization evident in the late Early Horizon is reminiscent of the collapse of Initial Period coastal centers some six centuries earlier. In fact, the societies that emerged along the north-central coast in valleys such as Casma and Nepeña at the beginning of the Early Horizon foreshadowed the kind of societies that came into being elsewhere in post-Chavín times.

If, as many scholars have suggested, stratified societies require a strong centralized state apparatus with coercive power to maintain long-term stability, then Chavín civilization was doomed by its structure. Lacking in fully developed state features, polities in the Chavín sphere of interaction attempted to compensate by using ideological and economic devices. If the spread and success of the Chavín cult profited from a sense of crisis induced by the deteriorating social and environmental conditions on the coast, the continuation of fundamental infrastructural deficiencies eventually undermined Chavín civilization itself and led to more radical attempts to resolve these difficulties by basic modifications in the political and social organization of these societies.

While the return to limited regional spheres of interaction in many cases followed territorial patterns similar to those of the Initial Period, it would be a mistake to presume that the earlier cultural patterns reemerged. On the contrary, the socioeconomic stratification and other changes that had appeared during the Chavín horizon persisted and intensified in many areas. The increased militarization in post-Chavín times probably reflected the interests of these dominant groups, as well as dangers presented by neighboring peoples. Thus, for most groups, the emergence of Chavín civilization represented a watershed in Peruvian prehistory from which there was no return.

Although many cultures of the late Early Horizon seemed to explicitly reject the pantheon, style, and all other elements linked to Chavín civilization, this crucial episode in Andean prehistory left a lasting impression. Centuries later, cultures such as the Moche began to revive the style and motifs of Chavín for decorating their ceramics. Still later, the people of Tiahuanaco began to worship a Staff God remarkably similar to the image on the Raimondi Stone.[3] The reputation of Chavín de Huántar as an ancient center of sacred power endured long after the Spanish Conquest. It was the indigenous veneration of Chavín stemming from the site's mythical status, rather than any memory of its crucial role in Andean prehistory, that led Father Antonio Vázquez de Espinoza in 1616 to describe the abandoned ruins at Chavín de Huántar as one of the most famous *huacas* or sanctuaries among the *gentiles*, like Rome or Jerusalem for the Christian world.[4]

Chronological Chart

Time Scale	Guayas Basin	Pacopampa	Bagua & Jaen	Cajamarca	Huamachuco	Moche & Chicama	Viru	Casma	Supe	Period / Horizon
A.D. B.C.	GUANGALA		EL SALADO TARDIO			GALLINAZO	GALLINAZO			
200				LAYZÓN	SAUSAGOCHA	SALINAR	PUERTO MOORIN	Chankillo	WHITE-ON-RED	Early Horizon
400		PACOPAMPA CHAVIN	EL SALADO	EL		Huaca de los Chinos		San Diego	Chimu Capac	
600	CHORRERA				PELON		LATE GUAÑAPE			
800			LA PECA							
1000				LATE HUACALOMA	COLPA	CUPISNIQUE	MIDDLE GUAÑAPE	Las Haldas	Bermejo	
1200	MACHALILLA	PACOPAMPA PACOPAMPA	BAGUA II					Moxeke		Initial Period
1400									La Empedrada	
1600	VIII		BAGUA I	EARLY HUACALOMA		Montegrande	EARLY GUAÑAPE	Tortugas		
1800		PANDANCHE A								
2000	VII									
2200										
2400	VALDIVIA VI					Huaca Prieta	CERRO PRIETO	Huaynuná		Late Preceramic Period
2600	V								Aspero	
2800	IV III									
3000	II									

Appendix: Radiocarbon Dates

Site	Valley	Phase or Provenience	Lab #	Uncalibrated Years BP	Calibrated Years BC	Reference
LATE PRECERAMIC SITES						
Huaca Prieta	Chicama	Pit 3, Layer Q	C-313	4257 ± 250	2901	Bird et al 1985:53
Huaca Prieta	Chicama	Pit 2, Bottom	C-598	4298 ± 230	2915	Bird et al 1985:53
Huaca Prieta	Chicama	Pit 3-Layer K	C-362	4044 ± 300	2581	Bird et al 1985:53
Huaca Prieta	Chicama	Pit 3-Layer M	C-316	4380 ± 270	3028, 2985, 2930	Bird et al 1985:53
La Galgada	Tablachaca	H-11, Floor 30	UGa-4583	3590 ± 75	1947	Grieder et al 1988:69
La Galgada	Tablachaca	H-11, Floor 30	TX-4447	3670 ± 70	2114, 2086, 2039	Grieder et al 1988:69
La Galgada	Tablachaca	Sector D Gallery	TX-2463	3740 ± 90	2181, 2166, 2142	Grieder et al 1988:69
La Galgada	Tablachaca	E-12:I-2 Floor 6	TX-4449	3790 ± 70	2273, 2245, 2205	Grieder et al 1988:69
La Galgada	Tablachaca	F-12, B-2	TX-4450	3820 ± 100	2288	Grieder et al 1988:69
La Galgada	Tablachaca	D-11, C-3	TX-3167	3820 ± 60	2288	Grieder et al 1988:69
La Galgada	Tablachaca	I-11, D-5	TX-3664	4110 ± 50	2857, 2821, 2691	Grieder et al 1988:69
Huaricoto	Callejón de Huaylas	Ceremonial Hearth XII	I-II,42	3970 ± 110	2689, 2660, 2637, 2623	Burger & Salazar-Burger 1985:122
Huaricoto	Callejón de Huaylas	Ceremonial Hearth XIII	PUCP-3#3	4210 ± 120	2883, 2796, 2784	Burger & Salazar-Burger 1985:122
Salinas de Chao	Chao	Unit C, cut 6	URI-812	3600 ± 90	1961	S. Pozorski & T. Pozorski 1990:484
Condorcerro A	Santa	Staircase of Circular Plaza	PUCP-95	4010 ± 70	2569, 2538, 2503	Cárdenas 1979:29
Condorcerro B	Santa	Cemetery	PUCP-113	4070 ± 60	2598	Cárdenas 1979:29
Cerro Obrero	Santa	Base of mount	PUCP-93	3690 ± 60	2130, 2074, 2045	Cárdenas 1979:29
Aspero	Supe	Huaca de los Sacrificios	UCR-242	3950 ± 150	2468	Feldman 1985:77
Aspero	Supe	Huaca de los Sacrificios	UCR-243	4060 ± 150	2587	Feldman 1985:77
Aspero	Supe	Huaca de los Sacrificios	UCR-244	4150 ± 150	2867, 2808, 2772, 2723, 2699	Feldman 1985:77
Aspero	Supe	Huaca de los Sacrificios	GX-3862	4260 ± 15	2903	Feldman 1985:77
Aspero	Supe	Huaca de los Idolos	GX-3861	3970 ± 145	2483	Feldman 1985:77
Aspero	Supe	Huaca de los Idolos	GX-3860	4360 ± 175	3018, 3001, 2926	Feldman 1985:77
Chupacigarro Chico	Supe	Uppermost level of pyramid	SMU-2012	3815 ± 140	2587	Zechentner 1988:519
Chupacigarro Centro	Supe	Lower level, Mound B	GX-13872	± 90	2554, 2548, 2491	Zechentner 1988:521
Alpacoto	Supe	Sector A	SMU-2014	3744 ± 125	2170	Zechentner 1988:520
Bandurria	Huaura	Funerary matting	I-7448	4420 ± 140	3040	Fung 1988:95
Bandurria	Huaura	Funerary matting	V-3279	4530 ± 80	3334, 3219, 3189, 3152, 3148	Fung 1988:95

Time Scale	Mosna	Callejón de Huaylas	Upper Huallaga	Central Ucayali	Rimac & Lurin	Paracas & Ica	Ayacucho	Cuzco	Lake Titicaca Basin	Period / Horizon
A.D. B.C. 200	HUARÁS	HUARÁS	SAJARA-PATAC	HUPA - IYA	BAÑOS DE BOZA	OCUCAJE 7-10	RANCHA CHUPAS	DERIVED CHANAPATA	PUCARA	Early Horizon
400	JANABARRIU	LATE CAPIILLA	KOTOSH CHAVIN	LATE SHAKIMU	Ancón	OCUCAJE 3-6	KISHKAPATA		LATE CHIRIPA	
600	CHAKINANI	EARLY CAPIILLA		EARLY SHAKIMU		Disco Verde	WICHQANA	CHANAPATA	MIDDLE CHIRIPA	
800	URABARRIU				Cardal / Garagay			MARCAVALLE A B C		Initial Period
1000		HUARICOTO	KOTOSH KOTOSH	LATE TUTISHCAINYO				D	LATE QALUYU	
1200										
1400						Erizo			EARLY QALUYU	
1600		TORIL	WAIRA-JIRCA							
1800				EARLY TUTISHCAINYO	La Florida					
2000					El Paraiso					
2200					Ventanilla					Late Preceramic Period
2400		CHAUKAYAN	MITO				CACHI			
2600										
2800										
3000										

Chronological chart for Peru, arranged from north to south, beginning far left. The site of Chavín de Huántar is located in the Mosna Valley. Phase names appear in upper case, and where no sequence of phases is yet established, representative sites are shown in upper and lower case. The period/horizon system follows that of John Rowe, and the time scale is based on calibrated C14 dates.

Site	Valley	Phase or Provenience	Lab #	Uncalibrated Years BP	Calibrated Years BC	Reference
Bandurria	Huaura	Layer 4	V-3277	4480±70	3295, 3242, 3104	Fung 1988:95
Bandurria	Huaura	Layer 3	V-3278	4300±90	2915	Fung 1988:95
Kotosh	Huanuco	Mito	TK-42	3900±100	2457	Izumi & Terada 1972:307
Kotosh	Huanuco	Mito	GaK-766b	3900±100	2457	Izumi & Terada 1972:307
Kotosh	Huanuco	Mito	GaK-766a	3620±100	2018, 2002, 1980	Izumi & Terada 1972:307
El Paraiso	Chillón	Unit IV, Pit 3	I-13,278	3650±100	2034	Quilter 1985:281
El Paraiso	Chillón	Unit IV, Pit 1, Level C	I-13,274	3790±100	2273, 2245, 2205	Quilter 1985:281
El Paraiso	Chillón	Unit I, Pit 2	I-13,276	3560±100	1908	Quilter 1985:281

COASTAL INITIAL PERIOD SITES

Site	Valley	Phase or Provenience	Lab #	Uncalibrated Years BP	Calibrated Years BC	Reference
Paita	Tumbes	Paita	GX-1136	3610±145	2010, 1973	Izumi & Terada 1966
Paita	Tumbes	Paita	GX-1003	3090±125	1400	Izumi & Terada 1966
Beach Ridge 6	Chira	Late Paita	SI 1422	2685±105	831	Watson 1986:121
Huaca Lucia	La Leche	Temple Summit	SMU-834	3273±163	1526	Shimada 1981:427
Purulén	Zaña		VRI-811	3120±80	1415	Felber 1984 personal communication
Huaca Prieta	Chicama	pre-Cupisnique	C-322	3310±250	1614	Bird et al 1985:53
Huaca Prieta	Chicama	Cupisnique	C-75	2665±200	821	Bird et al 1985:53
Caballo Muerto	Moche	Huaca Herederos Chica	TX-1938	3450±70	1749	T. Pozorski 1983
Caballo Muerto	Moche	Huaca Herederos Chica	TX-1937	3040±80	1314	T. Pozorski 1983
Caballo Muerto	Moche	Huaca de los Reyes, Mound F	TX-1974	3680±80	2123, 2042, 2080	T. Pozorski 1983
Caballo Muerto	Moche	Huaca de los Reyes, Mound F	TX-1972	3310±80	1614	T. Pozorski 1983
Caballo Muerto	Moche	Huaca de los Reyes, Mound F	TX-1973	3140±60	1424	T. Pozorski 1983
Caballo Muerto	Moche	Huaca de los Reyes, Mound F	TX-2180	2800±60	976, 965, 933	T. Pozorski 1983
Sechín Alto	Casma	Cahuachuco style	UCLA-279A	3400±100	1733, 1721, 1697	Beyer et al 1965:347
Cerro Sechín	Casma	Building with stone sculptures	H7205-6977	3240±20	1519	Samaniego et al 1985:184
Cerro Sechín	Casma	Post-sculpture construction	I-	3005±90	1265	Samaniego et al 1985:184
Tortugas	Casma	Unit 2-6	UGa-4525	3750±65	2191, 2161, 2145	S. Pozorski & T. Pozorski 1987:17
Moxeke	Casma	E of Huaca A	UGa-5461	3520±70	1883	S. Pozorski & T. Pozorski 1990:484

Site	Valley	Phase or Provenience	Lab #	Uncalibrated Years BP	Calibrated Years BC	Reference
Moxeke	Casma	Huaca A	UGa-5462	3515 ± 70	1859, 1848, 1769	S. Pozorski & T. Pozorski 1990:484
Moxeke	Casma	Mound, W sector	UGa-5801	3495 ± 85	1876, 1836, 1821	S. Pozorski & T. Pozorski 1990:484
Moxeke	Casma	E of Huaca A	UGa-4506	3490 ± 75	1875, 1838, 1818	S. Pozorski & T. Pozorski 1990:484
Moxeke	Casma	W sector	UGa-5799	3465 ± 55	1859, 1858, 1769	S. Pozorski & T. Pozorski 1990:484
Moxeke	Casma	E sector	UGa-4508	3425 ± 75	1741	S. Pozorski & T. Pozorski 1990:484
Moxeke	Casma	E sector	UGa-4507	3390 ± 150	1730, 1729, 1689	S. Pozorski & T. Pozorski 1990:484
Moxeke	Casma	W sector	UGa-5800	3345 ± 55	1672	S. Pozorski & T. Pozorski 1990:484
Moxeke	Casma	W sector	UGa-4509	3320 ± 85	1621	S. Pozorski & T. Pozorski 1990:484
Moxeke	Casma	W sector	UGa-5611	3310 ± 70	1614	S. Pozorski & T. Pozorski 1990:485
Moxeke	Casma	W sector	UGa-5610	3270 ± 50	1526	S. Pozorski & T. Pozorski 1990:485
Moxeke	Casma	E sector	UGa-5795	3245 ± 55	1520	S. Pozorski & T. Pozorski 1990:485
Moxeke	Casma	E sector	UGa-5609	3230 ± 60	1516	S. Pozorski & T. Pozorski 1990:485
Moxeke	Casma	E sector	UGa-5797	3220 ± 60	1514	S. Pozorski & T. Pozorski 1990:485
Moxeke	Casma	W sector	UGa-5630	3190 ± 60	1491, 1489, 1451	S. Pozorski & T. Pozorski 1990:485
Moxeke	Casma	Huaca A	UGa-5794	3185 ± 60	1448	S. Pozorski & T. Pozorski 1990:485
Moxeke	Casma	W sector	UGa-4511	3175 ± 90	1442	S. Pozorski & T. Pozorski 1990:485
Moxeke	Casma	E sector	UGa-4503	3165 ± 75	1436	S. Pozorski & T. Pozorski 1990:485
Moxeke	Casma	W of Huaca A	UGa-5798	3160 ± 85	1433	S. Pozorski & T. Pozorski 1990:485
Las Haldas	Casma	F/15, pre-Temple		3600 ± 95	1961	Matsuzawa 1978:666
Las Haldas	Casma	Exc 2, Layer 13	UGa-4534	3595 ± 75	1953	S. Pozorski & T. Pozorski 1987:10–11
Las Haldas	Casma	Exc 2, Layer 53	UGa-4532	3460 ± 75	1851, 1850, 1761	S. Pozorski & T. Pozorski 1987:10–11
Las Haldas	Casma	Cut 1	TX-631	3430 ± 80	1743	Grieder 1975:99
Las Haldas	Casma	F13		3150 ± 90	1428	Matsuzawa 1978:666
Las Haldas	Casma	Exc 2, Layer 12	UGa-4533	3140 ± 75	1424	S. Pozorski & T. Pozorski 1987:10–11
Las Haldas	Casma	Under structure	TX-648	3140 ± 80	1424	Grieder 1975:100
E1-15	Supe	Sector B	GX-13871	± 235	1643	Zechentner 1988:521
Cerro Colorado	Supe	Behind Sector A	QL-4196	± 80	1411	Zechentner 1988:521
La Empedrada	Supe	North arm	ETH-3925	± 90	1550	Zechentner 1988:520
La Florida	Rimac	Central platform	GX-04456	3645 ± 85	2033	Patterson et al 1985:64
La Florida	Rimac	North wing	W-87	3665 ± 170	2037, 2043	Patterson et al 1985:64
La Florida	Rimac	Central platform	GX-1210	3680 ± 120	2123, 2080, 2042	Patterson 1985:64
Ancón	Rimac	Early Colinas	GX-1240	3715 ± 110	2136	Patterson et al n.d.
Garagay	Rimac		TK-178	3340 ± 70	1643	Ravines et al 1984:135
Garagay	Rimac		CU-49	3170 ± 90	1439	Ravines et al 1984:135
Garagay	Rimac		TK-177	3090 ± 70	1400	Ravines et al 1984:135
Garagay	Rimac		CU-09	2730 ± 70	897	Ravines et al 1984:135
Cardal	Lurín	Sector IIA	I-14,121	3030 ± 90	1310	Burger & Salazar-Burger 1991:277
Cardal	Lurín	Sector IIA	I-14,122	2880 ± 90	1044	Burger & Salazar-Burger 1991:277
Cardal	Lurín	Sector IIA	I-14,123	2880 ± 90	1944	Burger & Salazar-Burger 1991:277
Cardal	Lurín	Sector IIA	I-14,130	3120 ± 90	1415	Burger & Salazar-Burger 1991:277
Cardal	Lurín	Sector IIA	I-14,770	2850 ± 90	1008	Burger & Salazar-Burger 1991:277
Cardal	Lurín	Sector IIA	I-14,772	2800 ± 90	976, 965, 933	Burger & Salazar-Burger 1991:277
Cardal	Lurín	Sector IIA	I-14,771	2690 ± 90	833	Burger & Salazar-Burger 1991:277
Cardal	Lurín	Sector IIIA, Atrium area	I-15,564	2850 ± 80	1008	Burger & Salazar-Burger 1991:277
Cardal	Lurín	Sector IIIA, Rm B	I-14,247	2730 ± 90	897	Burger & Salazar-Burger 1991:277
Cardal	Lurín	Sector IIIA, Rm B	I-14,238	2750 ± 90	905	Burger & Salazar-Burger 1991:277
Cardal	Lurín	Sector IIIA, Rm B	GX-1622	2850 ± 105	1008	Burger & Salazar-Burger 1991:277
Cardal	Lurín	Sector IIIA, Rm B	GX-1623	2935 ± 110	1156, 1144, 1134	Burger & Salazar-Burger 1991:277
Cardal	Lurín	Sector IIIA, Atrium area	I-14,249	2800 ± 90	926	Burger & Salazar-Burger 1991:277
Cardal	Lurín	Sector IIIA, Atrium area	I-15,565	2930 ± 80	1154, 1147, 1131	Burger & Salazar-Burger 1991:277
Cardal	Lurín	Sector IIIA, Atrium area	I-15,566	2920 ± 80	1124, 1113, 1108	Burger & Salazar-Burger 1991:277
Cardal	Lurín	Sector IIIA, Exc 3	I-15,567	2900 ± 80	1092	Burger & Salazar-Burger 1991:277
Cardal	Lurín	Sector IIIA, Exc 3	I-15,568	2930 ± 80	1154, 1147, 1131	Burger & Salazar-Burger 1991:277
Cardal	Lurín	Sector IIIA, Exc 3	I-15,569	2950 ± 90	1211, 1180, 1165	Burger & Salazar-Burger 1991:277
Cardal	Lurín	Sector IIIB	I-14,132	3050 ± 90	1376, 1346, 1318	Burger & Salazar-Burger 1991:277
Cardal	Lurín	Sector IIIB	I-14,133	3060 ± 96	1382, 1341, 1321	Burger & Salazar-Burger 1991:277
Cardal	Lurín	Sector V	I-14,124	3050 ± 90	1376, 1346, 1318	Burger & Salazar-Burger 1991:277
Cardal	Lurín	Sector V	I-14,131	2980 ± 90	1258, 1235, 1226	Burger & Salazar-Burger 1991:277
Cardal	Lurín	Sector V	I-15,570	3060 ± 80	1382, 1341, 1321	Burger & Salazar-Burger 1991:277
Cardal	Lurín	Sector V	I-14,125	2880 ± 90	1044	Burger & Salazar-Burger 1991:277
Cardal	Lurín	Sector V	I-14,?	3070 ± 90	1388, 1336, 1325	Burger & Salazar-Burger 1991:277
Cardal	Lurín	Sector V	I-14,251	2980 ± 90	1258, 1235, 1226	Burger & Salazar-Burger 1991:277
Mina Perdida	Lurín	East wing	I-14,252	2870 ± 90	1035	Burger 1991:277
Mina Perdida	Lurín	Central platform	I-14,253	2900 ± 90	1092	Burger & Salazar-Burger 1991:277
Mina Perdida	Lurín	Central platform	I-14,254	3120 ± 90	1415	Burger & Salazar-Burger 1991:277
Mina Perdida	Lurín	West wing	I-15,577	2960 ± 80	1252, 1245, 1216	Burger & Salazar-Burger 1991:277
Mina Perdida	Lurín	Central platform	I-16,761	3400 ± 90	1733, 1721, 1697	Burger 1990
Mina Perdida	Lurín	West wing	I-16,762	2870 ± 90	1035	Burger 1990
Erizo	Ica		GX-0185	3890 ± 90	2455, 2416, 2405	Rowe 1967b
Erizo	Ica		GX-0186	3820 ± 85	2288	Rowe 1967b
Hacha	Acarí		UCLA-153	2960 ± 90	1252, 1245, 1216	Rowe 1967b
Hacha	Acarí		UCR-2086	2970 ± 70	1255, 1240, 1221	Riddell & Valdez 1987:7
Hacha	Acarí		UCR-2087	2810 ± 69	985, 955, 944	Riddell & Valdez 1987:7
Hacha	Acarí		UCR-2088	2990 ± 70	1261	Riddell & Valdez 1987:7
Hacha	Acarí		UCR-2089	2730 ± 70	897	Riddell & Valdez 1987:7

HIGHLAND INITIAL PERIOD SITES

Site	Valley	Phase or Provenience	Lab #	Uncalibrated Years BP	Calibrated Years BC	Reference
Machaipungo	Chotano	Pandanche A(?)	—	3785 ± 100	2271, 2260, 2204	Rosas 1976:576, Kaulicke 1975:50
Pandanche	Chotano	Pandanche	ZK-333	3960 ± 115	2470	Kaulicke 1981
Pandanche	Chotano	Pacopampa Pacopampa	ZK-334	3345 ± 340	1672	Kaulicke 1981
Huacaloma	Cajamarca	Early Huacaloma	TK-341a	3080 ± 70	1394, 1331, 1329	Terada & Onuki 1985
Huacaloma	Cajamarca	Early Huacaloma	TK-409	2840 ± 90	1003	Terada & Onuki 1985
Huacaloma	Cajamarca	Late Huacaloma, Phase 1	TK-699	2750 ± 90	905	Terada & Onuki 1985
Huacaloma	Cajamarca	Late Huacaloma, Phase 1	TK-701	2620 ± 70	805	Terada & Onuki 1985
Huacaloma	Cajamarca	Late Huacaloma, Phase 1	TK-748	2630 ± 90	807	Terada & Onuki 1985
Huacaloma	Cajamarca	Late Huacaloma, Phase 1	TK-749	2820 ± 90	993	Terada & Onuki 1985
Huacaloma	Cajamarca	Late Huacaloma, Phase 2	TK-702	2630 ± 60	807	Terada & Onuki 1985
Cerro Blanco	Jequetepeque	La Conga	TK-710	3390 ± 70	1730, 1729, 1689	Terada & Onuki 1988

Site	Valley	Phase or Provenience	Lab #	Uncalibrated Years BP	Calibrated Years BC	Reference
Cerro Blanco	Jequetepeque	Tm-1	TK-714	3270 ± 70	1526	Terada & Onuki 1988:4
Cerro Blanco	Jequetepeque	Cerro Blanco	TK-713	2990 ± 80	1261	Terada & Onuki 1988:4
Cerro Blanco	Jequetepeque	Cerro Blanco	TK-751	2910 ± 170	1100	Terada & Onuki 1988:4
Cerro Blanco	Jequetepeque	Cerro Blanco	TK-712	2750 ± 60	905	Terada & Onuki 1988:4
La Pampa	Manta	Yesopampa	TK-174	3090 ± 70	1400	Terada 1979:174
La Pampa	Manta	Yesopampa	TK-192	3100 ± 70	1406	Terada 1979:174
La Pampa	Manta	Yesopampa	TK-187	3120 ± 110	1415	Terada 1979:174
La Pampa	Manta	Yesopampa	TK-186	3350 ± 100	1673	Terada 1979:173
Huargo	Junin		BVA Vierra#5	3560 ± 230	1908	Cardich 1973
Ondores	Junin	—	SI-486	3570 ± 80	1923	Matos 1975:60
San Blas	Junin	Fase Inicial		1870	2288	Morales 1977:35
Telarmachay	Junin	Pit, Layer 4	Gif-3481	3370 ± 180	1681	Levallée 1979:68
Telarmachay	Junin	Layer III	Gif-4189	3470 ± 100	1866, 1846, 1772	Levallée 1979:69
Telarmachay	Junin	Layer III	Gif-4188	3410 ± 100	1737, 1713, 1706	Levallée 1979:69
La Galgada	Tablachaca	G-12:H-4, Floor 8	TX-4446	3130 ± 80	1420	Grieder et al 1988:69
La Galgada	Tablachaca	H-11:G-10	TX-5606	3320 ± 270	1621	Grieder et al 1988:69
La Galgada	Tablachaca	Sector C shaft	TX-2464	3440 ± 80	1746	Grieder et al 1988:69
La Galgada	Tablachaca	G-11:G-8 Floor 9	TX-3663	3540 ± 50	1888	Grieder et al 1988:69
La Galgada	Tablachaca	C-11:J-6	TX-3166	3660 ± 80	2037	Grieder et al 1988:69
La Galgada	Tablachaca	H-11:FG-10, Floor 15	TX-4448	3650 ± 60	2034	Grieder et al 1988:69
Chavín de Huántar	Mosna	Urabarriu	ISGS-486	2770 ± 75	915	Burger 1984a:280
Chavín de Huántar	Mosna	Urabarriu	ISGS-493	2900 ± 150	1072	Burger 1984a:280
Chavín de Huántar	Mosna	Gallery of the Offerings	GX-1128	2700 ± 85	838	Burger 1984a:280
Chavín de Huántar	Mosna	Urabarriu	UCR-694	2715 ± 100	890, 845	Burger 1984a:280
Chavín de Huántar	Mosna	Urabarriu	ISGS-705	2580 ± 100	797	Burger 1984a:280
Kotosh	Huanuco	Waira-jirca	GaK-765	3750 ± 90	2191, 2161, 2145	Terada & Onuki 1972:308
Kotosh	Huanuco	Waira-jirca	GaK-262	3800 ± 110	2278, 2234, 2209	Terada & Onuki 1972:308
Waywaka	Andahuaylas	Muyu Moqo A	UCLA-1808E	3550 ± 100	1895	Grossman 1985:58
Waywaka	Andahuaylas	Muyu Moqo A	UCLA-1808A	3440 ± 110	1746	Grossman 1985:58
Waywaka	Andahuaylas	Muyu Moqo A	UCLA-1808J	3185 ± 160	1448	Grossman 1985:58
Waywaka	Andahuaylas	Muyu Moqo B	UCLA-1808F	2660 ± 250	818	Grossman 1985:58
Waywaka	Andahuaylas	Muyu Moqo B	UCLA-1808I	3240 ± 210	1519	Grossman 1985:58

EARLY HORIZON SITES

Site	Valley	Phase or Provenience	Lab #	Uncalibrated Years BP	Calibrated Years BC	Reference
Caballo Muerto	Moche	Huaca Guavalito	TX-1939	2390 ± 70	407	Burger 1981:594
Huacaloma	Cajamarca	EL	TK-704	2380 ± 90	405	Terada & Onuki 1989:241
Huacaloma	Cajamarca	EL	TK-705	2210 ± 40	358, 238, 252	Terada & Onuki 1989:241
Huacaloma	Cajamarca	EL	TK-703	2160 ± 120	196	Terada & Onuki 1989:241
Kuntur Wasi	Jequetepeque	—	NZ-998	2353 ± 92	401	Engel 1966:88
La Pampa	Manta	La Pampa	TK-195	2490 ± 60	762, 678, 662, 627, 600	Terada 1979:177
La Pampa	Manta	La Pampa	TK-176	2620 ± 70	805	Terada 1979:177
Huaricoto	Callejón de Huaylas	Late Capilla	TX-3583	2330 ± 80	397	Burger & Salazar-Burger 1985:129
Huaricoto	Callejón de Huaylas	Late Capilla	I-II, 151	2310 ± 110	394	Burger & Salazar-Burger 1985:129
Chavín de Huántar	Mosna	Chakinani	ISGS-507	2400 ± 100	408	Burger 1984a, Chart 24
Chavín de Huántar	Mosna	Chakinani	UCR-693	2456 ± 100	400	Burger 1984a, Chart 24
Chavín de Huántar	Mosna	Huarás	Gif-1079	2100 ± 100	151, 149, 117	Lumbreras 1989:112
Chankillo	Casma	Wooden lintel	L-4040	2292 ± 80	391	S. Pozorski & T. Pozorski 1987:123
Chankillo	Casma	Wooden lintel		2070 ± 100	101	S. Pozorski & T. Pozorski 1987:123
San Diego	Casma	Unit 1-12b	UGa-4514	2510 ± 115	767	S. Pozorski & T. Pozorski 1987:10–11
San Diego	Casma	Unit 1-4	UGa-4512	2490 ± 60	762, 678, 662, 627, 600	S. Pozorski & T. Pozorski 1987:10–11
San Diego	Casma	Unit 4-8c	UGa-4517	2455 ± 70	753, 704, 533	S. Pozorski & T. Pozorski 1987:10–11
San Diego	Casma	Unit 1-11	UGa-4513	2305 ± 55	393	S. Pozorski & T. Pozorski 1987:10–11
San Diego	Casma	Unit 4-3b	UGa-4516	2245 ± 60	372	S. Pozorski & T. Pozorski 1987:10–11
Pampa Rosario	Casma	Unit 1-8a	UGa-4536	2400 ± 70	408	S. Pozorski & T. Pozorski 1987:10–11
Cerrillos	Ica	Ocucaje 3	P-516	2408 ± 214	410	Burger 1988:109
Cerrillos	Ica	Ocucaje 3	GX-1345	2685 ± 140	831	Burger 1988:109
Site 14A-VI-16	Paracas	Paracas Cavernas	NZ-1087	2267 ± 191	382	Burger 1988:109
Cabezas Largas	Paracas	Paracas Necropolis	NZ-1127-2	2060 ± 170	96	Burger 1988:109
Usno Era	Ayacucho	Zone DB	UCR 676	2310 ± 100	394	MacNeish 1981:207
Usno Era	Ayacucho	Zone DA	UCR 671	2325 ± 100	396	MacNeish 1981:207

The calibrations employed are based on Pearson and Stuiver 1986, Pearson et al 1986, Stuiver and Pearson 1986

Notes to the Text

Chapter 1 (pp. 7–25)
1. See Rowe (1946, 1967a) for classic syntheses of the historical accounts of Inca civilization and its capital, Cuzco. 2. Sancho de la Hoz 1968[1534]:328. 3. Cobo 1979[1653]:96. 4. Guaman Poma de Ayala 1980[1614]:40–61, Adorno 1986:32–35. 5. Morgan 1967[1877], Redfield 1953:ix, Service 1975, Tylor 1958[1871]. 6. See Stocking 1987 for a detailed discussion of this theme. 7. Childe 1950, 1951; Daniel 1968; Frankfort 1951, Patterson 1981. 8. Adams 1966:13, Renfrew 1973:193–194, Sanders and Price 1968, Service 1975, Wenke 1990:54–57. 9. The original settlement of Andean South America remains a subject of vigorous debate; cf. Dillehay and Collins 1991, Gruhn and Bryan 1991, Lynch 1990, 1991. 10. In a 1928 paper at the 23rd International Congress of Americanists in New York, Tello (1930) placed Chavín in his Epoch 1 which corresponded to the Archaic Andean Epoch or Megalithic and preceded the cultures now known as Moche and Nazca. He more fully developed this position in his later writings (Tello 1942, 1943, 1960). 11. The idea of a Chavín horizon or civilization that predated the cultures of the Early Intermediate Period and Middle Horizon only became widely accepted outside Peru long after Tello's original formulation. The position statements of Bennett 1943 and Kroeber 1944 were particularly influential. 12. Willey 1945, 1951. 13. Rowe 1962a. 14. The calibrations employed in this volume have been calculated using the University of Washington software package based on the results of Pearson and Stuiver 1986, Pearson et al 1986, and Stuiver and Pearson 1986. Renfrew (1973) provides a useful discussion of radiocarbon dating and the calibration problem for those lacking technical background. 15. Lettau and Lettau 1978, Robinson 1964. 16. Hartline 1980, Schweigger 1947. 17. A large literature exists on the El Niño phenomenon in general and its impact on the modern Peruvian coast in particular; cf. Arntz 1984, Arntz et al 1985, Caviedes 1984, Fiedler 1944, Murphy 1926, UNESCO 1980. Research also has been done on the origins of El Niño and its impact on prehistoric Peru, cf. Rollins et al 1986, Nials et al 1979, Sandweiss et al 1983. 18. Pulgar Vidal 1972, cf. Dillehay 1979. 19. Torres and Lopez Ocaña 1982; for a short synthesis see Quilter 1989:3–5. 20. Robinson 1964; see Dillehay and Netherly 1983 for a short discussion of relic forests. 21. Robinson 1964. 22. Steinmann 1929, Wright 1984, Zeil 1979. 23. Robinson 1964, ONERN 1976. 24. Troll 1970. 25. Leon 1964, Pulgar Vidal 1972. 26. Brush 1977, Mayer 1985, Webster 1972. 27. For short syntheses of Amazo-nian climate and ecology see Lathrap 1970:22–44, Meggers 1971, cf. Moran 1981 for a guide to more recent literature on this theme. 28. ONERN 1976. 29. Richardson 1978, 1983; Rollins et al 1986, Sandweiss et al 1983. 30. Cardich 1976, 1985. Recent data from the Quelccaya ice core likewise shows major fluctuations in Holocene climate but thus far data have only been published as far back as 1,500 years (Thompson et al 1984, 1985). 31. Schoenwetter 1973. 32. Cardich 1985:312–313, fig. 6.14; Eddy 1977. A recent study (Friis-Christensen and Lassen 1991) appears to support Eddy's correlation of solar cycles and land surface temperatures on the earth, while recognizing that other factors also are involved. 33. Lanning 1967:51–52, Weir and Dering 1986. 34. R. Bird 1987, Bode 1989, Moseley et al 1981. 35. Moseley 1983a, 1983b; Moseley et al 1981; Nials et al 1979.

Chapter 2 (pp. 27–55)
1. Moseley and Willey 1973, Willey and Corbett 1954. 2. Feldman 1985:77. In cases such as the Aspero measurements, where the calibration curve has multiple intercepts. I have cited the middle intercept in the text; see the appendix for all the alternative measurements. 3. Moseley 1975:79–80. 4. Kirch 1990:216. 5. For detailed consideration of coastal diet and subsistence technology during the Late Preceramic see Bird et al 1985; Bonavia 1982; Matthiesen 1988; Moseley 1975:43–48, 52–55; S. Pozorski 1979, 1983; S. Pozorski and T. Pozorski 1979, 1987; Quilter 1991, Quilter et al 1991; Quilter and Stocker 1983; Weir and Bonavia 1985. 6. Engel 1963, Matthiesen 1988, Quilter et al 1991. 7. Feldman 1980; Moseley 1975, 1985; Moseley and Feldman 1988. 8. Moseley 1985:36–38. For an alternative interpretation of the evidence as suggesting an agricultural rather than a maritime economy, see Osborn 1977, Raymond 1981, Wilson 1981, Zechentner 1988. 9. Lathrap 1977; cf. Stephens and Moseley 1973, 1974; Whitaker and Cutler 1965; the term "Cotton Preceramic Stage" is employed by Moseley and Engel among others. 10. J. Bird et al 1985:229–244. M. Parsons 1970, Patterson 1971a, S. Pozorski 1983, Quilter et al 1991, Zechentner 1988. 11. Cohen 1979, Martins 1976, Moseley 1985, Ungent et al 1981, 1984. 12. Callen and Cameron 1960, J. Bird et al 1985:238–240, Weir and Bonavia 1985. 13. Tattersall 1985:60–64. 14. J. Bird et al 1985:240. 15. Patterson 1971a, S. Pozorski 1979. 16. West 1979; see Zechentner 1988 for the C14 dating of Supe settlements. 17. Burger and Asaro 1978, Wendt 1964. 18. Feldman 1985, Moseley 1985. 19. Burger 1985a:274–277. 20. Alva 1986a, Cárdenas 1979, Sandweiss et al 1983:287–293. 21. Grieder et al 1988:243. 22. Moseley 1975:60–62, Patterson 1971a, Wendt 1964. 23. Donkin 1979:5; see Engel 1963:figs. 177, 180 for illustrations of possible Late Preceramic digging sticks. 24. J. Bird et al 1985:219–228, Bonavia 1982:77–100, Quilter 1991:404–413. 25. Engel 1963:82. 26. J. Bird et al 1985:221–228. 27. For discussions of Late Preceramic textile technology see J. Bird et al 1985:101–218, Bonavia 1982:101–131, Fung 1972a, Moseley and Barrett 1969, Grieder et al 1988:152–181, S. Pozorski and T. Pozorski 1987. 28. Alva 1986a:fig. 21A, fig. 21B; Feldman 1985. 29. Bonavia 1982:201–214, Engel 1963, Quilter 1989:75–85, Wendt 1964. 30. J. Bird et al 1985:70–74, Lathrap et al 1975:28–29. 31. Feldman 1980, Feldman 1985:81. 32. Engel 1963: fig. 138. 33. Ravines and Isbell 1976:269, cf. Pasztory 1984. Moseley (1985) uses the term "preadaptation" to highlight the potential for turning the organizational mechanisms used to build Late Preceramic public buildings to the infra-structural needs of later times. 34. Alva 1986a, cf. Cárdenas 1979. 35. Feldman 1980, 1983, 1985; Moseley and Willey 1973. 36. Moseley 1975:82–83, S. Pozorski and T. Pozorski 1990. 37. Quilter 1985, Quilter et al 1991, Moseley 1975:26–28, cf. Engel 1967. 38. J. Bird et al 1985, Engel 1963:5, S. Pozorski and T. Pozorski 1979:342–344. 39. S. Pozorski and T. Pozorski 1979:349–351. 40. Bonnier and Rozemberg 1988, Burger and Salazar-Burger 1985, Grieder et al 1988. 41. Flannery 1973, Lynch 1980, MacNeish 1977, Pearsall 1978. 42. Burger and van der Merwe 1990:90–91. 43. Wing 1972. 44. Lanning 1967:63, cf. Bolton and Colvin 1981, Gade 1967. 45. Cardich 1988:44–45, Pires-Ferreira et al 1976, Wheeler 1984. 46. Lavallée and Julien 1976, 1984, Matos 1976, Matos and Rick 1981, Pearsall 1980. 47. Miller and Burger n.d. 48. Grieder et al 1988:152–181; see Bonavia 1982:132 for a rare discovery of camelid wool on the coast during the Late Preceramic. 49. Lavallée and Julien 1984. 50. Burger and Salazar-Burger 1980, 1985. 51. Izumi 1971, Izumi and Sono 1963, Izumi and Terada 1972. 52. Izumi 1971:68. 53. Izumi and Terada 1972:306. It has not been established whether the large mammal bones in the niches were camelids or deer (Yoshio Onuki, personal communication, 1991). 54. See Aranguren 1977 for a modern ethnographic case of burnt offerings in the Central Andes. 55. Izumi 1971, Izumi, Cuculiza, and Kano 1972. 56. Burger and Salazar-Burger 1980, 1985, 1986. 57. Bonnier and Rozemberg 1988, Bonnier et al 1985. 58. Grieder and Bueno 1985, Grieder et al 1988. 59. Grieder et al 1988:4–10, fig. 5, Bueno and Grieder 1979. 60. Grieder et al 1988:19–67. 61. Grieder et al 1988: 73–75. 62. Grieder et al 1988:24–27, fig. 20; the circular plaza at Huaricoto was an Early Horizon addition to the ceremonial architecture. 63. Burger and Salazar-Burger 1980, Feldman 1983, 1985:86–88. 64. Grieder and Bueno 1985:45, Grieder et al 1988:19–22. 65. Grieder et al 1988:73–102. 66. Feldman 1985:81, Grieder et al 1988, Lathrap 1973b, Quilter 1985. 67. Feldman 1985:81, Lathrap et al 1975:28–29, Lavallée and Julien 1984, Quilter 1985. 68. Steward 1949, Wittfogel 1957. 69. Moseley 1975:95, Burger and Salazar-Burger 1986. 70. It is not necessary to postulate even weak corporate authority for non-monumental sites such as Huaricoto where responsibility for ritual activities may have simply rotated between families, perhaps in a manner similar to modern "cargo" systems (Burger and Salazar-Burger 1986). Even in large sites like Kotosh, corporate authority may simply have been invested in a particular lineage with the power involved restricted to matters of public ritual.

Chapter 3 (pp. 57–103)
1. Cohen 1978, Quilter and Stocker 1983, Moseley 1985:36–41. 2. Feldman 1983:307–309. 3. Hill 1975, Meggers, Evans, and Estrada 1965. 4. Patterson 1985, Patterson and Moseley 1968:120–129, Rowe 1967b:26, Strong and Evans 1952:277–282. 5. Burger 1985b:506–510, Grieder et al 1988:185–191, Grossman 1985, Strong and Evans 1952. 6. Burger 1985b:528–529. 7. Izumi 1971, Izumi and Sono 1963, Izumi and Terada 1972. 8. Lathrap 1970, 1971, Izumi, Cuculiza, and Kano 1972:62–64. 9. Lathrap and Roys 1963. 10. Kano 1979. 11. Kaulicke 1981, cf. Morales 1980, 1982. 12. Williams 1971, 1985. 13. Patterson 1983. 14. Williams 1980:107. 15. Williams 1980:98, Cuadro I. 16. Quilter 1985:282, Williams 1985:231–232. 17. Bonavia 1965, Burger 1990, Patterson 1985. 18. Patterson 1985. 19. Burger and Salazar 1991a. 20. W. Isbell 1976, cf. Netherly and Dillehay 1986, Lathrap 1985. 21. Burger and Isbell 1976, Ravines et al 1984. 22. Salazar-Burger and Burger 1983:234–237; cf. Ravines 1984 for an alternative interpretation of the Middle Temple's iconography. 23. Williams 1980. 24. Ravines 1984. 25. Burger 1987, Carrión Cachot 1948, Engel 1956, Rosas 1970; cf. Lathrap et al 1975:54–55. It is possible that the figurines were once dressed in miniature clothing, as were the much later Inca figurines, but the perishable and delicate costumes do not usually survive in the archaeological record. 26. Burger 1987,

Burger and Salazar-Burger 1991a. **27.** Patterson 1983 is the source of these estimates, but his methodology is based on Thomas Pozorski's 1980 adaptation of an experimental methodology proposed in Erasmus 1965; cf. Ravines 1979. **28.** Burger and Salazar-Burger 1991a, Patterson 1971a, 1983, Ravines et al 1984. **29.** Scheele 1970. **30.** See Plowman 1984 for a summary of the varieties of coca and their appearance at archaeological sites. Unfortunately, the coca recovered in early contexts thus far (Dillehay 1979, Patterson and Moseley 1968, Cohen 1978:33, 1979:33) have not been studied in detail by botanists. Its apparent absence from recent excavations of Initial Period middens in Casma and Lurín underline the need for additional data before its Initial Period introduction to the coast can be established with confidence. **31.** Ludeña 1975, Marcus and Silva 1988, Patterson and Moseley 1968, Scheele 1970. **32.** Williams 1980, 1985. **33.** Netherly 1984; for modern accounts of the organization of Andean irrigation practices see Arguedas 1985, B. J. Isbell 1978, Mitchell 1973. **34.** Cohen 1978, Patterson 1971a. In the 1991 excavations by the author at Mina Perdida, maize was rare or absent in layers of well-preserved late Initial Period refuse. **35.** Burger 1987, Burger and Salazar-Burger 1991a, Thomas Patterson personal communication 1990. **36.** Patterson 1983. **37.** Matos 1968:227, 229. **38.** Patterson 1984, Patterson, Burger and Wallace n.d. **39.** Burger and Salazar-Burger 1991a:287, Quilter 1989. **40.** Reichel-Dolmatoff 1976. **41.** Burger and Salazar-Burger 1991a, Patterson 1983. **42.** Williams 1972, 1985:234–237. **43.** Ravines 1982:139, Silva 1978, Zechentner 1988:518–524. **44.** Tello 1943:139–150, 1956. **45.** Tello 1956:84–145, Samaniego et al 1985; cf. Bueno 1975, Samaniego 1980. **46.** Tello 1956:145–243, Kauffmann Doig 1979, Bischof 1986, 1987. **47.** Samaniego et al 1985:178–186, Roe 1974:34–37. **48.** See Samaniego et al 1985 and Tello 1956 for a description of the clay friezes; cf. Bonavia 1985, 1990 and Bischof 1991 for differences in opinion over the authenticity of the second painted feline. **49.** Proulx 1968, 1985, Roe 1974:36–38, Thompson 1962a. **50.** Fung and Williams 1979, S. Pozorski and T. Pozorski 1987:71–75, Tello 1956:79–83, Thompson 1964:201–206, 1964:207–208. **51.** Bischof 1986, Collier 1962, Tello 1956. **52.** Tello 1956:49–66. **53.** Fung 1972b, S. Pozorski and T. Pozorski 1986, 1987:30–51. **54.** S. Pozorski and T. Pozorski 1986, 1987. **55.** S. Pozorski and T. Pozorski 1986. **56.** T. Pozorski and S. Pozorski 1988, 1990a, cf. Burger 1989. **57.** S. Pozorski and T. Pozorski 1987:23, 74–75. **58.** Fung 1972a, 1972b, S. Pozorski and T. Pozorski 1987, T. Pozorski and S. Pozorski 1990b. **59.** S. Pozorski and T. Pozorski 1987:Table 1. **60.** S. Pozorski and T. Pozorski 1987:86–89, Tello 1943, 1956. **61.** Fung 1972b, Grieder 1975, Matsuzawa 1978, S. Pozorski and T. Pozorski 1987:26–28. **62.** Fung 1972b, S. Pozorski and T. Pozorski 1987. **63.** For an alternative interpretation of Casma's sociopolitical system see S. Pozorski 1987, S. Pozorski and T. Pozorski 1987. **64.** Burger and Salazar-Burger 1980, Cárdenas 1979, Daggett 1987b, Grieder et al 1988, Proulx 1968, 1985, Wilson 1988. **65.** Bischof 1987, Dagget 1987a, Proulx 1985, Tello 1943:136–137. **66.** Larco 1941, 1946:149–155. **67.** Alva 1986b, Keatinge 1980, Ravines 1982b, Shimada et al 1983. **68.** J. Bird et al 1985, Larco 1941, Strong and Evans 1952. **69.** Strong and Evans 1952 describes one of the few excavated mace heads; this late Initial Period piece was found in a Middle Guañape context. Some of the fine mace heads labeled as Cupisnique in museum exhibits and art catalogues may have been looted from Salinar tombs (Jose Pinilla personal communication 1991). **70.** Moseley and Watanabe 1974, T. Pozorski 1976, 1980, Watanabe 1976, 1979; Conklin 1985 proposed an eight-phase sequence for the architecture of Huaca de los Reyes, but aspects of it may be inconsistent with the available archaeological evidence (T. Pozorski personal communication 1990). **71.** Conklin 1985, T. Pozorski 1980. **72.** Alva 1987, 1988a. **73.** Alva and Meneses de Alva 1983. **74.** Strong and Evans 1952, Willey 1953:42–61. **75.** T. Pozorski 1983. **76.** Barreto 1984, Salazar-Burger and Burger 1983. **77.** Shimada 1981, Shimada et al 1983. **78.** Salazar-Burger and Burger 1983. **79.** Larco 1941, Willey 1971: figs. 3–46. **80.** J. Bird et al 1985:48, Cané 1985 and 1986, Schultes 1967, Sharon and Donnan 1977, Wassén 1965, 1967, Ralph Cané (personal communication 1990) reports that chemical analysis of seeds found in graves with snuff tablets in San Pedro de Atacama (northern Chile) yielded evidence of the psychotropic alkaloid dimethyltryptamine (DMT). See Frikel 1961 and Polykrates 1960 for examples of the continued use of snuff trays in the Amazon basin during the 20th century. See Engel 1963 for example of a snuff tray that may date to the Late Preceramic. **81.** Shimada 1981. **82.** Ravines 1982b, 1985a. **83.** Tellenbach 1986. **84.** S. Pozorski 1983, Shimada et al 1983. **85.** S. Pozorski 1983, Strong and Evans 1952. **86.** See Alva 1986b for good examples of the non-Cupisnique pottery styles found on the north coast, including "Tembladera" style ceramics (e.g. Alva 1986b: figs. 60–67, 88–94, 461–466). Although some scholars once believed that the Tembladera style might be post-Chavín because of similarities with the Paracas style of the late Early Horizon, this position has become less plausible with recent archaeological results from Jequetepeque and Kuntur Wasi. **87.** Burger 1984a:79–80, Kaulicke 1976, Lumbreras 1971: figs. 25a, 25b, Rosas and Shady 1970: lam. 15c, Terada and Onuki 1988: lam. 4b. **88.** Burger and Salazar-Burger 1991b Heather Lechtman personal communication 1992. **89.** Shimada 1990. **90.** Bennett 1948. **91.** Cárdenas 1979, Ishida et al 1960, Izumi and Terada 1966, Lanning 1963, cf. Guffroy et al 1987. **92.** Guffroy 1989:199. The chronology of the public construction at Ñañañique is being debated at present, and it is possible that the site was founded and occupied only during the beginning of the Early Horizon, prior to the expansion of the Chavín sphere of interaction. **93.** Zeidler 1986. **94.** Lathrap et al 1977, Marcos 1988. **95.** Marcos and Norton 1981. **96.** Coe 1960, 1967, Lathrap 1966, Lathrap et al 1977, Marcos 1986a, 1986b, Meggers 1966. **97.** Rowe 1967b:26. **98.** Gayton 1967, Riddell and Valdez 1988, Rowe 1967b:30.

Chapter 4 (pp. 104–127)

1. Kaulicke 1975, Daniel Morales personal communication 1990, Santillana 1975. **2.** Cueva 1982. **3.** Kaulicke 1975, 1981. **4.** Rosas 1976. **5.** Fung 1976, Morales 1980, Rosas and Shady 1970, 1974. **6.** Rosas and Shady 1976:25–29. **7.** Burger 1989. **8.** Kaulicke 1976, Morales 1980, 1982. **9.** Tello 1923, cf. Carrión Cachot 1958. **10.** Fung 1976, Morales 1980, Rosas and Shady 1970, and Kaulicke 1975, 1976, 1981 all offer detailed descriptions of the mid/late Initial Period ceramic style of Pacopampa, originally named Pacopampa Pacopampa by Rosas and Shady; it is roughly equivalent to Kaulicke's Pacopampa B, Fung's phases AB and C, and the Pacopampa Expansivo phase of Morales. **11.** Morales 1980, Rosas and Shady 1970: lam 15d. The author was shown the stone cup in 1983 by Tomas Perez, the site guard of Pacopampa. It was recovered from the mound of Yurac Sara near Pacopampa. **12.** Morales 1980; cf. I. Flores 1975. **13.** Kaulicke 1976:10–16. **14.** Alfredo Altamirano personal communication 1983, Daniel Morales personal communication 1991. **15.** Terada and Onuki 1982, 1985, 1988:33–47; cf. Reichlen and Reichlen 1949. **16.** M. Shimada 1982, 1985. **17.** Terada and Onuki 1982:53–54, 259, Terada 1985:195–198. **18.** Terada and Onuki 1985:19, pl. 2. **19.** Terada and Onuki, 1985. **20.** Ravines 1985b:72–82, Petersen 1985, Tello 1941. **21.** Williams and Pineda 1983. **22.** The role of the subterranean and celestial circulation of water in prehistoric, historic and modern indigenous Andean cosmology has been discussed by many scholars, including Bastien 1978, Reinhard 1985, Sherbondy 1982, and Urton 1981. **23.** Onuki 1990, 1991. **24.** Carrión Cachot 1948:149–151; cf. Roe 1974:27–28, Willey 1951:114–115. **25.** Onuki 1991. **26.** Carrión Cachot 1948. **27.** Terada and Onuki 1988:3–30. **28.** Terada and Onuki 1988:6–8. **29.** Dillehay and Netherly 1983, Netherly and Dillehay 1986. **30.** Alva 1987, 1988b. **31.** Alva 1987, 1988b:332–333. **32.** Thatcher 1979; Topic and Topic 1978, 1983, 1987. **33.** Krzanowski 1983, 1986a, 1986b. **34.** Research by Jorge Silva, Lucy Salazar, and the author did *not* substantiate preliminary accounts of a monumental U-shaped Initial Period complex in the Moyabamba area (Shimada et al 1983:148); the site appears to be much later in date. **35.** Church 1992:155. **36.** Shady 1974, 1987, Shady and Rosas, 1980. **37.** Shady 1987. **38.** Lathrap 1973b, Shady 1987. **39.** Izumi, Cuculiza and Kano 1972:39, 46–49, Kano 1979. **40.** Izumi and Terada 1972:308. **41.** Grieder and Bueno 1985, Grieder et al 1988. **42.** Burger and Salazar-Burger 1986. **43.** Wing 1972, Kano 1979. **44.** Izumi, Cuculiza and Kano 1972: pl. 27#1, pl. 46#3. **45.** Izumi, Cuculiza and Kano 1972:30–45. **46.** Grieder et al 1988:66–67. **47.** Grieder et al 1988. **48.** Izumi, Cuculiza, and Kano 1972:51–54. **49.** Grieder et al 1988:92–95. **50.** Izumi 1971, Lathrap 1971, 1973b. **51.** Burger 1984a:197, Smith 1988. **52.** Burger 1985b: Table 2, Miller and Burger n.d., Wing 1972. **53.** Izumi and Sono 1963; the archaeological survey of Christine Rudecoff (1981:7) in the Upper Huallaga near Huanuco covered roughly 200 sq. km. **54.** Onuki and Fuji 1974, Terada 1979. **55.** Ishida et al 1960, Thompson 1962a. **56.** Onuki 1985. **57.** Bonnier and Rozemberg 1988. **58.** Burger 1985b, Izumi and Sono 1963, Terada 1979. **59.** Hastorf et al 1989, Matos 1972, 1973, 1978, Parsons and Matos 1978. **60.** Browman 1975, 1977. **61.** Lavallée and Julien 1976, Matos 1976, Matos and Rick 1981. **62.** Lavallée 1979. **63.** Wheeler, Cardoza, and Pozzi-Escot 1979. **64.** Lavallée 1979, cf. Matos and Rick 1981. **65.** Pearsall 1980. **66.** Cardich 1964, 1973, Matos 1978, Morales 1977, Nomland 1939. **67.** MacNeish et al 1975: 40–41, cf. Lumbreras 1974b. **68.** Browman 1974, 1975, Burger and Asaro 1979, MacNeish et al 1975, Petersen 1970. Larco (1941:163) analyzed the bright red pigment sometimes used in Cupisnique burials and reported that they contained traces of mercury, the most important component of cinnabar. **69.** Grossman 1972, 1985.

Chapter 5 (pp. 128–164)

1. Lumbreras 1970:22, Tello 1923:227. **2.** Burger 1983:3–7, 1984a:6–10. **3.** B. J. Isbell 1978:13. **4.** Burger 1983, 1984a:221–231. **5.** Rowe 1962b; cf. 1967c for revised version of this architectural sequence. **6.** At the present time there is no definitive map of Chavín de Huántar and small discrepancies exist between the versions published in Rowe 1967c:97, Lumbreras 1971:2, and Tello 1960: fig. 4. Measurements provided in this volume for the constructions at this site should therefore be considered only as approximations. **7.** Tello 1960:253–299. **8.** Marino Gonzales personal communication 1975, Rowe 1962b:7–9, Tello 1960. **9.** Urton and Aveni 1983:229, Urton personal communication 1991. **10.** Reinhard 1985:397–407. **11.** Lathrap 1985. **12.** Lumbreras 1977. **13.** Martin Justiniano personal communication 1981. The author confirmed the presence of the gastropod impression in the floor. Lumbreras 1977:13 suggests that the dark E–W strip may be complemented by a N–S strip forming a cross on the masonry floor of the Circular Plaza. Completion of the Plaza excavations will eventually resolve this matter. **14.** Cordy-Collins 1976, 1977, Lumbreras 1977:23, Sharon and Donnan 1977. **15.** Tello 1960: 91–118. **16.** Descriptions of the gallery complexes appear in Lumbreras and Amat 1969, Lumbreras 1970, and Tello 1960. **17.** Tello 1960:104–109. **18.** Carrión Cachot 1958:406. **19.** Lathrap 1973a:95. **20.** Tello 1960: 176–177. **21.** Tello 1960: 109. **22.** Patterson 1971b, Tello 1960:177, 353–354. **23.** Lumbreras and Amat 1969. **24.** Lumbreras 1970:122. **25.** Lumbreras and Amat 1969, Lumbreras 1971, 1977, 1989. **26.** P. Reichlen 1974. **27.** Lumbreras 1989:130–132, 183–216. **28.** Lumbreras 1989:206–216, Miller 1984. **29.** Numerous descriptions and classifications of the assemblage from the Gallery of the Offerings have appeared, the most recent of which is Lumbreras 1989. The final report on the 1966/1967 excavations had not yet been published at the time this volume was completed. See Burger 1984a:172–183, Lumbreras 1971, 1989:187–204, and Lumbreras and Amat 1969 for discussions of the sources of the imported pottery found in the Gallery of the Offerings. 30. In Lumbreras's 1989 summary, the Ofrendas-style ceramics were subdivided further into four groups: Ofrendas, Floral, Dragonian, and Qotopukyo. 31. Alva 1986b:121, Lavalle and Lang 1981:94, Ludeña 1975, Proulx 1973:pl. 1A, Scheele 1970. 32. Silva 1978b. 33. Lumbreras 1977: 19–20. 34. Bustamante and Crousillat 1974. 35. See Morris 1974 and Silverblatt 1987 for summaries of archaeological and ethnohistoric material on the *acllawasi* and Reichel-Dolmatoff 1976:275 on the Kogi. 36. Lumbreras et al 1976. 37. Estete 1968 [*c.* 1535], Pizarro 1968[1571]; cf. Jimenez Borja and Bueno 1970, Rostworowski 1972. 38. There have been numerous treatments of the Chavín style including Bennett 1942, Kroeber 1944, 1947, Kubler 1962, Muelle 1937, 1955, Roe 1974, 1978, Rowe 1967c, Stone 1983, and Tello 1960. 39. Rowe 1962b. 40. Reichel-Dolmatoff 1976:285. 41. Roe 1974. 42. Roe 1974, 1978, 1982b. 43. Kubler 1975. 44. Rowe 1962b, Stone 1983. 45. Pasztory 1984. 46. Rowe 1962b. 47. Duviols 1976. There are ethnographic parallels to the Inca case, such as the production of ritual masks among the Piaroa of southern Venezuela; here religious specialists direct expert artisans to produce masks according to their exact specifications so that the end product is identical to the image of the mask in the mind of the religious leader (Boglár 1979:236). 48. Burger 1988:106–108, Menzel et al 1964, Roe 1974:31–32, Rowe 1962b. Lathrap (1985:249) suggested that the Obelisk could have come from a site further down the Marañon drainage, possibly Yauya. 49. Zerries 1968:255, 257, 238. 50. Rowe 1967c, Tello 1960:175. 51. Tello 1923:274–290. 52. Lathrap 1973a, 1977, 1985, Seeger 1981:214–215. 53. Rowe 1962b:19 has interpreted the tail as a fish tail and argues that it may be a misinterpretation of the cayman due to lack of first-hand observation. Lathrap (1973a:96) concurs with its identification as a fish tail but prefers to think that its inclusion was deliberate and highly meaningful. 54. Lathrap 1973a, Tello 1923, 1960. 55. Lathrap 1973a, 1977, 1985, Tello 1923, 1960:184; cf. Cané 1983, 1986. 56. Rivière 1969:260–261. 57. Lathrap 1971. 58. Reichel-Dolmatoff 1975:123, Rowe 1982:7, John Rowe personal communication 1977. 59. Lathrap 1973a:97, Reichel-Dolmatoff 1975, Roe 1982a. 60. Carrión Cachot 1958. Many of the "snake" representations incorporate non-ophidian elements such as upright ears; hence the term "cat-snake" is sometimes applied (Roe 1974:14). 61. Roe 1982a. 62. Arguedas 1957, Rostworowski 1985. 63. Other identifications of non-Amazonian fauna include that of the viscacha (Rowe 1962b), the bat or butterfly (Bruhns 1977), and the hawk (Rowe

1962b). Some scholars working on the north coast (e.g. Dillehay and Netherly 1983, Elera 1986) argue that many of the animals associated with the tropical forest today lived in forested habitats on the coast or western slopes of the Andes in prehistoric times and that these animals, rather than ones from the eastern lowlands, could have been the inspiration for their presence in the early religious iconography. 64. Lathrap 1970, 1971, Tello 1942. 65. Burger 1984a:37–80. 66. Harner 1972:120. 67. Cané 1985, Cordy-Collins 1977, 1980. 68. Tello 1960. 69. Reichel-Dolmatoff 1975:14. 70. This typology was suggested by Anne Dowd (personal communication 1985). 71. Tello 1960:300, lam. XIIV, von Reiss Altschul 1967, Wassén 1936, 1967. 72. Lathrap 1973b, von Reiss Altschul 1967. 73. Burger 1984a:28–36, 221–231. 74. Lucy Salazar-Burger personal communication 1981; cf. Fung 1976:199. 75. Espejo 1959, Tello 1960:118, lam. XLVII. 76. Burger 1984a:188–199, Tello 1960. 77. Burger and van der Merwe 1990. 78. Miller 1984, Miller and Burger n.d., Burger 1984a:188–190, figs. 380–388, Rowe 1962b:fig. 23 for a Chavin sculpture illustrating an atlatl and darts. 79. Burger 1984a, cf. Lumbreras 1989. 80. Burger 1983:30, fig. 19, Kauffmann Doig 1971:fig. 268, Rowe 1962b:fig. 17, Tello 1960:246, 247, figs. 80–82, 85. 81. Burger 1981, 1984a:277–281; cf. Lumbreras 1989 for an alternative interpretation of the measurements.

Chapter 6 (pp. 165–181)

1. Burger 1981, 1984a:277–281. 2. Burger 1984a:231–234, 246–247. 3. Burger 1984a:fig. 2, fig. 152. 4. Miller 1984, Miller and Burger n.d. 6. Miller 1979, Miller and Burger n.d. 7. Burger 1983, 1984a, cf. Espejo 1951, 1955. 8. Burger 1984a:234–250. 9. Burger 1984a:21–26, Miller and Burger n.d. 10. Burger and van der Merwe 1990. 11. Burger 1984a. 12. Burger 1983:12, 1984a:196–197. 13. Burger 1984a:107–155. 14. Burger, Asaro and Michel 1984; cf. Burger and Asaro 1979. 15. Burger 1984a:198–199. 16. Burger 1984a:214–217. 17. Burger 1984a. 18. Miller and Burger n.d. 19. Rowe 1962b. 20. Marino Gonzales personal communication 1975. While these columns have often appeared in photographs (Kauffmann Doig 1971:195, 201, Lumbreras 1970:84), little attention has been given to their iconography or chronological significance. The Monumental Stairway is referred to by Lumbreras (1970:84) as the Staircase of the Jaguars (Escalinata de los Jaguares) after the carved lintel discovered there (which is believed by most scholars to represent a supernatural cayman). 21. The trend towards increasing repetition of simple details in phase EF conforms to the process of pattern exhaustion at the end of a style cycle described by Kroeber (1963:137–144). An analogous style cycle occurred in the Nazca style of Peru's south coast during the 1st millennium AD. 22. Among the Kogi, the bivalve is associated with the female principle (and the left side) while the gastropod is associated with the

male principle (and the right side); they are buried in complementary pairs in burial ceremonies (Reichel-Dolmatoff 1974:298–299); cf. Cordy-Collins 1979a, Davidson 1982. 23. Rowe 1962b. 24. Cordy-Collins 1979a, Lyon 1978, Roe, 1982a. 25. Rowe 1960, Kauffmann Doig 1971:221–222. 26. Lumbreras 1970:114–118, Lumbreras and Amat 1969; Cordy-Collins 1979a:8. 27. Ayres 1961, Bruhns 1977, Rowe 1962a. 28. Tello 1960:68–69. 29. Lumbreras 1970:80–83, Mishkin 1940:240, Reichel-Dolmatoff 1974:298–299, Urton 1981, Urton and Aveni 1983, Zuidema 1982. 30. See Rowe 1962b for an alternative interpretation. 31. Lumbreras and Amat 1969. 32. Lumbreras and Amat 1969, Lumbreras 1970.

Chapter 7 (pp. 183–227)

1. For example, in the Rimac Valley the public centre of Garagay appears to have replaced Mina Perdida as the civic-ceremonial center of the local society when the latter was abandoned (Patterson 1985). This chapter is a revised and expanded version of an earlier synthesis (Burger 1988). 2. Burger and Salazar-Burger 1991a. 3. Ludeña 1975, Marcus and Silva 1988, Ravines and Isbell 1976, Ravines et al 1984, Patterson 1983, 1984, Patterson and Moseley 1968. 4. S. Pozorski and T. Pozorski 1987:77–78. 5. Grieder 1975, S. Pozorski and T. Pozorski 1987:86–89; cf. Fung 1972a:113–112, Matsuzawa 1978. 6. S. Pozorski and T. Pozorski 1987:86–89, Tello 1956:32–48. 7. S. Pozorski and T. Pozorski 1987:51–70. 8. Daggett 1987a, Proulx 1973, 1985. 9. Wilson 1988: 100–138, figs. 22–24. 10. Wilson 1988:104–110, figs. 28–49. 11. S. Pozorski and T. Pozorski 1987:95–103; cf. Fung and Pimentel 1973, Kroeber 1944:52–53, S. Pozorski 1987, Tello 1956:68–71. 12. Alva 1988a, T. Pozorski 1983, I. Shimada 1981. 13. T. Pozorski 1983, Watanabe 1976. 14. Alva 1986b:figs. 299–350, 356–369, Elera 1983, 1986, Lavalle and Lang 1981, Roe 1982b. 15. S. Pozorski 1987, S. Pozorski and T. Pozorski 1987:127–132. 16. R. Bird 1987, Moseley, Feldman, and Ortloff 1981:247, Nials et al 1979:10. 17. Rosas and Shady 1970, 1974, cf. Fung 1976, Kaulicke 1976, Lyon 1978. 18. Onuki 1990, 1991, cf. Ulbert and Eibl 1984. 19. Burger and Salazar 1985:131, Izumi and Terada 1972:309, Onuki 1982. 20. Larco 1941:809, 1946:149. 21. Bennett 1946:92, Carrión Cachot 1948:169–172, Willey 1948:10, 15. 22. Cordy-Collins 1976, cf. Lanning 1967:98, 102. 23. Werbner 1977a:ix. 24. Colson 1977:119. 25. Garbett 1977, Turner 1974:185, Werbner 1977a:xxxxiii, 1977b:212. 26. Kaulicke 1976:17–22, Keatinge 1981, Patterson 1971b:46. 27. Cieza de León 1967:196, Estete 1968:382–384, Pizarro 1968; cf. Patterson 1991:88–92, Rostworowski 1972, Spaulding 1984. 28. Cobo 1979:211–214. 29. Rostworowski 1972:39, 43. 30. Kaulicke 1976:55. 31. Burger and Salazar-Burger 1980, 28–31. 32. Cordy-Collins 1976:11, Jose Pinilla personal communication 1981, Tello 1959:fig. 1. 33. Lavalle and Lang 1979:55, Roe 1974:22. 34. Lumbreras 1974a:fig. 86, Roe 1974:fig. 18. 35. Lyon

1978:98–103, Cordy-Collins 1979b. 36. Cordy-Collins 1976:49, 1977:184, fig. 6, Lathrap 1973a, 1977, Lavalle and Lang 1979:51, 52, Lumbreras 1974a:79, Sharon and Donnan 1977:387, Tello 1960:fig. 50. 37. Lyon 1978:98–99. 38. Cordy-Collings 1979a. 39. Conklin 1971; cf. Sawyer 1972:92, figs. 1, 8. 40. Jose Pinilla and Carlos Elera personal communication 1991. 41. James Vreeland personal communication 1991. 42. Silverman 1991:374, Mejía Xesspe 1972:79–80. 43. Mejía Xesspe 1968:18–22. 44. Daggett 1987b, Kosok 1965:109, fig. 32, Tello 1943:136–139. 45. Tello 1937. 46. Kaulicke 1976:44, Larco 1946:pl. 65, Rowe 1946:292, von Reiss Altschul 1967:304. 47. Conklin 1971, 1978; also see Wallace 1979 for an analysis of regional preferences in spinning and plain weave during the Early Horizon. 48. Lechtman 1980, 1984, Lothrop 1941, 1951. 49. Lechtman 1980:275. 50. Kroeber 1947:429. 51. Willey 1962. 52. Burger 1984a, Fung 1972a, Lynch 1980. A radiocarbon measurement on the fire-drill hearth illustrated from Guitarrero Cave in the Callejón de Huaylas yielded a date of 2315 ± 125 BP (without calibration: Lynch 1980:243–245). Ground stone points appear in part of the northern highlands during the Initial Period. (e.g. Burger 1984a:194, Grieder et al 1988:98, Terada 1979:99) but their use becomes more general during the Early Horizon. They are introduced on the coast during the mid-Early Horizon (S. Pozorski and T. Pozorski 1987:119; cf. Muelle 1957). 53. Lothrop 1941. 54. Lothrop 1941. 55. Carrión Cachot 1948:63. 56. Onuki 1990, 1991. 57. Elera 1983, 1986, Shady 1983. Elite tombs of the Chavín horizon have been looted elsewhere, including in the Cayaltí zone of Zaña, the Tembladera zone of Jequetepeque, and the Huarmey area (Kauffmann Doig 1981:37, 131, Emmerich 1965:7–8, figs. 6, 8). Lavalle and Lang have illustrated gold objects said to come from the tombs in Cayaltí (Lavalle and Lang 1981:130, 142, 147, 168) and Jequetepeque (Lavalle and Lang 1981:128, 129, 132, 136–138, 152, 153, 164, 165). 58. Larco 1941:fig. 204, Lothrop 1951:56. 59. Lothrop 1941, Onuki 1990, 1991. 60. Kaulicke 1976, Morales 1980, personal communication 1983, Miller and Burger n.d., Rosas and Shady 1970, 1974, Santillana 1975. 61. Lavallée 1979, Lavallée and Julien 1976; cf. Julien 1981, Silva 1988. 62. Matos and Rick 1981, Pearsall 1980. 63. Matos 1978. 64. Morales 1977, Nomland 1939. 65. Browman 1974:190, 1975, 1977, Matos 1973, Parsons and Matos 1978. 66. cf. Casafranca 1960, Cruzatt 1971, I. Flores 1960, Lumbreras 1974b, Matos 1959, Ochatoma et al 1984, Ochatoma 1985. The excavations at Chupas and Wichqana have not been published in detail but the reports available seem to indicate that the public architecture is associated with the Chupas and Rancha styles of the late Early Horizon and that the Janabarriu-related Kichka Pata style pottery of this zone underlies these constructions. 67. Cohen 1979, Patterson 1971, S. Pozorski 1983, S. Pozorski and T. Pozorski 1987, Wallace 1962. 68. Dillehay 1979. 69. Miller and Burger n.d. 70. Browman

1974, J. Flores 1968:130–132. **71.** Beck 1979:108–115, 133–140. **72.** Burger 1984a, 1984b, Burger and Asaro 1979, Burger, Asaro, and Michel 1984. **73.** Burger 1980, cf. Cardich 1988, Silva 1988. **74.** Petersen 1970; chemical analyses by the author have confirmed the use of cinnabar at Atalla and Chavín de Huántar. **75.** Matos 1959, 1972. **76.** Browman 1975, Lumbreras 1974b, Matos 1973. **77.** Hodder 1977, 1982. **78.** See Burger 1984b:Table 1 and 1988:Table 2 for lists of sites where Janabarriu-related assemblages have been found; cf. Burger 1978, 1984b:42–45. **79.** Kaulicke 1975, 1976, Morales 1980, 1982, Rosas and Shady 1970, 1974; cf. Fung 1976. **80.** Elera 1983, 1986. **81.** Kroeber 1953, Menzel et al 1964, Sawyer 1972, Wallace 1962. **82.** Guffroy 1989, Guffroy et al 1987, 1989, Izumi and Terada 1966. **83.** Bruhns et al 1990, Burger 1984b, Lathrap et al 1975. **84.** Burger 1984b. **85.** Bruhns et al 1990, Idrovo 1992, Meggers 1966, Miller and Gill 1990. **86.** Rojas 1985, Shady 1987, Shady and Rosas 1980; cf. Miasta 1978 for related Early Horizon sites and ceramics in the tropical forest of northern Peru. The inclusion of the Huayurco materials in this section is based on Ruth Shady's recent discovery in Bagua of similar materials in association with Early Horizon assemblages (Ruth Shady personal communication 1992). The cross-dating of these materials to the Initial Period by Lathrap (1970:108–109) appears to be in error. **87.** Lathrap 1970:92–5, Ravines 1978, 1981. **88.** See Tello 1960:figs. 1–3 for the location of "Chavín" sites in the Marañon drainage. **89.** DeBoer 1975, Lathrap 1970:92–95, Ravines 1978, cf. DeBoer 1984:117–119. **90.** Grossman 1985, Mohr Chavez 1982–83, Rowe 1944, Yábar 1972. **91.** Chavez and Mohr Chavez 1976, Mohr Chavez 1988. **92.** Heine-Gelden 1959, Kidder et al 1963, Uhle 1923, 1930. **93.** Wittfogel 1957. **94.** Netherly 1984. **95.** Steward 1949, Steward and Faron 1959. **96.** Burger and van der Merwe 1990, Collier 1961, Kidder et al 1963, S. Pozorski and T. Pozorski 1987. **97.** White 1949. **98.** See Haas 1982 for a summary of variations on this theme. **99.** Cieza de León 1922, Chap. XIII:44–45; the English translation is taken from Lyon 1974:324. **100.** Carneiro 1970. **101.** Tello 1942, 1960.

Epilogue (pp. 228–229)

1. Topic and Topic 1987:50, 1978, Willey 1953. The late Early Horizon site of Mis Pasday, located in Otuzco near the upper limit of agriculture, is probably the oldest fortified settlement documented in the Peruvian highlands. **2.** Judging from a visit by the author, the late Paracas site (i.e. Ocucaje 9) of Tajahuana in the mid-section of the Ica Valley seems to have served primarily as a fortified redoubt (Rowe 1963:8). **3.** Rowe 1971. **4.** Vázquez de Espinoza 1948:491.

Further Reading and Bibliography

Abbreviations

Am. Ant. = *American Antiquity*
Am. Anth. = *American Anthropology*
ESPOL = Escuela Politécnica del Litoral, Guayaquil, Ecuador
INDEA = Instituto Andino de Estudios Arqueológicos, Lima
JFA = *Journal of Field Archaeology*
KAVA = Kommission für Allgemeine und Vergleichende Archäologie des Deutschen Archäologischen Instituts, Bonn
RMN = *Revista del Museo Nacional*, Lima
UNMSM = Universidad Nacional Mayor de San Marcos, Lima

For the general reader, the best overview of Andean archaeology is Michael E. Moseley's *The Incas and their Ancestors*. To go into further depth, I suggest the collection of essays in *Peruvian Prehistory* (ed. Richard W. Keatinge). Readers interested in the period prior to the one addressed in this volume are referred to Tom Lynch's article "The Paleo-Indians" in Jesse Jenning, *Ancient South Americans*. An excellent account of Inca society and political history is Thomas Patterson, *The Inca Empire*, while John Rowe's article "Inca Culture at the Time of the Spanish Conquest" in Volume 2 of *The Handbook of South American Indians* (ed. Julian Steward) still offers the clearest and most concise description available of Inca culture.

Adams, R. Mc. 1966 *The Evolution of Urban Society: Early Mesopotamia and Prehispanic Mexico*. Aldine, Chicago.
Adorno, R. 1986 *Guaman Poma: Writing and Resistance in Colonial Peru*. Latin American Monographs No. 68. U. of Texas Press, Austin.
Alva, W. 1986a *Las Salinas de Chao: Asentamiento Temprano en el Norte del Perú*. *Materialien zur Allgemeinen und Vergleichenden Archäologie* vol. 34. KAVA, Bonn. 1986b *Cerámica Temprana en el Valle de Jequetepeque, Norte del Perú*. *Materialien zur Allgemeinen und Vergleichenden Archäologie* vol. 32. KAVA, Bonn. 1987 Resultados de las Excavaciones en el Valle Zaña, Norte del Perú. In *Archäologie in Peru – Archäometrie: 1985*, ed. W. Bauer, pp. 61–78. Konrad Theiss Verlag, Stuttgart. 1988a Investigaciones en el Complejo Formativo con Arquitectura Monumental de Purulén, Costa Norte del Perú (Informe Preliminar). *Beiträge zur Allgemeinen und Vergleichenden Archäologie* 8(1986):283–300. Mainz. 1988b Excavaciones en el Santuario del Templo Formativo Udima – Poro Poro en la Sierra del Norte del Perú.

Beiträge zur Allgemeinen und Vergleichenden Archäologie 8:301–352. Mainz.
Alva, W. and **S. Meneses de Alva** 1983 Los Murales en el Valle de Zaña, Norte del Perú. *Beiträge zur Allgemeinen und Vergleichenden Archäologie* 45:335–60. Mainz.
Aranguren, A. 1977 Las Creencias y Ritos Mágicos-Religiosos de los Pastores. *Allpanchis Phuturinqa* 8(1975):103–132. Cusco.
Arguedas, J. 1957 *The Singing Mountaineers: Songs and Tales of the Quechua People*. U. of Texas Press, Austin. 1985 Puquio: A Culture in Process of Change. In *Yawar Fiesta*, trans. F. Horning Barraclough, pp. 149–192. U. of Texas Press, Austin.
Arntz, W. 1984 El Niño and Peru: Positive Aspects. *Oceanus* 27(2):36–39.
Arntz, W., A. Landa, and **J. Tarazona.** 1985 "El Niño" – Su Impacto en la Fauna Marina. *Boletín* (Volumén Extraordinario), Instituto del Mar del Peru, Callao.
Ayres, F. 1961 Rubbings from Chavín de Huántar. *American Antiquity* 27(2):239–244.
Barreto, D. 1984 Las Investigaciones en el "Templete" de Limoncarro. *Beiträge zur Allgemeinen und Vergleichenden Archäologie* 6:541–547. Mainz.
Bastien, J. 1978 *Mountain of the Condor: Metaphor and Ritual in the Andean Ayllu*. West Publishing Company, St. Paul, Minnesota.
Beck, C. 1979 *Ancient Roads on the North Coast of Peru*. Ph.D. thesis in anthropology, U. of California, Berkeley. University Microfilms, Ann Arbor.
Bennett, W. 1942 *Chavín Stone Carving*. Yale Anthropological Studies vol. 3. New Haven. 1943 The Position of Chavín in Andean Sequences. *Proc. of the American Philosophical Society* (1942) vol. 86:323–327. Philadelphia. 1946 The Archaeology of the Central Andes. In *Handbook of South American Indians*, vol. 2, ed. J. Steward, pp. 61–148. Smithsonian Institution, Bureau of American Ethnology Bulletin 143. Washington, DC. 1948 The Peruvian Co-Tradition. In *A Reappraisal of Peruvian Archaeology*, ed. W. Bennett, pp. 1–7. Memoirs of the Society for Am. Arch., *Am. Ant.* 13(4). Menasha.
Bird, J. 1948 Preceramic Cultures in Chicama and Viru. In *A Reappraisal of Peruvian Archaeology*, ed. W. Bennett, pp. 21–28. Memoirs of the Society for Am. Arch., *Am. Ant.* 13(4). Menasha.
Bird, J., J. Hyslop, and **M. Skinner.** 1985 The Preceramic Excavations at the Huaca Prieta, Chicama Valley, Peru. *Anthropological Papers of the American Museum of Natural History* 62(1). New York.
Bird, R. 1987 A Tsunami in the Peruvian

Early Horizon. *Am. Ant.* 52(2):285–303.
Bischof, H. 1986 Zur Entstehung des Chavín-Stils in Alt-Peru. *Beiträge zur Allgemeinen und Vergleichenden Archäologie* 6(1984):355–452. Mainz. 1987 Archäologische Forschung in Cerro Sechín (Casma) – Ikonographische und Stilgeschichte Aspekte. In *Archäologie in Peru – Archäometrie: 1985*, ed. W. Bauer, 1:23–46. Konrad Theiss Verlag, Stuttgart. 1991 La Pintura Occidental Del Felino de Cerro Sechín (Perú): Una Vista Diferente. *Latin American Antiquity* 2(2):188–192.
Bode, B. 1989 *No Bells to Toll: Destruction and Creation in the Andes*. Scribner, New York.
Boglár, L. 1979 Creative Process in Ritual Art: Piaroa Indians, Venezuela. In *Spirits, Shamans, and Stars: Perspectives from South America*, ed. D. Browman and R. Schwartz, pp. 233–239. Mouton Publishers, The Hague.
Bolton, R. and **L. Colvin.** 1981 El Cuy en la Cultura Peruana Contemporanea. In *Runakunap Kawsagninkupaq Rurasqankunaqa: La Tecnología en el Mundo Andino*, ed. H. Lechtman and M. Soldi, pp. 261–326. UNAM, Mexico.
Bonavia, D. 1965 *Arqueologia de Lurin*. Instituto de Estudios Etnológicos del Museo Nacional de la Cultura Peruana y Departamento de Antropología, UNMSM, Lima. 1982 *Los Gavilanes*. Corporación Financiera de Desarrollo S.A. Cofide and Instituto Arqueológico Alemán, Lima. 1985 *Mural Painting in Ancient Peru*. Trans. Patricia Lyon. U. of Indiana Press, Bloomington. 1990 La Pintura Occidental del Felino de Cerro Sechín ¿Es Original o Falsa? *Latin Am. Ant.*(1):86–91.
Bonnier, E. and **C. Rozemberg.** 1988 Del Santuario al Caserio: Acerca de la Neolitización en la Cordillera de las Andes Centrales. *Boletin del Instituto Francés de Estudios Andinos* 17(2):23–40. Lima.
Bonnier, E., J. Zegarra, and **J. Tello.** 1985 Un Ejemplo de Cronoestratigrafia en un Sitio con Superposición Arquitectónica-Piruru-Unidad I/II. *Boletin del Instituto Francés de Estudios Andinos* 14(3–4):80–101. Lima.
Browman, D. 1974 Pastoral Nomadism in the Andes. *Current Anthropology*, 188–196. 1975 Trade Patterns in the Central Highlands of Peru in the First Millennium B.C. *World Arch.* 6(3):322–329. 1977 External Relationships of the Early Horizon Ceramic Style from Jauja-Huancayo Basin, Junin. *El Dorado* 11:1–23.
Bruhns, K. 1977 Chavin Butterflies: a Tentative Interpretation. *Ñawpa Pacha* 15:39–47. Berkeley.
Bruhns, K., J. Burton, and **G. Miller.** 1990 Excavations at Pirincay in the Paute Valley of Southern Ecuador, 1985–1988. *Antiquity* 64:221–33.

Brush, S. 1977 *Mountain, Field and Family: the Economy and Human Ecology of an Andean Valley*. U. of Pennsylvania Press, Philadelphia.
Bueno, A. 1975 Sechín: Síntesis y Evaluación Crítica del Problema. *Anales Científicos* 4:135–165. Universidad del Centro del Perú, Huancayo.
Bueno, M. A. and **T. Grieder.** 1979 Arquitectura Precerámica de la Sierra Norte. *Espacio* 1(5):48–55. Lima.
Burger, R. L. 1978 The Occupation of Chavín, Ancash during the Initial Period and Early Horizon. Ph.D. dissertation, U. of California. Michigan Microfilms, Ann Arbor. 1980 Trace-element Analysis of Obsidian Artifacts from Pachamachay, Junin. In *Prehistoric Hunters of the High Andes*, ed. J. W. Rick, pp. 257–61. Academic Press, New York. 1981 The Radiocarbon Evidence for the Temporal Priority of Chavín de Huantar. *Am. Ant.*:592–602. 1983 Pójoc and Waman Wain: Two Early Horizon Villages in the Chavín Heartland. *Ñawpa Pacha* 20:3–40. 1984a *The Prehistoric Occupation of Chavín de Huantar, Peru*. University of California Press, Publications in Anthropology Vol. 14, Berkeley. 1984b Archaeological Areas and Prehistoric Frontiers: The Case of Formative Peru and Ecuador. In *Social and Economic Organization in the Prehispanic Andes*, ed. D. Browman et al, pp. 37–71. BAR International Series 194, Oxford. 1985a Concluding Remarks: Early Peruvian Civilization and its Relation to the Chavin Horizon. In *Early Ceremonial Architecture in the Andes*, ed. C. Donnan, pp. 269–289. Dumbarton Oaks Research Library and Collection, Washington, DC. 1985b Prehistoric Stylistic Change and Cultural Development at Huaricoto, Peru. *National Geographic Research* 1(4):505–534. 1987 The U-shaped pyramid complex, Cardal, Peru. *National Geographic Research* 3(3):363–375. 1988 Unity and Heterogeneity within the Chavín Horizon. In *Peruvian Prehistory*, ed. R. Keatinge, pp. 99–144. Cambridge U. Press, Cambridge. 1989 The Pre-Chavin Stone Sculpture of Casma and Pacopampa. *JFA* 16:478–485. 1990 A Preliminary Report on the 1990 Investigations at Mina Perdida, Lurin Valley, Peru. Paper presented at the Annual Meeting of the Northeast Conference of Andean Archaeology and Ethnohistory, SUNY, Binghamton. (Ms. in possession of author.)
Burger, R. L. and **F. Asaro.** 1978 Obsidian Distribution and Provenience in the Central Highlands and Coast of Peru during the Preceramic Period. *Contributions of the University of California Archaeological Research Facility* 36:51–83, Berkeley. 1979 Análisis de Rasgos Significativos en la Obsidiana de

los Andes Centrales. *RMN* 43(1977): 281–325.

Burger, R., F. Asaro, and H. Michel. 1984 The Source of the Obsidian Artifacts at Chavín de Huántar. In *The Prehistoric Occupation of Chavín de Huántar*, ed. R. Burger, pp. 263–270. U. of California Press, Berkeley.

Burger, R. L. and L. Salazar-Burger. 1980 Ritual and Religion at Huaricoto. *Archaeology* 36(6):26–32. 1985 The Early Ceremonial Center of Huaricoto. In *Early Ceremonial Architecture in the Andes*, ed. C. Donnan, pp. 111–138. Dumbarton Oaks Research Library and Collection, Washington, DC. 1986 Early Organizational Diversity in the Peruvian Highlands: Huaricoto and Kotosh. *Andean Archaeology: Papers in Memory of Clifford Evans*, ed. R. Matos et al, pp. 65–82. Institute of Archaeology, Monograph XXVII, UCLA, Los Angeles. 1991a Recent Investigations at the Initial Period Center of Cardal, Lurín Valley. *JFA* 18:275–296. 1991b A Preliminary Report on the Second Season of Investigations at Mina Perdida, Lurín Valley, Peru. Paper presented at the Annual Meeting of the N.E. Conference of Andean Arch. and Ethnohistory. New York.

Burger, R. L. and N. van der Merwe. 1990 Maize and the Origin of Highland Chavín Civilization: an Isotopic Perspective. *Am. Anth.* 92(1):85–95.

Bustamante, J. and E. Crousillat. 1974 *Análisis Hidráulico del Sitio Arqueológico de Chavín de Huántar.* Tesis de Grado, Programa Académico de Ingeniería Civil, UNI, Lima.

Callen, E. and T. W. Cameron. 1960 A Prehistoric Diet Revealed in Coprolites. *New Scientist* 8:35–40.

Cané, R. 1983 El Obelisco Tello de Chavín. *Boletín de Lima* 26:13–28. 1985 Problemas Arqueológicos e Iconográficos-Enfoques Nuevos. *Boletín de Lima* 37:38–44. 1986 Iconografía de Chavín "Caimanes o Cocodrílicos" y Sus Raíces Shamánicas. *Boletín de Lima* 45:86–95.

Cárdenas, M. 1979 *A Chronology of the Use of Marine Resources in Ancient Peru.* Publicación No. 104 del Instituto Riva-Agüero. Seminario de Arqueología, Pontificia Universidad Católica del Perú, Lima.

Cardich, A. 1964 Lauricocha, Fundamentos para una Prehistoria de los Andes Centrales. *Studia Praehistórica* III. Buenos Aires. 1973 Excavaciones en la Caverna de Huargo, Perú. *RMN* 39:11–29. 1976 Agricultores y Pastores en Lauricocha y Limites Superiores del Cultivo. *RMN* 41:11–36. 1985 The Fluctuating Upper Limits of Cultivation in the Central Andes and their Impact on Peruvian Prehistory. *Advances in World Arch.* 4:293–333. Academic Press, New York. 1988 *Civilización Andina: Su Formación.* CONCYTEC, Lima.

Carneiro, R. 1970 A Theory of the Origin of the State. *Science* 169:733–738.

Carrión Cachot, R. 1948 La Cultura Chavín: Dos Nuevas Colonias Kuntur Wasi y Ancón. *RMN de Antropología y Arqueología* 2(1):99–172. 1958 Ultimos Descubrimientos en Chavín–La Serpiente Símbolo de las Lluvias y de la Fecundidad. *Actas del 33 Congreso Internacional de Americanistas*, pp. 403–415. San José, Costa Rica.

Casafranca, J. 1960 Los Nuevos Sitios Chavinoides en el Departamento de Ayacucho. In *Antiguo Perú: Espacio y Tiempo*, ed. R. Matos, pp. 325–334. Editorial Juan Mejía Baca, Lima.

Caviedes, C. 1984 El Niño 1982–83. *Geographical Review* 74(3):267–290.

Chavez, S. and K. Mohr Chavez. 1976 Carved Stela from Taraco, Puno, Peru and the Definition of an Early Style of Stone Sculpture from the Altiplano of Peru and Bolivia. *Ñawpa Pacha* 13(1975):45–83.

Childe, V. 1950 The Urban Revolution. *The Town Planning Review* 21:3–17. 1951 *Man Makes Himself.* Watts, London.

Church. W. 1992 Summary of Investigations at Manachaki Cave in Current Research: Andean South America. *Am. Ant.* 57(1):155.

Cieza de León, P. 1922[1550] *La Crónica del Perú.* Calpe, Madrid. 1967 *El Señorío de los Incas*, Pt. 2 of *La Crónica del Perú.* Instituto de Estudios Peruanos, Lima.

Cobo, B. 1979 *History of the Inca Empire.* Trans. R. Hamilton. U. of Texas Press, Austin.

Coe, M. D. 1960 Archaeological Linkages with North and South America at La Victoria, Guatemala. *Am. Anth.* 62:363–393. 1967 Directions of Diffusion. *Science* 155(3759):185–186.

Cohen, M. 1978 Population Pressure and Origins of Agriculture: an Archaeological Example from the Coast of Peru. In *Advances in Andean Archaeology*, ed. D. L. Browman, pp. 91–132. Mouton Publishers, The Hague. 1979 Archaeological Plant Remains from the Central Coast of Peru, *Ñawpa Pacha* 16:23–50.

Collier, D. 1961 Agriculture and Civilization on the Coast of Peru. In *The Evolution of Horticultural Systems in Native South America – Courses and Consequences*, ed. J. Wilbert, pp. 101–109. Editorial Sucre, Caracas. 1962 Archaeological Investigations in the Casma Valley, Peru. *Proc. of the Thirty-fourth Congress of Americanists*, pp. 411–417. Vienna.

Colson, E. 1977 A Continuing Dialogue: Prophets and Local Shrines among the Tonga of Zambia. In *Regional Cults*, ed. R. Werbner, pp. 119–139. Academic Press, New York.

Conklin, W. J. 1971 Chavín Textiles and the Origins of Peruvian Weaving. *Textile Museum Journal* 3(2):13–19. 1978 The Revolutionary Weaving Investigations of the Early Horizon. *Ñawpa Pacha* 16:1–12. 1985 The Architecture of Huaca de los Reyes. In *Early Ceremonial Architecture in the Andes*, ed. C. B. Donnan, pp. 139–64. Dumbarton Oaks Research Library and Collection, Washington, DC.

Cordy-Collins, A. 1976 An Iconographic study of Chavín Textiles from the South Coast of Peru: the Discovery of a Pre-Columbian Catechism. Unpublished Ph.D. dissertation. U. of California, Los Angeles. 1977 Chavín Art: its Shamanic Hallucinogenic Origins. In *Pre-Columbian Art History*, ed. A. Cordy-Collins and J. Stern, pp. 353–362. Peek Publications, Palo Alto. 1979a The Dual Divinity Concept in Chavín Art. *El Dorado* 3:1–31. 1979b Cotton and the Staff God: Analysis of an Ancient Chavín Textile. In *Junius Bird Pre-Columbian Textile Conference*, ed. A. Pollard Rowe et al, pp. 51–60. The Textile Museum and Dumbarton Oaks, Washington, DC. 1980 An Artistic Record of the Chavin Hallucinatory Experience. *Masterkey* 54:84–93.

Cruzatt, A. 1971 Horizonte Temprano en el Valle de Ayacucho. *Anales Científicos* No. 1:605–631. Universidad Nacional del Centro de Huancayo.

Cueva Alarcón, N. 1982 *Pacopampa.* Seminario de Historia Rural Andino, UNMSM, Lima.

Daggett, R. 1987a Toward the Development of the State on the North Central Coast of Peru. In *The Origins and Development of the Andean State*, ed. J. Haas et al, pp. 70–82. Cambridge U. Press, Cambridge. 1987b Reconstructing the Evidence for Cerro Blanco and Punkurí. In *Andean Past* 1:111–163. Cornell University, Ithaca.

Daniel, F. 1968 *The First Civilizations: The Archaeology of Their Origins.* Thomas Y. Crowell Company, New York.

Davidson, J. 1982 Ecology, Art, and Myth: A Natural Approach to Symbolism. In *Pre-Columbian Art History: Selected Readings*, ed. A. Cordy-Collins, pp. 331–343. Peek Publications, Palo Alto.

DeBoer, W. 1975 Binó Style Ceramics from Iparia. *Ñawpa Pacha* 10–12:91–108. 1984 *Archaeological Reconnaissance in the Central Huallaga, Department of San Martín, Northeastern Peru.* Department of Anthropology, Queens College, CUNY, New York.

Dillehay, T. D. 1979 Pre-Hispanic Resource Sharing in the Central Andes. *Science* 204:24–31.

Dillehay T. and M. Collins. 1991 Monte Verde, Chile: A Comment on Lynch. *Am. Ant.* 56(2):333–341.

Dillehay, T. and P. Netherly. 1983 Exploring the Upper Zaña Valley of Peru. *Archaeology* 37:22–30.

Donkin, R. A. 1979 *Agricultural Terracing in the Aboriginal New World.* Viking Press Publications in Anthropology 56. U. of Arizona Press, Tucson.

Duviols, P. 1967 Un Inédito de Cristóbal de Albornoz: La Instrucción para Descubrir Todas las Guacas del Perú y sus Camayos y Haciendas. *Journal de la Société des Americanistes* 56(1):7–39. 1976 Punchao, Idolo Mayor del Coricancha, Historia, y Tipología. *Antropología Andina* 1–2.

Eddy, J. 1977 Climate and the Changing Sun. *Climatic Change* 1:173–190.

Elera, C. 1983 Morro de Eten, Valle de Lambayeque. *Boletín* 8:25–6. Museo Nacional de Antropología y Arqueología, Lima. 1986 *Investigaciones sobre Patrones Funerarios en el Sitio Formativo del Morro de Eten, Valle de Lambayeque, Costa Norte del Perú.* Memoria de Bachiller, Pontificia Universidad Católica del Peru, Lima.

Emmerich, A. 1965 *Sweat of the Sun, and Tears of the Moon.* U. of Washington Press, Seattle.

Engel, F. 1956 Curayacu – a Chavinoid Site. *Archaeology* 9(2):98–105. 1963 A Preceramic Settlement on the Coast of Peru: Asia, Unit 1, *Transactions of the American Philosophical Society* 53(3). 1967 El Complejo El Paraíso en el Valle del Chillón Habitado Hace 3,500 Años:

Nuevos Aspectos de la Civilización de los Agricultores del Pallar. *Anales Científicos de la Universidad Agraria* 5:241–280. Lima.

Erasmus, C. 1965 Monument Building: Some Field Experiments. *Southwestern Journal of Anth.* 21(4):277–301.

Espejo, J. 1951 Exploraciones Arqueológicas en las Cabeceras del Pukcha (Perú). *Cuadernos Americanos* LVI(2):139–152. Mexico. 1955 Gotush: Nuevos Descubrimientos en Chavín. *Baessler-Archiv.* n.f. III:123–136. Berlin. 1959 Rumi Chaka de Chavín (Pesquisa Bibliográfica). *Chimor* V–VI:32–38. Trujillo.

Estete, M. de. 1968 [c.1535] Noticia del Peru. In *Biblioteca Peruana*, Primera Serie I, pp. 345–402. Editores Técnicos Asociados SA, Lima.

Feldman, R. 1980 *Aspero, Peru: Architecture, Subsistence Economy and Other Artifacts of a Preceramic Maritime Chiefdom.* Ph.D. dissertation, Dept. of Anthropology, Harvard U. 1983 From Maritime Chiefdom to Agricultural State in Formative Coastal Peru. In *Civilization in the Ancient Americas: Essays in Honor of Gordon Willey*, ed. R. Leventhal and A. Kolata, pp. 289–310. U. of New Mexico and Peabody Museum of Archaeology and Ethnology, Cambridge, Mass. 1985 Preceramic Corporate Architecture: Evidence for the Development of Non-egalitarian Social Systems in Peru. In *Early Ceremonial Centers in the Andes*, ed. C. Donnan, pp. 71–92. Dumbarton Oaks, Washington, DC. 1991 Preceramic Unbaked Clay Figurines from Aspero, Peru. In *The New World Figurine Project*, vol. 1, ed. T. Stocker, pp. 5–19. Research Press, Provo, Utah.

Fiedler, R. 1944 The Peruvian Fisheries. *Geographical Review* 34:97–119.

Flannery, K. 1973 The Origins of Agriculture. *Annual Review of Anthropology* 2:271–310. Palo Alto.

Flores, I. 1960 Wischqana. Sitio Temprano en Ayacucho. In *Antiguo Perú: Espacio y Tiempo*, ed. R. Matos, pp. 335–344. Editorial Juan Mejía Baca, Lima. 1975 *El Mirador: Sitio Arqueológico.* Seminario de Historia Rural Andino, UNMSM, Lima.

Flores, J. 1968 *Los Pastores de Paratia: Una Introducción a Su Estudio.* Instituto Indigenista Interamericano Serie Antropología Social vol. 10, Mexico.

Frankfort, H. 1951 *The Birth of Civilization in the Near East.* Doubleday, New York.

Friis-Christensen, E. and K. Lassen. 1991 Length of the Solar Cycle: An Indicator of Solar Activity Closely Related with Climate. *Science* 254:698–700.

Frikel, P. 1961 Mori – a Festa do Rape. Indios Kachúyana: Río Trombetas. *Boletín do Museu Paraense Emilio Goeldi.* Antropologia, novo serie, 12:10–34. Belém, Brazil.

Fung, R. 1972a Las Aldas: Su Ubicación Dentro del Proceso Histórico del Perú Antiguo. *Dédalo* 9–10. São Paulo. 1972b Nuevos Datos para el Período de Cerámica Inicial en el Valle de Casma. *Arqueología y Sociedad* 7–8:1–12. 1976 Excavaciones en Pacopampa, Cajamarca. *RMN* 41:129–207.

Fung, R. and V. Pimentel. 1973 Chankillo. *RMN* 39:71–80.

Fung, R. and C. Williams. 1979 Exploraciones y Excavaciones en el Valle de Sechín, Casma. *RMN* 43:111–155.

Gade, D. 1967 The Guinea Pig in Andean Folk Culture. *The Geographical Review* 57:213–224.

Garbett, K. 1977 Disparate Regional Cults and a Unitary Field in Zimbabwe. In *Regional Cults*, ed. R. P. Werbner, pp. 55–92. Academic Press, New York.

Gayton, A. 1967 Textiles from Hacha, Peru. *Ñawpa Pacha* 5:1–14.

Grieder, T. 1975 A Dated Sequence for Building and Pottery at Las Haldas. *Ñawpa Pacha* 13:99–112.

Grieder, T. and A. Bueno. 1981 La Galgada: Peru Before Pottery. *Archaeology* 34(2):44–51. 1985 Ceremonial Architecture at La Galgada. In *Early Ceremonial Architecture in the Andes*, ed. C. Donnan, pp. 93–109. Dumbarton Oaks Research Library and Collection, Washington, DC.

Grieder, T., A. Bueno, C. Earle Smith, Jr., and R. Malina. 1988 *La Galgada, Peru: A Preceramic Culture in Transition*. U. of Texas Press, Austin.

Grobman, A., W. Salhuana, and R. Sevilla. 1961 *Races of Maize in Peru*. National Academy of Sciences Publication 915. National Research Council, Washington, DC.

Grossman, J. W. 1972 An Ancient Gold Worker's Tool Kit: the Earliest Metal Technology in Peru. *Archaeology* 25(4):270–275. 1985 Demographic Change and Economic Transformation in the South Central Highlands of Pre-Huari Peru. *Ñawpa Pacha* 21:45–126.

Gruhn, R. and A. Bryan. 1991 A Review of Lynch's Description of South America Pleistocene Sites. *Am. Ant.* 56(2):342–348.

Guaman Poma de Ayala, F. 1980[1614] *Primer Nueva Corónica y Buen Gobierno*, critical edition by J. Murra and R. Adorno, trans. and textual analysis of Quechua by J. Urioste. 3. vols. Siglo Veintiuno, Mexico City.

Guffroy, J. 1989 Un Centro Ceremonial Formativo en el Alto Piura. *Bulletin de l'Institut Francais d'Etudes Andines* 18(2):161–207. Lima.

Guffroy, J., N. Almeida, P. Lecoq, C. Caillaret, F. Duverneuil, L. Emperaire, and B. Arnaud. 1987 *Loja Prehispanique*. Editions Recherche sur les Civilisations, Paris.

Guffroy, J., P. Kaulicke, and K. Makowski. 1989 La Prehistoria del Departamento de Piura: Estado de los Conocimientos y Problemática. *Bulletin de l'Institut Francais d'Etudes Andines* 18(20):117–142.

Haas, J. 1982 *The Evolution of the Prehistoric State*. Columbia U. Press, New York.

Harner, M. 1972 *The Jívaro: People of the Sacred Waterfalls*. Doubleday/Natural History Press, Garden City, NY.

Hartline, B. 1980 Coastal Upwelling: Physical Factors Feed Fish. *Science* 208:38–40.

Hastorf, C., T. Earle, H. E. Wright, Jr., L. Le Count, G. Russel, and E. Sandefur. 1989 Settlement Archaeology in the Jauja Region of Peru: Evidence from the Early Intermediate Period through the Late Intermediate Period: A Report on the 1986 Field Season. *Andean Past* 2:81–129.

Heine-Geldern, R. 1959 Representations of the Asiatic Tiger in the Art of the Chavin Culture: A Proof of Early Contacts between China and Peru. In *Proc. of the 33rd International Congress of Americanists*, vol. I:321–326. Lehmann, San Jose, Costa Rica.

Hill, B. 1975 A New Chronology of the Valdivia Complex from the Coastal Zone of Guayas Province, Ecuador. *Ñawpa Pacha* 10–12:1–32.

Hodder, I. 1977 The Distribution of Material Culture Items in the Baringo District, W. Kenya. *Man* 12:239–269. 1982 *Symbols in Action: Ethnoarchaeological Studies of Material Culture*. Cambridge U. Press, New York.

Idrovo, J. 1992 *El Formativo Ecuatoriano*. Offset "Atlantida," Cuenca.

Isbell, B. J. 1978 *To Defend Ourselves: Ecology and Ritual in an Andean Village*. U. of Texas Press, Austin.

Isbell, W. 1976 Cosmological Order Expressed in Prehistoric Ceremonial Centers. *Actes du XLII Congres International des Americanistes* IV:269–299.

Ishida, E. et al. 1960 *Andes 1: The Report of the University of Tokyo Scientific Expedition to the Andes in 1958*. Bijitsu Shuppan Sha, Tokyo.

Izumi, S. 1971 The Development of the Formative Culture in the Ceja de Montaña: A Viewpoint Based on the Materials from the Kotosh Site. In *Dumbarton Oaks Conference on Chavin*, ed. E. Benson, pp. 49–72. Dumbarton Oaks Research Library and Collection, Washington, DC.

Izumi, S., P. Cuculiza, and C. Kano. 1972 Excavations at Shillacoto, Huanuco, Peru. *The University Museum Bulletin No. 3*. U. of Tokyo, Tokyo.

Izumi, S. and T. Sono. 1963 *Andes 2: Excavations at Kotosh, Peru, 1960*. Kadokawa Publishing Co., Tokyo.

Izumi, S. and K. Terada. 1966 *Andes 3 – Excavations at Pechiche and Garbanzal Tumbes Valley, Peru*. Kudokawa Publishing Co., Tokyo. 1972 *Andes 4: Excavations at Kotosh, Peru 1963 and 1966*. U. of Tokyo Press, Tokyo.

Jimenez Borja, A. and A. Bueno. 1970 Breves Notas Acerca de Pachacamac. *Arqueología y Sociedad* 4:13–25.

Julien M. 1981 La Industria Osea de Tellarmachay, Período Formativo. *RMN* 44:69–94.

Kano, C. 1979 The Origins of the Chavin Culture. *Studies in Pre-Columbian Art and Archaeology*, No. 22. Dumbarton Oaks Research Library and Collection, Washington, DC.

Kauffmann Doig, F. 1971 *Arqueología Peruana: Visión Integral*. Peisa, S.A., Lima. 1978 *Manual de Arqueología Peruana*. Ediciones PEISA, Lima. 1979 *Sechín: Ensayo de Arqueología Iconográfica*. *Arqueológicas* 18:101–42. 1981 *Introducción a la Cultura Chavin*. In *Chavin Formativo*, ed. J. de Lavalle and W. Lang, pp. 9–42. Banco de Crédito del Perú en la Cultura, Lima.

Kaulicke, P. 1975 *Pandanche. Un Caso del Formativo en los Andes de Cajamarca*. Seminario de Historia Rural Andina, UNMSM, Lima. 1976 *El Formativo de Pacopampa*. Seminario de Historia Rural Andina, UNMSM, Lima. 1981 *Keramik der Frühen Initialperiode aus Pandanche, Dpto. Cajamarca, Peru*. *Beiträge zur Allgemeinen und Vergleichenden Archäologie* 3:363–389. Munich.

Keatinge, R. 1980 Archaeology and Development: the Tembladera Sites of the Peruvian North Coast. *JFA* 7:467–475. 1981 The Nature and Role of Religious Diffusion in the Early Stages of State Formation: an Example from Peruvian Prehistory. In *The Transition to Statehood in the New World*, ed. G. Jones and R. Kautz, pp. 172–187. Cambridge U. Press, New York. 1988 *Peruvian Prehistory*. Cambridge U. Press, Cambridge and New York.

Kidder, A. II, L. Lumbreras, and D. B. Smith. 1963 Cultural Developments in the Central Andes. In *Aboriginal Cultural Development in Latin America: an Interpretive Review*, ed. B. Meggers and C. Evans, pp. 89–102. Smithsonian Miscellaneous Collections vol. 146(1), Washington, DC.

Kirch, P. 1990 Monumental Architecture and Power in Polynesian Chiefdoms: a Comparison of Tonga and Hawaii. *World Arch.* 22(2):206–221.

Kosok, P. 1965 *Life, Land and Water in Ancient Peru*. Long Island U. Press, New York.

Kroeber, A. 1944 *Peruvian Archaeology in 1942*. Viking Fund Publications in Anthropology No. 4, New York. 1947 Esthetic and Recreational Activities: Art. In *Handbook of South American Indians*, vol. 5, ed. J. Steward, pp. 411–492. U.S. Government Printing Office, Washington, DC. 1953 Paracas Cavernas and Chavin. *U. of California Publications in Am. Arch. and Ethn.* 40(8):313–348. Berkeley. 1963 *Anthropology: Culture Patterns and Processes*. Harcourt, Brace and World, New York.

Krzanowski, A. 1983 Ecología de Asentamientos Tempranos en las Andes Septentrionales del Perú. *Acta Archaeologia Carpathica* 22:245–266. 1986a *Cayash Prehispánico*. Polska Akademia Nauk – Oddzial w Krakowie, 25. Zaklad Narodowy im Ossolinskich-Wydawnictwo Wroclaw, Krakow. 1986b The Cultural Chronology of Northern Andes of Peru (The Huamachuco-Quiruvilca-Otuzco Region). *Acta Archaeologica Carpathica* XXV:231–264.

Kubler, G. 1975 *The Art and Architecture of Ancient America: The Mexican/Maya and Andean Peoples*. Penguin Books, Harmondsworth.

Lanning, E. 1963 A Ceramic Sequence for the Piura and Chira Coast, North Peru. *U. of California Publications in Am. Arch. and Ethn.* 46:135–184. Berkeley. 1967 *Peru Before the Incas*. Prentice-Hall, Englewood Cliffs, NJ.

Larco Hoyle, R. 1941 *Los Cupisniques*. Casa Editora La Crónica y Variedades, Lima. 1946 A Culture Sequence for the North Coast of Peru. In *The Handbook of South American Indians*, vol. 2, pp. 149–175, ed. J. Steward, US Government Printing Office, Washington, DC.

Lathrap, D. 1966 Relationships between Mesoamerica and the Andean areas. *Handbook of Middle American Indians*, vol. 4, ed. G. Eckholm and G. Willey, pp. 265–275. U. of Texas Press, Austin. 1970 *The Upper Amazon*. Thames and Hudson, London. 1971 The Tropical Forest and the Cultural Context of Chavin. In *Dumbarton Oaks Conference on Chavin (1968)*, ed. E. Benson, pp. 73–100. Dumbarton Oaks Research Library and Collection. 1973a Gifts of the Cayman: Some Thoughts on the Subsistence Basis of Chavin. In *Variation in Anthropology: Essays in Honor of John C. McGregor*, ed. D. Lathrap and J. Douglas, pp. 91–103. Illinois Archaeological Survey, Urbana. 1973b The Antiquity and Importance of Long-Distance Trade Relationships in the Moist Tropics of the Pre-Columbian South America. *World Arch.* 5(2):170–186. 1977 Our Father the Cayman, Our Mother the Gourd: Spinden Revisited, or a Unitary Model for the Emergence of Agriculture in the New World. In *Origins of Agriculture*, ed. C. Reed, pp. 713–752. Mouton Publishers, The Hague. 1985 Jaws: the Control of Power in the Early Nuclear American Ceremonial Center. In *Early Ceremonial Architecture in the Andes*. ed. C. B. Donnan, pp. 241–267. Dumbarton Oaks Research Library and Collection, Washington, DC.

Lathrap, D., D. Collier, and H. Chandra. 1975 *Ancient Ecuador: Culture, Clay and Creativity 3000–300 B.C.* Field Museum of Natural History, Chicago.

Lathrap, D., J. Marcos, and J. Zeidler. 1977 Real Alto: an Ancient Ceremonial Center. *Archaeology* 30:2–13.

Lathrap, D. and L. Roys. 1963 The Archaeology of the Cave of the Owls in the Upper Montaña of Peru. *Am. Ant.* 29(1):27–38.

Lavalle, J. de and W. Lang. 1979 *Arte y Tesoros del Perú, 3: Pintura*. Introductions by L. Lumbreras and J. Reid. Banco de Crédito del Perú, Lima. 1981 *Chavin Formativo*. Banco de Crédito del Perú, Lima.

Lavallée, D. 1979 Tellarmachay: Campamento de Pastores en la Puna de Junin del Período Formativo. *RMN* XLIII (1977):61–109.

Lavallée, D. and M. Julien. 1976 El Habitat Prehistórico en la Zona de San Pedro de Cajas, Junin. *RMN* 41(1975):81–127.

Lavallée, D., M. Julien, and J. Wheeler. 1984 Telarmachay: Niveles Precerámicos de Ocupación. *RMN* 46:55–127.

Lechtman, H. 1980 The Central Andes: Metallurgy Without Iron. In *The Coming of the Age of Iron*, ed. T. Wertime and J. Muhly, pp. 267–334. Yale U. Press, New Haven. 1984 Technical Examination of a Gold Alloy Object from Chavin de Huántar. In *The Prehistoric Occupation of Chavin de Huántar, Peru*, ed. R. Burger, pp. 271–276. U. of California Press, Berkeley.

León, J. 1964 *Plantas Alimenticias Andinas*. Boletin Técnico 6, Instituto Interamericano de Ciencias Agrícolas Zona Andina, Lima.

Lettau, H. H. and K. Lettau. 1978 *Exploring the World's Driest Climate*. Institute for Environmental Studies, Report 101, U. of Wisconsin, Madison.

Lothrop, S. K. 1941 Gold Ornaments of Chavin Style from Chongoyape, Peru. *Am. Ant.* 6(3):250–261. 1951 Gold Artifacts of Chavin. *Am. Ant.* 16(3):226–240.

Ludeña, H. 1975 *Secuencia Cronológica y Cultural del Valle del Chillón*. Tesis para optar el Grado de Doctor Especialidad Arqueología. UNMSM, Lima.

Lumbreras, L. G. 1970 *Los Templos de Chavín*. Corporación Peruana de Santa, Lima. 1971 Towards a Re-evaluation of Chavín. In *Dumbarton Oaks Conference on Chavín*, ed. E. Benson, pp. 1–28. Dumbarton Oaks Research Library and Collection, Washington, DC. 1974a *The Peoples and Cultures of Ancient Peru*. Smithsonian Institution Press, Washington, DC. 1974b *Las Fundaciones de Huamanga: Hacia una Prehistoria de Ayacucho*. Editorial "Nueva Educación" for El Club Huamanga, Lima. 1977 Excavaciones en el Templo Antiguo de Chavín (Sector R): Informe de la Sexta Campana. *Ñawpa Pacha* 15:1–38. 1989 *Chavín de Huántar en el Nacimiento de la Civilización Andina*. INDEA, Lima.

Lumbreras, L. G. and H. Amat. 1969 Informe Preliminar sobre las Galerías Interiores de Chavín (Primera Temporada de Trabajos). *RMN* 34(1965–1966):143–197.

Lumbreras, L., C. González, and B. Lietaer. 1976 Acerca de la Función del Sistema Hidráulico de Chavín. *Investigaciones de Campo No. 2*. Museo Nacional de Antropología y Arqueología, Lima.

Lynch, T. 1978 The Paleo-Indians. In *Ancient South Americans*, ed. J. Jennings. W. H. Freeman, San Francisco. 1980 *Guitarrero Cave: Early Man in the Andes*. Academic Press, New York. 1990 Glacial-Age Man in South America: A Cultural Review. *An. Ant.* 55:12–36. 1991 Lack of Evidence for Glacial-Age Settlement of South America: Reply to Dillehay and Collins and to Gruhn and Bryan. *Am. Ant.* 56(2):348–355.

Lyon, P. 1974 *Native South Americans: Ethnology of the Least Known Continent*. Little, Brown and Company, New York. 1978 Female Supernaturals in Ancient Peru. *Ñawpa Pacha* 16:95–140.

MacNeish, R. S. 1977 The Beginning of Agriculture in Central Peru. In *Origins of Agriculture*, ed. A. Reed, pp. 753–780. Mouton Publishers, The Hague. 1981 Synthesis and Conclusions. In *Prehistory of the Ayacucho Basin, Peru*, vol. II, *Excavations and Chronology*, ed. R. S. MacNeish et al., pp. 199–257. U. of Michigan Press, Ann Arbor.

MacNeish, R., T. Patterson, and D. Browman. 1975 *The Central Peruvian Prehistoric Interaction Sphere*. Papers of the R. S. Peabody Foundation for Archaeology, No. 7, Andover, Mass.

Marcos, J. 1986a De Ida y Vuelta a Acapulco con Mercaderes de Mullu. In *Arqueologia de la Costa Ecuatoriana: Nuevos Enfoques*, ed. J. Marcos, pp. 163–196. Biblioteca Ecuatoriana de Arqueología. ESPOL, Guayaquil. 1986b Intercambio a Larga Distancia en América: el Caso de Spondylus. In *Arqueologia de la Costa Ecuatoriana: Nuevos Enfoques*, ed. J. Marcos, pp. 197–206. Biblioteca Ecuatoriana de Arqueología. ESPOL, Guayaquil. 1988 *Real Alto: La Historia de un Centro Ceremonial Valdivia*. 2 vols. Biblioteca Ecuatoriana de Arqueología. ESPOL, Guayaquil.

Marcos, J. and P. Norton. 1981 Interpretación sobre la Arqueología de la Isla de la Plata. *Miscelánea Antropológica Ecuatoriana* 1:136–154. Guayaquil.

Marcus, J. and J. Silva. 1988 The Chillón Valley "Cocalands": Archaeological Background and Ecological Context. In *Conflicts over Coca Fields in the XVIth-century Perú*, ed. M. Rostworowski de Diez Canseco, pp. 1–32. Memoirs of the Museum of Anthropology, U. of Michigan, No. 21, Ann Arbor.

Martins, R. 1976 *New Archaeological Techniques for the Studies of Ancient Root Crops in Peru*. Ph.D. dissertation, University of Birmingham.

Matos, R. 1959 *Exploraciones Arqueológicas en Huancavelica*. B.A. thesis, UNMSM, Lima. 1968 A Formative Period Painted Pottery Complex at Ancón, Peru. *Am. Ant.* 38:226–231. 1972 Alfareros y Agricultores. In *Pueblos y Culturas de la Sierra Central del Perú*, ed. D. Bonavia and R. Ravines, pp. 35–43. Cerro de Pasco Corporation, Lima. 1973 Ataura: un Centro Chavín en el Valle del Mantaro. *RMN* 38(1972):93–108. 1976 Prehistoria y Ecología Humana en las Punas de Junin. *RMN* 41:37–80. 1978 The Cultural and Ecological Context of the Mantaro Valley during the Formative Period. In *Advances in Andean Archaeology*, ed. D. L. Browman, pp. 307–325. Mouton Publishers, The Hague.

Matos, R. and J. Rick. 1981 Los Recursos Naturales y el Poblamiento Precerámico de la Puna de Junin. *RMN* 44:23–64.

Matsuzawa, T. 1978 The Formative Site of Las Haldas, Peru: Architecture and Chronology. Trans. I. Shimada. *Am. Ant.* 43:652–673.

Matthiesen, D. 1988 Preceramic Animal Use at Huaca Prieta. In *Economic Prehistory of the Central Andes*, ed. E. Wing and J. Wheeler, pp. 18–30. BAR International Series 427, Oxford.

Mayer, E. 1985 Production Zones. In *Andean Ecology and Civilization: An Interdisciplinary Perspective on Ecological Complementarity*, ed. S. Masuda et al, pp. 45–84. Tokyo U. Press, Tokyo.

Meggers, B. 1966 *Ecuador*. Praeger, New York. 1971 *Man and Culture in a Counterfeit Paradise*. Aldine Atherton, Inc.

Meggers, B., C. Evans, and E. Estrada. 1965 *Early Formative Period of Coastal Ecuador: the Valdivia and Machalilla Phases*. Smithsonian Contributions to Anthropology, vol. 1, Washington, DC.

Mejía Xesspe, T. 1968 Pintura Chavinoide en los Lindes del Arte Rupestre. *Revista "San Marcos"* 9:15–32. 1972 Algunos Restos Arqueológicos del Periodo Pre-Paracas en el Valle de Palpa, Ica. *Arqueología y Sociedad* 7–8:78–86.

Menzel, D., J. Rowe, and L. Dawson. 1964 *The Paracas Pottery of Ica: A Study in Style and Time*. U. of California Publications in Am. Arch. and Ethn., vol. 50, Berkeley.

Miasta, J. 1978 *El Alto Amazonas: Arqueología de Jaen y San Ignacio, Perú*. Seminario de Historia Rural Andino, UNMSM, Lima.

Miller, G. 1979 *An Introduction to the Ethnoarchaeology of the Andean Camelids*. Ph.D. dissertation, Dept of Anth., U. of California, Berkeley. 1984 Deer Hunters, and Llama Herders: Animal Species Selection at Chavin. In *The Prehistoric Occupation of Chavin de Huantar*, ed. R. Burger, pp. 282–287. U. of California Press, Berkeley.

Miller, G. and R. L. Burger. n.d. We Don't Eat Caymans Here: An Exploration of the Ideoeconomic Universe of Chavin de Huantar. Manuscript submitted to *Am. Ant.*

Miller, G. and A. Gill. 1990 Zooarchaeology at Pirincay, a Formative Site in Highland Ecuador. *JFA* 17(13):49–68.

Mishkin, B. 1940 Cosmological Ideas among the Indians of the Southern Andes. *Journal of American Folklore* 53:225–241. Salem.

Mitchell, W. 1973 The Hydraulic Hypothesis: A Reappraisal. *Current Anth.* 14(5):532–534.

Mohr Chavez, K. 1982–83 The Archaeology of Marcavalle, an Early Horizon Site in the Valley of Cuzco, Peru. *Baessler-Archiv, n.f.* 28:203–329; 29:107–205, 241–386. 1988 The Significance of Chiripa in Lake Titicaca Basin Developments. *Expedition* 30(3):17–26.

Molina, C. de. 1943 *Relación de las Fábulas y Ritos de los Incas [1575]*. Los Pequeños Grandes Libros de Historia Americana. Serie 1, vol. 4, pp. 5–84. Imprenta Miranda, Lima.

Morales, D. 1977 Excavaciones en Las Salinas de San Blas. *Seminario Arqueológico* 1:27–48. Seminario de Historia Rural Andina, UNMSM, Lima. 1980 *El Dios Felino en Pacopampa*. Seminario de Historia Rural Andina, UNMSM, Lima. 1982 Cerámica Pacopampa y Mitología del Dios Felino. *Boletin de Lima* 19:45–53.

Moran, E. 1981 Ecological, Anthropological and Agronomic Research in the Amazon Basin. *Latin American Research Review*:3–40.

Morgan, L. 1967 [1877] *Ancient Society*. World Press, Cleveland.

Morris, C. 1974 Reconstructing Patterns of Non-agricultural Production in the Inca Economy: Archaeology and Documents in Institutional Analysis. In *The Reconstruction of Complex Societies: An Archaeological Symposium*, ed. C. Moore, pp. 49–60, American Schools of Oriental Research, Chicago.

Moseley, M. 1975 *The Maritime Foundations of Andean Civilization*. Cummings Publishing Company, Menlo Park, California. 1983a The Good Old Days Were Better: Agrarian Collapse and Techtonics. *Am. Anth.* 85(40):773–799. 1983b Patterns of Settlement and Preservation in the Viru and Moche Valleys. In *Prehistoric Settlement Patterns*, ed. E.Z. Vogt and R. Leventhal, pp. 423–442. U. of New Mexico Press, Albuquerque. 1985 The Exploration and Explanation of Early Monumental Architecture. In *Early Ceremonial Architecture in the Andes*, ed. C. Donnan, pp. 29–57. Dumbarton Oaks Research Library and Collection, Washington, DC. 1992 *The Incas and their Ancestors*. Thames and Hudson, London & New York.

Moseley, M. and L. Barrett. 1969 Change in Preceramic Twined Textiles from the Central Peruvian Coast. *Am. Ant.* 34:162–165.

Moseley, M. and R. Feldman. 1988 Fishing, Farming, and the Foundations of Andean Civilization. In *The Archaeology of the Prehistoric Coastlines*, ed. G. Bailey and J. Parkington, pp. 125–134. Cambridge U. Press, New York.

Moseley, M., R. Feldman, and C. Ortloff. 1981 Living with Crisis: Human Perception of Process and Time. In *Biotic Crises in Ecological and Evolutionary Time*, ed. M. Nitecki:231–267. Academic Press, New York.

Moseley, M. and L. Watanabe. 1974 The Adobe Sculpture of Huaca de los Reyes. *Archaeology* 2:154–161.

Moseley, M. and G. Willey. 1973 Aspero, Peru: a Reexamination of the Site and its Implications. *Am. Ant.* 38:452–468.

Muelle, J. 1937 Filogenia de la Estela Raimondi. *RMN* 6(1):135–150. 1955 Del Estilo Chavín. *Baessler-Archiv*, n.f. III:89–96. Berlin. 1957 Puntas de Pizarra Pulida del Perú. *Arqueológicas* 1:48–63. Lima.

Murphy, R. 1926 Oceania and Climatic Phenomena along the West Coast of South America during 1925. *Geographical Review* 16:26–54.

Netherly, P. 1984 The Management of Late Andean Irrigation Systems on the North Coast of Peru. *Am. Ant.* 49:227–254.

Netherly, P. and T. Dillehay. 1986 Duality in Public Architecture in the Upper Zaña Valley, Northern Peru. In *Perspectives on Andean Prehistory and Protohistory*, ed. D. Sandweiss and D. P. Kvietok, pp. 85–114. Latin American Studies Program, Cornell U., Ithaca.

Nials, F. L., E. E. Deeds, M. E., Moseley, S. Pozorski, T. Pozorski, and R. Feldman. 1979 El Niño: the Catastrophic Flooding of Coastal Peru. *Field Museum of Natural History Bulletin* 50(7):4–14; 50(8):4–10.

Nomland, G. 1939 New Archaeological Site at San Blas, Junin. *RMN* 8(1):61–66.

Ochatoma, J. A. 1985 *Acerca del Formativo en la Sierra Centro-Sur*. Tesis para optar el Titulo de Licenciado en Arqueología, Instituto Profesional de Arqueología e Historia, Facultad de Ciencias Sociales, Universidad Nacional de San Cristobal de Huamanga, Ayacucho.

Ochatoma, J., A. Pariahuamán, and V. Larrea. 1984 ¿Cupisnique en Ayacucho? *Gaceta Arqueológica Andina* 9:10.

ONERN (Oficina Nacional de Evaluación de Recursos Naturales). 1976 *Mapa Ecológico del Perú y Guía Explicativa*. Lima.

Onuki, Y. 1982 La Pampa Como Centro Ceremonial. Paper presented at the Dumbarton Oaks Conference on Early Ceremonial Architecture in the Andes, Washington, DC. 1985 The Yunga Zone in the Prehistory of the Central Andes: Vertical and Horizontal Dimensions in Andean Ecological and Cultural Processes. In *Andean Ecology and Civilization*, ed. S. Masuda et al, pp. 339–356. U. of Tokyo Press, Tokyo. 1990 Kintouro-Washi No Haka to Ōgon. *Bijutsu Hakubutsu Kan Niyusu* 25:2–4. Tokyo. 1991 Summary of Investigations at Huacaloma, Kolguitín and Kuntur Wasi in Current Investigations: Andean South America. *Am. Ant.* 56(1):154–155.

Onuki, Y. and T. Fujii. 1974 Excavations at La Pampa, Peru. *The Proc. of the Dept. of Humanities, College of General Education, University of Tokyo* 59:45–104. Tokyo.

Osborn, A. 1977 Strandlopers, Mermaids and Other Fairy Tales: Ecological Determinants of Marine Resource Utilization–the Peruvian Case. In *For Theory Building in Archaeology*, ed. L. R. Binford, pp. 157–205. Academic Press, New York.

Parsons, J. and **R. Matos.** 1978 Asentamientos Prehispánicos en el Mantaro, Perú: Informe Preliminar. In *Actas y Trabajos del III Congreso del Hombre y Cultura Andina*, vol. 2, ed. R. Matos, pp. 540–555. Lima.

Parsons, M. 1970 Preceramic Subsistence on the Central Coast. *Am. Ant.* 35:292–304.

Pasztory, E. 1984 The Function of Art in Mesoamerica. *Archaeology* 37(1):18–25.

Patterson, T. C. 1971a Population and Economy in Central Peru. *Archaeology* 24:316–321. 1971b Chavin: An Interpretation of Its Spread and Influence. In *Dumbarton Oaks Conference on Chavin*, ed. E. Benson, pp. 29–48. Dumbarton Oaks Research Library and Collection, Washington, DC. 1981 *Archaeology: The Evolution of Ancient Societies*. Prentice Hall, Englewood Cliffs, NJ. 1983 The Historical Development of a Coastal Andean Social Formation in Central Peru, 6000–500 BC. In *Investigations of the Andean Past*, ed. D. Sandweiss, pp. 21–37. Cornell U. Latin American Studies Program, Ithaca. 1984 The Ancón Shellmounds and Social Relations on the Central Coast during the Second Millennium BC. Paper presented at the annual meeting of the Institute of Andean Studies, January, 1984, Berkeley. 1985 The Huaca La Florida, Rimac Valley, Peru. In *Early Ceremonial Architecture in the Andes*, ed. C. Donnan, pp. 59–69. Dumbarton Oaks Research Library and Collection, Washington, DC. 1991 *The Inca Empire: the Formation and Disintegration of a Pre-Capitalist State*. Berg Publishers, Oxford and New York.

Patterson, T. C., R. Burger, and **D. Wallace.** n.d. *The Archaeology of the Ancón Shellmounds*. Book manuscript in possession of the authors.

Patterson, T. and **M. Moseley.** 1968 Late Preceramic and Early Ceramic Cultures of the Central Coast of Peru. *Ñawpa Pacha* 6:115–133.

Pearsall, D. 1978 Paleoethnobotany in Western South America: Progress and Problems. In *Nature and Status of Ethnobotany*, ed. R. I. Ford, pp. 389–416. Anthropological Papers of the Museum of Anth., U. of Michigan, vol. 67, Ann Arbor. 1980 Pachamachay Ethnobotanical Report: Plant Utilization at a Hunting Base Camp. In *Prehistoric Hunters of the High Andes*, ed. J. Rick. Academic Press, New York.

Pearson, G., J. R. Pilcher, Jr., M. G. Baille, D. M. Corbett, and **F. Qua.** 1986 High-Precision ^{14}C Measurement of Irish Oaks to Show the Natural ^{14}C Variations from AD 1840–5210 BC. *Radiocarbon* 28:911–934.

Pearson, G. and **M. Stuiver.** 1986 High-Precision Calibration of the Radiocarbon Time Scale 500–2500 BC. *Radiocarbon* 28:839–862.

Petersen, G. 1970 Minería y Metalurgia en el Antiguo Perú. *Arqueológicas* 12. Museo Nacional de Antropología y Arqueología, Lima. 1985 Cumbemayo: Acueducto Arqueológico que Cruza la Divisoria Continental. In *Historia de Cajamarca*, vol. 1, *Arqueología*, compiled by F. Silva Santisteban et al, pp. 97–100. Instituto Nacional de Cultura, Cajamarca.

Pires-Ferreira, J., E. Pires-Ferreira, and **P. Kaulicke.** 1976 Prehistoric Animal Utilization in the Central Andes. *Science* 194:149–154.

Pizarro, H. 1968 Carta de Hernando Pizarro "A Los Magníficos Señores Oidores de la Audiencia Real de su Majestad que Residen en la Ciudad de Santo Domingo." Biblioteca Peruana, Primera Serie, vol. I, pp. 117–130. Editores Técnicos Asociados S.A., Lima.

Plowman, T. 1984 The Origin, Evolution, and Diffusion of Coca, Erythroxylum spp., in South and Central America. In *Pre-Columbian Plant Migration*, ed. D. Stone, pp. 125–263. Papers of the Peabody Museum of Archaeology and Ethnology 76, Cambridge.

Polykrates, G. 1960 Einige Holzschnitzerein der Kashuiéna-Indianer. *Folk, Dansk Etnografisk Tidsskrift* 2:115–120. Danish Ethnographical Association, Copenhagen.

Pozorski, S. 1979 Prehistoric Diet and Subsistence of the Moche Valley, Peru. *World Arch.* 11(2):163–184. 1983 Changing Subsistence Priorities and Early Settlement Patterns on the North Coast of Peru. *Journal of Ethnobiology* 3(1):15–38. 1987 Theocracy vs. Militarism: the Significance of the Casma Valley in Understanding Early State Formation. In *The Origins and Development of the Andean State*, ed. J. Haas et al, pp. 15–30. U. of Cambridge Press, Cambridge.

Pozorski, S. and **T. Pozorski.** 1979 Alto Salaverry: A Peruvian Coastal Preceramic Site. *Annals of the Carnegie Museum* 48:337–375. 1986 Recent Excavations at Pampa de las Llamas-Moxeke, a Complex Initial Period Site in Peru. *JFA* 13:381–401. 1987 *Early Settlement and Subsistence in the Casma Valley, Peru*. U. of Iowa Press, Iowa City. 1990 Reexamining the Critical Preceramic/Ceramic Period Transition: New Data from Coastal Peru. *Am. Ant.* 91:481–491.

Pozorski, T. 1976 El Complejo de Caballo Muerto y los Frizos de Barro de la Huaca de los Reyes. *RMN* 41:211–252. 1980 The Early Horizon Site of Huaca de los Reyes: Societal Implications. *Am. Ant.* 45:100–110. 1983 The Caballo Muerto Complex and Its Place in the Andean Chronological Sequence. *Annals of the Carnegie Museum of Natural History* 52:1–40.

Pozorski, T. and **S. Pozorski.** 1988 An Early Stone Carving from Pampa de las Llamas-Moxeke, Casma Valley, Peru. *JFA* 15:114–119. 1990a Reply to "The Pre-Chavin Stone Sculpture of Casma and Pacopampa." *JFA* 17:110–111. 1990b Huaynuná, a Late Cotton Preceramic Site on the North Coast of Peru. *JFA* 17:17–26.

Proulx, D. 1968 *An Archaeological Survey of the Nepeña Valley, Peru*. Dept. of Anth. Research Report 2, U. of Massachusetts, Amherst, Peru. 1973 *Archaeological Investigations in the Nepeña Valley, Peru*. *Research Reports*, No. 13. Dept. of Anthropology, U. of Massachusetts, Amherst. 1985 An Analysis of the Early Cultural Sequence in the Nepeña Valley, Peru. *Research Report Number 25*, Dept of Anthropology, U. of Massachusetts, Amherst.

Pulgar Vidal, J. 1972 *Las Ocho Regions Naturales del Perú*. Editorial Universo, Lima.

Quilter, J. 1985 Architecture and Chronology at El Paraíso. *JFA* 12:279–297. 1989 *Life and Death at Paloma: Society and Mortuary Practices in a Preceramic Peruvian Village*. U. of Iowa Press, Iowa City. 1991 Late Preceramic Peru. *Journal of World Prehistory* 5(4):387–438.

Quilter, J., B. Ojeda, D. Pearsall, J. Jones, and **E. Wing.** 1991 Subsistence Economy of El Paraíso, Perú. *Science* 251:277–283.

Quilter, J. and **T. Stocker.** 1983 Subsistence Economics and the Origins of Andean Complex Societies. *Am. Anth.* 85(3):545–562.

Ravines, R. 1978 Antiguos Sitios de Ocupación en el Río Huayabamba, Perú. In *Homenaje a Jorge Basadre*, ed. F. Miró Quesada et al, pp. 521–532. Pontificia Universidad Católica, Lima. 1979 Garagay como Arqueología Experimental. In *Arqueología Peruana: Investigaciones Arqueológicas en el Perú 1976*, ed. R. Matos, pp. 75–80. Centro de Proyección Cristiana, Lima. 1981 Yacimientos Arqueológicos de la Region Nororiental del Perú. *Amazonia Peruana* 4(7):139–176. Lima. 1982a *Panorama de la Arqueología Andina*. Instituto de Estudios Andinos, Lima. 1982b *Arqueología del Valle Medio de Jequetepeque*. Instituto Nacional de Cultura, Lima. 1984 Sobre la Formación de Chavín: Imágenes y Símbolos. *Boletín de Lima* 35:27–45. 1985a Early Monumental Architecture of the Jequetepeque Valley, Peru. In *Early Ceremonial Architecture of the Andes*, ed. C. Donnan, pp. 209–226. Dumbarton Oaks Research Library and Collection, Washington, DC. 1985b *Cajamarca Prehispánica: Inventario de Monumentos Arqueológicos*. Instituto Nacional de Cultura de Cajamarca y Corporación de Desarollo de Cajamarca, Lima.

Ravines, R., H. Engelstad, V. Palomino, and **D. Sandweiss.** 1984 Materiales Arqueológicos de Garagay. *RMN* 46:135–233.

Ravines, R. and **W. Isbell.** 1976 Garagay: Sitio Ceremonial Temprano en el Valle de Lima. *RMN* 41:253–275.

Raymond, J. S. 1981 The Maritime Foundations of Andean Civilization: A Reconsideration of the Evidence. *Am. Ant.* 46:806–821.

Redfield, R. 1953 *The Primitive World and Its Transformations*. Cornell U. Press, Ithaca.

Reichel-Dolmatoff, G. 1974 Funeral Customs and Religious Symbolism among the Kogi. In *Native South Americans*, ed. P. Lyon, pp. 289–301. Little, Brown and Company, Boston. 1975 *The Shaman the Jaguar*. Temple U. Press, Philadelphia. 1976 Training for the Priesthood among the Kogi of Colombia. In *Enculturation in Latin America: An Anthology*, ed. J. Wilbert, pp. 265–288. UCLA Latin American Series vol. 37, Los Angeles.

Reichlen, H. and **P. Reichlen.** 1949 Recherches Archaeologiques dans le Andes de Cajamarca. *Journal de la Société des Americanistes*, n.s. 38:137–174. Paris.

Reichlen, P. 1974 Un Cráneo de Chavín de Huántar, Perú. *RMN* 39(1973):143–151.

Reinhard, J. 1985 Chavin and Tiahuanaco: a New Look at Two Andean Ceremonial Centers. *National Geographic Research* 1(3):345–422.

Renfrew, C. 1973 *Before Civilization: The Radiocarbon Revolution and Prehistoric Europe*. Knopf, New York.

Richardson, J. III. 1978 Early Man on the Peruvian North Coast, Early Maritime Exploitation and the Pleistocene and Holocene Environment. In *Early Man in America from a Circum-Pacific Perspective*, ed. A. L. Bryan, pp. 274–289. Archaeological Researches International, Edmonton. 1983 The Chira Beach Ridges, Sea Level Change and the Origins of Maritime Economies on the Peruvian Coast. *Annals of the Carnegie Museum* 52:265–276.

Riddell, F. and **L. Valdez.** 1988 Hacha y la Ocupación Temprana de Acarí. *Gaceta Arqueológica Andina* 16:6–10. Lima.

Rivière, P. 1969 *Marriage among the Trio: a Principle of Social Organisation among a South American Forest People*. Clarendon Press, Oxford.

Robinson, D. A. 1964 *Peru in Four Dimensions*. American Studies Press, Lima.

Roe, P. 1974 *A Further Exploration of the Rowe Chavin Seriation and Its Implications for North Central Coast Chronology*. Studies in Pre-Columbian Art and Archaeology No. 13. Dumbarton Oaks Research Library and Collection, Washington, DC. 1978 Recent Discoveries in Chavin Art: Some Speculation on Methodology and Significance in the Analysis of Figural Style. *El Dorado* 3(1):1–41. 1982a *The Cosmic Zygote: Cosmology of the Amazon Basin*. Rutgers U. Press, New Brunswick, NJ. 1982b Cupisnique Pottery: A Cache from Tembladera. In *Pre-Columbian Art History: Selected Writings*, 2nd edn, ed. A. Cordy-Collins, pp. 231–253. Peek Publications, Palo Alto.

Rojas Ponce, P. 1985 La Huaca Huayurco, Jaén. In *Historia de Cajamarca, Vol. 1, Arqueologia*, compiled by F. Silva Santisteban et al, pp. 181–186. Instituto Nacional de Cultura, Cajamarca.

Rollins, H., D. Sandweiss, and **J. Richardson.** 1986 The Birth of El Niño: Geoarchaeological Evidence and Implications. *Geoarchaeology* 1:3–15.

Rosas, H. 1970 *La Secuencia Cultural del Período Formativo en Ancón*. Tesis de Grado en el Programa Académico de Psicología y Ciencias Sociales. UNMSM, Lima. 1976 Investigaciones Arqueológicas en la Cuenca del Chotano, Cajamarca. *Actas del 41 Congreso Internacional de Americanistas (1974)* 3:564–578.

Rosas, H. and **R. Shady.** 1970 *Pacopampa, un Centro Formativo en al Sierra Nor-peruana*. Seminario de Historia Rural Andino, UNMSM, Lima. 1974 Sobre el Período Formativo en la Sierra del Extremo Norte del Perú. *Arqueológicas* 15:6–35. 1976 Investigaciones Arqueológicas en la Cuenca del Chotano, Cajamarca. *Actas del XLI*

Congreso de Americanistas 3:564–578. Mexico, DF.

Rostworowski, M. 1972 Breve Ensayo sobre el Señorío de Ychma o Ychima. *Boletín del Seminario de Arqueología* 13:37–51. Lima. 1985 Mitos Andinos Relacionados con el Origen de las Subsistencias. *Boletín de Lima* 37:33–37.

Rowe, J. H. 1944 An Introduction to the Archaeology of Cuzco. *Papers of the Peabody Museum of American Archaeology and Ethnology* 27(2). Harvard University, Cambridge, Mass. 1946. Inca Culture at the Time of the Spanish Conquest. In *Handbook of South American Indians*, ed. J. Steward, vol. 2, pp. 183–330. Bulletin 143. U.S. Government Printing Office, Washington, DC. 1962a Stages and Periods in Archaeological Interpretation. *Southwestern Journal of Anth.* 18(1):40–54. 1962b *Chavín Art: An Inquiry into its Form and Meaning*. The Museum of Primitive Art, New York. 1963 Urban Settlements in Ancient Peru. *Ñawpa Pacha* 1:1–27. 1967a What Kind of Settlement was Inca Cuzco? *Ñawpa Pacha* 5:59–76. 1967b An Interpretation of Radiocarbon Measurements on Archaeological Samples from Peru. In *Peruvian Archaeology: Selected Readings*, ed. J. H. Rowe and D. Menzel, pp. 16–30. Peek Publications, Palo Alto. 1967c Form and Meaning in Chavín Art. In *Peruvian Archaeology: Selected Readings*, ed. J. H. Rowe and D. Menzel, pp. 72–103. Peek Publications, Palo Alto. 1971 The Influence of Chavín Art on Later Styles. In *Dumbarton Oaks Conference on Chavín*, ed. E. Benson, pp. 101–124. Dumbarton Oaks Research Library and Collection, Washington, DC.

Rudecoff, C. 1981 Summary of Archaeological Survey in Huanuco. *Willay* 7:7. Cambridge, Mass.

Salazar-Burger, L. and R. Burger. 1983 La Araña en la Iconografía del Horizonte Temprano en la Costa Norte del Perú. *Beiträge zur Allgemeinen und Vergleichenden Archäologie* 4:213–253. Mainz.

Samaniego, L. 1980 Informe sobre los Hallazgos en Sechín. In *Gedenkschrift Walter Lehmann* 6:307–348.

Samaniego, L., E. Vergara, and H. Bischof. 1985 New Evidence on Cerro Sechín, Casma Valley, Peru. In *Early Ceremonial Architecture of the Andes*, ed. C. Donnan, pp. 165–190. Dumbarton Oaks Research Library and Collection, Washington, DC.

Sancho de la Hoz, P. 1968 [1534] Relación para su Majestad. In *Biblioteca Peruana*, Tomo I, pp. 277–343. Editores Técnicos Asociados, Lima.

Sanders, W. and B. Price. 1968 *Mesoamerica: The Evolution of a Civilization*. Random House, New York.

Sandweiss, D., H. Rollins, and J. Richardson III. 1983 Landscape Alteration and Prehistoric Human Occupation on the North Coast of Peru. *Annals of the Carnegie Museum* 52:277–298.

Santillana, J. I. 1975 *Prospección Arqueológica en Pacopampa*. Seminario de Historia Rural Andino, UNMSM, Lima.

Sawyer, A. 1972 The Feline Motif in Paracas Art. In *The Cult of the Feline*, ed. E. Benson, pp. 91–115. Dumbarton Oaks

Research Library and Collection, Washington, DC.

Scheele, H. 1970 The Chavín Occupation of the Central Coast of Peru. Ph.D. dissertation, Dept. of Anth. Harvard U., Cambridge, Mass.

Schoenwetter, J. 1973 Archaeological Pollen Analysis of Sediment Samples from Asto Village. In *Les Establissements Asto a l'Epoque Prehispanique*, ed. D. Lavallée and M. Julien, pp. 101–111. Travaux de l'Institut Francais d'Etudes Andines, Tome XV. Lima.

Schultes, R. 1967 The Botanical Origins of South American Snuffs. In *Ethnopharmacological Search for Psychoactive Drugs*, ed. D. Efron et al., pp. 291–306. Public Health Service Publication 1645, Washington, DC.

Schweiger, E. 1947 *El Litoral Peruano*. Compañia Adminstradora del Guano, Lima.

Seeger, A. 1981 *Nature and Society in Central Brazil – the Suya Indians of Mato Grosso*. Harvard U. Press, Cambridge, Mass.

Service, E. 1975 *Origins of the State and Civilization: the Process of Cultural Evolution*. Norton, New York.

Shady, R. 1974 Investigaciones Arqueológicas en la Cuenca del Utcubamba, Amazonas. *Actas del XLI Congreso Internacional de Americanistas* 3:579–588. Mexico. 1983 Una Aproximación al Mundo de las Creencias Andinas: la Cultura de Pacopampa. Patrones de Enterramiento durante el Formativo en la Sierra Norte del Perú. *Boletín* 8:17–24. Museo Nacional de Antropología y Arqueología, Lima. 1987 Tradición y Cambio en las Sociedades Formativas de Bagua, Amazonas, Perú. *Revista Andina* 10:457–487.

Shady, R. and H. Rosas. 1980 El Complejo Bagua y el Sistema de Establecimientos durante el Formativo en la Sierra Norte del Perú. *Ñawpa Pacha* 17:109–142.

Sharon, D. and C. Donnan. 1977 The Magic Cactus: Ethnoarchaeological Continuity in Peru. *Archaeology* 30:374–381.

Sherbondy, J. 1982 El Regadío, los Lagos, y los Mitos de Orígen. *Allpanchis Phuturinga* 20:3–32.

Shimada, I. 1981 The Batan Grande-La Leche Archaeological Project – the First Two Seasons. *JFA* 8(4):405–446. 1990 Summary of the 1989 season of the Sicán Archaeological Project. *Willay* 32/33:17–21. Cambridge.

Shimada, I., C. Elera, and M. Shimada. 1983 Excavaciones Efectuadas en el Centro de Huaca Lucía-Chólope, del Horizonte Temprano, Batan Grande, Costa Norte del Perú: 1979–1981. *Arqueológicas* 19:109–208.

Shimada, M. 1982 Zooarchaeology of Huacaloma: Behavioral and Cultural Implications. In *Excavations at Huacaloma in the Cajamarca Valley, Peru, 1979: Report of the Japanese Scientific Expedition to Nuclear America*, ed. K. Terada and Y. Onuki, pp. 303–336. U. of Tokyo Press, Tokyo. 1985 Continuities and Changes in Patterns of Faunal Resource Utilization: Formative through Cajamarca Periods. In *The Formative Period in the Cajamarca Basin, Peru: Excavations at Huacaloma and Layzon, 1982*, ed. K. Terada and Y.

Onuki, pp. 289–310. U. of Tokyo Press, Tokyo.

Silva, J. 1978a Acercamiento al Estudio Histórico de Bermejo. *Actas y Trabajos del III Congreso Peruano del Hombre y la Cultura Andina*, ed. R. Matos, I:310–324. Lima. 1978b Chavín de Huántar: un Complejo Multifuncional. *Serie Investigaciones* No. 1. Gabinete de Arqueología, UNMSM, Lima. 1988 La Alfarería de Pachamachay, Junin. *Boletín de Lima* 57:21–30.

Silverblatt, I. 1987 *Moon, Sun, and Witches: Gender Ideologies and Class in Inca and Colonial Peru*. Princeton U. Press, Princeton.

Silverman, H. 1991 The Paracas Problem: Archaeological Perspectives. In *Paracas Art and Architecture: Object and Context in South Coastal Peru*, ed. A. Paul, U. of Iowa Press, Iowa City.

Smith Jr., C. Earle. 1988 Floral Remains. In *La Galgada, Peru*, T. Grieder et al., pp. 125–151. U. of Texas Press, Austin.

Spaulding, K. 1984 *Huarochiri: An Andean Province Under Inca and Spanish Rule*. Stanford U. Press, Stanford.

Steinmann, C. 1929 *Geologie von Peru*. Heidelberg.

Stephens, S. G. and M. Moseley. 1973 Cotton Remains from Archaeological Sites in Central Coastal Peru. *Science* 180:186–188. 1974 Early Domesticated Cottons from Archaeological Sites in Central Coastal Peru. *Am. Ant.* 39(1):110–122.

Steward, J. 1949 Cultural Causality and Law: A Trial Formulation of the Development of Early Civilization. *Am. Anth.* 51:1–27.

Steward, J. and L. Faron. 1959 *Native Peoples of South America*. McGraw Hill, New York.

Stocking, Jr., G. 1987 *Victorian Anthropology*. The Free Press, New York.

Stone, R. 1983 Possible Uses, Roles and Meanings of Chavín-style Painted Textiles of South Coast Peru. *Investigations of the Andean Past*, ed. D. Sandweiss, pp. 51–74.

Strong, W. D. and C. Evans, Jr. 1952 Cultural Stratigraphy in the Viru Valley, Northern Peru: the Formative and Florescent Epochs. *Columbia U. Studies in Arch. and Ethn.* 4.

Stuiver, M. and G. Pearson. 1986 High-Precision Calibration of the Radiocarbon Time Scale, AD 1950–500 BC. *Radiocarbon* 28:805–838.

Tattersall, I. 1985 The Human Skeletons from Huaca Prieta, with a Note on the Audioexotoses of the External Auditory Meatus. In *The Preceramic Excavations at the Huaca Prieta, Chicama Valley, Peru*, ed. J. Bird et al, pp. 60–76. Anthropological Papers of the American Museum of Natural History, vol. 62, pt 1.

Tellenbach, M. 1986 La Excavaciones en el Asentamiento Formativo de Montegrande, Valle de Jequetepeque en el Norte del Perú. *Materialien zur Allgemeinen und Vergleichenden Archäologie* 39.

Tello J. C. 1923 Wira-Kocha. *Inca* I, pp. 93–320, 583–606. Lima. 1930 Andean Civilization: Some Problems of Peruvian Archaeology. *Proc. of the XXIII International Congress of Americanists* [1928]:259–290. New York. 1937 *El Strombus en el Arte Chavín*. Editorial

Antena, Lima. 1941 La Ciudad Inkaica de Cajamarca. *Chasqui* 1:3–7. Lima. 1942 Origen y Desarrollo de las Civilizaciones Prehistóricas. *Actas del XXVII Congreso de Americanistas (1939)*. Librería e Imprenta Gil, Lima. 1943 Discovery of the Chavín Culture in Peru. *Am. Ant.* 9(1):135–160. 1956 *Arqueología del Valle de Casma: Cultural Chavín, Santa o Huaylas, Yunga y Sub-Chimu*. Publicación Antropológica del Archivo "Julio C. Tello" de la Universidad Nacional Mayor de San Marcos, I. UNMSM, Lima. 1959 *Paracas: Primera Parte*, Empresa Gráfica Scheuch SA, Lima. 1960 *Chavín: Cultura Matriz de la Civilización Andina*. Publicación Antropológica del Archivo "Julio C. Tello" de la UNMSM, II. Lima.

Terada, K. 1979 *Excavations at La Pampa in the North Highlands of Peru, 1975*. Report 1 of the Japanese Scientific Expedition to Nuclear America. U. of Tokyo Press, Tokyo. 1985 Early Ceremonial Architecture in the Cajamarca Valley. In *Early Ceremonial Architecture in the Andes*, ed. C. Donnan, pp. 191–208. Dumbarton Oaks Research Library and Collection, Washington, DC.

Terada, K. and Y. Onuki. 1982 *Excavations in the Cajamarca Valley, Peru, 1979*. Report of the Japanese Scientific Expedition to Nuclear America. U. of Tokyo Press, Tokyo. 1985 *The Formative Period in the Cajamarca Basin, Peru: Excavations at Huacaloma and Layzon, 1982*. Report 3 of the Japanese Scientific Expedition to Nuclear America. U. of Tokyo Press, Tokyo. 1988 *Las Excavaciones en Cerro Blanco y Huacaloma, Cajamarca, Peru, 1985*. U. of Tokyo Press, Tokyo.

Thatcher, J. 1979 Early Ceramic Assemblages from Huamachuco, North Highlands, Peru. *Ñawpa Pacha* 17:91–106.

Thompson, D. 1962a Additional Stone Carving from the North Highlands of Peru. *Am. Ant.* 9:245–246. 1962b The Problem of Dating Certain Stone-Faced Stepped Pyramids on the North Coast of Peru. *Southwestern Journal of Anth.* 18:291–301. 1964 Formative Period Architecture in the Casma Valley. *35th International Congress of Americanists* 1:205–212. Mexico City.

Thompson, L. G., E. Mosley-Thompson, and B. M. Arnao. 1984 El Niño – Southern Oscillation Events Recorded in the Stratigraphy of the Tropical Quelccaya Ice Cap, Peru. *Science* 226:50–53.

Thompson, L. G., E. Mosley-Thompson, J. F. Bolzan, and B. R. Koci. 1985 A 1500-year Record of Tropical Precipitation in Ice Cores from the Quelccaya Ice Cap, Peru. *Science* 229:971–973.

Topic, J. 1986 A Sequence of Monumental Architecture from Huamachuco. In *Perspectives on Andean Prehistory and Protohistory*, ed. D. Sandweiss and P. Kvietok, pp. 63–83. Cornell Latin American Studies Program, Ithaca.

Topic, J. and T. Topic. 1978 Prehistoric Fortification Systems of Northern Peru. *Current Anth.* 119:618–619. 1983 Coast-highland Relations in Northern Peru: Some Observations on Routes, Networks and Scales of Interaction. In *Civilizations in the Ancient Americas: Essays in Honor of Gordon R. Willey*, ed. R. Leventhal and A. Kolata, pp. 237–259. U. of New Mexico and Peabody Museum of Arch. and Ethn., Albuquerque. 1987 The Archaeological Investigation of Andean Militarism: Some Cautionary Observations. In *The Origins and Development of the Andean State*, ed. J. Haas et al, pp. 47–55. Cambridge U. Press, Cambridge.

Topic, T. and **J. Topic.** 1987 Huamachuco Archaeological Project: Preliminary Report on the 1986 Field Season. *Trent University Occasional Papers in Anth.* 4. Peterborough, Ontario.

Torres, G., J. and **C. Lopez-Ocaña.** 1982 Estudio Bioecológico de la Loma Paloma. *Zonas Aridas* 2:61–66. Lima.

Troll, C. 1970 The Cordilleras of the Tropical Americas. In *Geo-ecology of the Mountainous Regions of the Tropical Americas*, ed. C. Troll, pp. 15–56. Ferd. Dummlers, Bonn.

Turner, V. 1974 *Dramas, Fields and Metaphors: Symbolic Action in Human Society.* Cornell U. Press, Ithaca.

Tylor, E. 1958 [1871] *The Origins of Primitive Culture.* Harper and Bros., New York.

Uhle, M. 1923 Civilizaciones Mayoides de la Costa Pacífica de Sudamérica. *Boletin de la Academia Nacional de Historia* VI (15–17):87–92. Quito. 1930 Desarrollo y Origen de las Civilizaciones Americanas. *Proc. of the 23rd International Congress of Americanists* (1928), pp. 247–258. New York.

Ulbert, C. and **K. Eibl.** 1984 Vorbericht über die Untersuchungen der Formativzeitlichen Anlage Kuntur Wasi am Oberlauf des Jequetepeque. *Beiträge zur Allgemeinen und Vergleichenden Archäologie* 6:559–572. Mainz.

UNESCO. 1980 *Proc. of the Workshop on the Phenomenon Known as El Niño.* UNESCO, Paris.

Ungent, D., S. and **T. Pozorski.** 1981 Prehistoric Remains of Sweet Potato from the Casma Valley of Peru. *Phytologia* 49:401–415. 1984 New Evidence for the Ancient Cultivation of Canna Edulis in Peru. *Economic Botany* 38:417:432.

Urton, G. 1981 *At the Crossroads of the Earth and the Sky: an Andean Cosmology.* U. of Texas Press, Austin.

Urton, G. and **A. Aveni.** 1983 Archaeoastronomical Fieldwork on the Coast of Peru. In *Calendars in Mesoamerica and Peru: Native American Computations of Time*, edited by Anthony Aveni and Gordon Brotherston, pp. 221–234. BAR International Series 174, Oxford.

Vázquez de Espinoza, A. 1948 Compendium and Descriptions of the West Indies. Trans. C. Upton Clark. Smithsonian Institution Collections vol. 102, Publication 3646, Washington, DC.

von Reiss Altschul, S. 1967 Vilca and Its Use. In *Ethnopharmacologic Search for Psychoactive Drugs*, ed. D. Efron, pp. 307–314. US Government Printing, Washington, DC.

Wallace, D. 1962 Cerrillos: an Early Paracas Site in Ica, Peru. *Am. Ant.* 27:303–314. 1979 The Process of Weaving Development on the Peruvian Coast. In *Junius B. Bird Pre-Columbian Textile Conference*, ed. A. P. Rowe, pp. 27–50. The Textile Museum and Dumbarton Oaks, Washington, DC.

Wassén, H. 1936 Some Observations on South American Arrow Poisons and Narcotics. *Ethnological Studies* 3, Göteborg Museum, Sweden. 1965 The Use of Some Specific Kinds of South American Indian Snuffs and Related Paraphernalia. *Etnologiska Studies* 28. Göteborg Etnografiska Museum, Göteborg. 1967 Anthropological Survey of the Use of South American Snuffs. In *Ethnopharmacologic Search for Psychoactive Drugs*, ed. D. Effron et al., pp. 223–289. Public Health Service Publication, Washington, DC.

Watanabe, L. 1976 *Sitios Tempranos en el Valle de Moche (Costa Norte del Perú).* Ph.D. dissertation, Programa de Ciencias Historico-Sociales, Especialidad Arqueología, UNMSM, Lima. 1979 Arquitectura de la Huaca los Reyes. In *Arqueología Peruana: Investigaciones Arqueológicas en el Perú, 1976*, ed. R. Matos, pp. 17–35. Centro de Proyección Cristiana, Lima.

Webster, S. 1972 An Indigenous Quechua Community in Exploitation of Multiple Ecological Zones. *RMN* 37:174–183.

Weir, G. and **D. Bonavia.** 1985 Coprolitos y Dieta del Precerámico Tardío de la Costa Peruana. *Bulletin de l'Institut Français d'Etudes Andines* 14:85–140.

Weir, G., J. Phillip, and **P. Dering.** 1986 The Lomas of Paloma: Human-environment Relations in a Central Peruvian Fog Oasis: Archaeobotany and Palynology. In *Andean Archaeology: Papers in Memory of Clifford Evans*, ed. R. Matos et al, pp. 18–44. Monograph XXVII, Institute of Archaeology, UCLA.

Wendt, W. 1964 Die Präkeramische Siedlung am Rio Seco, Peru. *Baessler-Archiv*, n.f. 11(2):225–275.

Wenke, R. 1990 *Patterns in Prehistory.*

Third edn. Oxford U. Press, Oxford.

Werbner, R. P. 1977a Introduction. In *Regional Cults*, ed. R. P. Werbner, pp. ix–xxxvii. Academic Press, New York. 1977b Continuity and Policy in South Africa's High God Cult. In *Regional Cults*, ed. R. Werbner, ch. 7. Academic Press, New York.

West, M. 1979 Early Watertable Farming on the North Coast of Peru. *Am. Ant.* 44(1):138–144.

Wheeler, J. 1984 On the Origin and Early Development of Camelid Pastoralism in the Andes. In *Animals and Archaeology: Early Herders and Their Flocks*, ed. J. Clutton-Brock and C. Grigson, pp. 395–410. BAR International Series 202, Oxford.

Wheeler, J., C. R. Cardoza, and **D. Pozzi-Escot.** 1979 Estudio Provisional de la Fauna de las Capas II y III de Telarmachay. *RMN* 43:97–109.

White, L. 1949 *The Science of Culture.* Farrar, Straus & Giroux, New York.

Whitaker, T. and **H. Cutler.** 1965 Cucurbits and Cultures in the Americas. *Economic Botany* 19(4):344–349.

Wiener, C. 1980 *Pérou et Bolivie. Recit de Voyage.* Librairie Hachette et Cie, Paris.

Willey, G. 1945 Horizon Styles and Pottery Traditions in Peruvian Archaeology. *Am. Ant.* 11:49–56. 1948 Functional Analysis of "Horizon Styles" in Peruvian Archaeology. In *A Reappraisal of Peruvian Archaeology*, ed. W. Bennett, pp. 8–15. Memoirs of the Society for Am. Arch. *Am. Ant.* 13(4). Menasha. 1951 The Chavín Problem, a Review and Critique. *Southwestern Journal of Anth.* 7:103–144. 1953 *Prehistoric Settlement Patterns in the Viru Valley, Peru.* Smithsonian Institution Bureau of American Ethnology Bulletin 155. US Government Printing Office, Washington, DC. 1962 The Early Great Styles and the Rise of the Pre-Columbian Civilizations. *Am. Anth.* 64(1):1–14. 1971 *An Introduction to American Archaeology: South America.* Prentice Hall, Englewood Cliffs, New Jersey.

Willey, G. and **J. Corbett.** 1954 Early Ancon and Early Supe Culture. *Columbia Studies in Arch. and Ethn.* vol. 3.

Williams, C. 1971 Centros Ceremoniales Tempranos en el Valle de Chillón, Rimac y Lurín. *Apuntes Arqueológicos* 1:1–4. Lima. 1972 La Difusión de los Pozos Ceremoniales en la Costa Peruana. *Apuntes Arqueológicos* 2:1–9. Lima. 1980 Complejos de Pirámides con Planta en U, Patrón Arquitectónico de la

Costa Central. *RMN* 44:95–110. 1985 A Scheme for the Early Monumental Architecture of the Central Coast of Peru. In *Early Ceremonial Architecture in the Andes*, ed. C. Donnan, pp. 227–240. Dumbarton Oaks, Washington, DC.

Williams, C. and **J. Pineda.** 1983 La Arquitectura Temprana en Cajamarca. *Gaceta Arqueológica Andina* 1(6):4–5.

Wilson, D. 1981 Of Maize and Men: A Critique of the Maritime Hypothesis of State Origins on the Coast of Peru. *Am. Anth.* 83:93–120. 1988 *Prehistoric Settlement Patterns in the Lower Santa Valley, Peru.* Smithsonian Press, Washington, DC.

Wing, E. 1972 Utilization of Animal Resources in the Peruvian Andes. In *Andes 4: Excavations at Kotosh, Peru 1963 and 1964*, ed. I. Seiichi and K. Terada, pp. 327–351. U. of Tokyo Press, Tokyo.

Wittfogel, K. 1957 *Oriental Despotism: A Comparative Study of Total Power.* Yale U. Press, New Haven.

Wright, Jr., H. E. 1984 Late Glacial and Late Holocene Moraines in the Cerros Cuchpanga, Central Peru. *Quaternary Research* 21:275–285.

Yábar, J. 1972 Epoca Pre-Inca de Chanapata. *Revista Saqsaywaman* 2:211–233, Cusco.

Zechentner, E. 1988 Subsistence Strategies in the Supe Valley of the Peruvian Central Coast during the Complex Preceramic and Initial Periods. Ph.D. dissertation, Dept. of Anthropology, UCLA.

Zeidler, J. 1986 La Evolución Local de Asentamientos Formativos en el Litoral Ecuatoriano: El Caso de Real Alto. In *Arqueología de la Costa Ecuatoriana: Nuevos Enfoques*, ed. J. Marcos, pp. 85–127. ESPOL, Guayaquil.

Zeil, W. 1979 The Andes, A Geological Review. *Beitrage zur Regionalen Geologie der Erde*, Band 13, Gebruder Borntraeger, Berlin.

Zerries, O. 1968 Primitive South America and the West Indies. In *Pre-Columbian Religions*, ed. W. Krickenberg et al, pp. 230–311. Holt, Reinhart and Winston, New York.

Zuidema, R. T. 1982 Catachillay – the role of the Pleiades and of the Southern Cross Alpha and Beta Centauri in the calendar of the Incas. In *Ethnoarchaeology and Archaeoastronomy in the American Tropics*, ed. G. Urton and A. Aveni. *Annals of the NY Academy of Sciences* 358:203–229. New York.

Sources of Illustrations and Acknowledgments

Abbreviations

AMNH = American Museum of Natural History
AMUT = Archaeological Mission of the University of Tokyo
RLB = Richard L. Burger
WL = Wilfredo Loayza
MNAA = Museo Nacional de Antropología y Arqueología, Lima
PRP = Pedro Rojas Ponce

Frontispiece After John Rowe 1967c: fig. 21.
1 After Guaman Poma de Ayala 1980 [1614]: Ch. 49.
2 Johan Reinhard.
3 After Tello 1943: pl. XIII.
4 RLB.
5,6 Servicio Aerofotográfico Nacional del Perú.
7 Neil Maurer.
8,9 RLB.
10,11 Pulgar Vidal 1972.
12 PRP.
13 RLB.
14 Redrawn from Feldman 1985:75.
15 (a) Redrawn from Bird et al 1985: fig. 122; (b) Grieder et al 1988: figs. 139 & 130; (c) Engel 1963; (d) Michael E. Moseley.
16 Redrawn from Bird et al 1985: fig. 130 and Grieder et al 1988: fig. 150.
17 John Hyslop, AMNH.
18 Robert Feldman.
19 AMNH, neg. 125150.
20 After Bird et al 1985:71.
21 After Alva 1986a.
22 Michael E. Moseley.
23,24 Jeffrey Quilter.
25 After Quilter 1985:283.
26 RLB.
27 After Wiener 1880:221.
28 Yoshio Onuki, AMUT.
29 Kazuo Terada, AMUT.
30,31 Yoshio Onuki, AMUT.
32 Redrawn after Izumi and Terada 1972: pl. 131.
33 Terence Grieder.
34 After Grieder and Bueno 1985:103.
35,36 Terence Grieder.
37,38 RLB.
39,40 After Patterson 1985:64.
41 RLB.
42 After Ravines and Isbell 1976.
43 Redrawn from Ravines and Isbell 1976.
44,45 WL.
46 Lucy Salazar-Burger.
47 WL (courtesy MNAA, Lima).
48 PRP (courtesy MNAA, Lima).
49–51 RLB.
52 Bernardino Ojeda and RLB.
53,54 James Kus and RLB.
55 Servicio Aerofotográfico Nacional del Perú.
56 Henning Bischof.
57 RLB.
58 After Tello 1957: 181, 151 & 202.

59,60 Bischof 1984.
61 Redrawn from S. Pozorski and T. Pozorski 1987:73.
62 Servicio Aerofotográfico Nacional del Perú.
63 RLB.
64 Redrawn from S. Pozorski and T. Pozorski 1986:384.
65 Redrawn after Tello 1956.
66 Donald Collier.
67 Redrawn from Johann Bastaroli.
68 Redrawn from T. Pozorski and S. Pozorski 1988: 117.
69 Redrawn from S. Pozorski and T. Pozorski 1987:86.
70 Hermilio Rosas La Noire, MNAA.
71 Enrico Poli.
72 Alfonse Jax.
73,74 Carlos Elera and Jose Pinilla Blenke, Museo de la Nación, Lima.
75 AMNH.
76 Thomas Pozorski.
77 Shippee-Johnson Expedition, AMNH.
78 Map after T. Pozorski 1976; reconstruction after Canziani 1989.
79 Redrawn from Alva 1987.
80 After Alva and Meneses de Alva 1983.
81 Izumi Shimada.
82 Lucy Salazar-Burger.
83 After Willey 1971.
84 Munson-Williams-Proctor Institute, Utica, NY.
85 RLB.
86 Courtesy Lowie Museum of Anthropology, Univ. of California, Berkeley). Photo RLB.
87 Nationalmuseet, Copenhagen.
88 After Guffroy 1989.
89 After Lathrap et al 1975: 43.
90 After Riddell and Valdéz 1988: 10.
91 Hermilio Rosas La Noire.
92,93 RLB.
94,95 Redrawn from Morales 1980.
96 After Rosas and Shady 1970: Lám. 15d.
97 RLB.
98,99 Redrawn after Morales 1980.
100 Yoshio Onuki, AMUT.
101 Jose Pinilla Blenke.
102 After drawing by PRP in Carrión Cachot 1948.
103–6 Yoshio Onuki, AMUT.
107 After Alva 1988b: fig. 13b.
108 Chiaki Kano, AMUT.
109 RLB.
110–12 Chiaki Kano, AMUT.
113 Terence Grieder.
114,115 Redrawn from Kano 1979.
116,117 After Izumi and Terada 1972: pls. 141–7, 142–8.
118 After Grossman 1972:275.
119 George Miller.
120 (Left) Annick Peterson. (Above) Redrawn from Lumbreras 1977.
121 Michael E. Moseley.
122–24 RLB.
125 Pauline Stringfellow.

126 Fernando La Rosa.
127 Michael E. Moseley.
128 Redrawn from Tello 1960:354.
129–31 WL.
132 After Lumbreras 1971:15.
133 WL.
134 After Lumbreras 1971:19.
135 Luis Caballero.
136 After Lumbreras 1971:4.
137 RLB.
138,139 After Rowe 1967c:10, 99.
140 RLB and Luis Caballero.
141 John Rowe.
142 After Rowe 1967c:102.
143 PRP.
144 Redrawn from Tello 1960.
145 The University Museum, Univ. of Pennsylvania.
146 PRP.
147–49 Cornelius Roosevelt.
150 WL.
151 Cornelius Roosevelt.
152 WL.
153,154 Cornelius Roosevelt.
155 WL.
156 Redrawn from Burger 1984a.
157 After Tello 1960.
158–61 RLB.
162 PRP.
163 After Tello 1960.
164 RLB.
165 Miller and Burger n.d.
166 RLB.
167 Redrawn after Burger 1984.
168,169 RLB.
170 Johan Reinhard.
171 After rubbing by Fred Ayres 1961.
172,173 RLB.
174,175 PRP.
176 After Burger 1988.
177 WL.
178,179 John Rowe.
180 WL.
181 Museo Arqueológico de la Universidad de Trujillo.
182–84 After rubbings by Fred Ayres, 1961.
185 Adapted from Lumbreras 1971.
186 WL.
187 After Roe 1974.
188 After Kauffmann Doig 1978.
189 WL.
190,191 RLB.
192 Redrawn from S. Pozorski and T. Pozorski 1987.
193 Aerial Explorations, Inc.
194 Servicio Aerofotografico Nacional, Peru.
195 After Willey 1953.
196 After Watanabe 1976.
197,198 WL (Col. Enrico Poli).
199 Hermilio Rosas La Noire.
200 Redrawn from Carrión Cachot 1948: fig. 17.
201,202 RLB.
203 RLB (courtesy Museo Amano, Lima).
204 Redrawn from Peter Roe.
205 WL (Col. Enrico Poli).

206 Photo Dumbarton Oaks; drawing after Rowe 1962b.
207,208 After Roe 1974.
209 Dumbarton Oaks.
210 William Conklin.
211 RLB (drawing based on photos by José Pinilla Blenke).
212 After Larco 1945:3.
213,214 Redrawn from Mejía Xesspe 1972.
215 Henning Bischof.
216 The Brooklyn Museum, New York.
217 After Larco 1941.
218 William Conklin.
219–21 Dumbarton Oaks.
222–24 National Museum of the American Indian, Smithsonian Institution.
225 After Lothrop 1941.
226,227 Yoshio Onuki, AMUT.
228 After Rosas and Shady 1970.
229 S. and T. Pozorski.
230 Courtesy John Rowe and the R.H. Lowie Museum of Anthropology, Univ. of California, Berkeley. Photo Gene Prince.
231 (A) Adapted from Fung 1975; (B,C,D,) RLB.
232 PRP.
233 After Elera 1983:26.
234 National Museum of the American Indian, Smithsonian Institution.
235,236 PRP.
237 WL (Col. Enrico Poli).
238 Chicago Museum of Art (on loan from MNAA, Lima).
239 WL (Col. Enrico Poli).
240 After Izumi and Terada 1966.
241 PRP.
242 WL (Courtesy MNAA, Lima).
243 PRP.
244 After Chavez 1988:20.

Acknowledgments

This volume draws upon my research in Peru over the last two decades. During this time, I was assisted by friends and colleagues too numerous to mention, but to whom I am deeply grateful. However, I do want to take this opportunity to thank Lucy Salazar–Burger without whose aid this volume would never have been completed; my teachers, Tom Patterson and John Rowe, who guided me into the strange and wonderful world of Andean archaeology; Jeffrey Quilter, who offered suggestions and encouragement on earlier drafts of the book; Elizabeth Kyburg, who typed the text; Luis Caballero and Heidy Fogel, who produced the original artwork; archaeology students from the universities of San Marcos, Trujillo, and Catolica for their assistance in my fieldwork; and my colleagues in Peru for their patience and friendship over the years.

Index